AF632981

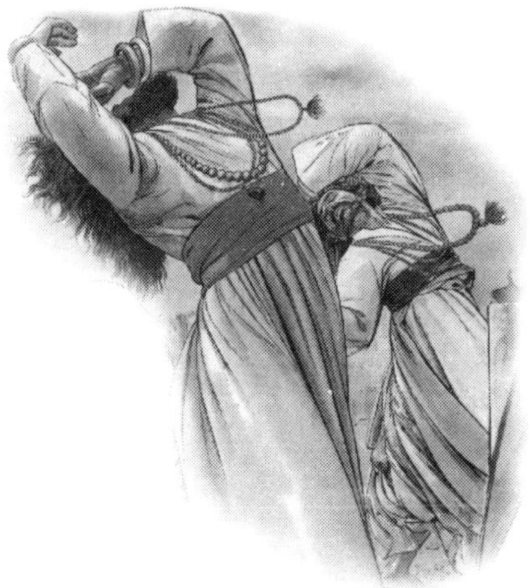

THE WANDERING SUFIS
Qalandars' and their Path

THE WANDERING SUFIS

QALANDARS AND THEIR PATH

Kumkum Srivastava

Indira Gandhi Rashtriya Manav Sangrahalaya
Bhopal

Aryan Books International
New Delhi

THE WANDERING SUFIS

ISBN: 978-81-7305-361-0 (HB)
978-81-7305-362-7 (PB)

© 2009, Indira Gandhi Rashtriya Manav Sangrahalaya, Bhopal

All rights reserved. No part of this publication may be reproduced, or transmitted in any form or by any means, electronic or mechanical, including photocopying, recording or by any information storage and retrieval system, without permission in writing from the publishers.

First Published in **2009** by:

INDIRA GANDHI RASHTRIYA MANAV SANGRAHALAYA
Shamla Hills, Bhopal - 462 013 (M.P.)

and

ARYAN BOOKS INTERNATIONAL
Pooja Apartments, 4B, Ansari Road, New Delhi-110 002 (India)
Tel.: 23287589, 23255799; Fax: 91-11-23270385; E-mail: aryanbooks@vsnl.com

Computer Typeset and Printed in India at
ABI Prints & Publishing Co., New Delhi

Foreword

The present work *The Wandering Sufis* by Kumkum Srivastava is theoretically well formulated and a good study on the anthropology of religion by combining both historical and anthropological perspectives. As regards the former, she delves into the concept, nature and origin of Sufism, different Sufi orders, and antinomian cults with special reference to the Qalandars and the Qalandariya path from various textual sources. On the other hand, in relation to anthropology, she has followed the method of participant observation in her study of two shrines – one at Purana Quila at Delhi managed by a family and the other at Panipat in Haryana managed by the Waqf Board. Thus, the author has been able to retain the methodological rigour required of both the disciplines in making it a holistic study. Secondly, she distinguishes between a theological study and anthropological study of religion, the former 'believing in divinity' and the latter studying religious practices of people from a distance dispassionately to know how people actively live in accordance with spiritual knowledge. Thirdly, the work bears significance also on the ground that not much emphasis has yet been given to the anthropological study of Sufi shrines, that too, by non-Muslims. Fourthly, she convincingly argues that although Sufism is presented in media and popular work as a homogeneous movement, this does not lead one to conclude that Sufism is monolithic and undifferentiated. Her emphasis on Sufism as a symbol of unifying different communities – Hindus and Muslims specially – is very relevant at a time when there is apprehension of 'clash of civilizations'. She shows how a large number of visitors to these shrines happen to be Hindus. Two more points are important about the work. Firstly, she has tried to understand the character of both shrines and their impact on the visitors. Secondly, she has shown that the Qalandar saints of both the shrines were 'individuals' who carved their own paths. As the author says, they were 'Qalandars in mind and not in morphology'.

While celebrating the cultural and religious diversities of our country, our Museum has also been emphasizing the syncretistic aspects of various religions also. The publication of this work is relevant to our museum since it strengthens our approach of emphasizing religious diversities on the one hand and the integrating and networking dimensions of the shrines studied on different communities, on the other.

I congratulate Kumkum Srivastava for successfully meeting the challenges of both the disciplines of history and anthropology. It is hoped that the work will be relevant to the disciplines of history, anthropology, sociology and religious studies. Sincere thanks are also due to our co-publisher, Aryan Books International, for a good output although in a short time.

9 September 2008

Professor Kishor K. Basa
Director
Indira Gandhi Rashtriya Manav Sangrahalaya
(National Museum of Mankind), Bhopal (M.P.)

Preface

This work is concerned with a comparative study of two Sufi shrines, one in Delhi, and the other in Panipat (Haryana), affiliated to the antinomian order of the Qalandars. Both the shrines are locally well known, visited by hundreds of people, and sometimes, they are also covered in media, both print and television, especially at the time of their *'urs* celebrations.

The Qalandars occupy an important role in people's imagery, especially because of the *qawwali*s (and some Hindi films and film songs) in which their reference figures. Their cultural practices and symbolism has also attracted people. However, barring a few historical writings, there have not been detailed empirical and historical accounts, or comparative studies of their shrines, which tell us who they are and what is their contemporary status: do we have Qalandars in the modern world? Has the concept of the Qalandar been deconstructed to mean a 'free, unattached, unshackled, almost bohemian, untrammelled' life? Are the shrines of Qalandar saints 'Qalandar', as we understand this term, with respect to their cultural profile? These questions have inspired me to undertake this study, where one shrine is family-managed, and the other, by the Waqf Board of Punjab and Haryana.

Sufi shrines are a part of the literate, reflective, and well-developed tradition. Most of these shrines came into existence during medieval times, and since then, historiographies and travelogues have been prepared on them, although like historical material in general, they are partial, incomplete, and scattered. A holistic study of Sufi shrines, therefore, would require not only a first-hand fieldwork account of the social life conducted there, but also, an introspection into their respective histories, thereby linking the present with the past, if the study is anthropological, or past with the present, if the study is historical. The historical literature on Sufism and its shrines is overwhelmingly in Persian and Urdu. Although much of it has been translated into English, it is expected that one reads the original, and offers the translation and interpretation one deems fit.

Being first a student of medieval Indian history, and then, of social anthropology, I have tried to bring together the approaches of these two disciplines. In doing so, the writings of Sir E.E. Evans-Pritchard, Ernest Gellner, and more recently, of Alan Macfarlane have greatly profited me. Today, historians of the modern world are exploring the possibility of conducting fieldwork in the locations of their study, and anthropologists are gradually moving away from a natural science conception of their discipline, and are paying attention to historical facts and methods.

The rituals performed at Sufi shrines are fewer in comparison to what one finds in Hindu temples. The major one is of veneration (*ziyarat*), which involves 'praying' in a way that pleases one, by folded palms or spreading them, by offering Fatiha, or by reading a holy litany. Washing the grave, covering it with sheets, distributing among the visitors the water with which the grave is washed, or the flowers that are offered to it, as 'transvalued food' (*tabarruk*), and *qawwali* renditions, are the other activities. Neither are there mediums in whom the saint descends nor are there complex rituals with strong symbolism. What compensates for this is the stout tradition of folklore about the saint – the stories of his presence and the miracles he performs and has performed in the past. People fondly talk about the petitions (*mannat*) they bring for the saint's intervention, and the miracles that have occurred in their lives and the miracles they have heard from others. Recounting the stories of miracles is also a meritorious act.

The saint's life, therefore, is of crucial significance. For the believer, the saint is 'alive' (*zinda*) and 'animate' (*javed*); he is 'there'; he listens to 'petitions'; he 'judges' people's faith and devotion; and he 'intercedes' on their behalf. In other words, the 'life-history' of the saint interests people. Each shrine is individual-centred. The belief is that if the saint finds one 'pure at heart' and 'unflinchingly devoted', he would pray for him, and the saint's prayers (and recommendations) would bring fruition. This belief keeps the shrine going.

Both the Qalandar shrines studied here were relatively quiet and non-political. The number of visitors on days other than Thursdays and Sundays was small, thus providing an ideal environ for long, intensive interviews with devotees as well as caretakers. These interactions familiarized me with the snippets from the life of the saint. Each respondent remembered that part of the story of the saint's life which interested him and with which he identified. Interestingly, when I examined the historical material, I found definite continuity between them, which show that the saint in the historical record is not separate or alienated from the 'life-history' account that the people construct, and transmit.

A visit to the shrine with devotion and firm faith is enough for seeking the saint's grace, but Sufi shrines all over South Asia have developed their own traditions of supernatural healing and counselling. To some shrines are chained mentally ill and challenged; to other shrines are brought the cases of snake and scorpion bites. A Sufi shrine was recently in the news for the copies of passports that the devotees hung on the branches of the trees in its vicinity, since it is believed that this saint would help them to go to foreign lands, for an affluent life, for job and settlement. Invariably, the specialists of supernatural cure, who are often descendants of the saint or caretakers of the shrine, establish themselves in the shrine, receiving clients, accepting whatever is gifted to them as fee, and also, demanding money in case a ritual is needed to be performed. However, any sort of supernatural service is independent of the shrine; it can be provided in any space, not necessarily within a Sufi shrine.

I spent days after days conducting a participant observation of the interaction between specialists of the supernatural remedy and their clients at the Delhi shrine. Being under the management of the Waqf Board of Punjab and Haryana, the Panipat shrine was not permitted any indulgence in supernaturalism, as it is contrapuntal to the ideals of puritan Islam, although it thrived surreptitiously. The amulets and talismans given to people had no relation with the Sufi ideology or the shrine, in the sense that the name of the saint was not written on the piece of paper that constituted the panacea. That is the reason why I have not dwelt much on supernatural cure and counsel.

This work submits that the Qalandar saints of both the shrines did not live the 'Qalandari way'; neither were they peregrinators nor did they sport the cultural artifacts and practices of Qalandars; neither were they weird, laughable and ridiculous characters from *The Arabian Nights* nor were they the antithesis of the Shariat-following Sufi saints. However, they were 'individuals', who carved their own paths; they were not part of an established system. They were 'Qalandars in mind', and not in morphology.

Many people have contributed to the successful completion of this work. First, I am extremely grateful to my supervisor, Dr. Soumendra Mohan Patnaik, much younger to me in age, who taught me the minutiae of anthropology and, at the same time, gave me freedom to arrange and present my work the way I wanted. I take this opportunity to thank Professor

Surinder Nath for various acts of kindness. I express my gratitude to Dr. Indu Anand, the Principal of Janki Devi Memorial College, for letting me take leave from my teaching work. I am indebted to all my teachers in history and anthropology for correcting my mistakes and helping me take up academic challenges. Whatever little I have learnt about life and love I owe it to Jai Mehra.

I would like to thank my husband, Vinay, for his immense support, infinite patience, and wholehearted encouragement; to Sonal, Tushar, and Rohan for their tolerant indulgence in allowing 'Mom to follow her heart'; to my father-in-law, Bharat Bhushan Srivastava, for helping me with translation of Urdu and Persian manuscripts; to my mother and sister, who believed in me; to Ajit, for his constant persuasion, and enquiry into the progress of my work; to Neera, for providing sound advice and moments of peace at Friday meditations; to Rehman, for helping me locate medieval texts; to Kishor Basa for alleviating my depression with his wit and humour, and commonsense; to Jagdish Chopra, my dear friend, for his genuine concern about my well-being in moments of stress; to Satish for his constructive criticism; to all my Sufi friends for teaching me that *ishq* (love) is the essence of life; and to my respondents at *dargah*s, who infused new hope and restored my faith in humanity. The story of the lives of the two great Qalandar saints, the subjects of this work, was my constant source of inspiration.

One who would have been very happy to see this dissertation finished was my brother-in-law, Paramjiet Pal Grover, more a friend than a relative. I dedicate this work to his memory.

Contents

Introduction

The study of Sufism is not only a subject of this work, it is also a part of my life. I do not recall exactly when and how I imbibed the philosophy and values of the great Sufi masters like Mu'in al-Din Chishti, Baba Farid, Nizamuddin Auliya, and started searching for the deeper meanings of the verses written by Rumi and Amir Khusrau, and lately those of Bu Ali Shah Qalandar.

Living in the largely Muslim dominated area of Daryaganj in the walled city of Delhi, with one wall of our *haveli* (mansion, named Akhtar Manzil) being shared with Masjid Daiwali, I woke up to the prayer call (*azan*) of the *imam* and slept after the evening (*maghrib*) prayers. Visiting Sufi *dargah*s (lit., 'royal court') seemed the normal thing to do when one was ill or when one wished for some boon, like wanting a child (particularly a son), or a job, or promotion, or redressal of some grievance, or a solution to some domestic or legal crises. Performing *hazari* (attendance) at the shrine, drinking charmed water, stirring small bits of paper, with verses of the Quran written on it in saffron ink, in water, wearing *tawiz* (amulets), tying *heraks* (strings) to the latticed grills at the shrine to make a vow (*mannat*) and removing them once the wish was fulfilled, eating *tabarruk* (*prasad*, blessed or transvalued food), be it rose petals, sugar-coated cardamom balls (*elaichidana*), sugar-wafers (*batasha*), offering sheets (*chadar*), asking the water-man (*bhisti, mashqi*) to sprinkle water in the shrine (as in Nizamuddin Auliya), was routine.

Every Wednesday, I would visit Nizamuddin Auliya's shrine with my friends, both Hindu and Muslim, since Thursday was a day which brought a great crowd there. Between November 14 and 28, when there was an exposition at Pragati Maidan, when parking of vehicles became a nightmare, we would often park it in the open space besides the *dargah* of Abu Bakr Tusi and chat with the shopkeepers, the caretaker Mohammad Naseem Sultani, or the visitors to the shrine. When these visits became a habit, I do not remember clearly. My face became familiar at both these shrines. Whenever I was despondent or elated, I would go there and receive some sort of solace. People visiting the saint's shrine also started sharing their stories with me, how the saint had worked miracles (*karamat*) with them, how they came there every Thursday, or sometimes as an 'outing' on Sundays. I would keep a record of these wonder stories, narrate them to my family and friends, write down the names and telephone numbers of the men and women I had met and talked to at length. I spoke with them often on phone, asked their welfare and in case of any problems how far they had progressed in litigation, or remedy of an illness, or birth of a child, or a son's admission to a college (engineering or medical), or a daughter's marriage, or divorce, or possession by a spirit. For fulfilment of any wish, the devotees were asked to light incense sticks (*agarbatti*) at the grave, or tie a *tawiz*, or bring the affected person there everyday for a week or two weeks or till the time he was completely cured.

People related similar tales about all shrines, be it the shrine of a Qalandar saint or a renowned saint of high merit and spiritual accomplishments. Most of my respondents belonged to middle and lower classes. They included a police officer of a high rank, many teachers of a nearby school, a cloth merchant of Chandni Chowk in old Delhi, a university lecturer of Arabic, a septuagenarian Unani specialist, office clerks and accountants, school going boys and girls, young college going and jobless youth, casual workers, labourers and masons, daily wagers, casual visitors, especially those who came on Fridays to pray at the mosque in the premises of Abu Bakr's shrine. A school peon and a young Punjabi boy and his father, dealing in velvet upholstery in Panipat, frequent Bu Ali's shrine regularly. Childless couples from India (and sometimes from abroad) visit Bu Ali's shrine as he is known to bless such people. Eunuchs form a part of the procession during the *'urs* ceremony of the saint. Mendicants, destitute, beggars, homeless, vagabonds also find solace and refuge here.

Islam is perhaps one of the most misunderstood religions in the world. Many non-Muslims have variously called it Mohammadism, Islamism, Moslemism or the Muslim religion (Armstrong, 2002; Ba-Yunus, 2002: 107). Many equate Islam with Sufi thought; to some it means violence and terrorism. For many others, it invokes images of exploitation of women.

Even in the academia, as Edward Said (1978, 1993) has pointed out, Islam has suffered from cultural and political biases. Ahmed (1988) argues about the sociology of Islam requiring the juxtaposition of the Islamic ideal with contemporary Muslim realities. The deficiency of the sociological literature on Islam was noticed by Ba-Yunus and Ahmed (1988). Turner (1975: 1-2) had earlier written:

> An examination of any sociology of religion textbook published in the last fifty years will show...that sociologists are either not interested in Islam or have nothing to contribute to Islam or have nothing to contribute to Islamic scholarship. ...There is consequently a need for studies of Islam which will raise important issues in Islamic history and social structure within a broad sociological framework, which is relevant to contemporary theoretical issues.

Even when they did focus on Islam, like Max Weber, they were often inconsistent in their approach. In Weber's sociology, one must start any research inquiry with an adequate account or description of the actor's subjective world. For Weber, the study of social action constituted the subject matter of sociology. Turner (1975: 3) observes that Weber in his study of Islam has abandoned his own guidelines. Much of the literature on Islam points out that Islam does not distinguish between religion and politics (Kedouri, 1972). It provides an overall societal ideology.

Islam is looked at in many ways, as identity, as political ideology and as faith (Ruthven, 1991). It is known in a bewildering diversity of ways in an increasingly interconnected world (Donnan and Stokes, 2002: 2). There is a diversity of contemporary knowledge about Islam. Donnan and Stokes (2002) believe that there are patterns that can be observed in the seemingly anarchic diversity of disciplinary approaches to Islam. Great differences between national scholarly traditions in the approach to the study of Islam can be observed. French Orientalist scholarship was marked by its involvement with north Africa and its erstwhile colonies in Morocco, Algeria and Tunisia. Throughout most of the twentieth century, much of Anglo-Saxon scholarship was characterized by an apprehension of Islam as localized and a diverse 'culture' rather than a unitary 'civilization'. Subsequently, the concept of culture adapted itself well to the mediation of relationships with 'minorities' in the Anglo-Saxon nation states in the post-colonial period.

Anthropology has produced some of the most intellectually persuasive accounts of the Muslim world by non-Muslim as well as Muslim scholars, depicting an Islam localized and embedded in plural cultural worlds. The Western world needed to find its 'others', and these had become hard to find after the collapse of the Soviet Union. Now understood more as 'civilization' rather than 'culture', Islam filled the gap conveniently. Islam became the 'other' of the West. Diverse colonial and post-colonial histories thus pattern distinct national trajectories in thinking about the Muslim world. Turner (1995: 31, 54) reminds us that Edward Said exaggerated the degree of coherence within Western discourse on the Orient. He has concentrated only on literary works in Islam and not historical and social scientific literature.

Islam has no complex symbolic systems, enigmatic ceremonies, obscure rituals and mythic narratives that anthropologists love to interpret, to reveal the hidden underpinnings, meanings, and contradictions of culture. In general terms, the dominant mode of Islamic thought disapproves of the mythic tales and symbolic patterns that many anthropologists think to be the core of religion. Because of its sober and pragmatic emphasis on practical application, Smith (1973) has described Islam as a case of orthopraxy. Western anthropologists often saw Islam as more or less transparent and treated it as taken for granted background, not requiring any deep analysis, but merely something to be mentioned. Any discussion of Islamic texts and practices was usually absent from anthropological inquiry during this period. The exemplary ethnographies by Emmanuel Marx (1967) (of the Bedouin of the Negev) and Robert Fernea (1970) (of Iraqi Bedouin) hardly mention Islam. Ethnographers would agree with Geertz (1979) who says that for most Muslims the religious truth contained in the Quran is neither subjected to argument nor changes with the dimension of time. It guides all practical activities, and therefore, need not be analyzed. That was the reason why most of these works did not deal with how Islam was actually practised.

Jamil Abun Nasr's (1965) account of the Tijaniya order was primarily historical. Gilsenan (1973) also conventionally presented religion as a dependant variable, reflecting its social context and the secular struggle for power among the Shadiliya order of Cairo. In different manners respectively, Lawrence Rosen (1984, 1989) and Dale Eickelman (1976, 1978, 1985) introduced new pathways for an anthropological study of Muslim life. Rosen, being a legal anthropologist, focused on the application of law in Islamic society. Since in this society, law is derived from the Quran and the Hadith, Rosen moved away from Geertz's emphasis on personality and towards the study of texts. Eickelman was among the first ethnographers of the Middle East to turn his attention to the study of classical Arabic texts. In other words, they followed Talal Asad (1986, 1993) who had said that one should learn about Islam as Muslims themselves would. Henceforth, the line between the historian, anthropologist, and Ulema would be blurred, though the anthropologist (the protagonist of the technique of participant observation) would continue to focus on the actual implementation and interpretation of sacred knowledge, while oriental historians and Ulema would continue to regard any study of the present as an avenue to understanding the past. Central texts in this new approach include: Michael Fischer and M. Abedi's (1990) important study of the debating Muslim scholars; Shaila Haeri's (1989) study of the institution of temporary (*mutah*) marriage among Shiites; Richard Antoun's (1989) ethnographic account of the life and sermons of a Jordanian mullah; Brinkeley Messick (1993) has written on the history and political implications of traditional Islamic law in Yemen; and Akbar Ahmed (1988, 1993) has used both historical and ethnographic material in his books on Islam. As anthropologists, we should not deny our role as outsiders, and are well advised to emulate the aspect of Islamic scholarship where Muslims scholars have had no qualms about making strong cases for their philosophical positions, and respecting their opinions and sensibilities (Asad, 1986).

An important observation in this context is from Ernest Gellner (1981), who says that Orientalists are at home with texts, while anthropologists are at home in villages. The natural consequence is that the former tend to see Islam from above, the latter from below. The former study Islam as it is conceptualized, the 'scriptural Islam' or 'normative Islam', whilst the latter study Islam as lived, or what may be called 'existential Islam'. Anthropologists are primarily interested in what people actually do with their lives and not in their textual or oral traditions. But in India, as in other contexts, the anthropological study of Islam requires that the community under study be situated in historical, regional, cultural and linguistic settings. The pluralist perspective and the comparative approach are therefore imperative in a study of Islam (Madan, 2001, 2007).

The pluralities were visible even in the early history of Islam: its regional variations during its expansive phase leading to the four schools of law with varying interpretations: through the early emergence of Sufism and sectarian divisions, the Khwariji, and the Shia, and later of secular law (*qanun*) in different countries. By the eleventh century, orthodox Islamic scholarship had taken a stand regarding plurality within the Muslim community (*ummah*) and more generally in the world. It was believed that there was but one true religion, Islam as propounded by the Ulema, and differences in it were due to corruption of true faith.

The history of Islam from the cultural, sociological, and political perspectives is the history of the meeting of peoples of diverse origins and contact of cultures. It has also involved the establishment of Muslim rule in non-Muslim areas. Therefore, it has been a history of accommodation, compromise and adaptation. Concomitantly, it has also been of intolerance, rigidity and exclusiveness. A fundamental problem, thus, in the anthropology of Islam in India, according to Madan (2007), has been of relationship of a single scripture of Islam and a variety of lived Islams. The story of the Islamization of Bengal (India), Roy (1983) tells us, makes it clear that a religion that is universal in its geographical spread is bound to appear before us in myriad cultural forms. It follows from this that the only significant way in which Islam could be made a live, vibrant religion was to bring it into line with the cultural tradition of people.

This work on Sufism is situated against the background of the plurality of lived Islams. It submits that in a plural society, a religious community is expected to be influenced by the others, and in turn influences them. Indian Muslims share many characteristics with non-Muslim communities, but at the same time, in their cardinal principles, they are like Muslims anywhere in the world. A cultural aspect that unites different communities in India is Sufism. At one time, it was thought that with increasing Sanskritization and Islamization, the veneration of Sufi saints would fall into oblivion. This, however, has not happened. My work shows that a large number of visitors (almost seventy per cent) to these shrines happen to be Hindu.

In addition, the veneration of graves is increasing day by day. Hitherto unknown graves have gradually become objects of worship. Souls resting in them are elevated to sainthood with hagiographies being created and systematized. Stories of miracles they have performed also come in currency. A group of administrators and custodians start looking after these graves. 'Keeping grave', so to say, has become an occupation. It is similar to Hindu fanes that emerge wherever godlings are placed. This phenomenon also needs to be studied in detail, for behind this spread of religiosity are purely economic motives.

The aim of my study is to understand the character of these shrines and their impact on the visitors. I have chosen to work on them because most works on Sufism pertain to the famous shrines, which have become more popular with the visits of national and foreign dignitaries. Every study of the shrine of Mu'in al-Din Chishti (at Ajmer) does not fail to mention that Dr. Rajendra Prasad, Begum Abida Ahmed, Indira Gandhi, Zia-ul Haq, and many others, had visited it in the past (Currie, 1989; Dhaul, 2004; Moini, 2004). The Qalandar shrines, in comparison, are lesser known. In addition to fieldwork, I have looked at the history of these shrines. This work is a contribution to the tradition of historical anthropology.

CHAPTER 1

Sufism: Concept, Nature and Origin

Many books and research articles have been published on Sufism and spiritual life in Islam. Each has dealt with a different facet since the colours in the palette of Sufism are myriad and varied, its appearance so intangible that it is difficult to describe it in totality. Keeping in perspective, this chapter introduces one to the concept, nature and origin of Sufism.

It is based on an analysis of the important literature available in English and Urdu. In addition, I have also incorporated here the ideas on and about Sufism I learnt from the respondents during the course of my fieldwork. Interestingly, what people, especially the literate, said about Sufism and the Sufi way of life, was similar to what the great masters of Sufism have said time and again. This implies that rather than remaining confined to its 'ivory-tower', so to say, the ideology of Sufism has percolated down to the level of masses. Older men and women, notwithstanding the strata to which they belong, tend to model their lives after that of the Sufi masters. These people – the pious souls – are honorifically called *buzurg* (literally, 'old people') or *bare log* ('great people'), and those who render supernatural assistance at Sufi shrines are also termed *pir baba*, but none of them is homologous with, or even comparable to, the posthumous Sufi masters. The contemporary world does not have Sufi saints of the ilk of Mu'in al-Din Chishti, Nizamuddin Auliya, or Ahmad Khattu, or Abu Bakr Tusi, but it has in plenty people who try to shape their existence according to the tenets that the Sufi masters have laid down. Undoubtedly, Sufism is a great cultural ideal, to be emulated in practice.

Every religious tradition has worked through two currents: the first strives to understand the Divine as transcendent, aloof, and inaccessible, while the second sees the Supreme in proximity, hence approachable and reachable. The role of the mystic in every religious tradition has been to provide the context and methods for this 'reaching out' to the Divine. Representing as it does, the inward and esoteric side of Islam, mysticism (*tasawwuf*) has been a very important stream within the Islamic thought. It emphasizes spirituality rather than ritual. Therefore, an understanding of Sufism is incomplete without an understanding of mysticism.

THE MEANING OF MYSTICISM

Mysticism is derived from the Greek word *myein*, which means 'to close the eyes'. Thus, it contains something mysterious, the great spiritual current which goes through all religions. It may be defined as the consciousness of the One Reality – which may be called wisdom, light, love, or nothing. Mysticism is understood in terms of the love of the Absolute. The power that separates true mysticism from mere asceticism is love. Divine love makes the seeker capable of bearing, even enjoying, all the pains and afflictions that God showers upon him in order to test him and purify his soul. The cruelty and tyranny attributed to Him are not regarded as reproaches but rather as praise of His independence (*istighna*). This idea is conveyed well in the following verses, the first from Sheikh Sadi, and the second, Rumi's *Mathnavi*:

ajab-ast ba vujudat ki vujud-e-man bi manad
tu bi-guftam andar a'i u-mara sukhan bi manad
(The wonder is that I survive the while I gaze on Thee,
that Thou shouldn't speak and the power of speech still be left to me.)
imruz shah-e-anjuman-e-dilbaran yakist
dilbar agar nazar buvad, dilbaran yakist
man behr-e-anyaki dujihan dada-am-bibad
'aybamj ma kun ki hasil-e-har du jihan yakist
(Today, at the Feast-of-the-Fair, one to one is assigned the throne,
for though of the fair, there are thousands there, in beauty He stands alone;
for Him, I forsake this world and that, and am counted in both undone,
withhold your blame, nor think it shame, for the sum of the worlds is One.)

Mysticism has no genealogy. There are several grounds for insisting that the mystical experience is not a religious phenomenon at all, and that its connection with religion is subsequent and even adventitious. But, there is no doubt that it is the eternal quest of man to have direct experience of the Ultimate Reality, whatever it is. A non-religious person can also have a mystical experience. As a concept, mysticism is important in both the Hindu and the Muslim traditions. The terms *ma'arifat* (gnosis) and *bhakti* (love or devotion) indicate the same basic urge of the finite to unite with the infinite. To put this idea in the Hindu idiom, it is the urge of the *sākār* (with form) to merge with the *nirākār* (the formless). Parrinder (1976) puts most of the eastern mysticism under the rubric of monastic mysticism that seeks identity with a universal principle, which may be called divine.

Mysticism wants to discover, experience and manifest the identity all beings already have with the One that is the root nature of everything. It is intuiting the 'essence of the mirror until one discovers it is made of light just as is the sun'. Bharati (1976) makes an initial attempt at defining and delineating the features of mysticism. A mystic is a person who has had an experience, incontrovertible to him, of oneness with an absolute matrix. This experience is in accordance with some theological postulates. That is why, a mystic experience, even of an atheist, is made intelligible and understood in religious idiom. The individual also identifies himself as a mystic by a term or terms that would translate operationally as mystic by the first part of the definition. In other words, a 'mystic is a mystic who calls himself a mystic.' In the same vein, Schimmel (1979) submits that in order to understand the Sufis, a research student ought himself to be somewhat a Sufi. Like the shaman, the mystic courts and manipulates ecstasy. Like the priest, he transmits his skills to a society generally through select neophytes. Mystics have also played an important role in the growth of civilization. Toynbee (1961) believes that the source of the creative acts of an individual lies in the 'inward' development of his personality.

Although mysticism is a universal constant, its variation can be observed clearly and it is characteristically shaped by the religious system upon which it is based. Therefore, Sufism is a term which pertains to Islamic mysticism. The mystic belief in gnosis (knowledge) and love is usually accompanied by characteristic ethics. The early Sufis imbibed many traditions of Christian asceticism, Arab piety and oriental esoteric cults. They were also influenced by the traditions of the Iranian, Greek and Indian civilizations. Sufism is believed to be a divine essence permeating the whole world. It is through mystical insight that man becomes oblivious of the material world through which he perceives divine truth and becomes one with him. The mystic attitude assumes the shape of a collective struggle for the spiritual and moral upliftment of society. Dumont (1970) says that the renouncer (or the mystic) is the initiator of ideological change in society.

ETYMOLOGY OF SUFISM

Idries Shah (1968: 13) says that the word Sufism is a German coinage of 1821. Different Sufis identified themselves by the order to which they belonged (such as Qadri, Naqshbandi, Chishti, Suhrawardi, etc.). Sufi became the generic category (or 'umbrella term') under which diverse mystic orders and traditions were classified. Shaikh Muhammad-bin-Khafif wore a coarse woolen frock (*palas*) for twenty years (*Kashf-ul-Mahjub*: 50-1). The mystics began to distinguish themselves in appearance by wearing an overgarment of coarse wool (Mujeeb, 1967). Some authors propose that the term Sufi is derived from *suf*, which means 'wool', as these mystics wore garments made of wool (called *khirqa*). Rose (1919: 33-4, 517) notes: 'The term [Sufi] appears to have been applied to wondering monks, who wore woolen garments in imitation of the Christian *rahibs* or the Arabian *hanifs*.' In an early definition of the Sufi, al-Rudhbari (quoted in Valiuddin 1971) is believed to have said: A Sufi is one 'who wears wool over his purity; gives his lusts the taste of tyranny and, having overcome the world, journeys on the path of the Chosen one.' Rizvi (1978: 28) notes that by Hasan Basri's time, the wearing of wool had become fashionable among Muslim ascetics. But, Hasan cautioned the ascetics: 'He who wears wool out of humility towards God increases the illumination of his insight and his heart, but he who wears it out of pride and arrogance will be thrust down to Hell with devils.' Baba Farid referred to himself as a devotee of God (*dervish*) wrapped in *kamli* (a woolen sheet). Some renouncers are popularly known as *kamli* (or *kali kamli*) *waley baba*, 'the renouncer wearing woolen (or of black wool) sheet'.

The author of *Ghiath-ul-Lugat* states that Suffa was an Arab tribe which in the *zamana-e-jahiliyat* ('Era of Ignorance', that is the 'time before the Prophet') separated itself from the others and began to serve in the Meccan places of worship; it was after them that the term Sufi came into existence. Other scholars think that the word Sufi is derived from *safa* (purity): a Sufi is one who has been purified from all worldly passions and vagaries. The Sufis lead 'pure' lives; have 'pure' hearts and spiritual elevation. 'Sufi' also seems to have been derived from the word *suf*, which means 'raw'. Mir Valiuddin (1971, 1972, 1974) gives two more derivations of Sufi: *suff* (rank, row) and *sofia* (wisdom). Of these, *suff* means that these pious men are expected to stand in the first row of men on the Day of Judgement (*roz-e-shumar*). The words *sofia* is from the Greek *sophos*, which means 'gnosis, knowledge or spiritual knowledge'. A Sufi would accordingly be one who has attained or seeks attainment through spiritual knowledge. Some others believe that this word comes from the word for 'bench' (*suffa*), referring to certain special companions of the Prophet or the 'first benchers' (Smith, 1957; Jackson, 1988: 254).

Another definition is that those Muslims who follow *tasawwuf*, the theology of the mystics, or contemplation, are called Sufi. Abu Hashim, 'the first spiritualist to be known as a sufi', first employed this term (Rizvi,

1978: 31). Some link the word Sufi with the Hebrew Cabalistic term 'Ain Sof' ('the absolutely infinite'), and say that the Cabbala and the Hasidim, the Jewish mystics, originated with Sufism or a tradition identical with it (Shah, 1968: 15). Dhul-nun Misri says that Sufi refers to that individual whose speech accords with his behaviour; whose silence indicates his state; and who discards worldly connections. Another opinion is that the Sufis 'regard the *sounds* of letters S, U, F (in Arabic, the signs for *soad*, *wao*, and *fe*) as significant, in this order of use, in their effect upon human mentation' (Shah, 1968: 16). In other words, the sound of SUF influences the brain, thus making the people have experiences beyond the normal.

All these probable etymological explanations have been subjected to criticism. Rizvi (1978: 28) notes that Jalalu'd-Din Huma'i, an Iranian scholar, points out that using the word Sufi for the wearer of woolen garments is incorrect from the point of view of Arabic grammar. The word was invented by some Iranian scholar on the pattern of the grammar of his language, and then assimilated into Arabic. Some important lexicographers stress that 'wool is the garb of animals'. The Sufi objective is not to emulate a hard life, but to perfect or complete the human mind (Shah, 1968: 14; Rodinson, 1973). The Sufis were highly sensitive to symbolism and would not adopt a name for themselves that misguided people. That SUF sound affects the brain may be criticized on the ground of a post-facto explanation, that is to say, a mundane derivation of the term Sufi (from wool) was given an esoteric thrust in terms of the sound theory (Shah, 1968: 17).

Attention may be drawn to al-Hujwiri's observation. In his *Kashf-ul-Mahjub* (what would literally mean 'The Revelation of What is Veiled'), he examines the roots of the word Sufi, and then asserts that no derivation, howsoever perfect it may appear, answers the etymological requirements expected of a saint. The reality far exceeds whatever is offered by etymology: there is much more to being a Sufi than simply wearing woolen garments or just assuming that by being a Sufi one would occupy the front row of dead men on the Day of Judgement. Perhaps al-Hujwiri knew that the issue of etymology might never be resolved, and therefore, it should not engage us beyond permissible limits. The Sufi way of living is far more a serious matter than the moot issue of its origin (Fakhry, 1970; Kramer, 1980).

TERMINOLOGICAL PLURALISM: THE SAINT

The orthodox saints among Muslims are called *salik* (a traveller in the path of Sufism), *faqir* (wedded to poverty), *sheikh*, *mir*, *miyan* (chief master, *pir* (old man), *wali* (a friend), *abdal* (one ordained by God to handle administrative affairs of the world), *qutub* (pole, axis, pivot), *ghaus* (one to whom one may cry for help), and *ghaus al-azam* (the head of them all, or refuge of the world, the saviour, whose merit can atone for the sins of other, without compromising his own salvation). Al-Hujwiri says that *wali* means 'near' and *wilayat* signifies 'nearness to God'. It has two grades: one is meant for all the believers, as the Quran says: 'God is near to those who believe and brings them out from darkness to light.' The other is reserved for those who annihilate themselves in God. The real *wali*, therefore, is he who lives in Allah and dies in Him. The word is also taken in two senses: (i) who is loved by Allah; and (ii) he who loves the worship of and devotion to Allah. Further, a *wali* has no identity of his own, but is merged in Allah's devotion. Etymologically, *wilayat* means the 'power to dispose' (*tasarruf*). It also means 'lordship' (*rububiyyat*). God has saints (*auliya*) whom He has especially distinguished by His friendship; whom He has chosen to be the governors of His kingdom. They have been marked out to manifest His actions for which they have been favoured with diverse kinds of miracles (*karamat*). They have been purged of natural corruptions and delivered from being a subject to their lower soul and passion, so that their thoughts are of Him and their intimacy is with Him solely.

The English term 'saint' has been used for *wali*, *sheikh*, dervish, *pir*, *sufi*, and *marabout*. The tendency is to regard these terms as synonymous. Turner (1975: 61) opines that 'when the western anthropologists talk about Islamic saints, they use the term as a shorthand for a diversity of roles.' Yet, there must be a unity in this diversity; therefore, a single term has been constantly in use to define the plurality of Arabic, Persian, and Urdu terms. The term *wali* expresses the idea of adherence, attachment, and nearness. In religious language, it also means the intermediary (*shafi*) between Allah and man. Darling (1930: 249) distinguishes *pir* from *murshid*; the former is a healer, and the latter, a guide. Weber (c.f. Turner, 1975) distinguishes between the *murshid* as the spiritual preceptor and member of a Sufi order and *pir* as the centre of the cult of saint worship. The *sheikh* is a venerable old man, chief of a tribe or head of a village. An Indian Muslim, when referring to his *sheikh*, will often refer to him as his *pir-o-murshid*. An ideal *sheikh* is a 'physician of men's souls', a man of the greatest learning and spirituality, who guides his disciples along the mystical path. A *sheikh* needs to possess certain qualities: an ability to perform miracles, tracing descent from the Prophet Muhammad or his companions, connections with a prestigious Sufi *silsila*, a mastery of Islamic doctrines and Sufi texts (see Mayer, 1966-7; Corbin, 1993).

Sufi, dervish, and *faqir* may be the terms by which a *sheikh*, *murshid*, or *pir*, might define himself, but not all *faqir*s or Sufis or dervishes qualify as *sheikhs*, *murshid*, or *pirs*. Sufi is one who tends towards the mystic life as it has developed within the framework of Islam. Dervish or *faqir* is one who is attached full time to the religious life either as a dependent of a Sufi

establishment or as an independent wandering mendicant. Rose (1919' wrote that in Punjab the institution of *piri-muridi* was typical of Sufism. Th *pir* is also known as *murshid* and corresponds to the *sheikh* of the Sufi. Nex in order to a prophet ranks the *sheikh*, a term which signifies being a deput or vicar (*khalifa*), whose duty is to call men by the path of the Prophe Muhammad to Allah. His condition is called *shuyukhiyat* and rules are lai down for his guidance in relation to his *murid* (pupil). He must show r greed for his property or services. The *murshid* is also called mystically, tl *saqi* ('cupbearer') or the *mutrib* ('minstrel'). The perfect *murshid* is term *khammar* (the 'vintner'). The *murshid* of love who calls the disciples to t path of Allah is called the *mallah* (the 'sailor') (see Alquadri, 1991).

Although the English term saint is used commonly for almost all h people in Islam, it hides the structural, spiritual, and social differen between their different categories. It has also been argued that 'using term *saint*...blurs the significant differences' [between Christian saints Islamic *walis*] and 'assumes the superiority of a Christian vocabulary conceptual framework against which Islamic ideas are to be interpre (*Encyclopaedia of Islam*: 80). Therefore, if the need is to specify the dis religious role of the personnel, the local terms should be used interpreting them satisfactorily.

CHARACTERISTIC FEATURES OF SUFISM

Against this background, Sufism may be defined as an 'awakening awareness of the un-manifest world'. The cardinal features of a Su may be delineated in following terms: (1) God exists in all and all e God; (2) Religion is only a way of life; it does not necessarily lead to salv a release from the world; (3) All happenings take place as per the God; nothing happens if He does not ordain it; (4) The soul is distinc the physical body and will merge into the Divine Reality accordir person's deeds; and (5) It is the teacher whose grace shows the w leads to union with God (Nasr, 1964).

The Sufis believe that there are four stages in one's jou realization: (1) leading a disciplined life as prescribed in Isl circumference of the Sufi circle is marked by the Shariat (the reveal (2) following the path (*tariqat*) delineated by the teacher (*murshid*); th acts as the radius connecting the esoteric-invisible and the exoteri periphery; at the centre of the Sufi circle stands the truth (*haqiqa*); (3 enlightenment (*haqiqat*); and (4) on the realization of truth, getting into the Divine Reality (*marifat*). The path that the Sufi treads in his of this circle encompasses three dimensions, three motives of asp God – these are *marifah* (knowledge or gnosis), *mahabbah* (love), an (fear). One of the best expositions of Sufism is in the work of Sha

Qadir Jilani. According to him, the Sufi combines in him eight characteristics, each exemplified by one or the other prophet. These characteristics are: (1) generosity (*sakhawat*) of the Prophet Ibrahim; (2) satisfaction (*rida*) of the Prophet Ishaq; (3) patience (*sabr*) of the Prophet Ayub; (4) suppliant (*munajat*) of the Prophet Zakariya; (5) expatriation (*ghurbat*) of the Prophet Yahya; (6) wearing of robe (*khirqa*); (7) travel (*safr*) of the Prophet Isa; and (8) poverty (*fuqr*) of the Prophet Muhammad. Sufi is he whose conduct towards Allah is sincere, and towards him, it is believed, Allah is also sincere. On him descend the blessings of Allah. Neither does the Sufi possess anything nor is he possessed, and if he possesses, spends it. A Sufi is one who is clean of impurity and full of meditation (Husain, 1956).

Withdrawal from people (*uzlat*) is one of the basic concepts of Sufism. A Sufi master advises his disciples to 'run away from the people as you run away from the beasts'. Because of this emphasis on isolation from the people, a persistent trend can be observed among the Sufis to leave human habitations and retire to jungles, closer to other desolate places. Three things that the Sufi are universally advised to follow are: to get used to hunger, wakefulness and silence, and withdrawal from people (*Al Risala al-Qushairiyah*: 16, 66; *Khairul Majalis*: 46, 68; *Siyar ul-Auliya*: 53, 275).

Self-abnegation is the hallmark of the Sufis: their ultimate aim is *fana fi'llah* (annihilation in God), for central to Sufism is the love of God for His creatures. Rabia Basri would say: "I am so absorbed in loving Allah that I have no time to hate Satan" (see Smith, 2001). The Sufis were the messengers of love, and advocated the principle of *sulh-i-kul*, i.e., peace with all and conflict with none. While all Muslims believe that they are on the pathway to God and will become close to Him in Paradise, after death and the Final Judgement – the Sufis believe as well that it is possible to become close to God and to experience this closeness while one is alive. Furthermore, the attainment of the knowledge that comes with some intimacy with God, Sufis assert, is the very purpose of the creation. Here, they mention the hadith *qudsi* in which God states: 'I was a hidden treasure and I loved that I be known, so I created the creation in order to be known.'

Knowledge (or gnosis, *marifat*) leads to the ability to discern between the Absolute and the contingent. This knowledge is supra-rational and derives its potency from the intellect, which is transpersonal rather than personal. Love creates bonding and generosity; the object of love in Sufi practice is Divine Beauty, an aspect of the Infinite. Fear is another dimension, which leads to the mindfulness of one's transgressions. It is inevitable that human beings should stray from the true path, for they are held in the web of contingency. Therefore, they must seek forgiveness of the Divine. When one is forgiven, one's awareness becomes realigned with the Divine, and one acts in accordance with it. From these dimensions of knowledge, love

and fear arise the Sufi practices of remembrance (*dhikr*, *wird*), which include *shahadah*, or attestation of faith in God, through such practices as 'There is no divinity other than the Divine' (*'sala-'ala'n nabi'*); the blessings of the Prophet; and the *istighfar*, seeking forgiveness.

It is erroneous to suggest that only those Sufis who manifest an attitude of love (such as Rumi, Hallaj, Farid) truly represent the mystical element of Islam. The spectrum of expression is far wider and includes Sufis like Ibn Arabi, Junayad and Suhrawardi, whose approach was primarily intellectual. However, man's ordinary state is one of forgetfulness and unconsciousness (*ghaflat*), oblivious to his spiritual connection with the Divine. Human beings also display many other forms of forgetfulness. The Sufi antidote is remembrance (*dhikr*) – the injunction 'remember God often' recurs constantly in the Quran.

Traversing through various states, *ahwal*, and stages, *maqamat*, on his journey, the Sufi pilgrim encounters 'proofs' of the degree of nearness in which he stands in relation to God: these are known as *karamat* (or graces). Guided and favoured, the Sufi then hopes to remove all traces of individuality and ego-confines. This is done through the act of *fana*, extinction, which would permit him to survive, beyond all forms, with God in a condition of *baqa*. Here is an experience of complete affirmation, *al baqa 'bad al-fana*.

A human being, through remembrance and practice, 'reaches out' in an attempt to aspire towards God. But it is the grace of God that 'draws in' the questing soul. The picture that emerges through the Sufi tapestries is that of a merciful Allah, always taking the first step towards man, the elect of His creation, showing him the path and its pitfalls, drawing him towards Himself by the powerful cords of love. Dhulnun Misri, the father of theosophical mysticism, explains that the knowledge of God has a 'three-fold' dimension – the theological, the philosophical, and the mystical. Bistami popularized the concept of pure love by denying one's own self (*Tazkiratul Auliya*, p. 177). The mystic strives for a deeper understanding of God though no mystic ever dare to know his essence. Dhulnun Misri says that to ponder about the essence of God is ignorance and to point to Him is associationism (*shirk*) and real gnosis is bewilderment.

In Islamic mysticism, both voluntaristic and gnostic aspects are equally strong. In their formative period, the Sufis admitted to a two-fold approach to God: as Hujwiri (d. 1071) says, there is a difference between one who is burned by God (His Majesty) in the fire of love and one who is illuminated by God's beauty in the light of contemplation. Jami describes two types of mystics in his *Lawaih Flash VI*: those who practise complete reclusion and are solely concerned with their own salvation and those who return to from their mystical experience in a higher state of mind and lead others on the right path.

The spiritual journey in Islam has two phases in opposition to the single-phased journey of mysticism in Christianity, Hinduism, Buddhism, Jewish Cabbalism and Hasidism, in which the goal is *fana* (stage of union). In Islam, the first phase is characterized by intoxication resulting in quietism and asceticism, while the second phase is that of activity and the fullest participation in worldly life. He now has the ability to guide others to the same goal by dint of his experience and the light he has gained (Rabbani, 2005). The reality, which is the goal of the mystic, cannot be understood or explained by the normal mode of perception. Only gnosis (or wisdom) of the heart may give insight into some of its aspects. Once the seeker (*salik*) has set forth upon the path to this last reality, he will then be led by an inner light. This light becomes brighter when he detaches himself from all worldly attachments – or, 'polishes the mirror of his heart' after a long period of purification or controlling his baser instincts (*nafs*). It is then that he reaches the last goal of his quest. That is *wisal* (union), or lifting the veil of ignorance, the veil that covers the essential identity of God and His creation. Khwaja Baqi Billah (quoted in Rabbani, 2005: 101) says:

> Nearness (*qurb*) and distance (*boad*) are imaginary. There was no distance which necessitated an effort for coming near Him, neither was there any separation which required an attempt for union.

EMERGENCE OF SUFISM

The approaches to the phenomenon of Sufism are varied. The tendency of most Western scholarship has been to glorify the classical phase of Islam and to debunk the 'medieval phase'. Gardet and Anawati (1988) state that there were three great periods in Islamic mysticism. The first phase was from the seventh to the ninth centuries, and this may be described as the phase concerned with the 'struggle for existence'. From ninth to the twelfth centuries was the second phase, attempting at reconciliation and doctrinal triumph of Sufism. The third phase, from the twelfth to the fifteenth centuries, ushered in the mystical orders. Nizami (1964, 1991) also endorses this view that by the middle of the thirteenth century, mystic thought, both in prose and verse, had reached its finale. Gardet and Anawati (1988) also speak of a fourth period from the sixteenth century onwards, where the decadence of Sufism took place.

Several theories about the origin of Sufism have been presented. Raising the question of the origin of Sufism today is as controversial as the question of the origin of the entire religion of Islam. The question of origin is two-fold. The basic point much argued by the Sufis themselves in search for the legitimization of their spiritual tendency is whether Islam as a religion contained within itself a spiritual ascetic tendency from the very beginning.

The second issue is one concerning the origins of Sufism itself. Regardless of where the original spiritual ascetic impulse came from, were the practices, aspirations, modes of expression used by the Sufis, developed within Islam? Or, were they the result of influences from another source (be that Christian, Indian, Iranian, etc.) and adapted to an Islamic style?

Many people have written on these issues; for instance, Arberry (1950) has presented the views of Western scholars on the origin of Sufism. One may broadly divide these opinions in two categories: first, those who consider that Sufism is a development within Islam; and the second, Sufism has its genesis in other exterior religious traditions. However, there are some who have put forth contradictory views. For instance, in an earlier thesis, McDonald (1903) submits that Sufism had the neo-Platonist patronage, combining it with a special reference to Christian ascetics and mystics. In a later work, he writes that like almost everything in Islam, the seeds of mysticism were also in the Prophet's mind.

Stoddart (1986) writes: 'There is no Sufism without Islam. Sufism is the spirituality or mysticism of the religion of Islam'. Further, he says that to 'attempt to separate the mystical element from the religion which is its outward support is an arbitrary act of violence.' He submits that one cannot be a Sufi without being a Muslim. Aziz Ahmad (1969) and Yusuf Husain (1957) confine the origin of Sufism to the Quran and the traditions of the Prophet. Wrote Tara Chand (1976): 'Sufism was born in the bosom of Islam.' Mohammad Habib (1974) attaches importance to the Arab phase of Sufism, but also feels that speculative Sufism can be traced to Persia. Trimingham (1971) traces the origins of Sufism within the Arabic and Persian spheres upon which the main emphasis is naturally placed. According to him, in terms of the wider setting, there was a vast movement of spirit spread throughout the Islamic world, influencing the ordinary person no less than a mystical elite. Sufism was a natural development within Islam, owing little to non-Muslim sources. In his introduction to the selections from Jalaluddin Rumi's lyrical poetry, Nicholson (1914) points out that neo-Platonism was certainly in the air. However, he believes that the early ascetic movement can be traced to its Islamic roots – a 'native product of Islam itself.' In his opinion, there are many things in the Quran which constitute a real basis of Sufism. Schimmel (1979) refutes the charge of a foreign origin of Sufism. According to her, Sufism traces its origin back to the Prophet and takes inspiration from the Divine Word as revealed to him in the Quran, which, for the Sufis, has been the 'unique lexicon'. The words and principles of Quran have formed the cornerstone of all mystical doctrines. Gibb (1957, 1970) remarks that the history of popular religion in Islam runs parallel to the history of the mystical movement. It was through the mystic channel that dynamic and progressive forces entered the structure of Islam and facilitated its adjustment with new situations and circumstances.

Some authors argue that most of the sources available about the Sufis in print in Europe and Middle-East in the nineteenth century were of late origin and unreliable about the early stage of mystical movement in Islam. That is why they think that Sufism must have been a foreign 'plant' in the 'deserts' of Islam. For some, Sufism is the development of the primeval religion of the Aryan people; for others, it is a typical Iranian development inside Islam. Margaret Smith (1973) has tried to explore the Christian influence on Sufism. However, Smith thinks that the impact of Quran and Sunnah is crucial on the life and work of Harith al-Muhasibi. Asin Palacios (of Spain) has put forward forty-five passages from the works of Muslim scholars for which he finds parallels in the Gospels. Writing on al-Hallaj, Massignon (1922 [1997]) says that he had given up Islam to embrace Christianity. Horton believes that al-Hallaj was a Brahmanical thinker. William Jones and John Marshall were deeply impressed by the Hindu influence on Sufism (c.f. Rabbani, 2005).

Goldziher (1967-71) was inclined to accept the Indian influence on Sufism. He pointed out parallel traditions in Islamic mystical tales and Buddhist stories. Since Abu Ali Sindi was the teacher of Abu Yazid Bistami, it is a clear and irrefutable proof of the Indian origin of Sufism. Another viewpoint is that Sufism was indebted to Parasimus, and on the western side, to Jewish Kabbals, Christian monasticism and neo-Platonism. The study of Fariduddin Attar shows the influence of Christianity on asceticism. al-Muhasibi (1857) especially borrowed from the New Testament. The wearing of *suf* (wool) was in imitation of Christian hermits; the *dhikr* (repeating God's name) was also considered to have been borrowed from the Christian mode of worship; and even the notion of *tawakkul* (total trust in God) and a total lack of possession and deprivation of any bodily comforts were the marks of a person who belonged to the monasticism of Christian Church. Given the geographical condition in which Sufism emerged in Baghdad, in the environment of the Christian heritage and in Khorasan, a former Buddhist Centre, it is not surprising that the elements of various religions, especially Christianity, should be present. Many authors believe that the monastic strain of Sufism was derived in particular from Christianity. R.C. Zaehner (1960) has emphasized the Hindu Buddhist heritage of Sufism. S.B. Sharda (1974) contends that Hindu thought and Yoga techniques exercised massive influence on Sufism. Sharafuddin Maneri, a Sufi of the mid-fourteenth century, had accepted certain yogic practices and social customs from the Hindus. Tara Chand (1976), who submitted that Sufism was 'born in the bosom of Islam', also compared

Sufism to a stream which gathers volume by joining of the tributaries from many lands.

Use of rosaries, the doctrine of *fana*, and the system of stations (*maqamat*) on the road thereto, would seem to be Buddhist in origin. For some, Sufism is a branch of mysticism, just like Tantra. Neo-Platonic philosophy and theology of Aristotle were translated into Arabic in AD 840. The mystical writings of the pseudo-Dionysus were widely known throughout western Asia. It is not a mere co-incidence that Dhulnun Misri worked out the doctrine of gnosis for the first time. On its theosophical side, Sufism was largely a product of Alexandrian speculation.

SUFISM IS ESSENTIALLY ISLAMIC

Undoubtedly, like any other system of thought and ideology in a world of diversity, Sufism did not exist as a windowless monad. The impact of several exterior thoughts on it was certainly unmistakable. Those ideas that were congenial to its spirit were adopted, and then assimilated. This process contributed to its dynamism. But the historical fact that it has borrowed unremittingly from outside does not deny the intrinsic spiritual nature of Islam that inheres Sufism. The knowledge that the Quran has imparted is of two kinds: *ilm-i-zahir*, or knowledge of rules and regulations of religion by books; and *ilm-i-batin*, or concentration of mind on God by worship (Rose, 1919). Those learned in the first type of knowledge are known as *mullah* and *maulvi*. Those who apply their mind on God in concentration call themselves Sufi. Therefore, the spiritual nature of Muslim is represented in the repository of Sufi thoughts. This line of reasoning submits that both the Quran and the life and acts of Muhammad support the mystical quest. The Sufis have time and again cited from the Quran and the Hadith and the Sunnah.

One of the submissions is that the general atmosphere of Islam during its formative era was fatalistic, with fear as the mainspring of its piety. At the centre were the fear of Allah, the ruler of the Day of Judgement, and the fear of hell, whose torments were widely depicted in the Quran. That God could reveal Himself through love did not seem to occur to many. To the Sufis, God was not punitive and distanced. Their search was for a personal, intimate, and warm God, one who dwells not only in the heaven and earth, but also in the hearts of human beings. For Sufis, God was always actively engaged bestowing His favours on people. The system they developed was more of a philosophy than a set of doctrines.

From the very beginning, the urge was felt by certain fervent believers to meditate on the Quran by constant recitation and also to internalize the text. The Sufis connected *dhikr* to the Quranic injunction to mention God often (33: 21). The constant repetition of the Kalimah (*la-illaha il-lillaha; Muhammad ur rasul Allah*, 'There is no God but one; Muhammad is His messenger') serves as the focal point of every Sufi group.

The Quran contains a number of ascetic and mystical elements. Some verses instantly recall the presence of God, the fear of judgement, the transience of all things human, and the beauty of virtue. Others offer the ways that can help in getting to the core of its faith. Many passages insist on the separation of the good from the evil. The Quran incessantly reminds the believer of the dogma of resurrection. The cycles of the prophets provide abundant examples of the ascetic aspect of life. The Quran describes the fall of Satan, the rivalry of the angels eager to please Mary in the temple; it calls God the 'Light of Lights', and states that everything will perish except God's countenance.

The Holy Prophet said *iman* is that 'you believe in Allah', His angels, His books, His messengers. The ideology of Islam submits that in a life after death and in *qadr* (destiny), in the good of it and the evil of it, Islam is that one bears witness. There is no Allah but Allah and that Muhammad is the messenger of Allah. One must keep up prayer, fast in the month of Ramazan, pay *zakat*, and carry out the pilgrimage to Mecca. If there is anything one worships, He is Allah. Whether one sees Him or not, He sees everyone. Thus, *iman* relates to matters of faith, of conviction.

Besides this, there is another concept, of *ihsan*, which refers to the state of sincerity in one's conviction and practice – to feel oneself in the Divine presence. According to the Prophet, there are two requisites of *ihsan*, which the Sufis call *mushahida* (vision of Allah) and *muraqaba* (meditation). The former implies that one should worship Allah as if one sees Him, while the latter signifies that if one cannot see Him, one should meditate on Him, because 'He surely sees you'. This is in essence the epitome of Sufi practice, which can be achieved by *zikr* (remembrance), *fhikr* (meditation), and *suhbat* (companionship of the righteous). It is because of this relationship that the Sufis describe *ihsan* as *umm-ul-tasawwuf* (the 'mother of Sufism'), and therefore, the basis of Sufism.

Muhammad's whole experience of revelation and his preparation towards receiving it are seen as models for ascetic life. The stories of Moses and al-Khidr in the *suras* have been elaborated into accounts of the mystic quest. Many aphorisms found on Muhammad's lips are applicable to the Sufi quest, and He is also portrayed as following an ascetic way of life. These traditions found their way in works such as the *Kitab al-Zuhd, The Book of Ascetic Practices* of Ibn Hanbal (d. 855). Ibn Hanbal cites the tradition from Aisha (Prophet Mohammad's wife), who was asked what the Prophet did in his house. She replied that he patched clothes, fixed sandals, and did similar things. When Muhammad died, 'he did not leave a *dinar* or a *dhirham*, nor any sheep or cattle, nor did he bequeath anything' (Ruthven, 1997).

Sufis subscribed to concepts that can be traced to the Quran. For instance, one of the concepts is of *tadhkiya zahir*, which refers to purification of the external self (such as *taharat*, *wudu*, *ghusi*, *salat*, *saum*, *zakat*, *hajj*, lawful earning, *nikah*, rights of men, etc.). The other concept is of *tadhkiya batin*, which signifies that one should purify one's inner self by observing trust in God, patience, fortitude, gratitude, sincerity, modesty, contentment, humility, decent manners, etc. It also implies that one should purify the inner self by abandonment of vices, such as falsehood, backbiting, envy, pride, anger, malice, and carnal passions.

Of these two concepts, Sufis laid great emphasis on *tadhkiya batin*, which they referred to as *tadhkiya nafs* (purity of self) and *tadhkiya qalb* (purity of character). The Quran also refers to them; for instance: 'He loves those who purify themselves' (Sura Bakr, 2: 222); 'Allah loves those that turn to Him in repentance and purify themselves'; 'He indeed is successful who purifies himself' (Sura Ala'ali, 87: 14). Statements concerning God are also popularly cited to prove that the source of Sufism is the Quran: 'Whenever my servants ask you about me, I am near to answer the call of the caller' (2: 186); 'Say, surely, we belong to God and to Him do we return' (Sura: 155); ' We are closer to Him than His jugular vein' (50: 16); 'He is the first and the last and the manifest and the hidden' (Sura Hadid, 57: 3); 'Whenever you may turn, there is the face of God' (2:115). 'God is with the God-fearing' (9: 23), whose way of life is echoed in the Quranic refrain; 'Remember God always; Remember me, and I will remember you' (23: 60); 'You who believe, remember God often' (33:41). And, the wandering way of the early ascetics is supported in Quran: 'Travel in the land and see how He began creation' (29: 20).

The traditions of the Prophet are on the same lines. The person who kills his carnal passions is called *mujahid*. The excellent *jehad* is that of the conquest of self. In the words of McDonald (1903), 'Muhammad was a Sufi, when on His way of becoming a Prophet.' According to Ibn Khaldun, the companions and successors of Muhammad followed this path of *tasawwuf*, of unfailing perseverance in working, utter devotion to Allah, turning away from the adornments of this world, renunciation from what men seek in the way of pleasure, and dignity and isolating oneself from all mankind, in spiritual retreat (Rippin, 1990). Later, when worldliness spread, those who dedicated themselves to the worship of Allah, were distinguished from the rest by the titles such as *Sufiyya* and *al-muta-sawwifa* (aspirants to Sufism).

That God is 'light' is one of the major themes in the Quran, and it has appealed to the Sufis the most. Its presence in the Quran is often claimed to be proof of the need for the mystic way:

> God is the light of the heavens and the earth. The likeness of His light is as a niche in which there is a lamp, the lamp is in a glass, the glass is just as if it were a glittering star kindled from a blessed tree, an olive, neither Eastern or Western, whose oil will ever glow, though the fire has never touched it. Light upon Light. God guides His light on anyone He wishes.

All Muslims believe that they are on the pathway to God and will become close to God in paradise, after death and final judgment. The Sufis believe that it is possible to become close to God and to experience this closeness while one is alive. Furthermore, the attainment of the knowledge that comes with some intimacy with God, Sufis assert, is the very purpose of the creation. Here, they mention the Hadith Qudsi in which God states: 'I was a hidden treasure and I loved that I be known, so I created the creation in order to be known.' Hence, for the Sufis, there is already a momentum, a continuous attraction in their hearts exerted by God, pulling them in love, towards Him. They experience the joyful ecstasy of being gently drawn to their 'eternal beloved', yet this primordially blissful return seems to have been interrupted. The story of the *miraj*, Muhammad's night journey (or ascension) (Quran, 17:1) is seen as a tale of the supreme mystical experience to which every mystic aspires. The emphasis frequently falls on the role of the journey as a prophetic initiation, leading the way for all mystics after Muhammad, to journey on their own union with the divine presence, not as prophets, but as *wali*, saints or friends of God.

All this attention to the Quran, *sira*, and Hadith on the part of Sufis simply indicates that they have, like all other Muslims, always gone back to the prime sources of Islam for inspiration as well as for justification of their position. The Quran contains verses which remind man of their vocation, building in his heart an edifice, founded on piety towards God. The life of this world is like running water, like a scorched harvest. A word of affection that pardons is worth more than a word that wounds. An abyss separates those with sincere hearts and hypocrites. The first are like the grain which sprouts, the tree which grows, the ear which swells; while the second are like captives, dumb, deaf, lost sheep. The Quran constantly reminds the believers that God who brings life to barren soil with water and produces fire from green wood will know well how to recall souls in their bodies like tamed birds.

However, it has frequently been pointed out that the ascetic lifestyle in Islam developed with a certain political motivation. Once again in Islam, a religious position appears to have been used as a rallying point, for rebellion against the political power. The whole early ascetic inclination is frequently shown as a renunciation and rejection of the political strife in the formative Islamic period. The early mystics were the true Muslim who held onto the Islamic spirit, in the face of religious manipulation by the ruling powers, for their own ends. The emphasis on *tawakkul* would be depicted in sharp contrast to the efforts of all other Muslims to secure their places on earth rather than in heaven, at least from the perspective of the mystics; one such mystic was al-Hasan al-Basri (d. 728), who denied the value of existence in this world and spoke of the hereafter as the realm free of the contamination of political self-interest.

THE SHARIAT AND SUFISM

We saw earlier that Sufism specializes in the spiritual dimension of Islam. It aims at the personal experience of the central mystery: *tauhid* (unity of God). It is through the realization of the fact that there is nothing to be worshipped, nothing to be adored and prayed, except God, that contact with the Holy is achieved. The religious complex of Islam pivots on *tauhid*.

Some scholars distinguish *tasawwuf* (or *tariqat*) from the Shariat, which is the Islamic doctrine and law. On this issue, explanations have been presented by the Sufis such as Abu Nasr-al-Sarraj (d. 988), Abu Talib-al-Makki (d. 996), Abu Bakr Mohammad-al-Kalabadhi (d. 995), Abul Qasim al-Qushairi (d. 1074), and al-Hujwiri (d. 1071). In addition, a lot of evidence is available in the *maktubat* (letters) and *malfuzat* (anecdotes) of early saints. All these rule out any question of *tariqat* being independent of the Shariat. The dependence of *tariqat* on the Shariat is well illustrated in a Sufi symbol in which Islam is compared to a walnut whose shell is the Shariat, which protects it from external force, its kernel is *tariqat*, and the oil, which though invisible yet present everywhere, corresponds to *haqiqat*, or the Ultimate Reality itself. Some Sufi teachers of the Shadhiliyah order liken the Shariat to the circumference of a circle at whose centre lies the *haqiqat*. The radii leading from the circumference to the centre are different paths (*turuq*), which connect the Shariat to the *haqiqat*. The Prophet said: 'Shariat is my word (*aqwal*), *tariqat* is my deed (*afaal*), *haqiqat* is my spiritual state (*ahwal*), and *maarifat* is my secret (*asrar*).'

While a person becomes a Muslim simply by repeating the Shahadah (*kalma*: 'There is no God but One; and Muhammad is his Messenger') and believing in it, a Sufi is one who explores its ultimate meanings and tries to live up to them. In doctrinal terms, the essence of Islam, which is known as *tauhid*, is contained in the first part of the Shahadah. Imam Malik (of seventh century AD) opines:

> One who indulged in *tasawwuf*, but did not learn *fiqah* (law of Islam) is a heretic; one who learnt *fiqah*, but did not practice Sufism is a sinner; and one who combined Sufism and *fiqah* found the truth.

The Sufi starts to contemplate on what it really means to actualize it. It is only in the second part of the Shahadah, where the priesthood is asserted, that he finds the answer. al-Hujwiri saw in the Sufi saints a vehicle by which the 'truth' and the 'proof' of the Prophet's veracity could be continued. Consequently, there is nothing which matters to a Sufi save Allah. A Sufi is different from a common Muslim only in that he wants to experience his religion more intensely, so much so that he has a personal will and the desire to die in the way of total obedience to God. At this stage, a Sufi deems to have completed his course and is considered dead to himself (having attained *fana*) and alive (*baqi*) with God.

The Shahadah starts with *la* (which means 'does not') and, thus, negates any other order of reality except Allah. The doctrine of *wahdat-ul-wujud* means that the real existence cannot be attributed to anything except God. The Sufis believe in the monistic view of reality: 'All is One – The Unity of Being.' This was not just a philosophy; it was also a spiritual and religious matter. The Sufis developed the concepts of *nasut* (mundane) and *lahut* (divine) to explain the duality that exists in the Unity of Being. Another point of difference between the Sufis and the exoteric scholars is the symbolism and allegorical expression of the Sufi poets and writers. They have tried to convey their spiritual experiences in human language, there being no other language to convey the definitionless, formless, colourless, speechless, boundless, timeless, spiritual states of the presence of God. God's Unlimited Being has been expressed as an 'Ocean'. The intoxication of Divine Presence and Divine Union has been expressed in terms of wine. The Sheikh has been called *saqi*, the tavern-keeper. It is this allegorical reference to wine, the cup, and the beloved on part of the Sufi poets and writers that made the orthodox oppose them in a bid to preserve the sanctity of Shariat.

In other words, the Shariat and Sufism, and the Muslim and the Sufi are perfectly complimentary since they both share the same ideological principle. But, as we shall later see, conflicts did surface as the practices (and cultural preferences) of certain Sufi saints were antithetical to the scriptural Islam.

SUFI PRACTICES

THE GLORY OF FUQR: WEARING OF THE 'PATCHED FROCK'

The wearing of a *muraqqa* ('patched frock') is the badge of aspirants to Sufism. The wearing of these garments is a custom (*sunna*) of the Prophet. He is supposed to have told Ayesha: 'See that you wear woollen raiment, that ye may feel the sweetness of faith. It is the inward glow (*hurqat*) that makes the Sufi, not the religious habit (*khirqat*)' (Ruthven, 1997). The patched cloak might be called the 'uniform' of the wandering dervishes. It has been seen in almost all parts of Asia and Europe for nearly four hundred years. Many Sufi masters have written about the method of sewing patches, whether they should be large or small, who should wear the robe, and who can confer it. The Sufi teachers enjoined their disciples to wear patched frocks, and did the same themselves in order that they might be marked men, and that all the people might keep watch over them, thus if they committed a transgression, 'every tongue would rebuke them'. And, if they wished to sin while clad in *muraqqa*, they would be held back in shame.

The patched cloak should be made with a view to ease and lightness. When the original cloth is torn, a patch should be inserted. Some Sufis hold that it is improper to sew the patch on the frock neatly and accurately. The needle should be drawn through the cloth at random and no trouble should be taken to repair it properly. Others say that the stitches should be straight and regular, as it is part of the practice of dervishes to keep the stitches straight and to take pains therein.

Some Sufis suggest that the garments should be blue (*kubud*) in colour. One of the reasons is the Sufis have made wandering (*siyahat*) and peregrination the foundation of their path, and on journeys, a white (or light coloured) garment does not retain its original appearance. It is not easily washed. Besides, everyone covets it. A blue dress, on the other hand, is the insignia of the bereaved and afflicted, and the apparel of the mourners. A Sufi is supposed to have said:

> In the flame of the candle, one part is pure light and the other pure darkness. The place of their union appears blue and that colour is suitable to the *hal* (state) of the Sufi.

Says *Kashf-ul-Mahjub*:

> This world is the abode of trouble, the pavilion of affliction, the den of sorrow, the house of parting, the cradle of tribulation; the Sufi disciples, seeing that their heart's desire is not to be gained in this world, have clad themselves in blue, have sat down to mourn union (with God).

Although blue is the choice of the Sufis, the form and colour of the *murid*'s garments depend on the Sheikh's intuition. Suppose the teacher finds his disciple inclined to fine garments, he would make him don a coarse robe of grass. But if he finds him disposed to hypocrisy and ostentation, he clothes him in soft silk! The white garment prescribed by the *sunnat* is only for Sheikhs who have gained freedom from the lusts of the flesh (*nafs*).

Only two kinds of men are fitted to wear the *muraqqa*: (i) those who are cut off from the world; and (ii) those who feel a longing for God. In many orders, the Sheikh invests the novice with *muraqqa* after a period of three years during which he is educated in the necessary discipline. The *muraqqa* is comparable to a winding sheet, the shroud (*kafan*), symbolizing that its wearer must resign all his hopes of the pleasures of life, and purge his heart of all sensual delights, and devote his entire life to the service of God and completely renounce selfish desires. After the Sheikh is convinced that the disciple has made considerable achievement in learning, he clothes him in that 'robe of honour'. The disciple has to see on his part that he fulfills the obligation which the robe involves.

With reference to the rending of garments, the doctrine is that when the Sufis pass from one stage to another, they immediately change their dress in thankfulness for having gained a higher stage. The patched robe is a dress which comprises all the stages of the path of poverty and purity, and therefore to discard it amounts to renouncing the whole path.

The robe was a symbol of the radical aspect of the Sufi life. It symbolized that the wearer was outside the mainstream of life, and did not indulge in fine raiment and rich food. As Sufism was founded on a belief in the transmission of saint-ship, the granting of a robe was significant, for it was a sign that the recipient had, according to his teacher, reached a satisfactory religious standard. The granting of a robe was an award in recognition of a disciple's personal spiritual achievement. It was also given to those who might not have been the disciples of Sufis, but had observed the Shariat and kept company with Sufis. After the receipt of a robe, the blessings accrued from it might lead to a total acceptance of the mystic path.

Devotions

The Sufi acts of devotion may be classified into general or special. The former are *namaz* (the ritual prayer), *tilawat* (the recitation of the Quran), and *awrad* (set forms of prayer). Notwithstanding their insistence on the regulation of the inward life of the soul, the Sufis also attach great importance to the ritual practices of Islam, such as *namaz, taharat* (ceremonial purification), hajj, etc. Like any Muslim, the Sufi believes that in *tilawat*, he pronounces the very words of Allah and so it seems to him that he hears the sound of the 'Beloved of his soul'. As a consequence, he enters into a state of ecstasy in course of his devotional reading. For Sufis of religious orders which forbid the use of music as a means of inducing ecstasy, the chanting or reading of the Quran supplies its place. But even in the case of those Sufis (like the Chishtis) who freely indulge in *sama'*, the reading of the Quran makes them get into rapture. It is said that one of the famous Chishti saints of Delhi, Khwaja Qutu'b-Din Bakhtiyar Kaki,

> on coming across a verse in the Quran containing some Divine threat of punishment used to strike his chest and become unconscious; but whenever he read a verse containing God's promise of His grace and reward, he would pass into a state of 'bewilderment' (*hayrat*), or ecstasy, and would remain in that state for quite a long time (Subhan, 1970: 94).

The third set of general prayers is called *awrad*, which constitutes set forms of prayers for daily recitation. There are many *awrad*, but the most popular of all is termed *durud*, 'prayer for the Prophet Muhammad'. *Durud* has several forms; however, the shortest one which the Muslims repeat whenever they utter the name of their Prophet, or hear it being pronounced, is as follows: 'Mercy and peace be upon him.' And its extended version is used in *namaz*. The importance of this *durud* for devout Muslims can be gauged from the following. I requested one of my Muslim friends, a scholar of Arabic language and literature, to have a close look at the first draft of my work. Amongst the suggestions he gave me was that I should write the acronym PBUH ('Peace be upon him') in brackets every time after I referred to Prophet Muhammad. He said it indicated that the 'intentions of the writer were clear'.

Other forms of prayer for daily recitation are called *dua-i-mathura* ('recorded prayers'). These were used by the Prophet and handed down in the Sunna. In addition, ninety-nine names of Allah and ninety-nine names of Muhammad, together with the titles of some saints are repeated every day. Besides these prayers, the Sufis also repeat the *shiajara* (genealogy, 'a chart tracing the line of succession in a particular religious order to Muhammad') of his order. The following prayers are also used for daily recitation with the help of a rosary (*tasbih*): (1) *tashbih* (viz., Subhan Allah, 'Holiness to Allah'); (2) *tahmid* (viz., *Al-hamdu li'llah*, 'Praise be to God'); and (3) *takbir* (viz., *Allahu Akbar*, 'Allah is great'). The special acts of devotion are *mujahada* ('acts of self-mortification'), *dhikr* ('remembering God through particular exercises of the breath'), and *muraqaba* ('contemplation'). The acts of self-mortification include prolonged fasting, repeating the names of God night and day, and denying to himself the ordinary comforts of life. Contemplation is usually done after *dhikr*. In this, the Sufi meditates upon some verse or verses of the Quran, such as 'He (Allah) is first, He is last. The manifest, the hidden, and who knoweth all things'; 'Whichever way ye turn there is the face of Allah'; 'We (God) are closer to him (man) than his jugular vein'.

THE DHIKR

Dhikr is 'repeating the name of Allah', the profession of his unity, in chorus, accompanied by certain motions of the head, hands, or whole body. It is performed near a saint's tomb, in a sepulchral mosque, or in a private room. It is an attempt to secure a mystical union with the divine through an emotional or subconscious bond. This effort is carried out under the direction of a teacher. Most of the Sufi orders distinguish between the 'daily' *dhikr* (or, *dhikr-ul auqat*) and the 'solemn' (*dhikr-ul jallula*). The former is recited silently, after each of the five daily prayers. The latter is used at ceremonials of the cult, especially at those observed on Fridays. There are various forms of the *dhikr*. It may be recited aloud (*dhikr-i-jali*), or mentally, or in a low voice; it is called *dhikr-i-khafi*. The type of *dhikr* that is given prominence varies according to the order. For instance, the Khalidia, a Turkish branch of the Naqshbandis, had accepted almost exclusively the *dhikr-i-khafi*, but the Naqshbandis generally belong to the Zahiria school, so they affect a deep-toned *dhikr-i-jali*.

A *dhikr-i-jali* is as follows: the worshipper (*zakir*) sits down in the usual way and shouts out Allah; then sitting as if for prayers, again in a louder voice, says Allah; then folding his legs under him says still louder, Allah. Again, placing himself in the correct attitude for prayer, he closes his eyes and shouts out the word *la*; drawing the sound from his navel then he says *ilaha* (God) as from his head, and lastly *illa'llah* (but God) from his left side with great energy. All this is repeated hundreds of times. The *dhikr-i-khafi* is made by the dervish closing his eyes and with the tongue of his heart saying: first, from his stomach, *Allhu sami'un*, i.e., 'God hears'; second, from his breast, *Allahu basirun*, i.e. 'God sees'; third, from his head, *Allahu 'alimun*, i.e. 'God the knower'. He keeps on going over these names, mentally, saying them to himself in an ascending and descending scale. Then, in a very low tone of voice, he says Allah; then he exhales breath and says, whilst so doing, *la ilaha*, and then inhales breath, saying *illa'llah*. This *dhikr* is very often repeated hundreds of times, and is always a most exhausting exercise. By long practice, a dervish gains great control over his breathing. It is said of one man that he used to say *la ilaha* exhaling his breath at the mid-day prayer, and *illa 'llah* inhaling his breath at the afternoon prayer. He held his breath for three hours.

Besides these two types of *dhikr*, there are some other exercises. The term 'the *dhikr* of all *dhikrs*' is used for *sultanu'l-adhkar*. Herein, the worshipper centres his mind on the exact position in the body of the various *lata'if* (subtle substances) and he makes them active with remembrance of God. Incidentally, some scholars of comparative religion find resemblance between the Sufi theory of *lata'if* and the theory of *chakra* as delineated in the Yoga system of physiology. Another practice is *habs-i-dam* ('restrained breathing'), where the devotee holds his breath and tries to repeat as many times as is possible the Shahadah. In *pas-i-anfas* ('guarding the respiration'), the worshipper imagines the word Allah engraved luminously in his heart. At the same time, he imagines that while inhaling he produces the sound Allah and while exhaling he makes the sound *hu*. Two other techniques are called *mahmuda* and *nasira*; in the first, the worshipper converges his eyes on the tip of the nose and in the second, towards the middle of the forehead. While doing so, he meditates on the thought that Allah is present and is seeing him. The last practice is called *naft-athbat*, 'negation and affirmation'.

Here, the devotee sits in the posture of *namaz* and faces Mecca. Then, he breathes as to imagine that he brings the phrase *la ilaha* from his navel, and then expels it by a jerk in the direction of his right shoulder. He then utters *illa 'llah* and jerks his head towards his heart intending to imprint these words on it.

It is by the strict performance of these exercises and by returning into privacy for devotional purposes (*khilwat*); by turning his face towards God (*tawajjuh*) by contemplating God with fear (*muraqabbah*); and by mystical spiritualism (*tasarruf*) that the dervish is supposed to gain the spiritual internal powers (*quwwat-i-ruhi wa batini*) which enable him to subdue the will of others. The mechanical repetition of the *dhikr* naturally weakens the intellect and personal will of the dervish. It produces a morbid state of mind in which he is easily led by the stronger will of the Sheikh and the *muqaddams*. The whole system is so developed that individuality is crushed out and the order is exalted. The Sheikh is the one absolute will and all obey him.

Another version (in Rose, 1919: 520-1) is that the worshippers sit cross-legged in a circle within which there are four candles. At one end of which are the *murshids* and the player on the flute. The Sheikh exclaims *al-Fatiha* and all recite the opening chapter of the Quran. Then begins the *dhikr* proper. The Shahadah ('There is no God but one') is chanted to different measures, first sitting, then standing. Before the end of the session, the worshippers speak out the words rapidly, turning their heads violently, shaking the whole body and leaping. *Dhikr* is solidly based on the Quranic injunction: 'Remember God with frequent remembrance and glorify Him, morning and evening.'

The early Sufis found in *dhikr* a means of excluding distractions and of drawing near to God by constantly repeating His name by rhythmic breathing either mentally or aloud. *Dhikr* is a pivot of mysticism. It can be translated as 'recollection' or 'remembrance', and was essentially a spiritual exercise designed to expel everything which separated the earthly individual from the divine. Through it Sufis were able to experience God's presence in every corner of their being. According to one Sufi, the first stage of *dhikr* is to forget the self and the last stage is the 'effacement of worshipper in the act of worship without consciousness of worship' (Nicholson, 1921 [1967]).

Dhikr popularized the use of rosary consisting of 99 or 100 beads. Some orders used rosaries of 301 beads, but ones of 1000 beads were not unknown. Contacts with Hindu *yogis* added a new dimension to the *dhikr* and involved the strenuous co-ordination of limb movements and postures associated with alternate exhalation and inhalation. The preliminary requirement for the *dhikr* of a Chishti disciple was to imagine that his Sheikh was personally present before him directing his contemplation.

POETRY (*KALAM*), MUSIC (*MAUSIQI*), AND SPIRITUAL CONCERT (*SAMA'*, LITERALLY 'HEARING')

The most charming expression of spiritual development is in the poetry of the Sufis. So essential was it to institutionalized Sufism that master poets were often co-opted into the mystic ranks, however great may have been their distance from its rigorous personal demands. For instance, two lyricists – Sa'di (the author of *Bostan, Gulistan*) and Hafiz (the author of *Diwan-e-Hafiz*) – were both revered as Sufi poets because the ambiguous imagery of their verses harkened to the pathos that the mystics experienced. It is typical of Persian lyrics that certain religious ideas from the centre of Islamic theology, certain images taken from Quran and the Prophetic tradition can turn into symbols of purely aesthetic character. Poetry provides almost unlimited possibilities, creating new relations between worldly and otherworldly images, a perfect interplay of both levels, and makes even the most prosaic poem bear a distinct religious flavour. There is hardly a verse in the poetry of the great masters of Persian, Turkish and Urdu poetry that does not reflect in some way the religious backdrop of Islamic culture. Persian lyrics would never have acquired their peculiar charm without Sufi theories. This is the background upon which the poetry develops and tries to resolve the tension between the worldly and the religious interpretation of life.

It is the Sufi poetry which provides the most captivating songs for a particular type of singing known as *qawwali* (its singers are called *qawwal*) at the shrines of saints. Sufi poetry is the product of their manifold spiritual states (*ahwal*) and as such, is saturated with ecstasy. When the *qawwals*, well versed in Sufi technique, sing these songs, they produce the same effect of ecstasy on the listeners, thereby elevating them. The mode of expression in Sufi poetry is generally the same as those of other themes. The Sufi poets make frequent use of the cup (*paimana*), wine (*sharab*), the tavern (*maikhana*), the cupbearer (*saqi*), the candle (*shama*), the moth (*parwana*), the rose (*gul*), and the nightingale (*bulbul*), to express their inexplicable spiritual experiences in human language as far as possible. Hafiz Shirazi clarified this in the following words:

> I am devoted to the *maikhana* which is a Khanqah for me and my thanks to the cupbearer (*saqi*) who is my morning recitation. My purpose in the mosque (or *maikhana*) is nothing but union with Thee. I have no other intention. Allah is my witness.

The songs sung in *qawwali* gatherings are arranged in a special manner to promote spiritual development. Their order enables the seeker to pass through the stages of the journey to God, with God and from God. First of all, they begin with the praise of God, the Holy Prophet and the saint. This is followed by general love songs to create a storm of love in the heart of the seeker. Then the verses relating to *fana-fi-Allah* are sung. The last stage of the spiritual journey is *baqa-bi-Allah* and towards the end of the gathering (*mahfil*), the song sung brings the seeker from 'intoxication' (*sukr*) to 'sobriety' (*sahw*).

Sufi poetry covers a wide range of subjects, such as praise of God, praise of the poet, the reality of the Creator, social behaviour, prayer and worship, intoxication and sobriety, man-God relationship, and so on. But its main theme is love (*ishq*) of the Divine Beloved (*mahbub-e-haqiqi*), and in the intensity and expression of this, the Sufis stand unsurpassed. The *ishq* in Sufi poetry is not worldly (*majazi*) but 'real' (*haqiqi*). From about the eleventh century, poetry became a medium for the Sufis. The most important Sufi poet was Jalaluddin Rumi whose *Mathnavi* became famous. He was the founder of the Mevleviya order, or the order of the Dancing Dervishes, in AD 1273. For Arberry (1950), Rumi was the greatest mystical poet in the history of mankind. Rumi's *Mathnavi* is perhaps the longest and voluminous single poem consisting of a thousand verses. His other collection of verses (*diwan*) called *Diwan-e-Shams Tabrez*, after the name of his Sheikh, is still bigger in volume. Amir Khusrau, the disciple of Nizamuddin Auliya, wrote five *diwan*s depicting the various stages of life he had passed through.

Scriptural or orthodox Islam is adversely predisposed to poetry, music, and entering into the states of ecstasy and trance. In my conversations with Muslims, I learnt that poetry sins when it equates one's beloved (a human being) with God; it is heretical when it encourages ideas contrapuntal to established religious institutions; and it also blasphemes religion by placing love for human above that for God. Music is also considered a distraction; a respondent of mine said that much of it satiates the base self (*nafs*), and so it is one of the factors responsible for the downfall of human beings. Other than the chanting of *azan* (call for prayer, *namaz*) and the Quran, music has no place in scriptural Islam. Writes Khalidi (1989: 257): '...the music which leads the listener to be more obedient to Allah has been encouraged; that which leads away from God and His directives has been avoided.' Scriptural Islam has also rejected moods of ecstasy inspired by music, vision, the glance of an imaginary or spiritual being, or any other extraneous social or psychological factor. As in the case of music, it was argued by scholars of Islamic law that *sama'* was likely to lead to 'sensuality than to spirituality' (Currie, 1989: 62; also see Rizvi, 1978). Baljon (1989: 195) writes: 'The reason why Muhammad himself did not practise poetry was its possible mix-up with religious exhortation.'

Closely related to anecdotal narratives and poetic musings, Sufi gatherings have a proclivity to music. Like poetry, music is by nature ambivalent. It could elicit purely sensual reactions, or it could lift the seeker out of his customary mood, his fixed routine of responses and expectations, to a new awareness of the Divine Beloved. Rumi, Sa'di and Hafiz advocated spiritual music and participated in assemblies where like-minded Sufi brethren enjoyed music and dance.

By contrast, certain Sufi traditions have overwhelmingly promoted poetry, music, and audition, others have been rather indifferent to them, and many orders in their attempts to get a foothold on Indian soil adopted some local religious practices. Poetry, music, and the states of ecstasy have been quintessential to religious performances of both little and great traditions of Hinduism. Concepts of devotional song (*bhajan*) singing, dancing in ecstasy (*masti*), crying and beseeching before the idols of gods and talking to them, and the idea of a personal god (*ishta devta*), who is also one's friend (*sakha*) and lover (*premi*), have been common to local Hindu cults. In shamanic practices as well as the contexts of spirit-mediumship, which are indispensable for healing, music has been an essential ingredient. The spirit entered the medium against the background of loud music and alleluia of the audience.

Rumi told his audience that 'like a good host, he gave them poetry because they demanded it; providing what was asked for' (c.f. Shah, 1968: 28). But, Rumi was also supposed to have said that poetry was trite in comparison to a high development of the individual; it was erroneous to reduce Sufi ideas to mere couplets and verses. Abu Bakr Sirajuddin said that composing mystical treatises or poems has never been an essential aspect of Sufism. Essential to Sufism are the doctrines, the grace of *dhang* ('direct intellectual intuition'), and the spiritual inspiration and practices which constitute the individual efforts of the mystic himself. Tara Chand (1961) also attaches importance to the practical aspects of Sufism: the 'practical aim of the Sufi is absorption in God.'

The Sufis thought that their ideas could be communicated in several ways and guises. They did not stick to any convention or format. Some of them conveyed their ideas in a strict religious framework using abstract language; others relied on abstract poetry. Some narrated anecdotes, tales and legends, which camouflaged Sufi teachings, and the masters interpreted them to reach the masses. Osho Rajneesh, in his discourses, often referred to the comic episodes from the life of Mulla Nasiruddin, a Sufi saint from Bengal, and in each episode, the saint gave a profound message to people. Some Sufis have also relied on art forms and products of artisans to popularize their views. But, none of them said, as we noted in Rumi's case, that amorous poetry, or any other mode of conveying the ideology, was sufficient. Sufi saints supported the point of view of holism, i.e., thought, ideology, practice, poetry, music, and ecstasy, must be used in togetherness to lift human beings from the mundane. Mu'in al-Din Chishti, the saint of Ajmer, popularly known as Gharib Nawaz, said:

> They know that we listen to music, and that we perceive certain secrets therein. So they play music and cast themselves into 'states'. Know that every learning must have *all* its requirements, not just music, thought, concentration (c.f. Shah, 1968: 135-6).

Mu'in al-Din Chishti belonged to the Chisti order (*silsila*) of Sufism. This order is well known for its fondness of 'musical parties', for which the term *sama'* is used. Of the four main Sufi orders popular in the Indian subcontinent (viz., Chishti, Qadiri, Naqshbandi, and Suhrawardi), the Chishti 'were alone in consistently seeking ecstatic inspiration in music' (Currie, 1989: 62). They rendered their constant support to music and *qawwali*. Most of the major Sufi theoreticians from Imam Ghazzali to Sharafuddin Maneri advocated at least limited participation in musical assemblies at the outset of the mystic quest. The *Siyar-al-Awliya* (p. 463) records that once Nizamuddin Auliya said:

> When a darwish claps his hands in a state of ecstasy, all the sins of his hands are removed, and when he shouts, all his evil desires are destroyed. There are cases on record where Sufis listening to such music have actually died of excessive ecstasy.

Today, *qawwali* performances have been highly secularized (Ahmed, 1992). They have also degenerated as sometimes these occasions are attended by dancing-girls who perform their nautch in honour of the saint (Subhan, 1970: 114). But it should not be forgotten that *qawwali* was primarily a 'religious musical concert', the *mahfil-i-sama'* (Sadler, 1963). Listening to the *qawwalis*, the Sufis entered into a state of trance.

However, Sufis were vehemently attacked for patronizing religious concerts. Rizvi (1978: 135-6, 161-2) documents cases where the Ulema were incited to protest against the *sama'* sessions of the Chishti saints. The 'age-old question of *sama''* was used as a weapon by all those who wanted to attack the Sufi saints (Rizvi, 1978: 161). For the Chishti, *sama'* was consonant with Muslim law. In his *Bawariq al-ilma*, Ahmad al-Ghazzali showed that *sama'* embraced three physical techniques: dance, whirl, and jump. Every movement is symbolic of spiritual reality. The *qawwal* sings Sufi poems to move them to ecstasy. Moreover, many Sufis thought that through their charisma, their devoted followers, and their convivial ceremonies, including musical assemblies, they would attract greater attention, sympathy and support than the sincere, but dull, educated and aloof Ulema.

The Chishti saints were, however, aware of the likely dangers of ecstasy. The Suhrawardi also listed its dangers. However, they approved its practice under correct circumstances. Qadiri were, however, opposed to music generally, and the instrumental music (*sama' bil-mazamir*) in particular, although music festivals were introduced in the Qadiri order in AD 1170 by

Sa'd Shamsu'd-Din, the immediate successor of Abdu'l Qadiri Gilani (Subhan, 1970: 113). The attitude of the Naqshbandi was even more hostile to music. al-Hujwiri made a distinction between two types of people in *sama'*. First, those who concentrate deeply upon the objective and moral lessons, the true meaning of the Sufi poetry and its delicate points; and the second are those who are instinctively attracted to and fond of musical concerts, although they do not understand the lessons of a religious concert. Thus, al-Hujwiri said, the beginners should not be allowed to attend the *sama'* gatherings. He further submitted that a Sufi should try to avoid *sama'*, but if he cannot, then he may practise it without overdoing it. He must resist from tearing clothes and passing any comments on the quality of music. A *sama'* concert should take place in proper surroundings in the presence of elders. Women, teenagers, and commoners should not be allowed to attend the music parties. The musicians should follow the Shariat, particularly the *namaz*. In a state of ecstasy, the Sufi must control his inner urge gracefully; al-Hujwiri calls dancing (*raqs*) in a state of ecstasy religiously tabooed. Thus, *sama'* by itself is not depraved; it all depends upon the context. Nizamuddin Auliya is supposed to have said that *sama'* is 'itself neither lawful nor unlawful'. A saint was once asked: 'What is *sama'*?' He answered: 'First tell me, who is the listener?' (Currie, 1989: 63).

MIRACULOUS EVENTS

One of the key signs of grace and authority, the most concentrated and dramatic for the believer, is those acts of wonder and power that we call miracles. For most of the Sufis, miracle was an integral part of Sufi discipline. The leading saints believed that the Sufi who had followed the mystic path could acquire supernatural powers. Sustained provocation from an antagonist or a disciple's dire straits could legitimately induce a Sufi to perform miracles, which manifest themselves either in the form of wrath (*jalal*) or grace (*jamal*). Crapanzano (1973), in his study of sainthood in Morocco, says that the saint made and makes miracles goes without saying. It is what makes him a saint and legitimizes his status. The successor to the saint is therefore linked to him by the chain of blessing (*silsilat al-baraka*). In fact, the legitimacy for the Sufis' claim of wielding miraculous power also came from the tradition of Islam, mainly the life and teachings of the Prophet. The Sufis claimed that they were emulating the Prophet. The followers of the Sufis considered themselves belonging to the community of the Prophet (*ahl-e-sunnat wal jamaat*) and hoped to be successful both 'here' and the 'hereafter'.

A miraculous event (called *khirqu'l-'adat*, 'violation of custom') belongs to one of the following four classes: 1. *mu'jirat* (lit. 'miracles'), which is the sign of priesthood; 2. *karama* or *karamat* (lit. 'favour from God'), meaning to work wonders; 3. *ma'unat* (lit. 'to help), a term used for describing wonderful works performed by ordinary men by mere accidents; and 4. *istidraj* (lit. 'stealth' or 'deception'), by which is meant the amazing deeds of the magician (Subhan, 1970: 108). A popular Sufi saying is: 'Prophets are accorded marvels (*mu'jirat*), saints miracles (*karamat*), and the enemies [of God] deceptions.' It is believed in Sufi circles that the ability to perform miracles is bestowed by God to His friends (*auliya*) (Gardet and Anawati, 1988).

According to Sufi beliefs, the miracles accorded to the saints come to them they know not whence, whereas the prophets know the origin of their marvels and speak in confirmation of them. The miracles of the saint consist in an answer to prayer, or the completion of a spiritual state, whereas the marvels accorded to prophets consist either of producing something from nothing or of changing the essential nature of an object. A saint is expected to hide his *karamat*, whilst a prophet must exhibit his power of performing miracles in demonstration of his prophetic office. However, opinions vary as to whether it is possible for a saint to know that he is a saint. Some maintain that it is possible for a saint to be aware of his sainthood: 'it is a grace (*karamat*) from God to man.' Once grace has been bestowed upon a person, he becomes 'miraculous'. In other words, his usual actions epitomize miracles; the person does not 'perform' voluntarily; they are 'performed' on their own.

Scholars of comparative religion opine that the 'ability to work miracles' is an important element of sainthood. Hasluck (1929: 255-6) writes that a dead man may become a saint posthumously, 'if certain phenomena considered characteristic of the resting place of saints, in particular luminous appearances, occur at his tomb'. To the concept of miracle, Nicholson (1914 [1975]) adds the concept of ecstasy; to quote him (p. 123), 'Anyone thus enraptured is a *wali*, and when such persons are recognized through their power of working miracles, they are venerated as saints.' In an analysis of some definitions of sainthood, Currie (1989: 11) says that in all of them 'an individual is a "saint" if he is believed to be able to provide for human needs through supernatural intervention.'

The problem with this view is that it does not distinguish between the cause and the effect. 'Working miracles' is a consequence of sainthood: once an individual acquires a 'ray of divine grace', he is able to perform miracles, or his actions become miraculous. It is not that the individual performs miracles first, and then moves up to become a saint. In fact, what makes a man a saint is the special relationship he has with God. Because of his nearness to God, he receives the special characteristic called *baraka*, which may be translated as the 'beneficent force, of divine origin, which causes superabundance in the physical sphere, and prosperity and happiness in the psychic order' (Colin, cited in Currie, 1989: 12). Once a person has *baraka*, he is able to work miracles.

Let us illustrate this with the example of Mu'in al-Din Chishti. His hagiographers depict him as having an elevated position; God communicates directly with him. The *Siyar al-Aqtab* has many entries which show God's love for the saint. For instance, Mu'in al-Din is 'summoned by a voice emanating from the tomb of the Prophet at Medina and ordered to go to India and settle at Ajmer' (Currie, 1989: 90). When he died, 'the inscription – The Lover of Allah died in the Love of Allah – appeared on his forehead' (*ibid.*). The belief is that because of his proximity with God, he was endowed with miraculous powers. Even after his worldly exit, it is believed, he makes predictions that come true; he miraculously helps those in difficulty; and conducts miraculous conversations. Stories of saints (not only of Islam but in other religions also) abound with miracles they have performed, and keep on performing after their departure from the mortal world.

Many of the anecdotes dealing with the *karama* of Sufi saints are recurring, repetitive and common to diverse traditions. The miracles that the saints perform are generally traversing long distances in a split second; walking on water; flying in air; conversing with inanimate objects; providing people with food, clothing, and other necessities of life; supernaturally protecting people in times of crises; and predicting future events. One of the reasons that explains the popularity of a shrine is the miraculous cure, victory, gain, and settlement that people achieve by having faith in it and visiting it regularly. In her work on Sufism in Sind, Ansari (1982: 23) says that the devotees of a saint saw in *karamat* a 'means of overcoming or at least confronting the problems which they faced in everyday life'. The belief that the Sufis had the ability to influence the destiny of their respective territories was given further impetus through their claims that the towns and cities would be destroyed if the *baraka* of the dervishes were stopped (Digby, 1984). The Sufis were also approached for protection from certain malevolent powers (such as *pari*, fairy or female djinn). Certain verses from the Quran were recommended as an antidote against the visitation of these spirits. The Sufis also referred to the belief in the evil eye (*nazar*) and black magic (*jadu*). Nizamuddin Auliya believed that *nazar* and *jadu* had the power to destroy their target.

When the descendants of a saint and the visitors to his shrine narrate the cases of his success, his popularity spreads, mainly by the word of mouth, attracting more people, which also implies more gifts and contributions to the shrine. The result is that the shrine prospers: the building is renovated, rest-houses are built, more shops selling ritual ingredients come into existence, etc.

The texts clearly show the relationship between *karamat* and power. For instance, there are also a large number of anecdotes in the texts about the opposition, disrespect and abusive epithets used by the kings (*sultan*), Ulema, and the other people of influence, leading to the provocation of the wrath (*jalal*) of the Sufis. In such situations, miracles served in a way, as a weapon to overawe, subdue, terrorize, and even, occasionally, to annihilate the opponents. The *Siyar-ul Auliya* (p. 94-5) notices that the curse of Shaikh Farid was said to have caused the death of the *wali* of Multan and *qazi* of Ajodhan. The saint's *jalal* affected even the common populace, as his curse was believed to have caused famine and epidemic.

There are many instances described in the texts which reveal an intense competition for power and prestige among the Sufis of diverse traditions. A symbolic miraculous contest was often held between the Sufis of different orders. Sheikh Farid spoke of a 'miracle show' in the hospice (*khanqah*) of Auhaduddin Kirmani-al Sistan. Kirmani caused the death of the local ruler who had no faith in him. The stories of miracles further confirm the Sufi's involvement in matters of political interest. Some Sufis had no qualms about advertising their own spiritual abilities. Khwaja Shahi-mui' Taab of Badaun would often claim that in case his followers ever needed his help after his death, they should visit his grave thrice and the problem would be resolved, and in case nothing happened till the fifth day, they should destroy his grave. However, some saints have detested such Sufis who sought to gain popularity in this manner. For instance, Nizamuddin Auliya felt that it was obligatory for the Sufis to downplay their *karamat*, even as it was binding upon the prophets to display their miracles.

Some scholars have looked into the phenomenon of *baraka* at the empirical level. Crapanzano (1973) notes that in the case of Sufism among the poor and petit bourgeoisie of Egypt, the miracle is a source of individual or group satisfaction rather than constituting a weapon against the broader social system. A challenge is there, but only of a very muted kind. For the Ahmediya order in Aswan and the Hamadsha of the Morocco slums, *baraka* and *karamat* become a dream in which one found refuge. In north Lebanon, it was noticeable that the conception of *baraka* was never referred to at all. One presupposed that *baraka* and *karamat* went together 'like cheese and biscuits' (O'Brien and Donal, 1971). But among the Muridiya, *baraka* is the key element in the making of money and the control of labour by a particular section of the brotherhood, and the pivot of authority. It is a valuable property to be dispensed or earned by the faithful through labour, to the point where work is even put above prayer as a duty.

SUFISM AND NATIONAL INTEGRATION

One of the famous sayings in the Sufi tradition is: *har quam rast rahe din-o-qibla gahe* ('Each people have their own path, their religion, their house of worship'). In other words, Sufism promoted the coexistence of diverse religions and communities, according respect to each of them (Mandal, 1994; Hasan and Roy, ed. 2005). Marc Gaborieau (1983) observed that it was through the works of the Sufis that the Indian continent saw the integration of different religious communities, particularly of the Hindu and the Muslim. Veneration (or worship) of the same saints by Hindus and Muslims created a common cultural and religious bond among them. In many Indian villages, the cult of the holy men cut across different communities, thereby uniting them. Saiyed (1989: 243) writes:

> One reason why communal harmony stands ruptured today is because the integrative role of the saints and their *dargah*s has been undermined by the forces of modernization.

Although this conclusion needs support from empirical studies dealing with the impact of modernization on Sufi cults, there is no doubt that the Sufis promoted the idea of oneness of human beings and the spirit of tolerating diverse religious practices, and these ideals continue till date. The Sufi strategy of creating unity in diversity is expressed beautifully in the following Persian verse that Nizami (1991: 1) has cited: 'Learn from the eyes the way to develop unity and oneness: the two eyes appear different but their vision is one.'

What did religion mean to the Sufis? It was not just conducting the prayer five times. Or, chanting the names of God mentally or on rosary. Pilgrimage, whether going for Hajj or to some local shrine, is also an important religious duty. But for Sufis, devotion (*ta'at*) to God is service to humanity. Nizamuddin Auliya (c.f. *Fawa'id al-Fu'ad*: 11-4) distinguishes two types of devotion to God. The first type called *lazimi* (intransitive) includes prayer, fasting, pilgrimage to Mecca, recitation of religious formulae, etc. The benefit of *lazimi* is confined to the devotee only. *Muta'addi* (transitive) is the second type of devotion. One performs it by spending money on the needy, showing affection to people, and striving to help fellow beings. Such actions bring comfort to others, and their award is endless. When asked about the highest form of devotion, Mu'in al-din Chishti opined that it was nothing but 'to redress the misery of those in distress, to fulfil the needs of the helpless, and to feed the hungry'.

The Sufis argue in favour of the unity of God and the fraternity of human beings, expressed in the idea that 'all men are brothers'. All humans are God's children and so, they are all dear to Him. As one brother or sister is different from the other, irrespective of common parentage and upbringing, in the same way, God's one child is different from the other. The parents love all their children, so does God love all humans He has created. Shaikh 'Abu al-Quddus (d. 1537) of Gangoh said:

> Why this meaningless talk about the believer (*momin*), the heretic (*kafir*, one who does not believe in the oneness of God), the obedient (*mati*), the sinner (*asi*), the correctly guided (*dar raha*), the misdirected (*beraha*), the Muslim, the pious (*parsa*), the infidel (*mulhid*), the fire worshiper (*tarsa*). All are like beads in a rosary.

The unity and oneness of human beings is clearly reflected in the views of the Sufis about non-Muslims. Among the nine principles that governed the early Chishtis in India were: service to others irrespective of their religious affiliations, and tolerance and respect for other religions (Currie, 1989: 65). It is also believed that Mu'in al-Din referred to a local Hindu as a saintly man (*wali*) of God (*ibid*.: 93; Nizami, 1991: 5). About Hinduism, Amir Khusrau said the following:

nist Hindu orche ki dindar chu man
hast basi jay ba qarar chu man
(Though Hindu is not like me in religion,
he believes in the same things as I do.)
ay ki zi but tana ba Hindu bari
hamaz way amuz parastushgari
(O You condemn the idolatry of the Hindu,
learn also from him how worship is done.)

Shah Waliullah (d. 1762) of Delhi reflects sociologically on the link between the individual and the society. The former is *insane-i saghir* ('small man') and the latter, *insane-i kabir* ('big man'). Unity emerges when the individual is integrated with the whole (the 'humanity'). The important concept, therefore, is unity rather than the multitudinous differences that exist between human beings. The Sufis promulgate the spirit of tolerance, not out of weakness or some political gain in perspective, but because they are spiritually and morally convinced about the essentials of goodness in all human beings albeit their religious connections. They also unflinchingly believe that all human beings are one, all have the same spiritual needs and the same origin.

The Sufis use the idea of the 'unity of human origin' to attack the man-made hierarchical institutions. At one time, they were critical of caste system and slavery. There are many stories of the Sufis liberating slaves and asking their followers to do the same. A rejection of caste also meant a concomitant rejection of its customs and practices. The Sufis also criticized the division of people into 'ritually pure' and the 'untouchables'. They were aware of the condition of the Hindu society at that time and the fact that certain groups (called *antyajas*) were denied the basic civic amenities. Rejecting the unequal system based on purity and impurity, their Sufis built their *khanqah*s outside the caste-towns in the midst of the people who were forbidden to live in the town with upper castes and thus led a marginal existence. Nizami (1991: 7) says that the earliest entrants to the Sufi order belonged to lower castes. Many Bhakti saints were impressed with Sufi ideas. Some of them also spent time in the *khanqah*s.

Nizami (1991: 15-24) writes that the Sufis worked at social, linguistic, and ideational and emotional levels to achieve harmony in Indian society. At the social level, the role played by the *khanqah*s was exemplary. People professing different religious faiths and belonging to different strata spent time in Sufi hospices. Food was freely distributed to all. Gifts to Sufi saints were redistributed to needy. The saints listened sympathetically to the problems of all and suggested probable solutions. The lifestyle the Sufis led, wherever they settled down, was similar to that of the local common people. This was crucial for their acceptance in the community. The love and attention they gave people, without any modicum of discrimination, made them the pivot of the local society. For them, the only basis of superiority of one over the other was piety (*taqwa*). But this certainly was not the monopoly of an individual or a group. Through *taqwa*, every individual could acquire the spiritual strength.

The Sufis did not discriminate between different languages. Each dialect had its own flavour and must be preserved, they thought. Thus, they promoted the languages of different regions and communicated their ideas in them, the examples of which are Hindivi, Punjabi, Bengali, Dakhni, Gujarati, and other regional languages. For the development of these languages, the *khanqah* worked like a 'nursery'. It was here that the dialects of the literati and the folk came together, and a common dialect intelligible to both was conceived. More attention was paid to the commoners. Shah Fakhruddin (of Delhi) said that the Friday *khutba* (sermon) should be delivered in Hindavi so that it was within a common person's comprehension. Amir Khusrau's contribution to the development of the local language (Hindavi) and communicating the highly abstract ideas in the vernacular was unparalleled (Mujeeb, 1967: 172-5). To sum up, the Sufis worked towards the linguistic unity of India.

The ideological and emotional integration of the country was a slow process. The most significant ideological support to the Sufis came from the doctrine of the 'unity of being' (*wahdat al-wujud*, or pantheism) that Muhiyuddin Ibn-Arabi had espoused. This doctrine had far-reaching implications as it considered all human beings, and indeed all created beings, as manifestation of God. Ibn-Arabi used to say: 'My heart is a mosque, a church, a synagogue, and a temple. God is love and my heart is the seat of love.'

Some authors also draw parallels between the Islamic *wahdat al-wujud* and the doctrines given in Upanishads. For instance, Shah Abd al-Aziz (d. 1823) of Delhi used to tell his disciples that the terms Allah and Parmeshwar were the same. This idea became integral to the Indian conception of religion as it is clear from the devotional song (*bhajan*) that was most dear to Mahatma Gandhi: *ishwar allah tero nam* ('Your name is Ishwar Allah'). *Mehfil-e-qawwali* spread these ideas to masses. The Hindu ascetic ideas in Kashmir were presented in terms of Islam. In other words, the Sufis made use of the local notions and micro-vocabulary to convey their ideas. Emotional integration followed the one at the ideational level.

CHAPTER 2

Sufi Orders

We can distinguish schematically three great periods within the historic sweep of Muslim mysticism. The first, which covers the first three centuries of Islam (seventh to the ninth), can be called the struggle for existence. Here, mysticism is searching for its right to exist and to overcome certain prejudices against it nourished by touchy and suspicious official authorities. The second period is marked by the attempt at reconciliation and the triumph of Sufism, due to al-Ghazzali, in the eleventh century. Finally, a third period is marked by the spread of the great works of mysticism (twelfth to fifteenth centuries), and from the sixteenth century onward, period of decadence (Levy, 1962).

The first period is a period of quest. Among the companions of Muhammad, the ascetic element is predominant: fasting, spiritual retreat, and meditation. In the seventh and eighth centuries, asceticism became more rigorous and complex. The ascetics still did not leave the community; they lived within it to fulfil the office of preachers or of 'censors'. At Basra, there was a group of open-air preachers, the *qussus*, who spoke to the people and told them anecdotes in rhymed prose. Among these ascetics, who gave themselves to devotion, some readers of the Quran made public exhortation to repentance; these were the 'weepers'. The preachers preached with vehemence expatiating on the end of the world.

The influence of Hasan al-Basri on Sufism was tremendous. His disciples handed down his method. Without wearing any regular religious habit, they had reached some degree of unity, by the second generation, and a coenobitic organization was formed at Abadan, near Basra, during the eight century. To this group belonged Rabia-al Basri, who, in the words of Louis Massignon (1922 [1997]), was the 'saint par excellence of Sunni hagiography'. Basra's contemporary was the school of Kufa. The former had realist and critical tendencies whilst the latter was idealist and traditional. Sufis of the school of Kufa swarmed to Baghdad, where at the beginning of the ninth century, they formed a group of disciples. At that time, many hermitages existed around the city. With the passage of time, Baghdad became a centre for many traditional and literary men in sympathy with the mystics. The famous masters [al-Sarraj (d. 988), al-Kalabadhi (d. 990), al-Hujwiri (d. 1072), and al-Qushairi (d. 1074)] strove to show in their respective writings that Sufis were good Muslims.

With the expansion of Sufi groups, a new attitude developed that transformed Sufism from the religion of the elite into a mass movement, spreading its tenets to all levels of the population. The Sufis not only shared their ideas but also their knowledge of the way leading to salvation with the populace. Gradually, the preaching of the Sufis began to attract wider groups of people. The basic rules of mystical education were elaborated during the eleventh century. Beginning in the early twelfth century, mystical fraternities that included adepts from all strata of society started emerging.

It is difficult to explain how the process of crystallization worked. However, it may be guessed that it might have been a response to an 'inner' (or 'internal') need of the community that was not being met spiritually by the scholasticism of orthodox theologians. People craved for a more intimate and personal relationship with God and the Prophet. When the fraternities came into existence, then the centre of mystical activity was not the private house or shop of the master. A more institutionalized structure proved to be necessary to cope with the growing number of disciples and adepts. Since the Sufis believed in the possibility of communication without physical presence, such a concept of a diffused order was easier for them to accept.

Branches of orders existed in guilds, in student bodies and in military formations. In modern times, the conventional monastery has become the exception (Brown, 1968). Outwardly similar in many ways to that of the Christian, Hindu, or Buddhist, the Sufi monastery is in reality the product of economic and political conditions, not of any esoteric necessity. The Sufis think that the 'monastery is in the hearts of people'. In places where a feudal life still continues, Sufi monasteries, tied to the products of land, continue to flourish. In urban life, Sufi centres are adapted to the tempo of town living, and derive their income from the shops set up in the shrine, or from a levy upon the earnings of the members of the order. The Sufi order, then, stands for the body of people who specialize in the acceptance, usage, and transmission of Sufism. It has no traditional shape, and its outward appearance will depend upon local conditions, and the type of spiritual assistance it provides.

We saw in the last chapter that the organization of religious institutions in Islam dates from an early period. Although Islam does not have the institution of monks and monastery, forty-five men of Mecca and Medina in AD 623 joined together, took an oath of fidelity to the doctrines of the Prophet, formed a fraternity to establish a moral community, and to perform daily penances. Abu Bakr (the first Caliph) and Ali had established the *jamaat* (assembly), wherein vows were taken and exercises practised. Uwais-i-Qarani, in AD 657, founded the first religious order of the Anchorites who practised the greatest austerity. Abu Hashim appears to have built the first *takia*, the convent (Trimingham, 1973). At one time or another, almost all the Sufis have been the members of one of the 'ways', which are called 'orders' by Western scholars, in allusion of their supposed similarity to the Christian religious orders of the Middle Ages.

CATEGORIZATION OF SUFI ORDERS

Abul Fazl (in his *Akbar Nama*) says that the disciples of a 'chosen' being, who introduced a new conduct (or practice), often desired to keep his tradition alive by founding an order, after his name, or by considering him as the founder of a new line. Abul Fazl found that during his time, fourteen orders ('families', *khandan*) were popular: Habibiyah, Tayfuriah, Karkiyah, Saqatiyah, Junaidiyah, Khazruniyah, Tusiyah, Firdausiyah, Suhrawardiyah, Zaydiyah, Idadiyah, Adhamiyah, Hubayriyah, and Chistiyah. The differences between them consist chiefly of personal loyalty to the founder(s) of the orders and the specific practices which they earmarked for their followers. But, membership was not necessarily confined to one order. As often happens, a Muslim (or, even a Hindu) may adopt the teachings and practices of several dervish orders without any paradoxical situation and without in any way affecting his original religious and social standing in the community. Since celibacy was not strictly observed even by the *pir*s themselves, as a result a strong tendency to form 'tribal' groups existed (Gellner, 1969, 1981). These groups arose because of the close spiritual affiliation among the members of the various orders and also because of the long lines of natural and spiritual descendants of the *pir*s. That is why, the term *khandan* ('family', 'extended kin group') was usually employed for the dervish fraternity.

The Hululia and the Ittihada

Many classifications of the Sufis have been offered. One of them is their division into the Hululia and the Ittihada. The Hululia (or, the 'inspired') believe that the divine spirit enters into the devout, whilst the Ittihada (or, the 'unionists'), as the name suggests, subscribe to the idea of attaining oneness with God. According to them, the soul by communing with God becomes God (Rose, 1919).

The distinction between the 'inspired' and the 'unionists' may be further elaborated by referring to Weber's (1963) distinction between asceticism and mysticism. When an individual considers himself as an 'instrument of God', living devoutly according to His commands, and envisaging his salvation or receipt of grace by perfecting himself in terms of the divine precepts, then he is said to be an ascetic, and his mode of existence, asceticism. In contrast, when an individual considers himself the 'vessel of God', carrying out those practices which eventually lead him to become one with God, with no difference of identity, he is said to be a mystic, and his mode of existence, mysticism. As we noted earlier, in the belief of the Sufis, the knowledge that the Prophet imparted was of two kinds: *ilm-e-zahir*, or knowledge by books, and *ilm-e-batin*, or the concentration of the mind on God by worship. It was the latter that led to mystic experiences.

From these two schools sprang five sub-orders: the Wasilia, 'joined to God'; the Ashaqia, 'lovers of God'; the Talqinia, 'instructed'; Zakia, 'penetrated'; and Wahidia, 'solitary'. Each one of them was distinguished in terms of the attitude they had for Allah. The term Batinia (esoteric) is applied to several Sufi sects and, according to Wilberforce Clarke (1891), to the 'Order of the Assasin'. al-Hujwiri (in his *Kashf ul-Mahjub*) writes that the whole body of aspirants to Sufism is composed of 12 sects (or 'schools'), which are: Hululis, Hallajis, Taifurias, Qassaris, Kharraziz, Sayyaris, Muhasibis, Tustaris, Hakimi, Khufaifis, Nuris, and Junaidi. Each of these schools was named after the Sufi saint who was believed to be the founder of the tradition. al-Hujwiri, however, condemned the feature of merging soul with God; he called it 'faithlessness' (*zindaq*) and a belief of the *kafirs* (non-believers). Since soul is not God, the two cannot merge. 'Soul is the creation which takes orders from Him,' so said al-Hujwiri. It is often said that Islam has seventy-two sects, but each sect asserts that all of them have gone astray and that the only true order is itself, the seventy-third, the *firqat-i-najat* or 'party of salvation'. This accords with the Prophet's prophesy that his followers would separate into seventy-three sects, and of these, all but one, the Najia, or the 'saved ones', would go to hell (Rose, 1991).

Ashab-i-sahw (The 'Sober Ones') and *Ashab-i-sukr* (The 'Intoxicated')

The Sufis had classified themselves into two main categories. The first was the *ashab-i-sahw*, the sober ones. The state of sobriety is sometimes called the second separation (*al farq-al-thani*); it is also called *farq baad-al-jama* (separation after union) or *jam-al-jam* (union of unions). They believed in systematic discipline, in patient and sustained spiritual effort, in generally restrained expression of enthusiasm and exaltation. They kept the *tariqah* (path, method) as close as possible to the Shariat. Then, there were the *ashab-i-sukr*, the 'intoxicated'. They were different, but when and why and in what way they became different varied in almost each individual stance. It cannot be said that they did not undergo any discipline or practice severe austerities; nor can it be said that they denied the value or necessity of sustained spiritual effort. What distinguished them was that they evinced a lack of concern with forms that amounted to a repudiation of all the recognized 'academic' methods of training, all standards of intellectual and spiritual attainment. They were intense and sometimes reckless in the expression of their views.

Bashara and Beshara sects

The third categorization of the Sufi movements is in Bashara and Beshara sects. The Bashara sects are orthodox and try to conform to Islamic traditions in spite of their freedom of thought. Their followers observe the customary Islamic practices of fasting, prayer, and consequently are in better standing within the world of Islam. The Beshara ('without the law') have openly flaunted the Islamic tradition and rejected the authority of the Shariat. The Bashara saints attempted to minimize their differences from the Ulema and sought to abide by the Shariat. By contrast, the Beshara saints were deliberately antinomian. The Beshara, and later the Tantric cults (such as the Nath tradition) had many similarities. In their personal lives, the Beshara do not show the orthodoxy of the Bashara, but some amount of licentiousness and corruption does creep in. Traditionally, the *taveez* (amulet), *tona* (magical cure), *jharphunk* (driving away illness through supernatural methods), boons, and curses are connected with the Beshara order. The ordinary Muslim *faqir*s (mendicants) roaming in towns (or villages) are likely to belong to this order.

One of the best accounts distinguishing the Bashara from Beshara was provided by Garcin de Tassy (1997):

> The former (ba-shar) practice the external precepts of the Muslim religion; the latter (be-shar), who are larger in number, do not take these precepts into account at all; they intoxicate themselves with bhang, opium, wine, beer, and other fermented drinks; they do not fast, do not offer the prescribed prayer, and some of them indulge their dissolute passions without any check. The be-shar faqirs do not marry; they live like vagabonds or tramps; they sleep wherever they find themselves; if anybody gives them something to eat, they eat it; if nobody gives, they go away. Muslims consider them generally to be saints and believe that

they do not submit themselves to the duties which an ordinary believer is obliged to, because they are absorbed in their meditation or interior doctrines.

In spite of their antinomianism, the Beshara Sufis commanded a wide following among the Muslim, and some of them rose to become extremely famous and boon-granting saints. The important point to note is that faith in a particular Sufi saint was of primary importance to commoners, and it was unimportant to them whether he was Bashara or Beshara.

Some of them are the Malamati (lit. 'blame-worthy'), Qalandari, and Siyahposh. Qalandaris were initially connected with men who were capable of performing magical tricks and miracles. Siyahposh moved about with a pair of iron tongs (*chimta*). The leaders of some of these sub-divisions resorted to hypnosis and the use of intoxicants. These sects cannot be called orthodox though they retained their Muslim identity. The *pir* became more important to their followers than Prophet Muhammad Himself and His teachings. More important than the Quranic laws, practices like blessings, magic, amulets and 'supernatural medicine', were associated with the Beshara order of Sufi saints. In their personal lives, they might show the austerity of the Bashara saints, as we shall see in the cases of Sheikh Abu Bakr of Delhi and Bu Ali Shah Qalandar of Panipat. The revolt of the Beshara sects was against the austerity and rigidity of the religions. Salvation was not possible to man, they thought, unless he was allowed to lead a free and unshackled life. In the beginning, the Beshara ideology started as a philosophy of freedom; in practice, it later degenerated into licentiousness among some sects. In the sixteenth century, there were a number of 'madmen' and 'naked men', who were respected because of the supernatural powers they were believed to possess (Mujeeb, 1967: 296). Against the background of the practices of these dervishes, some authors have submitted that an individual may be revered as saintly in Islam because of his 'insanity' or 'eccentricity'. Extreme asceticism is also a sufficient qualification for sanctity. Others may derive their sanctity from the millenarian ambition. Some are sanctified after their death if a miracle occurs at their tomb, or wherever they breathed their last. Goga Chauhan, the folk deity of Punjab and Rajasthan, worshipped by both Hindus and Muslims, is a good example of a saint venerated after his death (Lapoint, 1978).

The Suhrawardi order in particular has given rise to a number of Beshara sects (Nasr, 1964). In fact, it has both Bashara and Beshara sections. The Bashara section is further subdivided into the Jalalis (after Sayyid Jalalu'd-Din Shah Mir Surkh-posh of Bukhara), the Makhdumis (after the grandson of Jalalu'd-Din Mukhdum), the Miran Shahis (after Miran Muhammad Shah, a descendant of Jalalu'd-Din), Ismail Shahis (after Hafiz

Muhammad Ismail), and the Dawla Shahi (after Dawla Shah). The Beshara section of the Suhrawardis include Lal Shahbaziyya (founded by Sayyid Lal Shahbaz, d. AD 1324), the Suhagiyya (after Musa Shahi Suhag, a vice-regent of Jalalu'd-Din), and the Rasul Shahi (after Sayyid Rasul Shah of Ajmer).

A close study of the branches (and sub-branches) of the Suhrawardis reveals that although the Bashara and Beshara may be distinguished in ideational terms, continuity definitely exists between them. For instance, saints who were Beshara are also found in the Bashara section; take the example of Ahmad Ma'shuq who was one of the early Suhrawardi Sufis. There are examples of Bashara saints who in course of time became Beshara; some of the Sufis of the Jalali group became 'free' (*azad*) thinkers later in life. The example of Musa Shahi Suhag may be given here. In other words, transition from one category to the other is possible.

Some suggest that the Beshara group cannot be styled as a religious order in the same sense as the Bashara type is, even though some of them appear to be offshoots of the original 'respectable' orders. First of all, among them, the same attention is not given to the organization and control of the order as we find among the others. The same regard for learning is not there, and so the *pir*s of these groups are not among the society of the learned and the great. But, it does not mean that they are ignorant.

It is difficult to give a classification of the Beshara orders that may relate them either historically to the orders from which they sprang or to the specific circumstances of their origin. There are several of the Beshara orders that seem to be 'degenerate offshoots' of regular Bashara fraternities. Further, there may be other groups that appear to be connected with a historical founder, for the possibility of founding new order is not limited.

The concepts of Bashara and Beshara have also been applied to other social categories, such as princes of ruling lineages or poets. For instance, Aurangzeb believed that the law brought by the Prophet was complete and final; so he belongs to the Bashara category. Dara Shikoh had fifty Upanishads translated into Persian with the help of the Kayastha, the caste of scribes, under the title of *Sirr-e-Akbar* ['The Great Secrets']. His action could be interpreted as looking beyond the limits of the Shariat, so he was Beshara.

Poets have been similarly categorized. Meer Hasan Ali (1832 [1973]) made a distinction between two famous Persian poets: Sheikh Sadi and Hafiz. The former adhered to the model of a 'journeyman' on the Sufi path, assiduously following the Shariat. Hafiz, on the other hand, was 'soaked in the wine of divinity', that is to say, he was above the normal rules of moral and social conduct. A paradox here remains unmissed. Although Hafiz defied the rules of religious conduct, his grave is an object of veneration. It may be added here that the model Urdu poetry eulogizes the most is the Beshara lifestyle. Ridiculed are those who follow the religious instructions punctiliously; thus, *zahid* (the teetotaller religious person), *sheikh* (the Bashara scholar), *naseh* (the advisor in moral precepts), *muhtasib* (the enforcer of moral principles), and other religious officials constitute a negative reference group.

Other Classifications

In addition, orders have also been classified into urban and rural. Urban orders have an educated and sophisticated (or 'cultured') following. In north-west Africa, the Sufi orders vary with respect to their political attitudes, whether a particular order is peace loving or militant. The orders also interact with one another. In later centuries, it has not been possible to keep a rigid line of division. However, among the few exceptions, which have been able to keep exclusive membership, are the Tijanya in Africa and Mevleviya in Turkey (suppressed since 1925). The most widespread and probably the oldest existing Sufi order is the Qadiriya. With regard to most of the other orders, it has acted as a kind of lever, because of its looseness and adaptability.

THE NATURE OF THE SUFI ORDER

For the Sufis, the order is not a self-perpetuating entity with a fixed hierarchy and premise, forming a training system for the disciples. Like any other social phenomenon, Sufism is also a process in time; therefore, it is not possible for a Sufi body to take a permanent and rigid form. Schools of the Sufi appear in certain places and under individual masters and carry out activities for spiritual upliftment and human amelioration. The medieval mystics were keen to work out the concept of spiritual sovereignty to its full length. They assigned the importance of regalia to some of the articles of their daily use. The patched frock (*khirqa*), the prayer carpet (*sajjadah*), wooden sandals (*na'lainchubin*), rosary (*tasbih*), and the staff (*'asa*) of the chief saint constituted the mystic insignia in medieval India. To whomsoever the chief saint entrusted these articles in his last moments came to be regarded as his spiritual successor (*sajjadanashin*).

The Sufi orders have specific norms and set codes of dress and ritual. The extent to which a Sufi adheres to these forms is determined by his need for them as prescribed by his master. The basis of the Sufi group hinges on the belief that anyone who desires to seek salvation through the Sufi mode must choose a preceptor, or *pir* or *murshid*, i.e., 'leader'. A person who wants to 'traverse the path' without the guidance of a spiritual master 'is said to have Satan [Shaitan] for his guide'. He is 'compared to a tree that for want of a gardener's care brings forth "none or bitter fruits"' (Nicholson, 1914 [1975]: 32; Subhan, 1970: 87). The larger the following of a master, the greater will be its foundation; a large group of this type is termed a *silsila* (lit. a 'continuous chain'; 'order'). The men with a lesser following would form subgroups and would be termed *faqir*s or dervishes. Those with a larger following are called *pir*, *wali*, and *auliya*; *wali* means 'friend', 'helper', or 'patron', and its plural is *auliya*. The orders are generally named after the founder of the 'specialized technique' that they represent; for instance, the Rifai are called the 'howling dervishes'; the Qalandars, 'shaven'; the Chishti, 'musicians'; the Mevlevi, 'whirling dervishes'; the Naqshbandi, 'silent'. Many of the Sufi orders were highly secretive. It is said that when al-Hujwiri wrote his *Kashf ul-Mahjub*, it was assumed that he had concocted or made up a part of the material since details about many orders and individual mendicants were shrouded in mystery.

Sufi orders may be organized in a monastic form. On the other hand, the Sufi 'monastery' (or 'school') may consist of a linking of people and activities spread over a large area; hence there are orders (and especially branches of orders) with some members in India, others in Africa, some in Indonesia. Collectively they constitute the 'organism' of the school.

The objective of an order is to provide circumstances in which the members can attain the stabilization of their inner being comparable (or identical) with those of the early transmitters. All members know that it is not possible for the Sufi to attach himself to a personality alone. He knows that his interior powers are being guided from one objective to the next; hence there is a fixed succession of progress. The Sufi is a 'traveller'. He first attaches himself to the teacher. When he reaches the maximum development possible, the teacher transfers him to the 'reality' of the founder of the order. From here, he transfers his consciousness to the substance of the Prophet, from there to the reality of Allah.

MAJOR *SILSILAS*

The chief medium through which Sufi influences could filter down to the lower strata of the society was the Sufi *turuq* (or *salasil*), the Sufi brotherhood. The Sufi convents (*zawiah*, *khanqah*), which served later as the centres for the particular *silsila*, existed in the tenth century. But it was Hazrat Saiduddin Abul Khayr (d. 1049), who, for the first time, attempted to regularize convent life and give it a permanent basis by prescribing certain rules of conduct for the inmates of the Khanqah. In the early twelfth century, the first real Sufi orders, the Suhrawardi and the Qadiri, were founded. Later, many Sufi orders originated in Egypt and north Africa, but most of them were confined to their place of origin or to adjacent areas.

In the Indian subcontinent, besides the Suhrawardi and the Qadiri, first the Chishti and later, the Naqshbandi orders have been widespread. The Naqshbandis appeared in India before AD 1600. The Shattariya order, which flourished in the sixteenth and seventeenth centuries, found more fertile ground in Indonesia. Numerous other suborders emerged in the course of time as independent *silsila*s, but originally derived their authority from the main universal orders.

The Chishtis and the Suhrawardis belong to the Habibiyya order, founded by Habib Ajami in the eighth century. The Qadiris are an offshoot of Tartawsiyya, the order ascribed to Abu'l-Farah Tartawsi. The Naqshbandis sprang from the line of Junaydiyya, the order founded by Abu'l-Qasimu'l Junayd (tenth century); however, they can be traced back, from Junayd, through a different line of succession to Abu Bakr, the first Caliph. The main, sophisticated urban order has been that of Mevleviyah, instituted by Rumi (d. AD 1273).

Khwaja Abu Ishaq Shami Chishti, ninth in spiritual succession from Ali, is regarded as the founder of the Chishti order. He migrated from Asia Minor and settled at Chisht in Khorasan. Abu Ishaq Chishti had four spiritual descendants: Khwaja Abu Ahmad (d. AD 966); Khwaja Abu Muhammad (d. AD 1020); Khwaja Abu Yusuf (d. AD 1067); and Khwaja Mawdud (d. AD 1133). Fourth in the line of succession from Khwaja Mawdud appeared Khwaja Mu'in al-Din Chishti of Ajmer (popularly called Ajmerwale Baba or Gharib Nawaz), the sponsor of the order in India. He has been the most renowned saint in the history of the Chishti order; because of which some say that he, and not Khwaja Abu Ishaq, should be regarded as the founder of this order. The second, fourth, and fifth Chishti saints (Qutb al-Din Bakhtiyar Kaki, Nizamuddin Auliya, and Nasir al-Din Chirag Dehalvi), all have their separate tomb complexes. Their *dargah* complexes are respectively at Mehrauli, Nizamuddin, and Chirag Delhi. The last two areas are known after the names of the saints who had their hospices there. Only the third saint of the Chishti order, Farid al-Din Mas'ud Shakarganj, popularly called Baba Farid, is buried elsewhere, in Pakpattan, a town of Punjab (in Pakistan). The Chishti order is now indigenous to India (see Bhajjan 1991). From AD 1236, the year of the death of Mu'in al-Din of Ajmer, to AD 1887, when Sayyid Mir 'Abdullah Shah died, there have been 188 Chishti saints in India and Pakistan.

The Qadiri order sprang up from the Khanwada Tatawsiyya, and traces its origin to 'Abdu'l-Qadir Gilani. He is also called Hasanu'l-Husayni, on account of his descent, on his mother's side from Husain, and on his father's side from Hasan, Prophet Muhammad's grandsons. The order was established in India as late as three hundred years after the death of its original founder. Sayyid Muhammad Ghawth, tenth in the line of succession, founded this order in India. Between AD 1515, the year of the death of Shah Inayatullah, and AD 1881, Sayyid Ghawth 'Ali Shah's year of death, there have been 116 Qadiri saints in India and Pakistan.

The Suhrawardi order originated from the Junaydi Khanwada, and was founded by Diya'u'd-Din Najib Suhrawardi (d. 1167), the author of the Adabu'l-Muradin, 'Manners of the Disciples'. It was through some of his leading disciples that the order gained in reputation and influence. The history of this order in India began with the advent of some of the disciples of Shihabu'd-Din Suhrawardi from Baghdad. They were contemporaries of the famous Chishti saint of that time, Qutbu'd-Din Bakhtiyar Kaki. Many of these Suhrawardi disciples came under his influence, and in course of time their names were formally admitted to the calendar of the Chishti order. The man who did most to spread the influence of Suhrawardis in India was Baha'u'd-Din Zakariya (twelfth century AD). Before him, Sayyid Nuru'd-Din Mubarak, who is buried in Delhi, also played a significant role. From AD 1249, when Nuru'd-Din died, to AD 1832, the year of death of Sheikh Qalandar Shah Qureshi whose *dargah* is in Lahore, there have been in India and Pakistan seventy-two saints in the Suhrawardi order.

The origin of the Naqshbandi order is generally ascribed to Khwaja Baha'u'd-Din Naqshband, who died in Persia in AD 1389. The word *naqshband* literally means an embroiderer or printer of cloth, and, as applied to the founder of this order, it probably refers to his family occupation. The first Naqshbandi saint to enter India was Khwaja Baqi Bi'llah Berang, seventh in the line of succession from Khwaja Baha'u'd-Din, the founder. Acting on the instruction of his *pir*, he came to Delhi, where he died after three years. His disciple, Ahmad Faruqi, ritually established this order in India. There have been sixty-four Naqshbandi saints in India and Pakistan, from AD 1603 when Baqi Bi'llah Berang died in Delhi to AD 1860, the year of death of Imam 'Ali Shah whose shrine is at Gurdaspur.

In addition to the four main orders, there are others, called the 'minor orders', such as the Uwaysis, the Madaris, the Shattaris, the Qalandaris, the Malamatis, to count some prominent names. There are said to be 103 shrines of these saints in India and Pakistan.

From this description, we should not assume that a *murid* (pupil) belongs to one order only. The Muslims believe that although one should have exemplary loyalty to one's *pir*, he is permitted to visit pious people of other orders or their shrines to 'get benefits of grace' (*faiz*). It is not only that the same individual visits the shrines of saints of different orders, but also within the same family, different members may repose faith in two or more orders. In one of the Old Delhi families, I interviewed, the parents were Qadiri; of their eight children, seven (two sons and five daughters) were Naqshbandi, and one son did not belong to any order. The father, a devout

Qadiri, used to visit Maulana Abu'l Hasan Zaid Faruqi, a Naqshbandi saint, when he was alive. He was so impressed with him that he thought of handing over (*ba'it karna*) his children to Maulana Zaid as his 'disciples'.

As the 'orthodox' Sufis insisted on conformity with the Shariat, they did not come into conflict with orthodox Islam except on the question of *sama'*. Because of their individualistic approaches, and being organized into separate orders, the Sufis could not act as a unifying force for the entire Muslim community. But the *murid*s of an order did develop among themselves fraternal relationships (*pir-bhai*). The orders remained and were recognized as distinct, but the practice of pupils seeking spiritual guidance and benefit from Sheikhs of several orders became gradually common.

All the Sufi orders (and most of the Sufis) had their particular system of litanies and other devotions. Towards the sixteenth century, however, their difference on one issue became conspicuous. Some Sufis believed in *wahdat-al-wujud* ('Unity of Being' or Pantheism) so fervently that it became a central feature of their thought. Against this were others who brought to the forefront the doctrine of *wahadat-al-shuhud*, the unity of the phenomenal world, or unity as apprehended by one who sees God, the universe and himself. The doctrine of the 'Unity of Being' made Sufism metaphysical and intellectual; on the other hand, the representatives of *wahdat-al-shuhud* made a place for themselves in the official and social hierarchy.

THE KHANQAH

The first stage of Sufi organization was the circle of pupils and adepts around a master. In Khorasan (around AD 815-6), the location of such a group, was a centre called Khanqah (translated as 'convent'). This was not a building designed especially for the purpose, but simply a dwelling taken over, to house a Sheikh and his dervishes. Many such centres are recorded in the eleventh century during the lifetime of Abu Said ibn-Abul Khair (AD 967-1049). The Khanqah of Sultan Babur-sal at Cairo, built in AD 1310, provided for four hundred Sufis, whilst that of Siryaqus had one hundred rooms for individual Sufis. In the reign of Muhammad bin-Tughlaq, Shihabuddin Ahmad al-Umari was told that in Delhi there were two thousand large Khanqahs.

In Arab controlled regions, some of the frontier posts, known as *ribats*, had become centres of devotees. But these are not to be equated with Iranian Khanqahs because the master-pupil relationship did not figure in them. In the following stage of organizational development, the centre of a teaching and guiding master was frequently designated by the same term, *ribat*, on the banks of the Tigris, while the Iranian term *khanqah* was adopted in Iraq, Syria and Egypt, but not the Maghrib. Both types of institutions were especially designed for Sufi groups, but were different in construction. The *ribat* was centred upon a master, whilst the congregational outlook dominated the Khanqahs, and the officially appointed head was an 'administrator' (*mujadid*) rather than a 'shepherd of souls'.

In the development of organized Sufism, an earlier form of Khanqah was *zawiya*. It was a small modest establishment pivoted on a Sheikh. At first, it was relatively impermanent because the saints were frequently migrants. It was through these men that self-perpetuating *tariqa*s (the path) came into being. The *zawiya*s were not endowed like the Khanqahs and *ribat*s, although in time when becoming family residences, they tended to accumulate grants (*aufaq*). Khanqahs were sometimes endowed and sometimes not. If endowed, it was the testator's wish that the income of the convent should be spent on the purposes of those who had mastered their passions and on 'travellers' by the *tariqa*; it was unlawful to expend it on habituated and professional beggars. Most Sufi Khanqahs urged their disciples to pursue hard manual labour in order to crush the baser self (*nafs*).

The Khanqahs were not strictly guidance centres, but associations of people prepared to live a common disciplined life. They had their rules regarding the admission of Sufis into their companionship, whether for shorter or longer time. They had to assure themselves that those seeking admission were genuine and had been trained and initiated by a qualified Sufi teacher.

Over a period of time, the meaning of the term Khanqah has undergone change. It now means a tomb, especially of a *pir* or *faqir*, not necessarily one of the regular clergy. The tomb may be merely a mound of earth, but is more often a pile of stones or bricks, with a wall to enclose the grave. As it is usual to make vows to such tombs, branches of trees above them have often rags (*herak*) tied to the twigs. If a specific prayer has been answered, appropriate offerings are hung up, such as a cradle for a child bestowed, a halter for a stolen bullock recovered, earthen pitchers, clocks, etc. Such tombs become surrounded by trees, since no one dare cut them down, or remove fallen wood from the Sufi's grave. In this way, the tombs have also promoted ecological conservation.

The tombs also became sanctuaries for property as no one would venture to steal in its vicinity. The reasons of these prohibitions varied, but common to them was that such actions would desecrate the sacred geography, thus constraining the holy powers to punish offenders. The tombs are also attributed with curative powers; for instance, the tomb at Ishar in Shahpur is popular for the cure of toothache and ague. The sufferer offers cowries at the grave and the pain does not recur for as many years as he keeps on presenting cowries. In non-Arab Asia, the term Khanqah continued to be used, but the focal point was the tomb.

The institutions (*zawiya*, Khanqah, *dargah*), which were associated with a Sufi saint, survived as long as their founder's *baraka* (spiritual charisma, grace) continued to manifest itself. Veneration began for someone who was thought to have *baraka*, and it continued even after his death. If the charisma of a saint (whether living or dead) kept on working, pilgrims and offerings flowed in.

The Khanqah (or the *dargah*) thus became an institution among those Sufis who belonged to an order. As an institution, it lasted longer than the lives of its founders and individual inmates. In course of its survival, it was bound to develop characteristics, which did not harmonize with the principles and ideals of service. All institutions get routinized with time; Sufi orders were no exception.

Physical Structure of the Khanqah

A Khanqah normally consisted of a central courtyard (*qaa* or *sahn*), having cloisters (*riwaqs*) along two sides, within which were situated cells (*khalwas* or *tibaq*) of the Sufis. On one side was the main hall, the focus of their communal life, where their common devotional exercises took place. This was simple in construction. In front of the *mihrab* was the sheepskin of the Sufi upon which he reclined during ceremonies and receptions. Over the niche was engraved the name of the founder and religious phrases, such as the Shahada. Frequently, there was a separate mosque, whilst kitchens and other offices and sometimes a bathhouse were attached. Both resident and migrant Sufis were provided with food and lodging, and the residents with clothing and other perquisites. Many Khanqahs were not built specially for the purpose, but their owners bequeathed existing houses as pious foundations.

Rose (1919) has given a detailed description of al-Khanqah al-Qedim in Aleppo, founded by Nuraddin ibn-Zengi in AD 1148. Ibn Battuta (1953) has described Khanqahs in Cairo in AD 1326. He wrote that each Khanqah had a Sufi saint and a superintendent (*haris*) who were celibate. There were separate Khanqahs for the married. The duty of the saint and the *haris* included attendance at the five prayers, passing the night in the Khanqah, and attendance at the *dhikr* gatherings held in the hall. It was customary for each one of them to occupy his special prayer mat (*ja namaz*).

In the east, the concentration was on the *zawiya* mode of organization. It had a tomb, a small mosque, a Quran school and a room for indoor recitals. A couple of teachers taught the children to recite the Quran. Disciples of the saint taught legal sciences and principles of mysticism. There were rooms of the Sufi and other members of his line with their wives, children, and servants, together with housing for affiliates, pilgrims and travellers. The whole was self-sufficient, having land for cultivation and animals. It was like a *gemeinschaft* ('community').

Jamatkhana and *Dargah*

Though broadly used for hospices, these terms (*jamatkhana* and *dargah*) differ in their connotations. The Khanqah is a spacious building providing separate accommodation for each visitor and inmate. The *jamatkhana* is a large room where all the disciples study, sleep, and pray on the floor. The Chishti saints built *jamatkhanas*; the Suhrawardis constructed Khanqahs.

Sheikh Nizamuddin Auliya's quarters and *jamatkhana* were two separate units. A banyan tree was the main feature of the complex. The *jamatkhana* itself was a pillared hall with a few rooms on the first floor. Four walls surrounded an open space in front of the courtyard and access was through a vestibule. On both sides of the hall were small rooms, which the Sheikh used for his mid-day rest. A few other small rooms had grain stored in them for distribution to people. There was also a kitchen where food was cooked for the poor and visitors. The pillars and walls were made of mud and the roofs were covered with logs and earth.

The *zawiyas* were smaller places where the Sufis lived and prayed, but unlike inmates of Khanqahs and *jamatkhana*, they did not establish any vital contact with the outside world. This is one of the important characteristics of the *gemeinschaft* type of living. In the seventeenth and eighteenth centuries, the *dargahs* came into existence. Their primary aim was to provide a place to men of their affiliation to devote time to religious pursuits.

Khanqah residents

Khanqah residents were of three types. The first group was of the novice or servant class (*ahl-i-khidmat*, or 'servitors'). They were assigned such duties as waiting on others that enabled them to become acquainted with the company (*suhbat*) of mystics and to be initiated in humility. The spirit of service enabled novices to rise to the second group of mystics (called *ahl-i-suhbat*, 'associates'), who learnt the social ethics of Sufism. Members of the third category were aged Sufis (*ahl-i-khilwat*, or 'recluses'), generally living in seclusion, entirely dedicated to prayers and meditation. The rule was that in a Khanqah, the young should live communally, allowing older Sufis to reside privately. Inmates were supposed to cooperate and dine together, differences between Sufis be overcome and there be no hypocrisy in relationships.

The Suhrawardi divided the people of Khanqah into residents and travellers. The latter were the wandering dervishes, expected to reach the Khanqah before afternoon prayers, and if late, should spend the night in a mosque. The residents should extend warm welcome to the travellers, and serve the best food to them. The travellers should not be pestered with questions, although resident Sufis should themselves answer all queries. If an itinerant dervish was ignorant of the customs and practices of the Khanqah, the duty of the residents was to explain to him what was expected. The travellers to the Khanqah, after a stay of three days, must seek service in the Khanqah, unless their time is spent in devotion.

The Khanqah as the Mediating Institution

As the Khanqahs developed, they experienced an experimental form of community living. In almost every Khanqah, a person was sure to get a meal and with luck, a share of money or goods distributed as charity that would tide him over the next crisis. Khanqahs (great and small alike) dispensed hospitality to travellers and wandering Sufis. It was the Sufi (and those dedicated to a spiritual existence) who starved; inmates of the Khanqah got what they wanted. Food was freely distributed (*langar*) in Khanqahs. The Khanqahs distributed money, food, and worldly goods to poor, destitute, and needy. Saiyyid Mohammad Ghaus Shattari (d. 1563), singer Tansen's spiritual mentor, was fond of bulls and cows, which he kept in large numbers in his Khanqah. His genial and generous treatment of every visitor made his Khanqah at Gwalior a haven of refuge. The instruction in Khanqahs was to sweep and clean the stores everyday so that nothing remained of the worldly goods, which might distract the attention of people. However, a characteristic of Khanqah life (which may not be admirable) was the opportunity it gave a large number of people to live on the generosity of rich admirers of the Sufi, and thus introduce into Khanqah the 'odour of parasitism' (Mujeeb, 1967).

Suhrawardi (in *Awariful-Ma'arif*) observed that the Khanqah's corporate life provided an opportunity for individual members to exchange their views and experiences. Sufi Khanqahs were the only places where people professing different religions, enjoying different social statuses, and belonging to different social backgrounds met. To the Chishti Khanqahs came the Hindus and the Muslims, the *jogi*s and Qalandars, old and young, villagers and townspeople, and men and women (*Tarikhi Feruz Shahi*: 343). In the Khanqahs of Sheikh Farid of Ajodhan, Gesu Daraz of Gulbarga, Sheikh Ahmad Khattu of Ahmedabad, Rishi Nuruddin of Kashmir, views were 'exchanged between Sufis and *jogi*s in a cordial atmosphere' (*Fawaid*: 84-5; *Jawabni al-Kalim*: 186-7; *Tuhfat al-majalis*: 52-65; Nizami, 1991). The propinquity of life in a Khanqah produced a healthy rivalry between Sufis in the perfection of their morals and conduct. One of the main contributions these Khanqahs made was to the development of languages. In the early history of the Punjabi, Bengali, Hindivi, Dakhani, Gujarati, and other regional languages, it is the Khanqah which stands out prominently as the main nursery where the language of the elite and language of the common people came together and paved the way for their emergence.

The Khanqah might be said to have served as a mediating institution between the Sufi and his saintly qualities, on the one hand, and the believers, on the other. Through the medium of the Khanqah, a saint could definitely reach out to a vast multitude of the faithful. Being handed over to a Khalifa after a *pir*'s death, the main task of the successors was to cherish the memory of the dead saint. They observed the proper rites at his tomb and guided pilgrims and visitors to receive the saintly blessings of the dead *pir*. They also legitimized their alleged closeness to the saint as soon as possible after his death. Besides the supernatural benefits the saints gave people, in certain cases, they also acted as mediators between tribes, resolving their conflicts. They were also mediators between the rulers and the ruled (Gellner, 1981). Their closeness to state power was due to the matrimonial alliances with the daughters of ruling princes. For instance, the Amir Sultan Shamsu'd-Din Muhammad, the fourteenth century Suhrawardi saint, who was famous for exerting political influence on the state, married the daughter of Sultan Bayazid (Subhan, 1970: 185).

The attraction of a Muslim shrine is defined by the supernatural power of the saint who is buried in the tomb. From the eighth century, Khanqahs came to be established where admirers and disciples listened to the sermons on mysticism by the saint and spent their time in meditation. In some Khanqahs, a practice to sing devotional songs was also introduced. The role of the Sufi centres in spreading education made the influence of Sufism inseparable from the development of education in Islam. During the post-Mongol period, the formal educational system was destroyed in certain regions. But, at that time, the Sufi centres remained the sole repository of formal and academic knowledge, and they provided the base from which the traditional schools sprang up once again.

From the time of the Khorasanian Abu Said, Khanqahs provided a rendezvous for artisans and merchants. All Khanqahs in India followed this tradition for the mutual benefit of both Sufis and their visitors. Some Khanqahs operated a type of 'spiritual insurance' scheme in which financial pledges were made by merchants in return for Sufi prayers for protection during a journey. The chain of Khanqahs of Sheikh Abu Ishaq from Kazirun to China is a case in point. The network of Chishtis, Suhrawardis and Firdausia Khanqahs in north India, and those of the Kubrawiyya, and of other orders in Kashmir, offered greatly needed psychological comfort to merchants and other travellers during this period.

CONSTITUTION OF THE SUFI ORDER: THE HIERARCHY

The head of an order is called *sheikh*. He may be the founder of the order or the spiritual heir of the founder. A member of the order is expected to render absolute and unquestioning obedience to him. Subordinate to the *sheikh* are the *muqaddams* (chiefs). They are placed in charge of several monasteries. From among the 'brethren' (*ikhwan*) of the order, certain persons are elected as assistants to the *muqaddams*. These are the *wakil* who have charge of the property and funds of the order, and the *raqqabs* who are employed as couriers to carry dispatches. In the assembly of the members of the order, the *muqaddam* is assisted by the *chau'sh* ('leader'), the *muddah* ('percentor'), and the *qassad* ('chanter of elegies'). There are also the *allam*, or standard bearers, and the *suqqah*, or water carriers. Members of the order, who regard their duties as religious, fill these offices.

The simple members of an order are called *ikhwan* ('brothers') or *ashab* ('companions'), while the generic name of dervish covers all. A disciple is called a *murid*, and his spiritual guide, a *pir*. He who faithfully performs the religious rites of the order is termed *murabit*. Nicholson (1914 [1975], 1921 [1975]) writes that earlier, it meant a person who habitually lived in a *ribat*, or frontier guardhouse. Such buildings were occupied by troops, but pious individuals, wishing to participate in a holy war (*jihad*) against unbelievers, also joined them. He further observed that the word *murabit* has now got the exclusive religious meaning of a devotee or saint. Outside of these are, what may be called the 'associates', the lay members of the order. They do not live in the *zawiyas*. They are acquainted with the secret signs and words, by the use of which they can always claim the protection of the members. They do not join in the *dhikr*, but use the rosary in the same way as do the full members.

The founders of these orders were orthodox Muslims – they not only followed the injunctions of the Quran, but also those of the Sunna. The founders of the more modern orders follow the special teaching of some famous theologian, who can show that his instruction was based on that of the men who lived and taught in the earliest days of Islam. They maintain that their objective in founding an order is the glory of God, the extension of Islam and the perfection of men. They claim to be able to lead their disciples by successive stages to the one that they have attained, or at least have approximated to, the spiritual perfection.

A supernatural claim is made regarding the origin of many orders. The Sufis hold that the whole world is divided into circles (*wilayat*), each in charge of a living saint (called *sahib-i-wilayat*), who controls all temporal affairs therein. The doctrine of the *auliya* (or *wali*) appears to owe its origin to Abu Huzail Muhammad al-Altaf, who taught that there were at all times in the world these 'friends of Allah'. They were protected against all sins and could not lie. Members of a religious order are called dervish, but only those gifted by Allah with miraculous powers are the *auliya*. They stand under a regular hierarchy headed by the Qutb (also known as Wazir). Above him in holiness stand the companions of the Prophet Muhammad. Some Sufis also held that the *auliya* stood higher than even the Prophet, but many rejected this view. Many subscribe to the belief that there are always a fixed number of saints on the earth, four thousand of them according to some, and 356, according to others. At the summit of the hierarchy is the Ghaus ul-Azam – the 'great refuge' – the saviour whose merits can atone for the sins of others. To repeat, the Qutb follows him. After him are the *autad* ('picket'), one for each cardinal point with Mecca for the centre.

In addition, there is a category of the Pir Ghaib. They are a class of saints whose names are not known or whose miracle it was to hide themselves from the people at some particular period of their life, or it might be that the body of the saint disappeared after his death.

The *sheikh*s are skilful in dealing with new converts. They show great discernment in adapting their instructions to the various classes of men with whom they have to deal. All must absolutely obey the *sheikh*, keep secret the affairs of the order, and be loyal to it. The intensity of commitment a disciple should have for his teacher is expressed by Hafiz in the following words: 'If the tavern-keeper (i.e., *pir*) orders thee to stain thy prayer-mat with wine, do it: for the traveler is not unaware of the customs and manners of the stages of love's path' (c.f. Subhan, 1970: 87-8; Gaborieau, 1989: 214).

PIRI-MURIDI IN SUFI DISCOURSE

Sufism begins as an individual's effort to achieve a direct relationship with God. Its absolute necessity is some kind of blind submission to a *murshid* or inspired guide. The holy men, otherwise known as *pir* or *faqir*, in their capacity as spiritual leaders are called *murshid*s. Titus (1959) states that the spiritual guide is known as the *murshid*, *pir* or *sheikh* and it is necessary to have a *pir* or *murshid* (spiritual advisor, a guide on the right path). *Sheikh* or *murshid* is a spiritual guide, teacher, and example, and one whose presence is an inspiration to spiritual development, maturity and illumination. *Wali* (or saint) is one who possesses a direct experience of the reality of God demonstrated through extraordinary spiritual knowledge or miracles. According to Turner (1975), the Arabic term *marabout*, dervish, Sufi, or *wali* cannot be translated in the Christian term of saint, because the history, institutions and frameworks of these religions are distinct. There is no centralized, ecclesiastical machinery in Islam. There is no official or homogenous terminology of *marabout*ism. In Arabic, the term is *murabit*; in

Portuguese and Spanish, *marabuto*. Finally, the *marabout* is a Muslim, who devotes himself to the practice and teaching of religion (Geertz, 1968; Westermarck, 1926).

The Anatomy of Relationship

The Sufi accent on conduct (*ikhlaq*) follows from their sense of the sanctity of inner life: the Sufis believe that the company of a worldly person whose conduct is good is to be preferred over the company of a proclaimed *faqir* whose conduct leaves much to be desired.

They declare that God hid himself after creating man; to reveal the God dwelling within man, one must hide one's self. In order to break the eggshell of the gross body, the Sufis affirm the importance of three conditions: hardship (*illat*), humiliation (*zillat*), and poverty (*killat*). The Sufis revel in these adverse conditions. They abstain from the company of those who do not share their way of life. The reason for this is simple. It preserves the purity of the heart, saving it from foul influences of others. The Sufis go a step further – they abstain from reading books of religion, for such readings may be misleading. First, the Sufi must experience and then by way of confirmation, read his own literature, which is not only extensive but also intensive as most of it unfolded in meditation to its seekers.

Besides God, the Sufis do not turn their gaze in worship to anyone, except their *pir-o-murshid*, who is exalted to a near divine status as the agent through whom the voice of God makes itself heard. The flow of force (*twajeh*) from him transforms and transfigures the seeker: he is never the same person again. By remaining in the presence of such a master, the seeker acquires his attributes. It is believed that he attains communion (*fana*) with the master. The outcome is the death of the disciple and the birth of an enlightened one. By meditating on the *pir*, the disciple himself achieves illumination and becomes a master in his own turn (Nanda and Talib, 1989).

The Sufi masters expect only one thing from their disciples, obedience to the values that they have been taught. The seeker must show himself to be worthy of the blessing that has been conferred upon him. His life must be above reproach, as 'nobody would cast precious jewels in an unclean vessel'. It is thus that the Sufis declare seemingly in a spirit of paradox: 'It may take time to be a man, but it does not take any time to be God.'

The pivot of a Sufi fraternity is the *sheikh*, whose residence or place of teaching serves as a centre of the spiritual activities of his congregation. The membership is normally of two kinds. Besides the proper inmates (or the immediate circle), there is usually a large member of associates or lay members who pay visits from time to time in order to get fresh instructions. They are otherwise allowed to carry out their normal life. To teach and treat people according to their capacity and individual needs is a cardinal principal of the Sufi saints. An able disciple may succeed in obtaining the 'robe' (*khirqa*) and the privilege to teach the master's methods as his Khalifa. Other initiates, during the first stage of their apprenticeship, may be required to render prolonged services at the Khanqah, such as gathering food, cooking and cleaning. Among these dwellers, the first type is known as *ahl-i-suhbat* (those who share the company of the Sufi saint or his spiritual descendants); the second, *ahl-i-khidmat* (those who render service); and the third, *ahl-i-khilwat* (the associates, servitors and recluses).

The *ahl-i-khidmat* are novices who render service in order to become acceptable to the men of deeds and of stages, i.e., those engaged in practices and have advanced some stages on the way or 'path'. By service, they become fit for 'kinship', i.e., admission to the next degree in the order. Retreat (*khilwat*) is recommended to the old and *suhbat* (association) to the young. Some converts insist on fitness for service by outward appearance and inward and pure device whereby the candidate acquires kinship with Sufis. Exclusion was inflicted as a punishment, but the seeker of the pardon could be readmitted on payment of a fine (*gharamat*), which took the form of victuals.

The relationship between a spiritual master and his disciple is termed *piri-muridi* in Sufi parlance. *Piri-muridi* becomes more significant when one witnesses, day after day, a large member of Hindus and Muslims thronging to the *pirs* stationed at various *dargahs* of India. The visitor to the Indian subcontinent is amazed to see the innumerable shrines of saints, tombs and places of pilgrimage (Schimmel, 1975). For Sufis, the *pir-murid* relationship is the most fundamental person-to-person relationship. It is the relationship between a student with his teacher, between a spiritual seeker and the dispenser of spiritual benefits, between a devoted slave and his master, between a lover and his beloved. At its centre is the ultimate closeness between the saint and his follower. The saint, with his knowledge of the unseen (*ilm al-ghaib*), is believed to be aware of everything his disciple thinks, or does, or says. The *murid* also knows that his *pir* has penetrated his inner space. The *pir* is inside his follower and the *murid* refers all decisions back to him. Such a relationship makes for the personal, psychological security, strength, and stability within the disciple. When faced with difficulty, the *murid* handles them not alone, but with his *pir* (Pinto, 1995). A novice must treat his spiritual teacher with great respect and 'obey him like a corpse in the hands of corpse bearers'.

Jalaluddin Rumi firmly believed that to attain the truth, a guide is necessary, who must be selected with extreme care, for though there may be many, there are but few real guides to the truth. A true guide works for the common welfare of the creatures and a false guide for his own gain and vanity. The true guide brings union and harmony, while a false guide, discord and hatred (Schimmel, 1975: 75).

The relationship between the spiritual guide and preceptor (*pir-o-murshid bar Haqq*), on one side, and the seeker of truth (*murid, talib-i-Haqq*) on the other, receives utmost importance in all esoteric traditions. Its importance derives from the essential role that the master plays in transmitting his spiritual influence (*baraka*) to the innermost part of his disciples in the course of the initiatory rite (*ba'it wazifa*), thus legitimizing his membership in and sanctioning his indissoluble link with the spiritual tradition in question. Through this permanent bond, the Sufi assumes the role of a mediator between the effusion of Divine grace from the transcendental plane and those individuals eager to receive it, thus assuming the responsibility for the rebirth and inner transmutation of the disciple. The importance of the Sufi for the spiritual rebirth and growth of his protégé continues during the period of apprenticeship and spiritual emancipation (*tarbiyat*) that follows. *Piri-muridi* is thus an institutionalized form of socialization that aims at forcing the *murid* to give up his awareness of manifesting himself and take on the new awareness of manifesting God at each and every moment of his life (Nanda and Talib, 1989; Pinto, 1995).

The *murid* is completely dependent on his *pir* for his own personal qualities, with the result that he finds himself manifesting not himself, but the *pir*. From here, it is a step towards realizing that by manifesting the *pir*, he is actually manifesting God. He has now attained union (*wasl*) with God (Pinto, 1995).

The disciple's need to have a *sheikh* is inevitable. If a man does not have a *sheikh*, then, as we noted earlier, the Satan becomes his *sheikh*, luring him back into the temptation of his ego, and finally destroying him in confusion and error. A disciple keeps unswerving faith in the words of the *sheikh* and receives infinite love and care from him. The relationship is strictly based on the pattern of the Prophet's relations that enjoyed the Divine support.

The men of the path or Sufism are of three grades, the *mubtadiyan* (or beginners), whose will is surrendered to the *sheikh* and to whom no raiment goods or aught else is lawful save by his desires; the *mutawassilan* (the middle ones) are those who have surrendered their will to God, and who submit as occasion demands; and finally, the *muntahiyan* or perfected, who by God's will are absolute.

As far as the disciple is concerned, his first real step is finding such a person, who would first remove the rust from his mind, so that the external fact may be accessible to him. The guide should be free from subjective ransom or seeking leadership. He must not seek precedence in being a guide or have a desire to follow. The true leader will delay accepting applicants as disciples until he is sure that he has no such subjectivity. The *sheikh*s are very skilful in dealing with new converts. They show great discernment in adapting their instructions to the various classes of men with whom they have to deal. All must obey the *sheikh* absolutely and keep in perspective the affairs of the *silsila* and be loyal to them (Nanda and Talib, 1989).

Since the Sufi path is an arduous journey involving risks and impediments, it could be traversed only under the strict supervision of *sheikh* or *pir*, the mentor, who has himself traversed the 'path', and survived the raptures of states (*hal*), and experienced the severity of the divine majesty and clemency of the Divine Beauty. The *tariqa* involves a journey to a different spiritual station (*maqamat*), repentance (*tauba*), conversion (*inabat*), renunciation (*zuhd*), and trust in God (*tawakkul*). The stages were reached through self-mortification, performing *dhikr* and contemplation. All these need constant supervision by a *sheikh*. During a mystic journey, certain conditions such as *qabz* (contraction), *hast* (dilation), and illumination descend into the heart from God through *baraka*. Only a perfect *pir* can understand their significance and is able to distinguish between true illumination and the appearance of one, which in reality is a delusion emanating from the devil. The Sufi journey of a novice from the intellectual perception of God to an emotional involvement with Him is a personal experience, a mystery to be shared only with a perfect guide and revealed only to one's *pir*. Since there is a tendency requiring allegiance to a single Sufi order, this elevated the status of individual *sheikh*s in a manner reflected in ritual activities also (Rippin, 1990). Qadi Thana Allah Panipati (in *Mamulat-i-Mazhariyya*: 35) identified the positive aspects in a *sheikh* as consisting of the detachment of the heart from all worldly ties, the revival of the disciple's dead heart, refraining from committing sins, indigence from the desire to accomplish virtues and favourable actions (*amal-i-saliha wa husnat*).

But the *sheikh* has to show his availability, while selecting and accepting those seeking refuge at his service. Before reaching such a decision, the *sheikh* will, first of all, carefully scrutinize the innate qualifications of the aspirant, judging the degree of his sincerity, and right determination and submitting him to one or more proofs of his resolve. Once the *sheikh* has ascertained the suitability of the aspirant, the latter should entrust himself to the *sheikh*'s disposal, who will choose the auspicious moment to grant him initiation into the spiritual family (*khandan*) by asking him to pay a vow of allegiance to him and the ancestors of the lineage.

This process of socialization is painful. Some *murid*s take the easy way out: they run away. Some remain bound to the *pir* because of his friendliness and sympathy. Others wait, expecting material, magical and psychological assistance. Still others fear his miraculous powers. During this period, the *murid* falls in love with the *pir*, whom he regards as the representative of God. He observes the *pir*, serves him devoutly and believes that the hand of the *pir* is in everything that befalls him. He also frequently recalls and concentrates on the mental image of the *pir* before undertaking any action. Having thus attained union with the *pir*, he, one day, realizes that the *pir* is just a curtain or veil that hides something else: that which he has fully loved all the time in the image of the *pir*, is God Himself (Nanda and Talib, 1989).

There are different types of *pir*s in Pakistan (Gilmartin, 1979). Some are quiet hermits; others are active preachers; some take a useful part in the secular affairs of neighbourhood; some are mischievous stirrers of trouble; and some are charlatans. Ruling parties forge alliances with these *pirs* who command a vast body of hereditary followers, all of whom render unswerving support to various political parties. Unlike their ancestors, these *pirs* receive landed estates or money to build beautiful mausoleums and shrines in memory of their saints (Talbot, 1995). When referring to his *sheikh*, an Indian Muslim will often talk of his *pir-o-murshid*. He would enumerate the characteristics of his *pir*, such as poverty, religious and spiritual teaching, asceticism, humility, ecstasy and ability to perform miracles. To the population at large, they represent sources of power to all in need of superhuman intervention, as expressed in the following quartet.

Had tape tan auliya
Anhad tape tan pir,
Had anhad dono tape
O hai faqir.

Pir – Human as well as Divine

Essentially, the Sufi saint is human. Shaikh Abu Said of Nishapur avers that the true saint goes in and out amongst the people, eats and sleeps with them, and buys and sells in the market. He marries and takes part in social intercourse, but all through, he never forgets God for a single moment. In the literature, the Sufi saint is depicted as a servant worshipping and fulfilling the duties of a servant. In the words of Syed Ahmed Moinuddin Habibi (d. 1973), a Sufi saint is truthful, faithful and righteous. He prefers the poor man to the rich, the small quantity to the large, low to the high. He is of genuine feeling in the opinion of men. The saint is one who smiles if saluted, in conversation, he is pleasant; when asked, he shall give; when others divulge secrets, he conceals; of princes, he knows, but is not proud, and the poor he does not disdain; the next world he does not sell for the present; through Allah he is rich, before Him he is humble, from Him he gives, on Him he depends, he fears none other than Allah. His trust is only in Allah. In fact, the *pir* ranks next to the prophet.

The ideal Sufi is a physician of man's soul; a man of great learning and spirituality, who guides his disciples along the mystical path. A Sufi needs to possess certain qualities: (a) ability to perform miracles and have magical powers; (b) descent from the Prophet or his grandson or other Ashraf companions; (c) connection with a prestigious Sufi saint or *silsila*; and (d) a mastery of Islamic doctrines and Sufi texts (Gellner, 1969). Nicholson (1975) identifies ecstasy as a necessary qualification of a saint. He reminds us that knowledge of the nature of leadership (*rububiyya*) depends on servant-ship (*ubududiyya*).

The ideal *pir* potrayed in Sufi hagiography is one who has great learning and spirituality, guides his disciples along the mystic path, and dispenses help and advice, mediating disputes. He is both a teacher and spiritual guide to his disciples. Mujeeb (1967: 121), however, believes that devotees come to the *pir* to exploit his spiritual powers, to seek the cure of an ailment or fulfil a wish, to heal both mental and bodily problems, and worldly problems, through amulets, blessings, or recommendations.

Accepting a Sufi in his time as a great *sheikh* was dependent upon the recognition that he possessed to an impressive degree the qualities which showed that he was the recipient of divine grace, and had mastered the Islamic doctrinal or Sufi texts or an abundance of literary compositions. He worked miracles, cared for his disciples, and accepted hangers-on. In many cases, a ruler and his kingdom were under the protection of a *faqir*. The latter were averters of natural disasters in the kingdom (*Sujar al-Auliya*: 32-5, 151-2). In the words of Nasr (1972: 35), to become a saint in Islam is to realize all the possibilities of the human state to become the Universal Man. The mystical quest is none other than the realization of this state, which is also union with God, for the Universal Man is the mirror in which are reflected all the divine names and qualities. Through the Universal Man, God contemplates Himself, as all things that He has brought into being.

The humanness of *pirs* has been emphasized in many works. Like humans, *pirs* also get angry. Discussing the traits of the Sufi *sheikh*, Digby (1984) believes that along with the patterns of holy life and of Sufi organization transmitted from Khorasan to the Delhi Sultanate were traits such as an uncompromising arrogance, despite professions of humility, display of *jalal* (splendour), but in practice, the wrath that led to the suffering of those who opposed the *sheikh*. The character of the disagreeable and terrifying dervish of Persian folklore who exercises his supernatural powers with malignance comes closer to it.

Rose (1919) mentions that in Muzaffargarh, every Muslim has a *pir*, but he need not be learned or even of known piety. Indeed, many are notoriously immoral. He, however, should have the reputation of being able to secure the objects of his *murids*' vows. The *murid* secures his *pir's* intercession by an annual offering called *buhal*, which is collected by the *pir* himself or his deputies.

But, when the *pir* is elevated to a quasi-divine status, the structure of institutional Sufism has to deal with certain aspects. One of them relates to mortality. As the *pir* does not sin, he also does not die (Hodgson, 1974). His spirit is presumed to live on eternally in the presence of God, whom he had served loyally throughout his ascetical and usually long-lived life. As a result, the *pir* is supposed to pierce the curtain of death through the tomb that enclosed his earthly remains. He was thought to be more strongly present in that place than elsewhere, and also to be more receptive to the intercessory pleas his followers offered there on that occasion when he came to make his departure from this life to the next. Appropriately, that moment of celebrating the *pir*'s triumphal passage from earth to heaven is known as *'urs* (wedding ceremony). He, the lover, the bridegroom, is joined to God, the Beloved Bride, in an eternal marriage.

Though often derided as a degenerate form of pure Islam, the Sufi tomb cults embodied the logical outcome of cumulative unbridled devotion to living saints. There was also greed involved, both on the part of relatives and hangers-on, each wanting to derive personal benefits from their special association with the deceased saint. Without greed, Lawrence (1982) says, the magnificent tombs and ancillary *masjid madrasa* complexes would never have been constructed and maintained. Yet, the root motive for all such attention to saints' tombs was belief in the special spiritual importance of those who resided within the tombs.

Often there was also a network of associative saints' tombs. If a South Asian Muslim affiliated himself with the Chishti order, for instance, he would attend not just one but as many as five annual *'urs* ceremonies. They would also know about the lives of the first five saints. They would know the locations of their tombs, dates of their *'urs*. Hence, the strength of one's saint's presence and the persistence of his reputation were often reinforced by association with other saints. While the tomb cults were peculiar to each saint, the network of saints' tombs cumulatively linked one Sufi to the other throughout the calendar year, decade after decade, in the minds and lives of their devotees. This would explain that when people visit a town to attend the *'urs* of their favourite saint, they would also visit the shrines of all those saints, who, in one way or the other, were connected to their saint. On their way to Ajmer, for example, the devotees stay in Delhi for a few days, during which they visit the *dargah*s of Nizamuddin Auliya and Abu Bakr Tusi.

It is the posthumous function of saints' cults which is essential to understanding local contexts. Saints' cults were not consistent in tenor with the teaching or example of the venerated deceased master. Lawrence (1982) thinks that many of them seem to have functioned in a manner antithetical to the doctrines and deeds of the saints interred in their cultic tombs. Undoubtedly, that widespread devotion of living saints and also the tomb edifice containing the deceased saints characterized the spiritual outlook of Muslims as well as non-Muslims, both elites and commoners. Within the Sufi orders, too, there were differences in the manner of their accommodation to local contexts.

Initiation

There is no uniform pattern of training for the novice. After some preliminary instructions, the aspirant is introduced by two of his brethren (*ikhwan*) to the whole assembly of dervishes. In the presence of the *sheikh*, he swears that he would be loyal to the order and obedient to him. The *sheikh* touches the head of the novice and breathes into his ear the Shahadah – which he has to repeat 101, 151, or 301 times, as the case may be. This practice is called *talqin*.

The initiate gains admission to and promotion in an order slowly, only after a long ascetic training. Initially, he is a *tilmidh*, a disciple, then a *murid*, an aspirant, then a *faqir*. He now enters the 'path' and has dreams and supernatural revelations. Thus, he becomes a *salik* (traveller) on the mystical path, on way to still higher stages of life. He now becomes a *majdhub* – the attracted – drawn towards God and finally illuminated and inspired.

The probation period depends on the progress made by the novice, some needing only a short period, others a lengthy period of training, lasting three years. In the first year, he devotes himself to serving the people; in the second year, he spends his time in the service of God; and in the final year, he is devoted to guarding his heart. The servicing of God necessitates a severance from all self-motivation related to both worlds (Nicholson, 1921 [1975]).

After the *talqin*, the aspirant is taught the *dhikr*. Then, he recites the Fatiha (the first verse of the Quran). The novice, then, retires into seclusion, meditates and enters a state of semi-consciousness (*khilwat*). He repeats his dream to the *sheikh*, who utters in his ear 'Ya Allah'. This goes on for forty days, after which the novice becomes a *murid*. In some orders, the novitiate extends over 1001 days during which time, the novice has to perform the humblest domestic duties in order to test his obedience and to develop a spirit of humanity. In addition to retreats, watchings, and fasting, the *ikhwan* (brothers) must observe the *ziarat hadiyah*, which is an expiatory offering made for the violation of some rule or neglect of some duty.

It is by strict observance of the exercises like *dhikr, tasbih, tahmid, takbir* everyday, by retiring into privacy for devotional purposes, by *tawajjuh, muraqabbah*, and by mystical spiritualism (*tassaruf*) that the dervish is supposed to gain the spiritual internal powers – *quwwat-i-ruhi wa batini*

(Naqshbandi order), which will enable him to subdue the will of others (*iradat*). Abu Said of Nishapur speaks of his own experience as a novice, wherein he bound himself to eighteen things: (1) fasting continually; (2) abstaining from unlawful food; (3) practicing *dhikr* uninterruptedly; (4) keeping awake at night; (5) never reclining on the ground; (6) sleeping in the sitting posture; (7) sitting facing the Ka'aba; (8) never leaning against anything; (9) never looking at a handsome youth or woman (other than those in his family); (10) not begging; (11) remaining content; (12) resigning to God's will; (13) always sitting in the mosque; (14) not going to the market; (15) following the Prophet; (16) every twenty-four hours, completing a recitation of the Quran; (17) behaving as if blind, deaf, and dumb; and (18) for a whole year, conversing with no one. This entire set of practices led people to call him a lunatic.

Every order has a different process of initiation. In the Chishtia order, a disciple first recites two *rakat*s of *namaz*, and is then given instructions, which he is directed to observe without demur, such as: (a) a *faqir* takes food in the name of God; (b) he spends his life in Yad-e-Ilahi; (c) he sleeps with death (remembrance of God); and (d) arises with Kalima. He is told: 'O disciple, thou hast become a *faqir* and should follow these precepts; the word *faqir* contains four letters *fe, qaf, ye, re*, expresses *faqah* or fasting, *qaf* representing *qanaat* (or contentment), *ye* for *yad Ilahi*, and *re* for *riyazat* (repentances), so should thou possess these four qualities' (*Bagh-o-Bahar* of Mir Umman).

After this, he is bidden to give all his attention to his *murshid* in a certain way everyday. Then, some *ism* (or sacred name) is disclosed to him. He is directed to go to a shrine, to fast there for forty days (*chilla kashi*) and to keep on repeating the sacred name. Lastly, the spiritual pedigree of the order is disclosed to him. By degree, he progresses and sees visions and places (*arsh* or heaven). In this state, when the two stars *nasira* and *mahmuda* become one, he falls into a spiritual waking consciousness and reaches the *loh mahfuz* (or protected plank). Now, when he repeats his meditations from his very heart, a condition of *taqwin* (or deep trance) supervenes and his own self is revealed to him (*isme-zat*) (Rose, 1919: 47-48).

In the Qadiri method of initiation, the founder, Abdul Qadiri, represents the *atwar-i-saba* or seven paths (the seven names of Allah with their colours). The initiatory rites include the giving of the right hand clasped in the *sheikh*'s right hand with the two thumbs raised up against each other (Brown, 1968: 80, 89-95). The Qadiris have three grades of dervishes: the *murid, khalifa*, and *sheikh*. Sir Richard Burton was initiated into this order first as a *sheikh*, then as a *murshid* (i.e., one allowed to admit *murid*s or apprentices). In this *silsila*, the disciple is instructed to attain union with God or reach him by the practices of *yak zarbi*, *du zarbi*, *seh zarbi* and *chahar* *zarbi*, the four methods of repeating the name of Allah. He must recite these names in a voice not to arouse sleeping people. In *yak zarbi*, he repeats the word Allah in a certain pitch from the heart and throat with emphasis once; in *du zarbi*, he sits in the posture of the *namaz* and recites the name Allah, turning his head once to the right, and again in the heart; in *seh zarbi*, he sits cross-legged and recites the name Allah, first to the right, then left, and thirdly, in the heart in a loud voice. In *chahar zarbi*, he sits cross-legged and recites Allah first to the right, then left, thirdly in his heart, and fourthly, in front, in a loud voice. They are also taught to pronounce the words *la-illaha illallah* in a certain way with eyes closed (*Al Medina*:14).

The seven names of Allah, which the *murid*s of the Qadiri *silsila* use have their peculiar light, prayer and the number of times they must be repeated.

Name	**Colour**	**Frequency**
1. La-illaha illallah	Blue	100,000 times
2. Allah	Yellow	8,586 times
3. Ismi Hu	Red	44,630 times
4. Ismi Hai	White	20,092 times
5. Wahid	Green	93,420 times
6. Aziz	Black	74,644 times
7. Wadud	No light	30,202 times
Total		**447,574 times**

It used to be necessary to recite the names the above number of times in order to qualify for the degree of *sheikh*.

At initiation into the Suhrawardi order, the *murshid* first bids the disciple repent his sins (*tauba*), great and small. He then has to recite five Kalimas, and to attain full conviction of the true faith, to recite the names of God regularly, and to observe fasts (*roza*). This is called *murid hona*. Jalaluddin Rumi instituted religious dancing (or *hal khelna*) among his disciples. On this account, they earned the name of dancing or whirling dervishes.

In the Naqshbandi order of Sufism (founded by Khwaja Bahauddin of Turkestan [d. 792 AH/AD 1414]), the disciple is first directed to put aside all external and internal anxieties and to sit in solitude having no thought of enmity or anger, to be moderate in eating, and to bring death before his mind, and to ask God to pardon his sins. Then, he must close his eyes and lips and draw breath into his heart or stomach, or, in other words, stop breathing. This is called *habs-i-dam*. After this, he must utter the word *la* from his heart and prolong it from his *naf* (navel), to his right side right up to his shoulder, and then repeat the word Allah and then *Il-la-Allah* (*Phulkean States Gazetteer*, 1904, Vol. III: 157).

Until the time of Mazhar Jan-i-Janan and his successors, it was customary for the *sheikh* to ask the newly arrived seeker to look for an auspicious Divine sign, often sought from the Quran, to confirm the righteousness of the decision to join the order (*istikhara*), and then to wait for about seven days until the decision had fully matured in the applicant. The ritual consists of the conclusion of a non-dissolvable treaty between the master and the disciple, which sanctions the establishment of a lifelong bond. At the moment chosen for formal initiation into the order, the disciple is asked to kneel down before the *sheikh*, join his right hand with that of his master, and express his regret and repent (*tawba*) for all sins and negligence committed in the past (*istighfar*). He is then asked to pronounce three times the Kalima-i-Shahada, followed by a vow to observe faithfully the five Islamic pillars (*arkan-i-khamsa*), and the Sunna of the Prophet to abstain from any unlawful innovation (*bidat*), or associating anything to the rank of god, except Allah (*shirk*). The novice symbolically leaves behind the stags of his previous profane existence, preparing himself for his rebirth in a new life as a member of the spiritual family of which the *sheikh* represents the nearest and most immediate link. Soon afterwards, the neophyte receives for the first time the spiritual attention (*tawajjuh*) of his new *sheikh* combined with the instruction in the method of focusing the mind of the *latifa-i-qalb* in order to prepare it for the reception of the spiritual grace (*faiz*). The impact created at a subtle level through the transmission and infusion of the master's *tawajjuh*, aided by the repentant attitude of the novice, creates a favourable condition for leaving an immediate imprint on the latter's subtle heart organ (*naqshband*), which opens the gate for the reception of the Divine effusion and participation at God's mercy (*abwat-i-ahmad*).

The initiation rites of the Beshara orders are very different from those of the Bashara. Some of the prominent Beshara orders are the Bektashis, the Rifai, Mevlevi of Central Asia, and the Malamatis, Siyahposh, and Qalandars of India. The Bektashis' rites are numerous and elaborate, and with them, religious symbolism reaches a high development. At initiation, the *murid* is deprived of nearly all his clothing, if he intends to take the robe of celibacy (*mujarrad iqrar*). His breast being bared, and anything metallic or mineral on his person is taken from him, to symbolize his renunciation of the material world. A sheep is sacrificed, as among the Rifais of Egypt, and with a rope made of wool, he is led into the halls of the *takia* (hermitage) by two *tarjumans* (interpreters). In the octagonal centre of the square hall is one stone called the *maidantash*, on which stands a lighted candle, while around it are twelve seats of white sheepskin (*postaki*). At an initiation, the candle is replaced by one placed in front of each post. The *murshid* or *sheikh* is seated on one post, and the eleven members of the order on the others. The *murid* is led to the central stone on which he stands with crossed arms, his hands resting on his shoulders, his whole body leaning towards the *sheikh* in a prescribed attitude. The *murid* kneels before the *sheikh*, their knees touching, while each holds the other's right hand, the two thumbs raised straight as the Arabic letter *alif*. The *maidantash* represents the altar on which Abraham was asked to offer his son to God. Twelve members seated on the posts represent the twelve *imams*. The *sheikh* is said to represent Ali, but the *murid* makes his vows to the *pir* or founder of the order, and not to the *sheikh*.

Before his initiation, the supplicant is tested for a full year during which he is styled a *mahaqq* (or catechumen), being tested with false secrets to test his powers of guarding the real mysteries of the order. He is guided to the *takia* by two *rahpars* armed with a *tabbar* (a halberd). The *iqrar* (or vow) is comprehensive and concludes with the *murid*'s acceptance of Mohammad as his *rahpar* and Ali as his *murshid*. The dress of the Bektashis consists of a sleeveless vest (*laidri*), with a streak supposed to be the word Ali and twelve lines symbolizing the Imams: a *khirqa* with a similar streak, a girdle of white wool: a cord (*kambaria*) of goat's hair to which is attached a crystal called *naif*; earrings (*mangosh*) like those of the Rifais and a cap (*taj*) (the *sheikh*'s cap has twelve *tarks*), *dolak* (or leggings), the *lavank* or (long robe), and the *muliffah* (or wide dress), the *kashkul* (or beggar's bowl), the *figni* (or pilgrim's staff), the *chillik* (or rod used in punishment), and the *luffar* (or horn) (*Dictionary of Islam*: 691-692; Brown, 1968: 153).

Let us finally have a look at the system of *bai'at* (initiatory rites). The system of accepting an intermediary for the attainment of spiritual guidance is known as *bai'at*, which means taking an oath or promising earnestly to follow. When a man takes a *bai'at* from another person, by placing his hand in the others, he accepts the other as his spiritual guide, and makes a firm commitment to him to follow his dictates unquestioningly. The holding of the hand symbolizes the acceptance of the spiritual power of the *murshid* by the aspiring *murid*. The *murid* promises that he would do what the *pir* bade him do, and direct his life according to the tenets of Islam. It also affirms that the *pir* has accepted him as his *murid* and would henceforth provide him with assistance in resolving his worldly problems, so that he could attain his goal.

Once the *bai'at* is made, the *murid* joins the fraternity of other *murids*. Other *murids* are now his *pir-bhai* (*murids* of the same *pir*). The *murid* now evaluates himself, recollects his sins, and the *pir* supports the *murid* in his determination and protects him from evil forces. The system of *bai'at* infuses new hope and provides strong assurance to lead a pious life. If a person has no *pir-o-murshid*, he is taunted and derogatorily called *be pira* (or *be murshada*). The *pir* is very selective in choosing a *murid*. It is likely that many companions may have been with him for ten to twenty years, but he does not make them his *murid*. They are not considered able for that (Leibeskind, 1998: 8,

69). The prospective *murid* also takes care in choosing the right *pir*. The individual seeker does not always find it an easy task to select a saint to his liking (Leibeskind, 1998: 69-70). It is also not appropriate for a *pir* to actively solicit for *murids*. The giving and taking of *bai'at* involves obligations and responsibilities on both sides, and therefore each party has to be convinced of the other's sincerity and love. The search for the right *pir* does not necessarily take place during the waking hours. The prospective *murid* also receives guidance or sees his future *murshid* in his dreams and receives *bai'at* from him (Pinto, 1989). The method of initiation, which is held in absence, without a living person, is called *uwaisi bai'at*. The women were also initiated. The only difference was that while the *pir* touched a male *murid*, a woman was initiated while holding on to a cloth.

Worship of living saints

Due respect is shown to the guide: disciples prostrate themselves in front of him, a mark of respect due to Allah. The *murids* follow the guide's advice blindly. If he says that day is night, you must say, 'Look! Here are the moon and stars.'

The third image of the guide is that of an intermediary to get access to Allah; this is called *fanafil sheikh*, which is an allusion to the technique among Naqshbandis called *muraqaba* (Troll, 1989: 32-51). Wahabis regard saint worshippers as *mushrik* or *kafir* and saint worship as *fitna*. Saiyed (1989) posits a question: Can the veneration of Sufi saints be considered a part of Islam? Rahman (1979: 130) says that saint veneration came into existence and has persisted because the saints inspired confidence, particularly among the masses, who turned to them for spiritual guidance. For such Muslims, the Sufis had brought Allah and divinity within reach. While emotional attachment and loyalty of faith in Sufis have mystical roots and religious overtones, the hold the saints have over their followers has not survived on these grounds alone. Secular and 'mundane' considerations also play an important role (Gaborieau, 1983). Veneration of saints creates a common religious and cultural bond. It serves as one of the most powerful integrative mechanisms between the two communities. It is the personal and spiritual influence of the various saints that has allowed a peaceful coexistence of the two communities for several centuries on the Indian subcontinent.

The formation of well-defined orders was instrumental in the introduction of the custom of spiritual initiation. The Sufis were now allowed to freely participate in the activities of an order and to follow the spiritual discipline prescribed by the master of that order provided they undertook to remain firmly committed and loyal to the representative of that order. The relationship between the Sufi and his master assumed a new dimension.

In the Khanqah phase, both the teacher and disciple were placed on an equal footing as far as their respective capabilities to attain the spiritual goal were concerned. But in the *tariqa* phase, there was a clear-cut line of demarcation between the *pir* and the *murid*. It was incumbent on the *murid* to completely surrender himself to the *pir*. In this phase, there also emerged a special category of disciple, namely, the Khalifa, apart from the ordinary *murid*. The Khalifa was virtually the successor who was authorized by his *pir* to initiate other *murid*s into the *silsila*. Thus, the *tariqa* phase can be considered as the 'beginning of the processes whereby the creative freedom of the mystic was to be channelled into an institution'. The last stage was the *taifa*, in which the mystic dimension of Sufism was relegated to the background. The conspicuous feature was the elevation of the *pir* to the stature of a living deity, who was an object of adoration and worship by the *murid*s. Indeed the *pir* then emerged as the medium through which alone a *murid* could attain oneness with God. In other words, the *pir* was an intermediary between the *murid* and God.

*Pir*s thus became saints (*wali*). Sufi orders, which in the second stage had been schools of spiritual discipline, then became saint cults centred on the spiritual power of a single individual. Moreover, the headship of most *taifa*s, particularly in India, became mainly hereditary as blood replaced merit as the chief criterion of succession. This, in turn, gave rise to a whole new class of individuals who by virtue of their blood descent from a saint could claim special spiritual status.

Saints now began to be seen as wielders of infinite mystical power, which could be transmitted not only to the descendants of a saint but also to his *dargah*. Thus, with the replacement of the Khanqahs by *dargah*s, Sufism became more devotional than mystical. Soon, it took the shape of a popular movement.

The behavioural aspects of cults are: 1. personal visits to the shrine; 2. giving offerings in cash or kind; 3. Fatiha, which has to be recited; 4. the guardians and worshippers share the offerings; and 5. *'urs* celebrations. A *pir* with considerable following went to the extent of equating the Islamic concept of *nabi* with the Hindu concept of *avatar*. The mystical concepts of the concerned *pir*s tended to lean towards an absolute non-dualistic model.

According to Smith (2001: 244):

> The shrine is a place in which women can be together, or alone, and can be in communication with a personage considered in some senses to be able to help them with the kinds of personal problems in which the high God may seem too remote to be interested.

Social factors also draw women to the shrines; the *dargah* is the 'functional alternative of the mosque'. An additional social structural reason for women's strong faith in the shrine and its saints arises out of insecurities and anxieties in their daily life in which they are fully involved. Since they do not attend the mosque, they look elsewhere for support; and that support comes from the *dargah*.

For a fuller understanding of the phenomenon of saint and *dargah* veneration, Gellner (1981) thinks, it is necessary to comprehend both the religious and mystical, as well as sociological existential dimensions. But, the most important factor, at least sociological, seems to be this inescapable requirement of religious organization and leadership. Sufism provides a theory, terminology and technique of leadership far more generally usable in tribe, village or town under government, or in anarchy (Gellner, 1981). The important thing about Sufism is that it creates a quasi-church.

A Critique of the Cult of the Tomb

The Quran does not explicitly recognize saints, or sanctions the institution of sainthood. In fact, it emphasizes that God and God alone is the *wali* of the believers, and there is no *wali* or helper but Him (3:68, 2:107, 2:120, 9:116, 18:26). Humankind is sternly warned against taking friends or seeking help from anyone, but God (6:14, 42:9). In addition, the Quran disallows intercessions (*shafa'ah*) by anyone but God (2:48, 74:48). There is neither *wali* nor *shafi* except Him (6:51). Contrary to this, the saint is typically recognized after his death and he seems to have played, as we saw, much more active and critical political roles than did the Jewish *zaddikin*. Reformist Muslims (including Mohammad Iqbal) wanted to do away with *pir*-ism, which appeared to them as one of the reasons for the poverty and backwardness of people. Lawrence (1982) seeks an opinion whether posthumous cults rather than actual saints' lives are the source of what Gardet and Anawati (1988) calls 'degeneracy', and Trimingham (1971), 'the paved Way'.

Trimingham (1971) claims to offer a historical construction of Sufi brotherhoods. He stakes out a thinly disguised critique of their very existence. The only true Sufism, for him, existed in the classical phase. This development into orders, and the integral association of the saint cult with them, contributed to the decline of Sufism as the 'mystical way'. Spiritual insight atrophied and the 'way' became paved and milestoned. The *tariqa* phase (AD 1100-1400) represented for him a bourgeois movement after which the decline of Sufism in the *taifa* phase (after AD 1400) was inevitable.

What Trimingham (1971) fails to note is the complementary function of the *silsilas*/*tariqas* in the medieval Islamic world. As Eaton (1973, 1978) has documented, institutionally affiliated Sufis performed a variety of functions. Lawrence (1982: 28-9) says that judgements posed in dichotomous categories (such as vibrant/decadent, creative/stagnant or orthodox/

unorthodox), do not begin to allow a value-free descriptive approach to the historical evidence of the orders, yet, apart from such an approach, the assessment of their influence in any region of the world is impossible. However, the doctrine of complete surrender to a fellow human being could not be reconciled with Islamic orthodoxy, which rejected even when orthodox Ulema cautiously joined the Sufi movement and participated in some of its moderate forms.

In *Al Balagh Al-Mubin*, a mid-nineteenth Wahabi text (trans. Gaborieau, 1989), the author gives an inventory of the objectionable practices of Indian Muslims (Schimmel, 1979: 150-88). The book denounces all forms of cults directly addressed to dead saints, supposed to be residing in their tombs. People address the prayers of supplication (*du'a*) and make vows (*nadhr-o-niyaz*) in order to receive specific favours. This collective devotional endeavour, classified according to Ibn Taymiyya's terminology, gives an account of the *'urs* celebrated on fixed days (*id zamani*) at a fixed place (*id makani*).

> When they celebrate the death anniversary of a saint (*buzurg*), they come in crowds from far and near to his tomb, and perform more devotions than they do obligatory rituals. To solve their worldly problems, they address their supplication to the tomb. ... they pray to the saint to ask for children and food, they offer costly veils for the tomb, sprinkle perfume on it, burn incense, thinking it meritorious, they adorn the tomb with light-lamps. They think this will please the saint and they would reach his proximity (*qurbat*) (Urdu Text: 38).

The tomb worshippers adore the saint in the same way as one worships Allah in the Holy Ka'aba. For instance, they spread on the graves cover of all kinds of colours; they kiss them; they circumambulate them, reciting verses or silent *dhikr*; they make vows to them; they sacrifice animals in their names; they consider the water used to wash them as a benediction (*tabarrak*) comparable to the water of Zamzam well. They consider that seeing or making a pilgrimage to the saint (*pir*) is an act of worship, comparable to seeing the Holy Ka'aba. They consider the tomb as *qibla* for prayer and think it is better to worship there than at any other place (Urdu Text: 159).

He also mentions the pilgrims carrying standards (*nishans*) in procession; women, musicians and dancing girls; fairs with games and dances; the drinking of liquor and consumption of drugs; recitation of canonical prayers at the tombs; taking away of relics, part of the offerings or a bit of the veils of the tombs, or a handful of earth (Urdu Text: 125-35). The text also describes the whole complex of institutions, which have grown around the tombs, *qabr* or *gor* (derogatory term); in actual practice they are referred to as *mazar*, in case they are modest-sized, and *dargah,* in case they are prestigious ones. He mentions raised stone tombs and the cupolas (*qubba*) erected over them. Relics of the saints such as their staffs (*asa*), their blankets and their robes (*khirqa*) are preserved and worshipped (Urdu Text: 59-62).

The beliefs underlying such devotions and institutions are varied. The saint hears their prayers, if pleased with the offerings he can grant the favours requested – food, children, cure of ailments, redress of torts, recovery of misplaced and stolen objects. The good man by his mystical exercises, piety and austerity has reached near Allah and become a *shafi*, then, when dead, his soul gets great power, and when the faithful visit the tomb, the saint is informed of his problems and intercedes for him in this world and the next.

CHAPTER 3

Antinomian Cults with Specific Reference to the Qalandars and the Qalandariya Path

A key to understanding the antinomian cults is the distinction between the Bashara and the Beshara. The path identified as the Qalandariya is the name of an antinomian Sufi cult and Muslim 'path' (*tariqa*). The individual members of this path are called Qalandars. Also written with K (Kalandar) and C (Callandar), but more generally with Q (Qalandar), this word has found its way in popular imagery and lexicon, chiefly because of the musical hits, *dam mast mast dum mast mast*, and *dama dum mast qalandar*. Several contemporary *qawwali* performers (such as, the late Nusrat Fateh Ali Khan) and Sufi and pop singers (like, Abida Praveen, Runa Laila, Hans Raj Hans, Kailash Kher, and Wadali brothers) have included in their musical repertoire the verses which were composed in the past in honour of Lal Shahbaz Qalandar of Sehwan (Sindh, Pakistan), a Sufi of the first half of the fourteenth century, and Bu Ali Shah Qalandar of Panipat (see Appendix II).

The image which the Qalandars conjure up in minds of people is of a renouncer, a *faqir*, totally indifferent to the external world and its normative order, always in a state of ecstasy (*masti*), which can be further intensified through almost uninterrupted musical concerts and consumption of barbiturates (such as *bhang*, *ganja*, *charas*). There are cases of Muslim renouncers (such as, *faqirs*, *majhdubs*), who in fact indulged in practices tabooed for the community as a whole. For instance, Eaton (1978 [1996]: 269-70) gives the example of saints of Bijapur who attracted the attention of the general public by their nakedness and indulgence in *bhang* and wine. Digby (1984: 97) writes that the saints were 'irresistibly drawn away' individuals, who were not 'accountable for their actions', and what distinguished them was 'divine frenzy or madness'. Groups of such renouncers have been called 'antinomian', for they were (or are) contrapuntal to the established religious type. Although the reference to Qalandars figures commonly in politico-religious literature, to our knowledge only two works in English provide a detailed account of this cult: Digby (1984), in his detailed article on Qalandars in the Delhi Sultanate of the thirteenth and fourteenth centuries, has attempted to collate the literature available on this *tariqa* and provide a substantial review; and Liebeskind (1998) focuses on three Sufi shrines (based in Awadh in north India) that belong to the Qalandariya path. Some information on Qalandaris also available in Lawrence's *Notes from a Distant Flute* (1978). In Urdu, *Silsila-e-Qalandariyya* (July 2005), written by Maulana Ubaid Allah Koti Nadvi, also presents an introduction to the *silsila*. More recently, a booklet titled *Adhai Qalandar* has also been published.

BESHARA CULTS

Let us first describe the three Beshara sections of the Suhrawardi order. Sayyid Uthman Marwandi, popularly known as Lal Shahbaz or 'Red Falcon' of Marwand, his natal province, the founder of the Lal Shahbaziya section, the prominent character in a number of songs, was an ascetic from Seistan, who had settled in the mid-thirteenth century in Sehwan, in the lower Indus Valley, site of an old Siva sanctuary. Zia-ud-din Barani speaks of his visit to the court of Balban's son in Multan. Bahauddin Zakariya is alleged to have granted him Khilafat (Digby, 1984). Although he was a strict ascetic, he is called a Malamati and a Qalandar, which points to his unusual and libertine lifestyle, manifested in his wearing of red garments and using narcotics and intoxicants. He expressed his ideas in the following verse:

I am a falcon with no habitation,
I cannot be contained in any place,
I am a phoenix with no trace,
I cannot be contained in name,
At one time, I wore the sacred thread,
At another, I read the Holy Quran,
Yet at another, I was tutored in Christian religion (as a Christian),
I have worn two hundred robes,
Put on even the cloak of poverty,
But the tower I am occupying now,
Not even one out of one thousand can reach.

Another hypothesis of why he was called 'red' is that once, imitating Ibrahim, he sat for a whole year in an iron pot placed upon a broiling fire, as a result his skin turned a deep rubicund hue.[1] It is believed that once he assumed a winged form to rescue a deeply religious man from the stake, because of which he earned the title of Shahbaz ('falcon'). He was reputed to be a grammarian, a logician, and a philologist, besides being an embodiment of divinity. His followers believed that he indulged in an antinomian mode of life because he wanted to conceal his spiritual dignity from people. In fact, many Malamati and Qalandari saints addressed the spiritual dangers of a pious reputation by intentionally acting in apparent contradiction to religious law or social standards. They might drink (or feign to drink) wine in public, and shear themselves of all outward signs of social respect, such as the hair and beard, respectable clothes, and so forth. The basic idea was that they wanted less crowd around them, since it would obstruct their pursuance of the spiritual path.

A Persian poem ascribed to Lal Shahbaz takes up the motif of dancing ecstatically in the fire and the gallows. Such lines place him in the succession of Hallaj, the martyr of love. In AD 1324, he died, and was buried in Sind. Feroz Shah built his mausoleum in 1357. Since then, his tomb is a place of pilgrimage. As he wore garments of red colour, his devotees, confined mostly to Sind, also dress in red, use intoxicants, believe in reciting God's praise, and meditate in a demonstrative way. With shaven heads, these devotees still perform their ecstatic songs on Thursday evenings. However, the festivities at the time of *'urs* have been lately purged as they had become immoral affairs. The devotees also perform *dhamal* (dance), which is akin to the *mehfil-i-sama'* of the Mevleviya dervishes.[2] The hymn in honour of Lal Shahbaz (i.e., *dama dam mast qalandar*) has become a hit in both India and Pakistan. Richard Burton, in his travelogue on Sind, wrote that every year, a girl of the Khonbati caste was married to the tomb of Lal Shahbaz, and was not permitted to contract a real marriage.

The Suhagiya section was founded by Musa Shahi Suhag of Ahmedabad. He is also described as the hidden Sufi of his time. He concealed his spiritual attainment by living with eunuchs. The epithet *suhag*, affixed to his name, indicates that he used to dress and adorn himself like a woman; he regarded God as 'his husband' (Subhan, 1970: 248). He, too, did not observe the precepts of Islam regarding prayer and fasting. In imitation of their teacher, the followers of this sect wear bangles and bracelets on their wrists. If someone refuses to give them alms, they threaten to break one of their bracelets and eat the glass pieces (de Tassey, 1995: 164).

The Rasul Shahi section of Beshara sect was founded by Sayyid Rasul Shah. Incidentally, the title of the Prophet is Rasul. The Rasul Shahi shave off the facial hair, wear a cap, and a loin cloth. They carry a sheet to use in hot, cold, and wet weather. They drink spirits, do not marry, and live by begging. The followers of this sect regard the drinking of spirits as a virtue. It is a very small sect and its followers are mostly in Lahore, in Pakistan, and Punjab and Gujarat, in India. In Punjab, they are said to be men of respectable families, but in Gujarat, they are notorious for insobriety, and their ascetic practices, which are believed to be for 'appearance' only (Sharif, 1832 [1921]).

From the Junaydi order, one of the fourteen orders mentioned by Abul Fazl, is the Rafai sub-order. In some parts of India, it is known as Gurzmar, because the *faqir*s of this order carry a mace (*gurz*) with which they strike their bodies, sometimes even inflicting upon themselves grievous wounds. They heal these wounds with their saliva. This belief in the therapeutic value of saliva is based on the initiation ceremony, wherein the teacher (*murshid*) transmits his saliva on to the tongue of his disciple. The *murshid* had received the saliva of his teacher, and this *silsila* goes back to the founder of the order, whose saliva was believed to have had the curative powers. So, the belief of this order is that let the *faqir* strike his body with the mace, and in case, it is cut, he is advised to apply his own spittle, for it has the healing power descending from the founder.

The Madari order of Sufis is also Beshara. It is ascribed to a charismatic leader, Shah Badi-ud-Din Shah Madar, a Jew by birth, a fifteenth century emigrant, who lived in different cities of India. According to Abdur Rehman Chishti, on the basis of Qazi Mahmud Kinturi's work (*Risala-i-Iman-i-Mahmud*), Shah Madar's father was from Aleppo (Syria) (*Mirat-e-madari*, manuscript in Khuda Baksh Library, Patna, ff. 3b-5b).

In Jaunpur, Shah Madar had differences with the chief *qazi*, Shihabuddin Daulatabadi, who was the religious guide of Sultan Ibrahim Sharqi (AD 1400-40). The reason was that Shah Madar had abstained from the Friday prayer. The chief *qazi* asked him the reason for his absence. The Shah replied that as he was a wayfarer, he was legally exempt from attending the prayer meeting. The *qazi* was not satisfied with this explanation. He thought that as the Shah had been living there since three days, he could not be treated as a wayfarer. Under these circumstances, he left for Makanpur (Kanpur), where he stayed till his death. Badauni (in *Nijat-al Rashid*) states that nobody ever saw the Shah eating food or anyone cooking for him. His clothes were also not taken out for laundry.

The Madari order is small, mostly popular with Hindu and Muslim jugglers, acrobats and those who earn their livelihood by exhibiting tricks with monkeys and bears. The accounts of the Madaris, dated to the reign of Shah Jahan (1628-1658), indicate that like many Hindu renouncers, the Madaris were scantily clothed and smeared their bodies with ash. It was also said that those who had attained the height of 'spiritual perfection' remained sky-clad even in the winters of Kashmir and Kabul. They kept their hair uncombed and tangled. They wound iron chains (like the Qalandars, as we shall see) around their heads and necks. Black turbans and black flags were their diacritical marks. In common with the other Beshara groups, they did not observe prayers and fasting. Believing that a state of inebriation was a prerequisite to mystic experience, they encouraged the excessive consumption of intoxicating drugs, especially Indian hemp. One of their splinter groups was termed *Be Qaid wa Be Nawa* ('Without Ties and Material Concern'). Its members did not accept anything beyond a small quantity of food and drink. They made their cloaks (*khirqa*s) from shreds and rags they collected from garbage (Subhan, 1970: 302-6; Rizvi, 1978: 319).

During the seventeenth century, the followers of Shah Madar were divided in two groups. The followers of one group were ritualistic. They also had a mosque constructed in the *dargah* complex. The second group comprised wandering dervishes, who attached no importance to the performance of rituals. They practised celibacy, wore loin-cloth, and moved in groups with banners. *Dabistan-e-mazahib* informs us that they remained nude, and consumed *bhang* in heavy quantity. They believed that when the Prophet was blessed by God, He was permitted to take a round of the Paradise. But, He was unable to enter, since the gate was narrower than the eye of a needle. Thereupon, Jibril advised Him to recite the words *dam madar* ('by the breath of Madar'). No sooner He did this, that the door opened. The Shah, they believed, shared in God's nature, whereas the Prophet was required to benefit from the recital of these words.

Although there has been a decline in such orders, we come across Madaris in the towns of Uttar Pradesh. Shah Madar's *dargah* is visited by thousands of people. As is common with other orders, the followers of Shah Madar are usually from lower classes. It is said that even Aurangzeb, whom we classify as a Bashara ruler, visited the tomb (Rizvi, 1978: 319). As is common with other Sufi shrines, Shah Madar's tomb is visited by Hindus and Muslims, although women are not permitted entry. About Shah Madar's shrine, it is said that if women defied the taboo, they would be seized with violent pains as if their bodies were 'wrapped up with flames of fire' (Subhan, 1970; 305; Rizvi, 1978: 319).

Another special characteristic of Madar's tomb is that on the occasion of the saint's *urs*, the ritual of fire-walking is performed by *faqir*s: burning coals are spread on the ground and the mendicants walk on it shouting 'Dam Madar; Dam Madar', i.e., 'By the breath of Madar'. It is also believed that the foot (or, any other part of the body) does not receive any injury in this ritual performance. Worthwhile it is to note that fire-walking is common in many other religious denominations, but its interpretation may vary from one context to another. Common to all of them is that fire-walking is an act of austerity (Obeyesekere, 1981).

An important Beshara order is of the Malamatis. Derived from the word *malamat* ('blame'), it means "one who is 'blameworthy'". The followers of this order believe that they stand in a special relationship to God and, therefore, are not 'subject to the divine ordinances'. The first Sufi to follow the Malamati path was Dhun Nun-Misri; he is regarded as a *zindaq* ('freethinker'). His disciple, Hamdunu'l-Qassar, founded the Malamati order. Many types of *faqirs* have been noted in this order; to follow Subhan's classification (1970: 318), they are:

1. Libertines, who consume intoxicants, lead a free life, and do not practise any religious duty. They claim to be the followers of Jalal-ud Din Rumi, the founder of the Mevlevian order, which in its process of initiation gives importance to a lengthy orientation rather than the trials typical of other Sufi orders. It regards 'audition' (*sama'*) as a form of meditation.
2. The second category is of renouncers who take opium and other drugs to produce quiescence of spirit. These noxious drugs are sometimes taken in excessive doses for stimulating imagination.
3. The third category is of *faqirs* who are devoted to music. They imitate the Sufis of the Chishti order in their external practices, but do not follow the precepts of Islam.
4. Then there are those who are given to hallucinations. Because of their 'wild talk', they have come to be looked upon as Sufis.

Abu 'Abda Rahman-as Salamai (d. 1021) regarded the Malamati as the highest grade of God's slaves, above both the legalists (*fuqaha*) and the theosophists (*ahl-e-ma'arifa* or *suffiya*). According to him, the Malamati is he whose 'veins are saturated with the nourishment of pure virtue', who is really sincere, who does not want anyone to be acquainted with his ecstatic states and experiences. He wants to be despised by men, so that he may lose himself in God. A Malamati rejects all outward show and does not wear the special dress which characterizes the Sufi. He also does not have a *sheikh* who would initiate him, but he is ready to seek guidance.

Besides these, one comes across some small groups of Beshara saints. For instance, Imam Shahi, who shave their facial hair, wear a sleeveless shirt (*alfa*), a waist band, and a thread or necklace. Their distinguishing mark is a narrow, perpendicular line, extending from the tip of the nose to the top of the forehead. They are celibates, live by alms, and claim miraculous powers. Another group known from the Punjab is called Nikalseni (or Nicholsoni). They worship the British General, John Nicholson, who was killed at Delhi in 1857. Another case is of Baba Budan, also known as Hayat

Qalandar or Hayat ul-Bahr, a saint of the fourteenth century, who was reputed to have introduced coffee in Mysore. Baba Budan Hills, in which his shrine is located, take their name from him (Rice, in Sharif, 1832 [1921]: 140).

ANTINOMIAN GROUPS IN THE DELHI SULTANATE IN THE THIRTEENTH AND FOURTEENTH CENTURIES

Digby (1984: 60-108) has undertaken a detailed study of the Qalandars of the thirteenth and fourteenth centuries in Delhi. One may not come across many groups of Qalandars in contemporary India, but they are far from being extinct (Liebeskind, 1998). Ewing (1979, quoted in Digby 1984: 77), from her observations of 1976, says that the Qalandars still enjoyed a part in the ceremonial of the *'urs* of Mu'in al-Din Chishti of Ajmer.

Digby (1984: 60) says that the hagiographical tradition of the Delhi Sultanate is quite strong. Certain groups in these sources can be distinguished by the (1) peculiarities of their appearance; (2) costume and insignia; (3) failure to perform prescribed Muslim duties (*faraid*) and other supererogatory pious acts (*tarawih, nawafil*); (4) occasional violent attacks on the Sufis; and (4) episodes of immoral conduct (such as, 'gazing at young, handsome boys'). These groups are denominated Qalandari, Haydaris, Jawaliqs (or, Juwaliqs), and Muwallihs. The terms used for these groups are *tai'fa*, *tariqa*, *silsila*, and *mashrab*. Of these, the term chosen by the author, writing on them, depends upon whether he considers them to be orders in the same way as are the main orders found in India, or whether they constitute a loosely organized band of people claiming to practise austere measures. Another term which figures in literature is Malang; it has been popularized by Nusrat Fateh Ali Khan's musical hit, *Ali da Malang main te Ali da* (I'm the Malang of Ali'). Haydaris and Jawaliqs wrapped blankets round their body. They wore collars and iron blankets (*dastaklak*) round their necks and arms. The iron-clad *faqir*s had no *khirqa*, nor any garment on their body except a *langoti* round their loins, and carry a blanket under their arm-pits. They had strange manners and practices, such as walking on burning faggots, and shaving off hair on head, beard, eyebrows, moustache, and practising celibacy.

These Beshara groups of the Delhi Sultanate have a 'family resemblance' among them. Rizvi (1978: 303) writes that 'the *Fawaidu'l-Fu'ad* and the other Indian mystical writings do not distinguish between the Qalandariya and the Jawaliqi traditions.' Hasan al-Jawaliq, the founder of the Jawaliq tradition, is also regarded as the founder of the Qalandariya tradition (*Ibid.*). Digby (1984: 63) submits that irrespective of the relationship between these groups, the terms Qalandar, Haydari, and Jawaliq are not interchangeable. All Haydaris and Jawaliqs can be called Qalandars, but not all Qalandars can be called Haydaris and Jawaliqs.

A Haydari is a follower of Qutb al-Din Haydar, a thirteenth century Sheikh of Khorasan, the eponymous founder of the tradition of the Haydari. A Jawaliq, on the other hand, is a follower of Hasan al-Jawaliq, an Irani at the close of the thirteenth century. The Jawaliqs are distinctly identified as the wearers of a garment (called *juwal* or *palas*) of red (or, ochre) colour, symbolizing a 'colour of those who kill themselves'. By comparison to other groups, historians are less informed about the Muwallihs, the followers of Sidi Muwallih, who played an important role in the political life of Delhi in the late thirteenth century. This order was also known in the Middle East. In the literature of that time, there is a brief reference to Sulayman Turkman Muwallih who was one of the founders of this tradition. In Delhi, a Suhrawardi Sheikh (named Jalal al-Din) of the late fourteenth century said that the Muwallihs were well known for their practice of lamentation (*walwalah*).

In other words, each of these social categories (Qalandar, Haydari, and Jawaliq) can be defined with reference to their respective founders and a set of cultural features. However, we also come across collocations such as Haydari-Qalandari or Jawaliq-Qalandari. A saint may combine the elements of both the traditions in himself. Abu Bakr Tusi (of Delhi) is one example of this collocation: he is Haydari-Qalandari. Digby (1984: 63) suggests that in such cases, both the nouns are used synonymously. These traditions are known are *ahan-poshan* (the 'wearers of iron', i.e., those who wear iron chains, bracelets, bangles) and *chiram-poshan* (the 'wearers of leather', i.e., those who wear garments made of leather, or just wear leather sheets). In fact, Haydari-Qalandari distinguished themselves from others by wearing over their cotton clothes iron chains and rings in their ears. The Jawaliqs, who were the disciples of the Sheikh Jamaluddin of Sava, wore leather garments. Apart from the apparent differences, they were similar in their attitude to religion and worldly life. Influenced by non-Muslim mystics, they laid emphasis on the need for spiritualists to practise celibacy, disown any house or hospice, put on coarse clothes, and depend for their existence on God's mercy.

The term Malang is the most general; it can be used for anyone completely immersed in devotion. So much is his involvement with the divinity that he forgets to take care of his bodily self, demeanour, and outfit. One of my respondents, brought up in Multan, remembered that the Malangs were notorious for their unhygienic ways: 'their noses always used to run, they were often unwashed.' They wore a black cloak, hanging slightly below the knees. The Malangs were, however, treated with deference by the natives of Multan. In the busy and overcrowded bazaar of Multan, they were always given right of way and room to walk comfortably. 'Give way, the Malangs are coming,' the people used to shout. Apparently, none wanted to annoy them, for fear of being cursed. Sometimes, the Malang read palms of their supplicants and predicted their future, and provided other types of supernatural assistance. I heard several stories from my respondents of being given amulets and talisman by wandering *faqirs*, who were Malang.

THE QALANDARS

Paul Jackson's *The Mystical Dimensions of Islam* has a section titled 'The Qalandars – Beyond the Law?' Here, Jackson says that the Qalandars are Sufis with no affiliations. Lewis (2000: 34-5) calls them 'unaffiliated' who 'signaled their withdrawal from all social conventions.' They paid scant attention to the prescriptions of Islamic law. Often seen in Persian miniature paintings, they first seem to be Hindu *yogis* (renouncers) – with shaven heads and beardless faces, they are depicted as wearing little clothing as opposed to the rather fulsome clothing of the other Sufis. They are shown as roaming about in groups in comparison to other Sufis who moved as individuals. Lewis (2000: 134) writes that Rumi chose Shams Tabrez as the focus of his devotion and provided a literary persona for his poetry. In legends, Shams is portrayed as an 'untutored, charismatic Qalandar, possessing miraculous powers'. This caricature of Shams is reflected in the writings of Jami, Dowlat Shah, and Aflaki.

The word Qalandar has a wide spectrum of meaning. Rabbani (2005) says that the Qalandars are the mystics who have an 'overdose of inspiration', resulting in constant ecstasies and raptures, and are therefore, unable to guide others. They are *mast* (overwhelmed) in their own *hal* (state), and do not, or cannot, look for others. J.P. Brown in his work titled *The Darweshes* (reprint 1968) says that this word in Spanish means 'pure gold'. Qalandar is said to be one of the names of God in Syriac Ebrani. According to some, it is derived from the Persian *qalandar*, which means a 'thief', 'ugly, uncouth, ungainly man'; it also means a 'whittled piece of wood put behind a door to stop it from opening'. One of Burke's (1979) respondents told him that this word in Persian also means a 'chief of some sort'. Some hypothesize that it could be from another Persian word *qalantar*, which means 'large' or 'great'; or, from Greek *kaletor*, meaning 'truth-workers'. In Persia, says Seyyed Hussein Nasr, the undisciplined and lax dervishes, oblivious to the injunctions of the Shariat, were usually called *qalandar ma'ab*. The word *qalandar* was also used for a particular type of cloth (canopy, or *shamiyana*) called *sarapardah*. It was 150 by 150 yards and contained sixteen divisions. It had a double roof; the upper one, called *qalandari*, was tent-like in shape (*Ain-i-Akbari*: 48, 55-7; Mujeeb, 1967: 373). Interestingly, writing on the Salar Masu'd Ghazi *dargah* at Bahraich, Schwerin (1981: 149-50) notes that copper coins which pilgrims throw at the dome of the *dargah* are called *qalandar*.

Some scholars opine that this word has been derived from the Turkish word *qurinda* or *qalandari*; the word *qala* means 'pure'. In Turkish, the word Qalandar means a 'dervish who has withdrawn from the world and who wanders about like a vagabond; a man who has renounced all worldly things and who has seen the truth; a philosopher' (c.f. Yazici 1973: 472). Qalandar has also become the name of a certain tune in Turkish; it is sometimes also spelt *karendal* or *kalender*. In old Ottoman texts, the words *ishik* and *torlak* are used as equivalents of Qalandar. In the Ottoman period, the Qalandars were also referred by other names, such as Abdalan-i-Rum and Shamsiyan. Abdals are recorded from the early fourteenth century. Later authors allege that the Qalandariya derives from Mevleviya (the order founded by Rumi); they are however misled by the fact that the dress of the Shamsiya (after Shams Tabrez), which is a branch of Mevleviya, resembled that of the Qalandars.

Rizvi (1978: 301) begins his chapter on the Qalandars with the following statement: 'The history of Sufism has been made infinitely *colourful* by the role of qalandars' (emphasis mine). Qalandars were made butts of jokes, of cruel humour, as figures of fun, as is evident from the stories of *The Arabian Nights*. They are 'colourful', to borrow Rizvi's word, because of their quaint physical appearance, dress, behaviour, and habits. Several poems describe the arrival of Qalandars in the market towns as a disruption of the social order. The presence of Qalandars is described to be overpowering, creating chaos, with shopkeepers and townspersons trying to please them (Lewis, 2000: 34-5). Many writers understand the Qalandars as a cultural species.

The Qalandars have been most numerous in Persia and a great bulk of them were concentrated in Ardabil, the stronghold of the Safawiyas. Some of their groups established themselves in India. In Anatolia, and even in Rumelia, in the early Ottoman period down to the sixteenth century, the Qalandars played a dangerous part several times, attacking the authority of the state and leading serious uprisings. Even in the Seljuk period, similar risings seem to have been led by the Qalandars. In the Indian context, there are cases of Qalandars attacking the Sufis of other orders.

The term Qalandar is applied to an ensemble of *faqir*s, of which we have varying descriptions. The Qalandar (the 'Calendar') of *The Arabian Nights* are not really an 'order'. Some writers think that these renouncers form a group of 'begging monks' (Sharif, 1921: 295); some have wives, some not; some are 'within', others 'without' the Law. They occupy thatched huts outside, or retired spots within towns, where they pass their time in solitude, trusting to providence, with laymen providing them food and drinks. The places where they resort are called *takia*.

Others say that they constitute a tribe of nomads (Sell, 1928 [1985]: 176), who eke out their subsistence by conjuring tricks and entertaining, by performing monkeys and bears (Titus, 1959: 135). In Punjab, Rose (1919: 543) writes, they are said to make excellent pipe bowls. They have a secret argot and settle their own disputes with order and dignity. The People of India Project, undertaken by the Anthropological Survey of India, found a Muslim community in Delhi, which went around with performing animals and called itself Qalandar. The people of this community used this term interchangeably with Madari (see Ghosh and Nath, eds., 1996: 301-3). *The Times of India* issue of 29 July 2000 carried a picture of Qalandars on its front page, describing them as 'people who earn their livelihood by staging dance shows of monkeys and bears'. In north India, the stereotype of a Qalandar is that he is a Muslim, who goes from door to door singing and asking for alms. If the householder responds, divine blessings are bestowed upon him, but if he refused, then the *faqir* hurls abuses at him.

Another set of writers regard the Qalandars as pious people, who peregrinate, generally without footwear, and carry out the severest acts of austerity and mostly live in a state of ecstasy (Rose, 1919: 169-70). In the hagiology of Indian Islam, the Qalandars constitute an order of renouncers 'who are so absorbed in religious reveries or overcome to such an extent by ecstatic experiences that they are unable to distinguish between things lawful and unlawful' (Subhan, 1970: 310). Jami, the poet of the early sixteenth century, defined the Qalandars as those 'who have pulled from their necks the bridle of Islam', and 'one should rather name them *hashawiyya*'. In mystical terminology, Abu Hafs Umar-bin Abdul-al Suhrawardi says, a Qalandar is a saint who totally and finally annihilates himself in the love of God by reaching the stage of *fana-i-fillah* ('disappearance in oneness'). Qalandar also means *ishq* and love is God. Through love, the Qalandar becomes one with the creator. Muhammad Hussain-bin Khalaf Tabrizi, the compiler of the famous dictionary in Persian (known as *Burhan-e-Qate*), defined Qalandar as a person who is so much spiritualized that he is free from the social and customary inhibitions and taboos. He leads a life of self-detachment from the world and is entirely absorbed in contemplation of the divine beauty and majesty (Yazici, 1973). Inam Muhammad (1978) feels that the conception of Qalandars that he is in a state of ecstasy, does not care for rules or laws of society or religion, is not true. A Qalandar is basically well versed in all religious teachings and has reached a zenith of spiritual divinity through hard perseverance, practice and prayers. He adheres to three concepts of life: love of the creator, love of his fellow beings, and indulges out of divine ecstasy in certain acts and practices of extreme devotion which are within the limits of ethical rules and values. This motif of the Qalandars appears in the eleventh century poems of Abu Said Abial Khayr (967-1049) and recurs throughout the work of Sana'i, Attar, and others.

Let us have a look at another meaning. In his meeting with the Qalandars, Burke (1979) found that they generally declined to discuss the matter concerning their order and its practices. However, one of his respondents was a bureaucrat and a Sufi named Akbar Baig. Speaking of the Qalandars, he described them as 'mystics and also as Sufis'. According to him, they are Qalandars 'when they are in a certain period of their lives.' In this period, they are totally absorbed in divinity, with the result that they have no time for mundane concerns. Their state is eloquently expressed in the following verse from Kurratu'l Ayn:

Sikandar's pomp and display be thine;
the Qalandar's habit and way be mine;
That, if it pleases thee, I resign, while this
though bad, is enough for me.

They may die as Qalandars, and then, they are venerated and enshrined. 'But generally to be a Callandar is only a phase in the life of a Sufi.' Baig's conclusion was that 'Callandarism is a condition, not a permanent status.'

An interpretation of Baig's comments on the state of Qalandarism could be that every Sufi, notwithstanding the order of his allegiance, has a phase of ecstasy, and this is the condition of 'being a Qalandar'. But when this state overcomes a Sufi for his entire life, he is forever a Qalandar. Thus, the Qalandar is not a contrapuntal ideal type of a Khanqah Sufi; rather, it is a phase in the spiritual development of a person. Every Sufi has a Qalandar in him. Another respondent of Burke was a Qalandar, named Imtiaz, who showed him a picture of Hazrat Bu 'Ali Shah Qalandar whom he called the 'greatest Callandar teacher'. The picture showed a Sufi 'plentifully endowed with facial hair', sitting on a tiger skin rug with his hands upraised, the fingers linked together. (Perhaps, it was the same picture which has been reprinted in John A. Subhan's book. The superscription on the picture reads: 'The Blessed Presence of Bu Ali Shah Callandar, Year 1000 Hijri.') The explanation of sporting 'plentiful' facial hair was that he grew it after completing (or, transcending) his Qalandari status.

We have now two concepts: (1) Qalandar is a cultural type; and (2) it is a stage to be understood in processual terms. The first is a relatively 'fixed' status group, and can be contrasted to the other Sufi cultural types. We understand it in terms of physical appearance, the material cultural traits, attitudes and behavioural characteristics. The second meaning of Qalandar is a state of mind; it is a process which seizes every Sufi. Both these meanings are interspersed in the writings on the Qalandar path, however, most writers do not make clear distinction.

Let us now have a look at the distinction between the two orders, classified as 'minor orders' (Subhan, 1970: 299-318), the Malamatiya and the Qalandariya. It was Shihabu'd-Din Suhrawardi's *'Awarif al-Ma'arif* that advanced a distinction between two types of dervish: the Qalandars and the Malamatis. The Qalandariya is applied to people so possessed by the intoxication of a 'tranquility of the *qalb* (heart),' that they have no respect for customs or usages. They reject the regular observance of society and the rules of mutual relations. They perform the minimal obligatory prayers, which are allowed by the indulgence of divine law. They do not concern themselves with earthly pleasures. The Malamatis, in comparison, try to conceal their mode of life and spiritual achievements. They resort to offensive behaviour, for they disdain people bothering them. The Qalandar, on the other hand, seek to destroy the accepted customs. In fact, many Sufis have taken recourse to the malamati technique, in order to hide from people, so that the spiritual practices could be pursued without any disturbance. Mendicants of other religious orders have also variously adopted highly offensive and degrading stratagems, desiring that the people loathe them and eventually, stop taking an interest in them (Parry, 1994; Lewis, 2000).

THE PAST OF THE QALANDARS

According to some scholars, the Qalandariya school was started by Prophet Muhammad who educated Hazrat Ali (son-in-law of the Prophet) with its principles. In fact, Islamic mysticism is traced to him; in the Shahbaz Qalandar song (*Ali da malang mein te Ali da*), Ali is given the first place amongst the Sufis (the refrain is: *Ali da pehla number*); Ali also figures in other Sufi songs (for instance, *Ali more angna daras dikha*). Waseem in his introduction to de Tassy's (1997: 23) essays writes: "Even the illiterate porter would cry 'Ya Ali! Madad' ('O Ali, help me') when lifting a heavy load. Among other things Ali represents, like Hanuman, devotion and prowess." The Qalandariya system was entrusted by Ali to Hazrat Syed 'Abdu'l-Aziz Makki, one of the Sahabas and member of the Ashaba-i-Sufa ('brethren of purity'), a companion of the Prophet himself (Sahaba-i-Rasool). He had been called a Qalandar by the Prophet Muhammad. He lies buried in Pakpattan, district Sahwal in Pakistan, close to the tomb of Baba Farid. Another view is that one of his disciples, Sayyed Khizr Rumi Qalandari, founded the Qalandari order. The members of the order went about with shaven heads with a view to follow the footsteps of the Master, 'Abdu'l-Aziz Makki, who had lost his hair owing to a very long life.

It is said that Mohammad Chelebi, a descendant of Sultan Valad, Rumi's son, through his daughter, combined several practices in his person, viz., Mevlevi, Shiite, Harufi, and Qalandari. On his journeys, he would wander the hills and valleys, sometimes with dishevelled hair, and sometimes with hair, face, and eyebrows shaved, wearing only a long smock open at the chest (*tennure*), a Qalandari cloak, and occasionally a Mevlevi hat, and sometimes a twelve-pointed crown or headgear (*taj*), belonging to Shams Tabrizi order. He was an antinomian figure, who smoked opium and even drank in the mosque, and tossed wine on the walls out of his Malamati beliefs. This example also clearly shows the coexistence of the practices of different antinomian orders in one person (Lewis, 2000: 446).

Another legend is linked with Makki. It is said that he was so profoundly absorbed in asceticism and solitude that he shaved his head, beard, and moustaches. When the Prophet saw him, he greatly approved and remarked that people in the Paradise (*jannat*) looked just like him. At his request, the Prophet allowed him to lead a recluse's life in a mountain cave. The Prophet himself prayed for his welfare and longevity. Makki reappeared from the cave on three occasions: once to show allegiance to the Caliph Abu Talib; second time in the ninth century to become the disciple of Bistami; and finally, after two hundred years to initiate Khizr Rumi, who brought the Qalandariya tradition to India. After this, he went to Ajodhan and disappeared in a grotto in the outskirts of the city.

According to a Sufi legend, their Master Makki is still alive. He is said to have been living through the ages from the time of Abraham until now! A small mound (*sardaba*) is considered the place inside which he is said to be existing in a state of self-induced unconsciousness by holding his breath (*habs-i-dam*). So, according to this tradition, the whole structure of the Qalandariya order begins with the Prophet. Another contemporary of the Prophet, Uways-u'l-Qarani, is also regarded as a Qalandar. The Prophet gave His cloak to Uways-u'l-Qarani, from which it is inferred that he greatly loved the Prophet.

Writers of Sufi history agree that the term Qalandar is much older than the institutionalization of the 'path' of Qalandars. The eleventh century Sufis, Abu Sa'id bin Abi'l Khair, Baba Tahir Uryan, and Khwaja 'Abdu'llah Ansari, were aware of the word Qalandar, and they used it more in the sense of a peregrinator. The origin of the term Qalandar has yet not been established, but it is first encountered in the following quatrain (*ruba'i*) attributed to Uryan:

I'm a wanderer whose name is Qalandar;
I've neither home, nor goods, nor kitchen;
[no country, no lair;]
When day comes, I wander round the world;
When night falls I lay my head on a brick.
[By day, I wander aimless over the earth,
and when night falls, my pillow is a stone.]

The second reference to Qalandar is a short treatise by a Sufi, Khwaja 'Abdu'llah Ansari (d. 1088-9), titled *Qalandar-nama*, which is an exposition of the doctrines of the Qalandars. It contains the Khwaja's conversations with a Qalandar who visited his school (*madarsa*), wearing a garment of coarse cloth (*namd*), and spoke to him and his students about divinity. The Khwaja was profoundly impressed by the Qalandar's discourse, and wished to follow him in his wanderings. But the Qalandar dissuaded him from the stressful life of a mystic wanderer. He taught the Khwaja that one experienced real spirituality by reducing oneself to the state of a beggar.

By the end of the twelfth century, the Qalandars had emerged as a separate and identifiable group. It is attested, as Digby (1984: 62) shows, by an anecdote in Attar's poem, the *Mantiq-al-tayr*, composed around AD 1177. An Arab, coming to 'Ajam, had an encounter with a band of shaven Qalandars. He had never seen these people earlier. He was overcome by their style of living. Not only did he join them, he also shaved his hair and accepted their customs. The Qalandars, however, maltreated, assaulted, and robbed him. The Arab finally returned to his native land. This anecdote shows that Qalandars were active in Khorasan in the twelfth century, and by that time some of their cultural practices had crystallized.

In literature and poetry, the Qalandars are described as wanderers. They are also portrayed as enjoying moods of exaltation, sometimes aided by barbiturates, sometimes induced by meditation and auto-hypnotic techniques of ecstasy. In the eleventh century Khorasan, the word Qalandar was used for a 'very poor, ill-clad, wandering religious mendicant, probably weak in learning and in the performance of prescribed Muslim religious observances, but with a popular appeal and charisma deriving from the intensity of his poverty, which was often closer to the ideal of *faqr* than the actual behaviour of settled Sufi Shaykhs established in hospices' (Digby, 1984: 62). In other words, the Qalandars formed an anti-thesis of the Khanqah or the settled Sufis.

In the *Encyclopedia of Islam*, the Qalandar is classed as a Sufi religious order, founded in early thirteenth century by Qalandar Yusuf, an Arab of Spain, who was a contemporary of Hadidji Bektashi, the founder of the Bektashi order. The group of Qalandars appeared in Damascus in AD 1213-4. al-Maqrizi (d. 1442) provided an account of the early Qalandars. He said that during Yusuf's time, the Qalandars did not wear garments of coarse cloth. Neither did they subject themselves to mortification nor to rigorous religious exercises. Sufficient for them was that their 'hearts were at peace with God'. It was their ideal, and to attain this, they unhesitatingly threw off all the etiquettes of politeness in society.

Another founder of the group of Qalandars was Sheikh Muhammad ibn Yunus Jamalu'd-Din of Sawa. He was also well known in Damascus.

From 1210 to 1225, he was in Sawa, and then moved to Damietta on the Nile in Egypt. In his life-history account given by Ibn Battuta, Sheikh Jamal was a very handsome man. When he was in Sawa, a woman fell in love with him, but she could not entice the Sheikh. Once, on the pretext of having a letter read, being illiterate, she invited the Sheikh to her house. As soon as he realized her real intentions, he hid in the lavatory, shaved off his beard and eyebrows, and then accosted her. The woman looked aghast at his appearance and asked him to leave her house. Since then, the Sheikh kept his shaven appearance because it saved him from what would have been an end of his virtuosity. His disciples followed his way – they also kept their facial and body hair (including the scalp and eyebrows) shaven, and for this, they always kept a razor (*ustara*) with them. What was an expedient strategy adopted by a person to stave off a woman's advances became a revered tradition and an identifying mark of a Qalandar. We earlier saw that it is after Makki that his followers kept shaven scalps; however, this does not explain the custom of shaving of other facial and body hair. Sheikh Jamal's case is able to explain the origin of this tradition. The Sheikh's disciple was Qutb al-Din Hayder, who later became the founder of the Haydari tradition. This would also illuminate the closeness of the traditions of Qalandars and Haydaris.

The Qalandars were present in Syria at the beginning of the thirteenth century, but the dispersal of the followers of Jamalu'd-Din and Qutb al-Din came about in AD 1220-1 when Khorasan was devastated by the Mongols. Jamalu'd-Din of Sava fled and settled in Damascus where he breathed his last in AD 1232. Qutb al-Din Hayder also advised his disciples to flee before the advent of Mongols, and he was never seen again. The Qalandaris were initially disapproved of in Damascus and exiled. The Qalandariya was reintroduced with the Haydari group, a *zawiya* being built in AD 1257. A pupil of Makki, known as Khizr Rumi, is credited with the introduction of the Qalandariya path into north India, at the time of Iltutmish which developed into a definite line of ascription as a Qalandari order.

A Persian *faqir* called Hasan al-Jawaliq came to Egypt during the time of Adil Ketbugha (1294-6) and founded a *zawiya* of Qalandars. In course of time, it came to be known as that of the Jawaliqs. He then went to Damascus where he died in AD 1322. al-Makrizi remarks that they were 'quietists', seeking inward peace, but their means of attaining this involved discarding normal social restraints.

Another tradition traces the Turkish Qalandaris as being the original ones. The group claims to derive from a Spanish Arab immigrant called Yusuf Andalusi. Expelled from the Bektashi order because of his arrogance, he tried in vain to enter the order of the Mevlevis, and ended by forming a distinct order under the name of Qalandar. During the reign of Muhammad II

(1451-81), a Qalandar convent with mosque and school (*madarsa*) made its appearance in Istanbul. Evliva Chelebi refers to an Indian Qalandari convent at Kaghid Khanah (Scutari) whose *faqirs* were provided with supper by Sultan Muhammad. There was a Qalandari order in Aleppo too. Another Qalandar *zawiya* existed in Jerusalem in the middle of the Namitta cemetery. It was formerly a church and was taken over by one Ibrahim-al Qalandar for his *zawiya*, but before 1488, it fell into disuse. Ira Lapidus confirms that Sufi beggars called Qalandari had their own community in Bukhara.

In India, some think that Shah Khizr Rumi introduced the Qalandari tradition. He was a resident of Delhi before AD 1235. However, according to Sell (1928 [1985]: 31), the order was introduced into India by 'Ali Abu Yusuf Qalandar, known as Bu Ali Qalandar, a native of Spain. After being connected with the Bektashi and Chishti ordes, he finally left both of them, and organized an order of his own. In his travels, he came to India and settled down at Panipat. Titus (1959) says that the tomb of Bu Ali Qalandar is the chief shrine of this order and is venerated by his followers. It is said that the Haydari cult reached India very early. We first hear about a Haydari saint in Lakhnauti. Barani writes that he enjoyed patronage of the rebel governor of Bengal, Tughril Khan, in AD 1279, because of which he was known as Sultan Darwesh. Tughril gave him three maunds of gold so that the rings and the bracelets of this saint might be made of gold instead of iron (Rizvi, 1978: 304). This also shows the closeness between the Haydaris and Qalandars. Barani (see Rizvi, 1978) also writes that when Balban marched against Tughril, he executed the Haydari saint and put his head on the gibbet. In the reign of Balban, a dervish named Sidi Muwallih (the founder of the Muwallih order) founded a Khanqah outside the gates of Delhi. At the same time, a Haydari-Qalandari saint, Abu Bakr Tusi, had established himself in Delhi. In the following reign of Alauddin Khilji, a 'free kitchen' (*langar*) was run by a Qalandar known as Ramzan. Contemporaneous to Abu Bakr at Delhi, Sharfuddin Bu Ali Qalandar had make his mark at Panipat after having spent twenty years at Mehrauli (Delhi).

At this juncture, it is relevant to consider the idea of the Daor-i-Qalandar, the 'era of Qalandars'. Abdul Ghani Munsiff has made an important observation about it. He says that we use the word Qalandar for a type of dervish or Sufi of distinctly unorthodox tendencies, and one who is not affiliated to any dervish order. He defines the essential meaning of the Qalandari era as the 'garment of religion turned inside out amounting to the universal dissemination of psychological and spiritual truths.' He says that the era of Qalandars was 'fulfilled' (or, completed) in the person of a female Qalandar named Bibijan, ethnically a Pathan, who was settled in Poona in the early twentieth century. The Daor-i-Qalandar refers symbolically to the end of the world being precipitated by the completion of three Qalandari manifestations. Earlier it was thought that it is two-and-a-half (*adhai*): Bu Ali Sharfuddin Qalandar of Panipat ('one'), Lal Shahbaz Qalandar of Sehwan Sind ('one'), and Rabia Basri ('half'). To this, Ghani adds the name of Bibijan ('half'), thus giving the concept of three Qalandars of the Daor-i-Qalandar. Ghani extrapolates that 'half' here is a scale of feminine equivalence in the Islamic context. He posited the interpretation of the completion or end of a cycle producing a new world view in the Qalandari vein.

The fact that the Qalandars were able to proliferate and diffuse does not mean that their success was without opposition. During the phase of their historical development, the Qalandars were also subjected to vitriolic criticism. For instance, *ishq-i-majazi* (platonic love) was very popular among the Sufis since the last decades of the fourteenth century. It was influenced by the expression of divine love and beauty in Sufi poetry as well as Ibn-al Arabi's (d. 1240) portrayal of women as an embodiment of virtue, spiritual excellence, and love (Corbin, 1993). Against this background, even the great Sufi saints began to show faith in the efficacy of platonic love. To them, contemplation of all earthly beauty was a preparatory stage for envisaging God's eternal beauty, which is beyond all comparison. It may also be noted here that it had an adverse effect on the morality of some dervishes, particularly Qalandars. They stopped performing obligatory duties (*farz*) of Islam, and showed eagerness for *ishq-e-majazi*, considering it a means of spiritual evolution. They fell for a boy or girl at the very first sight and then pined for a love relationship.

Often, they were forbidden to live the way they desired. For instance, in his sixteenth century Turkish chronicle, *Menakib-i Hvica-i-ahan ve netice-i-can*, Vahedi vehemently denounces the socially deviant dervishes of Baraq Baba's ilk and a group which called itself Shams-i-Tabrizis, who shaved their heads and faces, walked barefoot, wore felt clothes and caps of black and white, played music and chanted, and in addition, also drank wine (Lewis, 2000). The Mamluke Sultan al-Malik al-Nasir Hasan, the grandson of Kalaun, forbade the Qalandars in AD 1360 to shave their beard. Ghiasuddin Azam Shah, the Sultan of Bengal, embarked upon a scheme to expel all Qalandars from the town. The Qalandari habits were interpreted as outrageous and being an order of mystics whose rule required perpetual wandering and *faqr*, it was a 'catch-all' term for beggars whose ornate bowl was a mere pretension of spirituality. Those who take on other cultural traits to indulge in debaucheries should not be confused with the 'real' (the 'true') Qalandars. (This was also the view of Suhrawardi and Jami.) Nizamuddin Auliya is said to have informed his audience in 1307 that while the outward form and peculiarities of the Haydaris had remained, their real spirit had disappeared (*Fawaid ul-Fuad*: 20). In this line of thinking, the Beshara were treated as a group of outcasts, pariah and mentally incompetent, who would more 'accurately be called unbelievers'. Nevertheless, the Beshara sects flourished and many of its saints were (and are) the objects of worship, cutting across religious boundaries.

The Ulema and Sufi *sheikh*s found the way of life of the Qalandars aberrant. The Suhrawardi and Chishti saints described the Qalandars as 'pseudo-dervishes'. The sixteenth century Shattari saint, Sheikh Rizq Allah Mushtaqi, also shows his dislike for them. The Governor of Jaunpur, Khan Azam Ahmad Khan Lodi Sarang Khani, during the reign of Sultan Sikandar Lodi (1489-1517) entertained every dervish as his esteemed guest for three days, but showed no regard for the Qalandar, who was immediately sent away with the gift of a buffalo (*Waqiat-e-Mushtaqi*: 97). But, there were many who provided refuge to all types of dervishes, including Qalandars. Masad-i-Ali Khawas Khan (the leading noble of Sher Shah Sur) maintained a large number of Hindu and Muslim holy men. Sheikh Rizqullah Mushtaqi says that he was always found in their company. Ni'matullah Harevi mentions their names along with the names of their orders to which they were affiliated. He refers to the Malang, *jogi*s, *muni*s, and *gabri*s (fire-worshippers).

QALANDAR AS A CULTURAL SPECIES

Earlier, we said that it is amply clear from literature that the Qalandars constitute a cultural species. To understand this fully, we shall examine here the set of material objects and symbols (the diacritical signs) which define a Qalandar.

The Qalandars are distinguished from other Muslim orders by their physical appearance. In Turkish works, there exists vivid and detailed information about the morphology of a Qalandar. He is depicted as 'clean shaven, with shaven eyebrows and heads, wearing a conical hat of woven hair and a yellow or black shawl, and carrying a drum and a standard (*'alam*; 'ceremonial flag')' (Yazici, 1973: 472). In an illustration to Nicolas de Nicolay's *Les Navigations* (Lyons, 1567, in Yazici 1973: 472), the Qalandar is shown as wearing a coarse garment of horse-hair which reaches to just below the hips. His head and face are completely clean-shaven. On his head is a felt hat with a horse-hair brim of one hand's length. And, he wears rings in his ears, on his wrists and on his genitals.

Another source of a vivid description of a Qalandar is *The Arabian Nights*, especially the tale of 'The Porter and Three Ladies of Baghdad'. This tale not only provides an account of the physical appearance of a Qalandar, but also throws light on why those 'bizarre' looking men became Qalandars. In this tale, the Qalandars are regarded as a source of 'great amusement and fun'.

The tale begins with the portress answering the knock at the door. She soon returns, saying: "Truly our pleasure for this night is to be perfect ... . At the gate [stand] three Persian Qalandars with their beards and heads and eyebrows shaven ... . They are foreigners from Roumland with the mark of travel plain upon them." She further states that the Qalandars require lodgings for the night: "And, O my sisters," she continues, "each of them is a figure of fun after his own fashion, and if we let them in we shall have matter to make sport of." These Qalandars are addressed as 'mendicants' and *faqir*s.

The women (who happen to be sisters) request the Qalandars to amuse them with a story or rare adventure. The Qalandars drink wine: 'the warmth of wine ... mount[s] to their heads' (p. 52). They seem to be adept at playing the musical instruments. After having drunk the inebriating liquid, they call for musical instruments – 'a tambourine of Mosul, a lute of Irak, and a Persian harp' (p. 52). Each of them takes one instrument, starts playing on it, and strikes up a 'merry tune'. The women sing 'lustily' to the accompaniment of the music, and a 'great noise' is produced. The story does not refer to any orgiastic revelry during the drinking and singing session.

The women ask the Qalandars whether they are brothers. The Qalandars deny any consanguinity between them. However, a coincidence worth noting is that they are all monocular. They say that each one of them hails from a different country, they are sons of kings (p. 60). And then, the women ask the Qalandars to narrate their individual life story. Each story ends with a set of reasons accounting for why they adopted the Qalandari garb. We shall refer to this later.

Ibn Battuta describes the Qalandar as being distinctive. To the characteristics cited above, he adds the perforation of hands and ears for insertion of iron rings as symbols of penitence. The Qalandar also wears a ring on his penis (the practice called *tathqib-al-ihlil*). Jamali adds that the Haydari passed a round iron rod through his penis and both its ends were sealed; the rod was called *sikh-i-muhr* (Rizvi, 1978: 307).

Well known in literature is Ibn Battuta's account of a Haydari party he met in a village near Amroha in AD 1342. He wrote that they were a 'company of poor brethren who had iron rings on their necks and arms, whose chief was a coal black Negro.' The leader asked Ibn Battuta to supply him with fire-wood so that he could light it for a dance. Battuta requested the governor Aziz al-Khammar to furnish it. After lighting the fire, the Qalandars began their musical recital and danced. The chief of the Qalandars borrowed a shirt from Ibn Battuta and beat the fire with its sleeves. He returned the shirt which showed, so wrote Battuta, not a single burn mark (Rizvi, 1978).

Hamid Qalandar has placed the Qalandars above the Sufis, and he does not mention the Haydaris as a separate group. He says that the Qalandars have scarification of their bodies. They have their own distinct type of turban and wear short garments. Although different, they observe the ceremonial cleanliness of the Sufis. He also says that wearing of the iron rings through the ears is more a cultural practice of the Jawaliqs. *Siyaru'l-'Arifin* (p. 119) notes that the Qalandars do not wear the cloak (*khirqa*), which is particularly associated with the Sufis in India. *Khairu'l-Majalis* (p. 185) describes a group of Qalandars as wearing neither clothes nor *khirqa*, in fact nothing but iron chains and rings, fragments of blanket and loin cloths. Some Qalandars wrapped their body with a blanket (often a coloured one) and fastened either a piece of blanket or a small sheet of cotton round the loins (*Khairu'l-Majalis*: 131). Those who wrapped the blanket round their body were called the Jawaliqs (*Ibid.*). Some of them used to walk quite naked (Burke 1975: 70). That the Qalandars wore iron rings round the neck and on the arms was recorded in *Fawa'idu'l-Fu'ad*. Ziya'u'd-din Barani (d. after 1357) refers on several occasions to the *palas*, or coarse garment apparently reddish ochre (*gerwa bhes*, *tesu* colour), worn by the Qalandars. In addition, some of their garments used to be of leather; the garment (called *duwal*, *juwal*, *juwaliq*, *jaulakh*, *dilaq*), which gave the Jawaliqs their name, may have been of leather (Digby, 1984: 63).

Of the Qalandaris, the most strong association with the wearing of iron objects is of the Haydaris. We earlier saw that the Qalandars (and members of other similar groups) wore iron bangles, bracelets, necklaces, and chains. A related observation is that iron in one form or the other is associated with the Qalandari groups. Take for instance, an anecdote from the life of Abu Bakr Tusi, the Haydari-Qalandari saint of Delhi. A person intending to test the much acclaimed miraculous power of the saint sent him as a gift a plate of iron balls resembling the roasted horse-grams (*bhuna chana*). The eponymous founder of the Haydaris, Qutb al-Din Haydar, is said (and this anecdote was narrated by Sheikh Nizamuddin Auliya) to have held red-hot iron bars with bare hands and bent them into rings. Digby (1984: 64) conjectures that they [Hayder and the Haydaris] 'practiced the actual working of iron as smiths'; they might have been nomadic smiths. But this hypothesis cannot be supported unless we have relevant hagiographical material on occupational groups from which the Qalandaris and Haydaris hailed. Apart from historical reasons, the contexts in which they identified themselves with iron, the wearing of iron also symbolized carrying the load, a measure of austerity. In light of the information so far available, it does not seem that the Qalandars ever used the iron ornaments, they wore, as weapons. We also cannot interpret iron bangles and bracelets as 'restraining' the 'use of the weapon,' as Uberoi (1996: 1-18) did in his interpretation of the five Sikh symbols, because the Qalandars did not carry a weapon. Uberoi interprets symbols in a relationship of complementarity – thus, the bracelet (*kara*) is understood in relationship with the sword (*kirpan*).

The Qalandars used to carry a razor (*ustara*) for shaving hair; a large needle (*juwal-doz*) for sewing patches on their garments; a begging bowl (*kachkul*); and by the late fourteenth century, they used to travel with a banner (*alam*) and a drum (*dhul*). The former was for letting the others know that they were the Qalandars; and the latter was for producing music to the tunes of which they danced. Though they were all functional implements, the razor, the sacking-needle and the begging bowl had been used by them as weapons (Digby, 1984: 91). In addition, the Qalandars developed their own patois and vocabulary, which helped in the formation of their identity. He further said that the Qalandars 'unmindful of life around them go without shoes and practice the severest acts of austerities in a state of ecstasy.'

Why did the Qalandars shave their facial and body hair? Although literature does not specifically mention this, one of our respondents remembered that the Qalandar he had known in Delhi and visited him many a times thirty years ago, cut even his eyelashes. The literature does not mention anything about shaving pubic or armpit hair. (However, it is mentioned in Hadith that either of these should not grow longer than a grain of rice.) It only mentions 'body hair', leaving the rest to the imagination of the reader.

One of the reasons we mentioned earlier was that this practice came into existence after the founder of the Qalandari *tariqa*. Makki, a very old Sufi, had lost all his hair and his disciples started keeping a shaven scalp in emulaton of their master. In case Jamal al-Din of Sawa is regarded as the founder of the Qalandar path, then the tradition of keeping the face and the body hairless came into existence after the master defeated the amorous advances of a woman by shaving his face.

At the ideological level, the Qalandars wanted to reveal the beauty of the face. It is not known when and why this reason came into existence, and who was its advocate. Digby (1984: 63) says that one might speculate a medical reason for adopting this practice of shaving all hair and also, the scarification of body. To quote him (*Ibid.*): '...these [practices] might have contributed to the elimination of bodily parasites among groups of men who were ill-clad, traveling in conditions of hardship and dependent upon charity.'

But both these explanations (one attributed to the actors [the Qalandars] and the other speculated by the observer) may not be convincing, for they justify the practices after they have become commonly accepted. In a typical functional mode of explanation, if a practice or custom exists, it must be functional, otherwise it will cease to exist; in the same logic, if the Qalandars shave off their hair, its manifest function is that it enhances the actor's beauty which otherwise remains hidden behind hair, and its latent function is that as the Qalandars keep their bodies hairless they are relatively free from germs. Therefore, these explanations from the actor's and the observer's perspectives are in fact the consequences (the effects); they certainly are not the causes. That the Qalandars started shaving off because they wanted a beautiful face (uneclipsed by hair) is supported nowhere by hagiographies. Perhaps, these practices came into existence after the personal styles of the masters and teachers, and with the passage of time, they became the diacritical signs – the 'public signs' – of the members of a sect. Thus, amongst the 'personal signs of Qalandars' was the practice of shaving hair and keeping a razor. It will be preposterous to say that they kept a razor as a weapon, but indubitably if the occasion demanded, they used it.

The Qalandars did not wear the Sufi cloak (*khirqa*); rather, they covered themselves with a garment of coarse cloth (*namd*). Some of them covered their pubic area with pieces of blankets; on record are the Qalandars who remained sky-clad. All this symbolized the value of *faqr*, the Sufi concept of poverty. The Jawaliqs and also, some Qalandars, wore leather garments because they lasted longer. The concept of changing clothes was perhaps not encouraged as can be understood from the fact that they carried a needle to sew the torn garments. And, the leather-clad Qalandar did not have to worry about change or damage to his sheet. That some Qalandars wore the ochre-robe (*palas*) can be explained in terms of the influence of Hindu renouncers on them. Walking without footwear is interpreted as an austere measure, subjecting the body to sufferings which is a kind of *faqr*.

The *kaasa* or *kachkul* (a special wooden bowl for begging) served a utilitarian purpose; on one occasion it was used by a Qalandar to strike a Sufi (Digby, 1984). The drums the Qalandars carried with them announced their arrival in a human settlement and also produced music for their dances and audition. The insignia on the banner was a marker of their identity. The passing of an iron ring through the penis has been reported among non-Hindu ascetics (Briggs, 1938; Ghurye, 1953; Das, 1982). Some Qalandars also resorted to this practice, which symbolizes an annihilation of one's sexuality, and thus reproductive ability. This act is un-Islamic, for all, notwithstanding their locus in the spiritual hierarchy, are required to marry and have progeny. Digby (1984: 66) suggests that this practice of emasculating – thereby, desexualizing oneself – is a case of 'Indianization'; the Qalandars imitated their counterparts in Hindu renunciatory orders who resorted to this practice. This shows that the Qalandars (like the Chishti, but unlike the Suhrawardi) adopted certain non-Islamic practices from diverse spiritual traditions. Siddiqui (1979: 36) believes that syncretism is discernible in the teachings and practices of Qalandars (and also, Chishti).

RECRUITMENT TO THE QALANDARIYA PATH

The Sufis, like Muslims in general, as said earlier, are required to get married and have progeny. Remaining celibate is un-Islamic. However, a number of Sufis in contravention to Shariat, remained unmarried. In fact, most of the Chishti Sufis were celibate. The Qalandaris (and the other related paths), as we saw earlier, adhered to the value of celibacy. Thus, recruitment to their sect was external, which means people of different strata joined it. Although no study has been carried out on the social and cultural background of the Qalandars, Digby (1984: 66), citing Ibn Battuta, says that most of the recruits to the group of Qalandars were from lower strata.

The myths surrounding the founders of the Qalandariya path are of a different order. For instance, take the life-history account of Bu Ali Qalandar. After his birth, he neither opened his eyes nor would he drink milk. He wept uncontrollably with not even a moment's respite. A couple of days later, a dervish came to his house and asked his father to bring the child outside so that he could see him. The child was brought to him; the dervish picked him up and uttered the words: 'Oh, Qalandar! You have come to the world. Now open your eyes and stop crying.' The child stopped weeping. He was destined to become one of the most famous Qalandars of India (Siddiqui, 1979).

In other words, the myths of these founder-Qalandars begin with the premise that they were destined to become Qalandars. But, when we examine the Qalandar stories of *The Arabian Nights*, the reason invariably is that the individual is devastated to such an extent that eventually he is optionless and becomes a mendicant. It is a coincidence that he enters into the Qalandari *tariqa*. Take, for instance, the first story. This son of the king, who later becomes a Qalandar, is betrayed by his Wazir who kills his uncle and usurps his property. The prince now feels that he has no way of escaping, 'save by shaving off ... beard ... and eyebrows.' He says (p. 66): '... I shore them off and changing (changed) my fine clothes for a Kalandar's rags.' In the other two stories also, the princes are finally left with no option but to tread the renunciatory path.

Two types of men joined the Qalandari path: those who found it more attractive, i.e., those pulled towards it; and those who sought to escape from the struggle of life, from oppression and punishment, and from being caught by the state. The Qalandari path provided an alternative and since the Qalandars were expected to lead a peregrinating life, the chances of wanted men being noticed by the state personnel were remote. Digby (1984: 68) writes: 'Many recruits were evidently run away children or adolescents, but older men might also abandon their professions and join the Qalandars.' Once, the Chishti Sufi Gesu Daraz asked a Qalandar the reason for his joining the order. The reply was that he had had an argument with his parents, which upset him so much that he ran away from home. On the way, he came across a group of Qalandars who greatly encouraged him to join the order. And, there he was, a Qalandar. In other words, there was no explicit religious motive, no spiritual yearning, and also no providential meeting with a Sheikh or *pir* which could have been inspiring. A common stereotype of the Qalandars, as we noted earlier, was that they were not the 'men of learning' (*mard-i-muta'allimi*); thus, illiterate and people of low intelligence found a place in the Qalandari order.

Thus, those who joined either the orthodox Sufi orders or the Bashara sects were 'opting out' from the demands made on them by high medieval Muslim society, and the life history of an individual can illuminate the set of predispositions which make him leave the standard life of a householder and live as a mendicant. In this sense, the orthodox Sufis and the Qalandars share many things in common vis-à-vis the householders (the pious Muslims), but when these two are separated, the reasons for choosing the Qalandar *tariqa* would appear to be different from those of the Bashara orders.

RELATIONS OF THE QALANDARS WITH OTHER RELIGIOUS ORDERS

Earlier, we saw that barring minor differences, the Qalandars, the Haydaris, and the Jawaliqs are closely related. The *Fawaidu'l-Fu'ad* and other mystical writings do not distinguish between the Qalandars and the Jawaliqs. These groups are depicted in literature as being strongly antagonistic to the settled (and also, highly respected) Khanqah life of the Suhrawardis and the Chishtis. The Chishti records are the only source of information about the Qalandars and other related groups (Rizvi, 1978: 303). The behaviour of the Qalandars was condemned, since it was regarded as shocking and sacrilegious. The Suhrawardis of Multan reserved the right of admission to their Khanqahs. The founder of the Suhrawardi order in Multan, Baha'u'd-Din Zakariya, one of the vice-regents of Shihabu'd-Din Suhrawardi, had decided not to welcome Qalandars and Jawaliqs to his portals. They were immensely disliked for their propensity to use unrespectful language and behave insolently. But, the Qalandars persisted in forcing entry to the Suhrawardi Khanqahs (Mujeeb, 1967: 147).

A famous Chishti saint of Gulbarga (Karnataka), the successor of Sheikh Nasiru'd-Din Chiragh-i-Dehli, Sayyid Mir Gesu Daraz, accused the Qalandars of enticing boys. He forbade his grandchildren and other young members of his family to have any contact with the Qalandars or listen to their conversations (Digby, 1984: 69). Gesu Daraz allocated primacy to the

Shariat over *tariqat* (path), and in accordance with this any sect or individual deviating from the Shariat was the target of his anger. In his posthumously published biography (*Tarikh-i-Habibi*), the Qalandars are listed as the eighth in the list of causes of Gesu Daraz's displeasure. He is believed to have once said: the Qalandars 'bring the children of Musalmans into evil courses and lead people astray' (*Ibid*.: 79).

The Sufis as well as their followers, even a large number of commoners, were suspicious of Qalandars, since they vehemently rejected the Islamic assumptions of what constituted a good life. In addition, the public demeanour of Qalandars provoked opposition. The Qalandars were aggressive; their clothes were bizarre. Their *'sama* gatherings (right from the days of Jamal al-Din of Sava) had the practice of 'gazing at good-looking boys' (*nazar ila 'l-murd*). Although not mentioned explicitly in literature, the homosexual tendencies on the part of Qalandars cannot be totally ruled out, as the next section shows. On record are the examples of the groups of Qalandars who had 'beautiful' boys in their company (Digby, 1984: 69).

The impact of Hindu renouncers (especially, of the Nath tradition) on them had been tremendous. Some Qalandars perforated their ears and started wearing ear-rings, thus emulating the *kanphata jogi* (split-ear renouncer). Another custom some of them shared with Hindu renouncers was of perforating the penis and wearing a ring. The Qalandars followed the Indian *sadhus* in consuming a type of grass called the Indian hemp (*kunnab*) and some other drugs (Rizvi, 1978: 303). Further, it is said that Qutb al-Din Haydar, the founder of the group of the Haydaris, permitted his dervishes the use of hemp (c.f. Rastogi, 1982). Habib (1950, 1974) opines that the Qalandariya movement was strongly under the Buddhist influence; its adherents in the eleventh century might have been the Buddhist ascetics maintaining their Buddhist beliefs and way of life under a Muslim guise. Alternatively, the early Malamatis had been inspired by such Buddhist ascetics. Yazici (1972: 473) says that since the Qalandars looked in envy at the way of life of these Indian ascetics, the second alternative is more likely.

In Chishti sources, there are references to many cases of violence in which the Qalandars were involved. Sheikh Nasiru'd-Din Chiragh-i-Dehli was violently stabbed by a Qalandar. Baba Farid was always ready to receive Qalandars and Jawaliqs in his Khanqah, but he also did not escape their criticism and disrespectful behaviour. A Qalandar sprinkled a preparation of hemp leaves on the prayer-carpet (*sajjada*) of Baba Farid. When the Baba's *murid* tried to stop the Qalandar from doing this, he got enraged and hit the *murid* with his begging bowl. He calmed down only when the Baba intervened. It is also said that when Sheikh Baha'u'd-Din Zakariya did not fulfil the demands of the Qalandars, they gathered round the Khanqah and pelted it with stones. Then, there is a case of a Haydari *faqir* who attacked

Sidi Muwallih. Many other cases of this type have been described in detail by Rizvi (1978) and Digby (1984). The conclusion from all of them is that the Qalandars demanded alms and accommodation in the Khanqah in a highly aggressive and threatening manner. In case their demands were not met with, they resorted to violence and hurled curses. The Sufis pacified them, gave them gifts, saved them from being prosecuted by authority, and sent them away with respect. For instance, Sheikh Nasiru'd-Din gave the Qalandar who stabbed him eleven times, twenty silver coins (*tanka-yi-safed*) 'on the grounds that perhaps when he was stabbing [him] with the knife, his own hand had been injured' (Digby, 1984: 94).

In spite of the impudent behaviour of the Qalandars towards the Khanqah Sufis, the latter tried their best to accommodate them. They believed that in the garb and appearance of a Qalandar, there might be a learned man. The sources point out that a Qalandar who visited the Khanqah of Sheikh Nasir-al Din was described as erudite. Barani wrote that the sons of Sultan Balban and the Suhrawardi Sheikh, Baha'u'd-Din Zakariya, attended the *'sama* session at the Qalandar shrine at Sehvan (Sind), of Lal Shahbaz. In fact, the title Shahbaz (the 'noblest falcon') was given to him (Mir Sayyid Uthman Marwandi, which was his real name) by Baha'u'd-Din Zakariya. The Qalandars were given effective organization as a recognizable group by Jamal-al Din of Sava who was described as *mufti* and 'mobile library' by Nizamuddin Auliya (Rizvi, 1978: 302).

It is said that a disciple of Nizamuddin Auliya, Sayyid Nazmuddin Ghawthudahar Qalandar, is also credited with having introduced the Qalandari path in India. At the suggestion of his *pir*, he became the disciple of Khizr Rumi as well. It is said that he had journeyed to England and China, besides having gone on pilgrimage to Mecca not less than forty-two times. Innumerable are the legends about his austerities. For instance, it is said that he fasted for a period of forty years, breaking his fast daily with the leaves of the palm tree. He remained seated on one stone for thirty years. He had a long life, alleged to have died at the age of two hundred in AD 1432. His successor was Qutubdin Bindal Qalandar Sarandaz-i-Ghawthi, who was also alleged to have a long life, dying in 1518 at the age of 145. The title Sarandaz was indicative of a miraculous phenomenon. His head would get detached from his neck at the time of prayer (Rastogi, 1982: 53).

Bu Ali Qalandar (and some other Qalandars of renown) gave the Qalandari order a status, and their adoption of the belief in the 'unity of being' made it difficult for the orthodox Sufis to reject them. Defending the Qalandari way, Sheikh Fakhruddin of Jaunpur commented: 'A Qalandar could appear to be neglecting prayers in one bodily form and be offering them elsewhere in another embodiment. They [the Qalandars] prefer one way, the *sufi*s another' (c.f. Mujeeb, 1967: 304).

Many Sufis and poets described themselves as Qalandars. Baba Tahir Uryan, aPersian Sufi poet, referred to himself as a 'wandering dervish' (*dervish-i-Qalandar*). In more recent times, one of the greatest Indian Muslim poets, who wrote in Persian and is highly honoured in Afghanistan and Central Asia, was Mirza 'Abdul Qadir 'Bedil', who adopted the 'guise of a Qalandar and depended on God alone for his sustenance' (Mujeeb, 1967: 331). Quite a few writers were Qalandar; for instance, Ahmad Chiramposh, 'Ali Anwar Qalandar, Shah Taqi 'Ali Qalandar Kakorawi, Turab 'Ali Muhammad Kazim Qalandar (Rizvi, 1978: 414, 423; Liebeskind, 1998).

The policy adopted towards the Qalandars by the Chishti Sufis was one of reconciliation and accommodation. Why was it so when the Qalandars displayed an aggressive behaviour? The Qalandars were Muslim and in their style of living adhered sincerely to the value of *fuqr*, and in this they equalled the Khanqah Sufis. They displayed *karamat* with which the Sufis were also accredited. The stories of the miracles performed by the Qalandars were well known and they were considered by people as possessing extraordinary qualities, by the grace of Allah, for which one may use the word charisma. The Qalandars were charismatic, and the stories of their charisma were strongly supported by the strict austerities they performed. Besides, the Qalandars were frequent visitors at he court of the Lodis and the doors of a large number of their nobles' houses were open to them.

The Qalandars were antithetical to the Khanqah. Rizvi (1978: 303) writes: 'From the Punjab, the displeased qalandars moved to Delhi creating scenes wherever they saw a Khanqah.' Khanqah symbolized the routinization of charisma, whereas the Qalandar was the bearer of charisma, 'pure charisma', which is individualistic. If Khanqah was the embodiment of order, the Qalandar was its opposite. The relation between the Khanqah and the Qalandar may be expressed in following terms:

Disorder: Order :: Charisma : Routine :: Qalandar : Khanqah

But pure charisma cannot survive for long. The long-drawn process of reconciliation and accommodation gives birth to mediating (hybrid) categories between the opposites, so were created the Qalandariya-Chishtiya order or the Qalandariya-Suhrawardi order. Some place Bu Ali Qalandar in the category of Qalandariya-Chishtiya. In *Akhbar-al-Akhyar*, Qalandriya-Chishtiya is treated as one of the fourteen subsidiary branches of the Chishti *silsila*. By thirteenth century, many Qalandars began to adopt a settled life of the Khanqah (Rizvi, 1978: 304). The routinization of the charisma had begun.

THE ISSUE OF HOMOSEXUALITY AND DRINKING LIQUOR

'Gazing at good looking boys' seems to be a recurring feature in the anecdotes relating to Qalandars, though they were warned against 'sodomy'.

Shamsaldin condemned Owhad al-Din Kermani for his practice of *shahed-bazi*, in this case his attention to beautiful boys, in the Hellenistic tradition of the ephebe. Rumi held a very unfavourable opinion of this (Lewis, 2000: 320-32). He believed that Owhad's relationship with the boys in his circle was not chaste. In the state of *sama'* ecstasy, Sufis would often tear open their cloaks or shirts. Poets refer to this repeatedly, but it was more than just a metaphor or hyperbole, as Sufi manuals like the *Kashf al-Majhub* and *Talbis-e-Eblis* confirm it. It was in the contexts of *sama'* that some would rub their bare chest against the chest of young boys.

Rumi says that the Sufis tore the garment (*jabbe*, a close-necked one) out of pure motives, but others who followed them had perverted the purpose. For Rumi, this act symbolized the rending of the body so that the soul could escape and ascend towards purity. It does not mean that one should remove conventions, ignore piety and the law, and commit sodomy. He wrote (cited in Lewis, 2000: 321):

If you want spirit, son, then tear your cloak
and head for purity, quickly wing your way.
A Sufi is one who quests for purity
not for patches, woollen garb, and buggery!
Vile folks have reduced Sufihood these days
To nothing but patched cloaks and sodomy.

Though condemned by Islamic law, sodomy doubtless did take place among certain Sufi orders. The chapter on Bu Ali in this work cites many examples of 'love for young boys'. The occasional legal cases demonstrate that it was a real phenomenon. The example is given of Sheikh Naser al-Din in Konya, who cultivated a circle of sodomizers around him because of his unnatural inclination. As a result of his disgrace, people came to refer to it as the 'disease of Sheikhs'. Another story related by Rumi himself (*Ibid.*: 322) is about two travelling brothers, one bearded and the other without facial hair. The latter became the 'object of attention by other men'. Rumi expressed the 'pain' of the boy in the following verses (*Ibid.*: 323):

A better place for me is the Sufi lodge
but even there I've not a moment's peace.
A crowd of porridge guzzlers look me over
eyes full of ejaculants, hands on their balls.
Even those vowed celibate among them
steal furtive glances and massage their cocks!

The boy concludes that when the Sufi convents behave like this, there is no hope for him among the worldly folk. Rumi did employ the symbol of homoerotic, or androgynous love, in his poems addressed to Shams Tabrez as the 'divine beloved', but this merely adopts an already three hundred years' convention of poetry of praise in Persian literature.

Drinking of wine and other liquors is forbidden in Islam, but not so in the context of some Sufi orders. Historians tell us that wine-taverns outside of major towns made not only liqours, but also music, dancing girls and prostitutes available. Some Sufis, particularly Malamati, did indeed drink wine. Even those who did not, however, used wine as a symbol of divine or mystical intoxication. It represented the *mysterium tremendum*, the sense of God's presence in the mind and heart of the devotee. It was opposed to the knowledge of God's law, which the conventional Ulema made the object of their religious studies.

These are, however, poetic tropes. Though they may overlap with personal practice in case of many Sufis, it is extremely difficult, as my study shows, to conceive of Bu Ali drinking wine. His poetry certainly intends this symbolic meaning of wine, which Persian poets like Sana'i and Attar had firmly established. Several passages in his *Mathnavi* refer to the unhealthy and undesired effects of earthly intoxication. His idea was that the symbolic wine, which comes from the covenant with God, does not bring intoxication for a night, likely earthly wine. Lust also acts like wine, while cannabis, a wise man should not touch.

STATUS OF THE QALANDARS

We have seen that the Bashara orders believe that the Qalandars seek to destroy all customs and traditions. The Suhrawardis regarded them as reprehensible. The Qalandars were said to be uncaring of social and moral restrictions, leading a free and unshackled life, having negligible respect for etiquette and public censure, demanding accommodation and alms threateningly, and cursing people if their wishes were not carried out (Titus, 1959: 135).

The Qalandars have also been compared to Nath Yogis, who wandered in towns and established monasteries. By the fifteenth century, some Naths became professional beggars and acrobats (Ghurey, 1953; Gross, 1992). Mixed with the Muslim followers of Shah Madar and Qalandars, a section of Nath renouncers also popularized these ideas (Rizvi, 1978: 354). Namdeva, a Marathi devotional poet, called God the Qalandar in one of his poems (Rizvi, 1978: 356):

> Come God, the Qalandar
> Wearing the dress of an Abdali (the mystical officer of the divine court).

Yazici (1973: 472) has compared the Qalandars with the hippies of the Western world. There exists a strange and superficial parallel in the garb of leather, metal studs, crude jewellery adopted by a number of youth of the United States of America and the United Kingdom, and their rejection of the values of their society. In the 1960s, the hippies seemed committed to a nomadic and ecstatic way of life, sustained by drugs and hallucinogens, and licence in sexual conduct.

But, the similarity between the two cannot be stretched beyond these superficial levels. Both hippies and Qalandars were created in different contexts. One was rooted in a religious society where *fuqr* was valued, where belief in supernatural powers was extremely strong and so were the functions of holy and pious people. The hippie culture had its origin in an affluent society where religion had little or no influence on civic values. As individuals, the hippies might have been in search of happiness to be acquired through the religious methods, but as a group they certainly were not religious; and certainly they were not renouncers. Qalandars, on the other hand, were mendicants, who had a claim to charisma and magical powers. They performed miraculous acts. The hippies were neither the bearers of charisma nor did they work miracles. They were also not passionately assertive, violent or aggressive. The Qalandars, as described in the Chishti literature, were proverbially aggressive.

But, what is the reaction of the Qalandars to the characteristics attributed to them as a group? Not many accounts of encounters with Qalandars are available; however, of sufficient merit is Burke's (1979) with Qalandars in Meerut and Delhi. Let us summarize this first-hand experience, for it tells us about the status of Qalandars.

Burke learnt from his respondents that Qalandars were not only in 'short supply' (p. 70), but were not always living in the stereotyped Qalandari outfit. In other words, a perfectly normal (common) looking person might turn out to become Qalandar for a stipulated period of time, or they might adopt a short wandering life at the behest of their teacher.

Near Meerut was the shrine of Sheikh Pir Shattari, which was often visited by Qalandars. Sometimes they came in disguise, sometimes not. Burke met a Qalandar in Meerut who was a retired officer of the Indian Civil Service. He familiarized Burke with the concept of Qalandar as a stage in the life of a Sufi. Burke also met a Qalandar who had come to see him at his guest house in Meerut. In addition to the usual material objects the Qalandars carry with them, this Qalandar had a small fur rug which he unrolled before sitting down on the floor. He was clad in a blue robe and had shaved off all his facial hair. Burke asked him how he was (*apka mizaji mubarak kaisa hai*)? His answer, which Burke thought was a typical Qalandari reply, was: "*ap ap hain, mizaj mizaj hai, kaisa kaisa hai* ('You are you, health is health, how is how'); it all depends on what you mean by 'How're you'?"

He made it clear to Burke that the Qalandars were not connected with Hindus. Yoga, the technique adopted by a large number of Hindu renouncers, was nothing more than, the Qalandar said, 'self-deception', and it could be learnt easily (p. 73). The Qalandar learnt to perfect themselves; their aim was to become *insan-i-kamil* ('universal man', 'perfect man').

One of the Qalandars Burke met in Delhi was a bank employee. He did not wear any of the Qalandari signs and accoutrements. His uncle, sympathetic to the Qalandari path, knew a group of Qalandars. Both these men took Burke to a meeting of the Qalandars.

About a dozen Qalandars were present. Of them, three had shaven heads and faces. And, the audience consisted of about fifty people including children. We do not know whether women and girls were also present. The meeting began when their leader, a printing magnate of Delhi, addressed all in Persian. He said that the Qalandars performed the ritual of concentration; they shouted the word 'Hu', a short name of Allah; then, they started a series of movements to the beat of a small drum and the thin trill of flute music (p. 76), and someone also sang.

Then, all the hand and body movements stopped. The Qalandars sat 'immobile, impassive, their faces showing no signs of life' (p. 76). This was the moment of 'remembering'; and after this came the moment of listening in which a tape-recorder was played and all listened with rapt attention to discourses interspersed with music. The length of the entire session was dependent upon the wish of the leader of the group – called Badshah ('Monarch').

Burke had the honour of having supper with the Badshah and other Qalandars, after the Qalandari performance was over. The Badshah told Burke that the Qalandars were neither 'being swallowed up or dying out' (p. 78). However, much of the 'picturesqueness' associated with them is passing out, he said, and it is because of the changes in society. Further, the Qalandars were not hostile to other religious traditions. The Badshah, whose actual name is not given by Burke, opined: 'Anyone may benefit from anything' (p. 79). There is no conflict between different ways of achieving 'completeness', and the tradition of Qalandariya is one of them. Referring to the Western culture, the Badshah said: 'You preach equality', and pointing to his path, he submitted: 'We, here, practice it' (p. 80). Burke was so overwhelmed by his philosophy and world-view that he talked to him on various other subjects. He also learnt from the Badshah a series of callisthenic exercises which were a part of the Qalandar's tradition of health lore.

It is clear from this account that contemporary Qalandars are qualitatively different from their counterparts of the fourteenth and fifteenth centuries. Today, they do not display the Qalandari morphology. They may renounce the world, but do not lead the life of a spiritual nomad. They are far from being overtly aggressive and demanding. They let only a select group of people – their confidants – know of their spiritual allegiance. They may be part of a small group, or may work as individuals. However, their aim is the primordial one – to acquire the state of a 'completed being' (*insan-i-kamil*). This was also the aim of their spiritual ancestors, the Qalandars of the past.

I personally did not look around for the Qalandars. But, some of my respondents told me of the meetings they have had with the Qalandars. One of them told me of two Qalandars in Ghaziabad he knew personally, but they preferred to remain 'concealed' (*parde main*). One of them, Basharat Ali, was a peon in a school. He was unwashed, and always chewed betel leaves (*pan*), the juice of which had stained his teeth and entered the crevices of his lips also. He had matted hair, and often used coarse language.

Another respondent, belonging to Qadiri *silsila*, was in touch with a Qalandar, who died three decades ago. The Qalandar was not part of a group. He practised alone, and followed some of the Qalandari practices, such as shaving facial and body hair, however he did not wander. His grave is at Nizamuddin, close to where Nizamuddin Auliya's shrine is located. Our respondent visits the Qalandar's shrine as and when he happens to be in that area. Once, while praying at the Qalandar's shrine, he experienced strong vibrations, a phenomenon for which the term *riqat-tari hona* is used. Another respondent narrated to me his experiences with two independent Qalandars. None of them kept a shaven pate and face. One of them retired from a government school where he worked as a peon. The other man, who always wore white, was also working in a semi-government department. They both followed the Qalandari path without being 'morphological Qalandars'. And, they did not let others know of the path they tread. Perhaps, it was because of the stereotypes associated with Qalandars that most of these people wanted to keep their faith concealed.

The most famous Qalandariya shrines in India and Pakistan are of Lal Shahbaz (in Sind, Pakistan) and Bu Ali (in Panipat and also, Karnal, India). Delhi has Matka Pir, Abu Bakr Tusi, a Qalandari Sufi who was Haydari as well. This shrine is also very popular, although not much has been written about this saint and his shrine. Just opposite Nizamuddin, in close proximity of Oberoi Intercontinental Hotel, is the *dargah* of a female Sufi, Fatima Bi. It has recently been repaired and white-washed. But before this, at the entrance of the shrine, the name of the female saint was followed by the appellation 'Qalandar', but after it has been white-washed, the latter has been eliminated. Some of my respondents were doubtful of her Qalandari status.

NOTES AND REFERENCES

1. Ibrahim was unjustly accused by his father, Azar, an idol-maker, of impiety. The wicked emperor, Nimrod, ordered to throw him in a fiery furnace, which miraculously became a bed of roses. This story is contained in the Quran.
2. Incidentally, *dhamal* is the name of a musical note in which the *dhul* drum induces a special kind of ecstasy

CHAPTER 4

The Shrine of Hazrat Sheikh Abu Bakr Tusi Haydari Qalandari, The Matkey Shah of Purana Qila, Mathura Road, Delhi

Coming from Red Fort towards south Delhi, one crosses Appu Ghar, Pragati Maidan (Exhibition Ground, since 1972). As you cross the last gate to Pragati Maidan on Mathura Road, you see a petrol pump, in close proximity a few shops, tea stalls, a garage, inside a compound. Here, one is struck with a strange sight: clay vessels (sing. *matka;* plu. *matkey*) of various sizes, old and new, decorated and plain, painted and embellished, placed upside down, in a row, on the boundary wall of a place of worship, a shrine, obviously Muslim, because of the presence of a mosque in the compound. The shrine is on a mound (*tila*), twenty-eight feet above the level of the ground. If one looks up at the trees, even on the dry branches, hedges and bushes, you can see *matkey* hanging. So carefully are they placed on the sturdy branches that neither strong winds nor rain or hailstorms can dislodge them. Sometimes the pots are suspended from the farthest branches, indicating the effort taken by those who manage this shrine. The reason is to 'consecrate' as many branches of the trees as possible, so that they can be seen from a great distance. If you happen to visit this shrine on a Thursday, when it is frequented by a large number of people, you can see its 'servitors' (*khadim*) directing young boys to climb trees and place the 'offered' (*nazar, niyaz*) *matkey* at the end of branches.

As you enter the shrine through the arched doorway, on your right is a vendor selling cigarettes and betel leaves (*pan*). Facing you are two shops with signboards written in Devanagri and Persian scripts – Abdul Hamid Phoolwale and Qadimi Dukan ('Old Shop'). The items sold here – *elaichidana* ('sugar-coated cardamom') and roasted *chana* (horse/black gram) – constitute what will become 'transvalued food' (*tabarruk*; the Hindi word *prasad* is also used) after being offered at the shrine. Flowers, rose petals and garlands, sheets (often green) bordered with golden lace, of different fabrics, *itr* (tiny phials of local perfume), incense sticks (*agarbatti*), and earthen vessels (clay water pots), all constitute the ritual ingredients. These shops also sell incredibly low-priced religious books on various topics, cassettes of *qawwalis* and other devotional songs, and posters of religious import. *Behishti Zevar* of Maulana Thanvi (of the nineteenth century) is a commonly sold book. Till July 2008, there was no popular book (or booklet) on the saint of this shrine, Sheikh Abu Bakr Matkey Shah, as is the case with the shrines of Nizamuddin Auliya, Muin al-din Chishti, or Bu Ali Shah Qalandar of Panipat. A highly academic booklet on Abu Bakr, with references and footnotes, was written by the then President of the Abu Bakr Dargah Committee, Syed Akhlaq Hussain Dehalvi, and was published in 1960. It was not sold at the shops located in the shrine and was available only at Jama Masjid book stores. The books sold here are those about other Sufis, particularly Nizamuddin Auliya whose shrine is hardly two kilometres from Matkey Shah. What is unique about the stalls at this *dargah* is that they sell *matkey*. None of the shops at any other tomb stocks this item.

Once you have stepped inside the sacred territory of this shrine, on the right is a mosque called Masjid Nur-al-Islam. Just outside the mosque sits a vendor selling radish in winters and cucumbers in summers. Before you is a long flight of stairs. Every seventh step is a broader one. On a Thursday, you will find beggars, mostly male and children, squatting at almost every step. On your way up, they will not beg for alms, but when you return, after paying obeisance, their entreaties and pleas deafen one. But, they do not follow you around as in the *dargah* of Nizamuddin Auliya.

After you have climbed thirty steps, on a raised platform to the left sits a woman (daughter-in-law of Bhajni, the woman who earlier used to sit here), tending the footwear that you remove before entering the shrine. Set against the wall is a wooden rack of fifty slots for keeping the footwear. It is used only on Thursdays when the shrine receives a larger number of visitors. On other days, the shoes are left on the floor, and, like in Hindu and Jain temples, when you want them back you are expected to tip the caretaker; you may also give him a little *prasad*, although he will not ask you for any money. The woman hailing from Gazipur in Bihar is addressed as Amma ('mother', as was her mother-in-law) by all. Her family has been serving the shrine for the last thirty-three years. An old man at the shrine since 1992 assists the family in its work. On the right side on the same landing are two (sometimes three) large earthen water pitchers kept against the wall for the weary and thirsty. You may also wash your hands with the water stored in them. There are no glasses or bowls except an aluminum ladle placed near them.

After another eight steps, you can see a set of three rooms and a passage leading to the backyard and the bathrooms. You also see a water tap in the courtyard. A couple of goats and some birds could be seen earlier, but not these days as they are housed elsewhere, and the shed in which they were kept has now been converted into a living room. Till many years, the shrine did not have a water cooler, but in 1999, a regular visitor to the shrine, a Hindu, donated one. It is installed in a corner of the landing so that the visitors and the residents may use it. Some cots (*khat*) are placed in the open courtyard (*sahn*). A portion of the *sahn* is covered with asbestos sheets, a donation that has come from another Hindu devotee of Matkey Shah. Earlier, an old sofa with frayed upholstery used to be kept here, but now its place has been taken by a bench and a couple of chairs. Opposite the bench and chairs, is a rectangular wooden cot (called *takht*), behind which stands a wooden almirah, in which bottles (which are used for giving charmed water to the clients seeking supernatural cure), books, and papers are kept. Next to it is a chair. A large desert air cooler cools the room behind the *sahn*.

The *takht* has double drawers (*peti, sandukchi*) built into the headrest (*sirhana*). In the *peti* are kept long sheets of paper, pens, and books. The *takht* is covered with a mattress and a bed sheet. On this is placed another small rectangular seat with a velvet cover. This is placed near the *peti*. A bolster (*gav takia*) kept on the *takht* is used as a backrest. The *takht*, especially the small cushion, is called the *gaddi* (seat, euphemistically called, 'throne'), and on it sits the *sajjadanashin* (lit., 'of the holder of the prayer-carpet', *locum tenens*), the person who looks after the *dargah* complex. He is also called *gaddinashin* ('one who sits on the seat'), but this term is also applied to all his brothers. In his absence, no person, without the ties of patrilineal descent, can sit on the *gaddi*. His eldest son is well versed with the lore of working blessings; thus, in his father's absence, he occupies the seat. Children are however absolved from these rules and prohibitions. The wall has two photographs of the present *sajjadanashin*'s father, of which one was taken as he was leaving for *hajj*. Also hangs a glass-framed enlarged photocopy of the *sajjadanashin*'s *khilafatnama* ('certificate of succession'). The entire complex houses the families of the *sajjadanashin*, his mother, brothers, their families, his own family, and also the *khuddam* (*khidmat karne waley*, the 'servitors', the 'workers') of the shrine. The family that looks after the shoes lives in the same complex.

The covered *sahn* is the 'office' of the *sajjadanashin*. He receives his clients and guests there, working blessings for all those who approach him. He advises the visitors on various matters, from health to success in business, marriage to possession by a harmful spirit. In his absence, his younger brothers and sons (who are being trained in it) perform this task.

On your left is another flight of stairs of sixteen steps, facing the water cooler, and you reach another courtyard (*sahn*). Earlier, it used to be an open *sahn*, but in 1998, a group of regular visitors to the shrine, under the direction of another devotee, a Hindu, covered it with asbestos sheets for protection against the harsh sun, strong winds, and rain. The covered *sahn* has fans and tube-lights. The parapet of this *sahn* also has earthen-pitchers placed upside down. On the left is a row of earthen-pitchers; they have all been offered by the visitors to the shrine, waiting to be placed elsewhere. As the consecrated objects are theoretically not to be recycled, these earthen pitchers remain either on the wall or on the floor of the *sahn*, or they are suspended from the branches of trees.

On the floor level, on your right, is the grave (*mazar*) of the Khalifa of Sheikh Abu Bakr Tusi, Hazrat Sheikh Rahimuddin Iraqi, whose name some suggest was Hazrat Jalaluddin Khilji. According to the *sajjadanashin*, earlier it used to be lower than this resting place; in fact, it was just six feet above the 'office' of the *sajjadanashin*. Now an alcove (*ala*) reminds the people of its earlier location. It has since been moved up a few feet. This decision was taken by elders (around fifty-five years ago), for they thought that because of its location, Sheikh Iraqi's *mazar* was not being visited by many. Now that it is relocated, visitors to Sheikh Abu Bakr's tomb visit it first.

Now, in front of you is the tomb of Hazrat Abu Bakr. An inscription on the main entrance to the grave (*rauza*) in Devanagri and Urdu describes the shrine as a *dargah*. On both sides of the door to the *rauza* are fitted two desert air coolers. Take three steps and you are inside the grave, the sanctuary (sanctum sanctorum). The grave is covered with many sheets (*chadar*), in resplendent colours, generally green or yellow, either embroidered or with golden lace (*gota*), borders and edging. Below these are other satin, chenille, or blue sheets. On the top sheets are strewn rose petals (*gulab*) and marigold (*genda*). The devotees wish to place the flowers they offer on the grave and are careful about not dropping them elsewhere. At the end of a busy day, the duty of the *khuddam* is to collect the flowers and brush them into a pile in a corner.

The shrine of Abu Bakr Tusi is a one-storied tomb, a flat roofed building (*baradari*). It stands within an enclosed courtyard (*baramda*). Its elevation consists of four vertical walls, the sole relief being formed by three metal arched and latticed doorways on the three sides. The western wall has no portal. The floor is tiled, but usually covered with a green carpet. This gives a rich plastic appearance as well as a scheme of variegated colours. The roof is painted in bright colours and so are the arches around the cenotaph, red and green being favourite colours. This shrine lacks the usual lattice or trelliswork in its doorways and walls. It impresses anyone with its plainness; lack of embellishment and ornamentation, it is almost austere, except for the coloured glass chandeliers atop the grave. From the roof of this cloister hang a few lamps and three fans. The western wall (or the *qibla*) has a large plaque in the centre and shelves on each side. The plaque has a Quranic injunction and an inscription in Urdu stating that 'this is the *rauza* of Sheikh Abu Bakr Tusi Haydari Qalandari who died on 20 Ramzan 655 AH.' A dislodged sign-board (in fact, upside down) at the main entrance also gives the same information.

At the main entrance, i.e., at the feet of the saint, facing the left, sits the *khadim*, the 'ritual officiant', who takes 'ritual ingredients' from the visitors, offers them to the saint, and returns the 'blessed food and flowers' as *tabarruk*. One may make the offerings of flowers and sheet (*chadar*), and money, oneself, without the intervention of the *khadim*. On Thursdays, two *khuddam* sit there, one on the left and the other on the right, to cope with the crowd. No one is permitted to enter the pillared, arched cloister, the inner chamber (*baradari*); however, males may kiss or touch the grave of the revered saint, or the *chadar* and lift its corners, and touch it to their eyes and forehead to receive the saint's *baraka* (grace). But, the feet of the supplicant are generally outside the inner chamber since there is a paucity of space. On the right is placed a *golak* (*danpeti*, metal donation box); people drop monetary offerings and sometimes, pieces of jewellery, in it.

The inner chamber has a separate roof which has a couple of rows of beautifully painted earthen pitchers. At the main gate of the shrine are earthen pitchers painted in green colour; the rest are brick coloured. The arches are engraved with flowers even on the capitals and base. If one has to delineate an insignia of this shrine, it will be an earthen pitcher. Now, we understand why Hazrat Abu Bakr is popularly known as Matka Pir, Baba Matka Pir, Matkey Shah, and Matkey Waley Baba.

Once they have reached the inner sanctum of the shrine, the devotees bow low and kiss the grave or the covering sheet (*gilaf*). Prayers are offered and thanks given for favours received, and petitions made for favours required. The prayer is a sort of spiritual bargaining. Offerings to the shrine will be made if the devotee's prayers are answered. The devotees scatter rose petals over the tomb, and the privileged are given petals which have been lying there to keep as *tabarruk* or to eat. There is a tradition according to which the Prophet declared the red rose to be the manifestation of the glory of Allah. *Tabarruk* is something particularly laden with *baraka*, usually through close physical association with the saint or his shrine. Pilgrims

The *heraks* (rags) tied to the grill of the gate of the sanctum sanctorum of Abu Bakr Tusi or Matkey Shah.

The clay pots being bought by the women visitors to the shrine to be offered to the saint at the fulfilment of the vow.

The *matkas* or clay pots hang from every branch of the tree in the *dargah* premises, giving an exotic look to the shrine.

Getting ready to hang another *matka* on the branch of the tree.

The pots on the roof proclaiming the *mazar* (grave) of the revered saint Abu Bakr Tusi.

Another view of the inner vestibule where the saint lies buried.

A signboard proclaiming the method of offering the clay pot to the saint after fulfilment of the vow.

The *qawwal* and his assistant in the courtyard of Abu Bakr's shrine. A cloth is spread for collection of tips.

also spend time circumambulating the mausoleum and sitting in its vicinity in passive and receptive silence to absorb the spiritual presence of the saint and to meditate on his life and teachings.

At the entrance to the *rauza* is written in Devanagri: 'Please do not burn incense sticks (*agarbatti*) inside.' But, it is an important ritual ingredient; so on the right of the mausoleum is a squarish alcove, darkened with thick deposits of carbon. An earthen lamp (*diya*) is always kept lit here. It is for igniting incense sticks, which are placed/stuck in any of the two neckless pitchers kept there that are filled with sand (and, of course, the ash of *agarbattis*). These *agarbatti*-holding *matkey* are kept on two stands. Near them is a display board, painted green, on which is written in Urdu: 'After the fulfilment of the wish (*mannat*), the items to be offered to the saint are: one *matka*, one *chadar*, one and quarter kilogram of milk, one and quarter kilogram of sugar, one and a quarter kilogram of jaggery (*gur*), and one and quarter kilogram of *chana*.' Facing the mausoleum, outside its boundary wall, sit a group of *qawwals*. On Thursdays, since the *qawwali* session lasts the entire day and most of the evening, finishing around nine in the night, two groups of *qawwal* are called to perform.

Across the road from the *dargah* is the famous Bagh-i-Bedil, which has the *mazar* of Abu Bakr's contemporary, Sheikh Nuru'd-Din Malik Yar Parran. But, his cult is not very popular, and also, there is no ritual of paying respects to him before or after visiting the shrine of Abu Bakr Tusi. Bagh-i-Bedil is named after Mirza Abdul Qadir Bedil, the famous Persian poet, who had adopted the way of a wandering mystic, a Qalandar.

Earlier, I referred to a booklet in Urdu on Matkey Shah, written by the President of the Dargah Committee, which is a good source of information in so far as the reference to this saint in medieval literature is concerned, but often the author conjectures about the activities that might have been carried out during the Shaikh's lifetime. He also enters into several theological issues that concern only the believers.

From a survey of literature on Muslim shrines in India and Pakistan, we learn that those generally selected for study are either famous for treating cases of psychic ailments (such as Mira Datar Dargah, Gujarat), or leprosy (the Sayyid Salar Mas'ud Ghazi Dargah at Bahraich, Uttar Pradesh), or because of their popularity with people (like that of Mu'in-al Din Chishti at Ajmer or Nizamuddin Auliya at Delhi), or their material assets (such as the *dargah* of Shah Jamal Sahib of Aligarh). Then, some authors (e.g., Desai, 1989; Jackson, 1989; Jeffery, 1981; Pfleiderer, 1981; Schwerin, 1981) provide short descriptive accounts of all the prominent *dargahs* or *rauzas* in a town, without concentrating on any one of them for a detailed description. Highly generalized articles on the place of *dargah* in Islam or the relations of the disciples (*murids*) with their *pirs* are in plenty.

In none of the *dargah*s and *rauzas*, I have so far visited, are women allowed inside the inner chamber. This has been the observation of other researchers as well (Pfleiderer 1981: 198). One of the theories why women are not permitted in Sufi shrines is that the saints prefer to remain 'hidden' (in *purdah*) and in 'seclusion' (*takhliya*), and they think that women are a great distraction in their concentration. Siddique (1979: 23) writes that since the fourteenth century the *'urs* celebrations provided anti-social elements an opportunity for merry-making and promiscuous enjoyment. Because of repeated occurrences of these incidents, Firoz Shah and Sikandar Lodi, the two Sultans of Delhi, disallowed women's admission to the Sufi shrines.

Later, women were permitted entry into the *dargah*, but not to the tomb. Today, with their heads covered, they have to remain outside the sanctum sanctorum of the mausoleum. They may tie threads, rags ('petition-strings', *herak*) to the latticed arches, trellis, or grills in the wall. By contrast, women are permitted to enter the shrine of Abu Bakr; however, they are not allowed entry into the limited space around the grave. Barring the *khuddam* and *mujawirs* (administrators), who are all male, this rule also applies to the general male visitors, but they can kiss and touch the grave. This norm, however, is not strictly enforced because the number of visitors to the shrine on other days (besides Thursdays and Sundays) is substantially less. During daytime, no *khadim* is around, and people unaware of the prohibition may do as they please.

A visitor to Matkey Shah is bound to be impressed by the simplicity of its structure, and the fact that it does not have those institutions which are generally associated with *dargahs*. Moreover, it is perhaps the only Muslim shrine (in Delhi) on a mound, and one has to climb fifty-four steps to reach it. Most shrines consist of several other tombs, where those related to the saint by consanguinity or affinity are also buried. Also buried in the same complex are the disciples of the saint, or in case the saint was a warrior (for instance, Salar Mas'ud Ghazi), then other soldiers also rest there. In the case of Sharaf ud-Din Maneri's *dargah* in Bihar, those who wanted to be buried close to him have staked their claim in the grounds just outside the *dargah* (Pemberton, 1997).

The *dargahs* also have mosques, rest houses, dispensaries, kitchens, *langar khanas*, etc. The *dargah* of Mu'in al-Din Chishti has four mosques, where Muslims come together to perform prayer (*namaz*) five times a day. In the *dargah* complex of Nizamuddin Auliya, where besides the mosque, the offices of the *sajjadanashin* and those who specialize in supernatural treatment (*ruhani ilaj*), meat shops, cigarette and *pan* kiosks, *dhabas* (wayside eating places), tea stalls, book sellers, shops selling *chadar* and flowers, and a number of other commercial enterprises have come up. Mahmood (1989: 31-2) writes of the *dargah* of Salar Mas'ud: besides the Sangi Qil'a (stone fort), which is the mausoleum, and the Qil'a-i Kalan (big fort), which surrounds the shrine, the outer complex of the *dargah* has administrative offices, a hospital, a garden, a school, a library, a police post, a guest house and an auditorium. The Salar Mas'ud *dargah* also gives financial support to a college in Bahraich (*Ibid*.: 41). The *dargah* of Matka Pir has none of the conventional and expected buildings or facilities surrounding it or in its complex.

The actual burial ground of the saint, the *mazar*, is the most sacred place, but there exists a network of smaller places where the saint's *baraka* (grace, power) has manifested itself over a period of time. These places are holy in their own right, such as the chamber (*hujra*) in which the saint is believed to have meditated, the place (called *chillah gah*) where he must have performed particularly difficult austerities, the place where assemblies (*mehfil*) were held, the Khanqah, even the places where the *sajjadanashin* lives, etc. These units of the sacred geography are also venerated.

These structures are absent at Matka Pir. The mosque is not administratively a part of the *rauza* complex. Apart from the *mazar* of Abu Bakr's Khalifa, no other grave exists here. Other institutions (such as hospital, school, dispensary, etc.) are also absent. The two shops selling ritual ingredients at the entrance to the shrine are also not within its boundary as demarcated by the Delhi Development Authority (D.D.A.). Compared to the shrines of Nizamuddin Auliya and Mu'in al-Din Chishti, which 'unfortunately have a shabby appearance and unclean surroundings' (Mahmood, 1989: 32), the Matka Pir is noticeably neat and clean and is situated by the side of the main road linking north to south Delhi.

No noisy scenes (*shor-sharaba*) are witnessed here; no loud customer-calls by florists, no *pankhewala* who fans the pilgrims, and no beggars trailing you. Pfliederer (1981: 204) writes of Mira Datar dargah: 'Competing voices catch the visitor's ear as he approaches the main door.' A common experience when you enter the *dargah* of Nizamuddin Auliya is that the *pirzade* (plu., the 'sons of the *pir*'), dressed in black caps and white long shirts (*kurta*) and *salwar*, call out to you to get your name registered in their books. No such registers are kept at Matka Pir. Firstly, there are no *pirzade*; and the *mujawars* do not approach the visitors to provide assistance in rituals. In fact, all those who manage the shrine are employed elsewhere, or they have their independent businesses, unlike the *pirzade* of Nizamuddin *dargah*, whose full-time occupation is to look after the interests of the shrine (and, of course, themselves). They have the 'turn' system (*rota* or *pari* system), quite like those of the Mahabrahmins at funeral grounds (Parry, 1994; Srivastava and Srivastava, 1997). No such system has evolved at Matka Pir. It is because of the fewer number of people (just three brothers and their sons) who manage this shrine. Once the number of descendants increases, family disputes regarding their share in income from the shrine are bound to surface (Mann, 1989).

Matka Pir is perhaps the only Qalandari shrine in Delhi. Earlier, I referred to the grave of Fatima Bi, proximate to Oberoi Intercontinental Hotel, where till quite recently, the word Qalandar was written below her name but was effaced after the door of this shrine was repainted. The enquiries I made did not yield anything substantial. The *mujawars* of Matka Pir unambiguously said that the only Qalandari shrine in Delhi is of Abu Bakr Tusi; the other of this order is at Panipat (of Sharfuddin Bu Ali Shah). Abu Bakr is the only Haydari-Qalandari saint in India. In that sense, it is of especial interest.

However, people visiting the shrine are unaware and also unwilling to learn of distinctions of denominations and their hierarchy: Why the term Qalandar after his name? Who are the Qalandars? Where are they placed in the hierarchy of Sufis? The answer to my question if the Qalandars visit the shrine was that nowadays the Qalandars do not live the way they used to live in the past; thus, it would be impossible to identify a Qalandar unless he wishes to reveal himself. Qalandars have not disappeared; but they are also not visible, at least in morphological terms. Qalandari is now more an 'interior' state; in that sense, Qalandars may be visiting the shrine, but then, who knows?

Not only the visitors but also the administrators term it a *dargah* ('Dargah Sharif', as they call it honorifically), but in my opinion it is just a *mazar*, and as we saw, the plaque in the mausoleum calls it *rauza*. The institutions and appurtenances associated with a *dargah* are absent here. Let us clarify the terms. The term used for the grave is *qabr*, but one which is venerated (*ziyarat*) is called *mazar*. It is always covered with a velvet cloth (*gilaf*). Thus, a *dargah* includes the *mazar*. There are examples of *mazars* that do not have *dargahs*, or it may come to be established as the popularity of the saint and his *baraka* grows. A *mazar* may be defined as a raised, rectangular, cement platform underneath which rest the mortal remains of the venerated saint. It may or may not have a 'ceiling' – which means, with or without a 'room' (or 'structure', *maqbara*). When a *mazar* is on its way to becoming a *dargah*, the first step is the construction of a *maqbara*, preferably of marble. The distinction between *mazar* and *dargah* is also important socially – women may be permitted entry into the *dargah* but not the *mazar*. When the saint is buried at the same place where he had lived, it is called *rauza*, a word which literally means 'garden' (de Tassy, 1997: 40). Since Abu Bakr's Khanqah and his *mazar* are at the same place, the term *rauza* is used for it.

MATERIAL FOR THE LIFE-HISTORY ACCOUNT OF ABU BAKR TUSI

We begin the story (or legend, life-history account) of a Sufi master by looking into the literature that was produced when he was alive. This literature consists of the writings of the Sufi, memoirs of the *murids*, the letters (*maktubat*) written by the Sufi, the descriptions of the travellers who visited the Sufi and his Khanqah, and perhaps, in more recent times, the historiographic accounts. But, it seems that the Sufis have nurtured some kind of an innate bias against writing. In the Sufi tradition, writing is regarded as a 'vehicle' inferior to oral expression. The spoken word or silence is deemed closer to the Truth. For them, 'writing is a rational rather than an intuitive endeavour' (Lawrence, 1982: 31); in fact, the latter is revelatory. Because of this philosophical tenet, many Sufis deliberately refrained from writing. Some wrote letters to their disciples or to other Sheikhs with the assumption they would be destroyed after they had served their purpose. The Sufis also thought that the reader of the written words should be trained and mature, and should be able to understand the meaning in the context, for there was always a danger that an ignorant or bad-tempered person might misinterpret the Sufi's words and defame him for blasphemy.

Notwithstanding this orientation of the Sufis to writing, there was always an impulse to record the sayings of the saint, his biographical details and travels, the austerities and penances he performed, the first-hand account of his discourses, his participation in assemblies (for instance, *mehfil-i-'sama*), and his opinion of other Sufis, if he ever expressed this. But, unfortunately, under the rubric of such writings have flourished several apocryphal and fictional accounts (Rizvi, 1978: 5). The researcher should, first of all, be able to distinguish the authentic writings from the spurious.

An important work in this context is that of Lawrence (1982: 31-3). He identifies four kinds of literary evidence that have proved notable in the institutional phase of Sufism. The first is the genealogical tree (*shijra*). A Sufi does not become famous because of the genealogical connections, but once he is renowned, the family trees are used to affirm and explain that he was destined to reach the spiritual height he has attained. The pedigree (or, what we may call, 'biological genealogy') functioned to confirm the consanguineous relation of the Sufi to the earliest generations of Muslims, and perhaps even to Prophet Muhammad Himself or His family members. Take, for example, the case of Salar Mas'ud Ghazi, who is shown as related to 'Abd al-Muttalib, the Prophet's grandfather (Mahmood, 1989: 26-7). The other genealogy, which has precedence over the consanguineous links, is of spiritual relationship; we may call it the 'spiritual genealogy'. It describes the relations of initiation (*ba'it*): Who initiated whom? How spiritual relations were transmitted? So, Qutb al-Din Bakhtiyar Kaki is the spiritual descendant of Mu'in al-Din of Ajmer. The Chishti masters used to send their disciples to different parts of India so that their ideas and practices could diffuse among varieties of people. Each one had his distinct 'work area' ('spiritual territory', *wilaya*).

The second literary evidence consists of anecdotes. Lawrence (1982: 31) writes: 'Sufis delighted in anecdotes on every topic – whether moral, having to do with sensual restraint and subtle codes of conduct, or miraculous, pertaining to food, procreation, conversion, and the like.' These conversations of the Sufis were committed to writing by their disciples (for instance, Amir Hasan kept an account of the assemblies of Nizamuddin Auliya which he had attended, and this book of discourses is called *Fawa'idu'l-Fu'ad*), and this literary genre is known as *malfuzat*. The letters (*maktubat*) and didactic essays (*isharat*) of the Sufis had the same content. Their purpose was to illuminate a point of spiritual, social, legal, and even behavioural import (see Digby, 1991).

Lawrence (1982: 33) regards poetry and proclivity to music (*sama'*) as the third and the fourth aspects. These two are of particular significance to the Chishti *silsila*, but not for those orders that were negatively predisposed to them. Poetry eulogized the Sheikh; for instance, the verses of Amir Khusrau that he wrote in a state of love for Nizamuddin Auliya (see Faruqi 1991). Have a look at the following verse of Khusrau:

Khusro, Nizam pe bali bali jaiye;
Mohe suhagan kihni mose naina milaye ke.
[Khusrau sings praises of Nizam (Nizamuddin Auliya);
Whose one look at me made me his bride.]

Poetry also described the pathos experienced by the 'journeyman' on the path to Truth (Ibn-Haqq). Rumi's *Mathnavi*, Sa'di's *Bustan* and *Gulistan*, and Hafiz's *Diwan* are fine examples of this tradition. These Persian poets were classified as Sufis. Musical concerts also expressed certain aspects of the Sufi ideas and their creators. The *karamat* of the saint was often included in poetry and musical gatherings.

SALIENT ASPECTS OF THE STORY OF ABU BAKR TUSI

No biological or spiritual genealogical tree of Abu Bakr has been found. Nor do we have his *malfuzat*, *maktubat*, or *isharat*. We do not know if he ever lectured or wrote letters. No eulogy of this saint is known to us. We know that he was fond of *sama'* gatherings, but no information is available on his role in them. We find reference to him in 'Abdu'l-Ha'i's *Nuzhatu'l-Khawatir*, Hamid bin-Fazlu'llah's (also known as Dervish Jamali Kamboo Delhavi) *Siyaru'l-'Arifin*, Shaikh 'Abdu'l-Haqq's *Akhbaru'l-Akhyar*, Mir (also Amir) Khurd's *Siyaru'l-Auliya*, and Muhammad Shah's *Ma'ariju'l-Wilayat*. On the basis of these sources, we reconstruct certain aspects of the life of Baba Matka Pir Hazrat Sheikh Abu Bakr Tusi Haydari Qalandari Rahmat-ullah, as he is referred to in honorific terms. Before we do that, a point needs to be reiterated here. The visitors to Matka Pir are least interested in the genealogy of the saint. Even the knowledge of the administrators of the shrine is extremely limited. The biography of Abu Bakr is unimportant to them. They believe that their wishes would be fulfilled once they present themselves before the saint and ask him for his intercession. Devotion and faith supersede the academic quest.

The problem of chronology exists with respect to Abu Bakr Tusi. We noted earlier that the inscription on the plaque (installed after 1971) inside the mausoleum reads that he left his mortal remains (*wisal paya*) in 655 AH (AD 1235). But *Nuzhatu'l-Khawatir* (p. 123; c.f. Hussain 1960: 7) records that between 664 AH (AD 1244) and 684 AH (AD 1264), he came to Delhi. Hussain's booklet (1960: 54) notes that Abu Bakr died on 22 Rajab 700 AH Confusion prevails with respect to these dates, but it seems certain that he was in Delhi in the mid-thirteenth century. The usual information one receives from the *sajjadanashin* is that he came to India from Iran about 762 years ago, and started living on a hill on which his *dargah* is located today.

Abu Bakr was a resident of Tus, a city of Khorasan (Oxus); that is why the suffix to his name is Tusi, and he was also popularly known as Tusi Baba. When he migrated to India, at that time, Ghiasuddin Balban was the Sultan of Delhi. Abu Bakr established his Khanqah at the banks of river Yamuna, which was a favourite resort for mystic scholars. According to *Akhbaru'l-Akhyar* (pp. 73-4; Rizvi, 1978: 307), he demolished a temple which was there, and built his Khanqah. He organized *sama'* gatherings (*Ibid.*). Rizvi (1978: 308) writes that Abu Bakr's relations with his contemporaries were not very cordial. One of the first conflicts he had was with another Sufi, Nuru'd-Din Malik Yar Parran, attached to the *silsila* of Shaikh Abu Ishaq Kaziruni. This *silsila* was known as *silsila-i-ishaqia*, and its founder used to wear purple clothes and carried purple banners with him (*Siyar ul-Arifin*, p. 68). Nuru'd-Din was a resident of Lar in Fars and also came to Delhi during the reign of Balban.

By that time, Abu Bakr was fully established and held in great esteem. He was the most notable figure of the order of Haydari Qalandari in Delhi (*Siyar ul-Arifin*, p. 67; *Akhbaru'l-Akhyar*, p. 73). Nuru'd-Din planned to build his Khanqah in proximity of that of Abu Bakr. But, the latter considered this action of Nuru'd-Din as an encroachment on his spiritual territory (*wilayat*). Abu Bakr asked Nuru'd-Din to bring an order (*farman*) saying that he could establish himself on the banks of Yamuna, from the Sultan and also permission from his *pir*. *Siyaru'l-Arifin* (p. 68) says that at that time the Sultan was out of Delhi (maybe in Thatta or Bengal), but Nuru'd-Din brought the *farman* from both of them (the Sultan and his *pir*) so quickly that Abu Bakr was really impressed with his 'flight'. The title he bestowed upon Nuru'd-Din was Parran, meaning 'flier' (Hussain, 1960: 7-8; Rizvi, 1978: 308). We noted earlier that his *mazar* is in Bagh-i-Bedil.

Abu Bakr's year of birth is not known. Hussain (1960: 54) estimates that he lived to be seventy or eighty. We have no knowledge of his *pir*, and how he entered into the Haydariya-Qalandariya *tariqa*. Not much is known about his learning and accomplishments (*ilm* and *fazl*). His contemporaries (*ham-asar*) were Sheikh Nizamuddin Auliya, Sheikh Nizamuddin Panipati, Sheikh Ali Zanbali, Maulana Husamuddin Inderpati, Sheikh Parran, Sheikh ul-Quzzatwa'l Khutabo, and other Chishti saints (*Akhbaru'l-Akhyar*, p. 73; Hussain, 1960: 14). They used to visit his Khanqah and were aware of his external (*zahiri*) and internal (*batini*) spiritual achievements. He was well known for his attempts to transcend his baser self (*nafs*) and was educated in the precepts of Islam (*tabligh-i-din*). 'Abdu'l-Ha'i (p. 123) wrote that Abu Bakr was committed to prayer and closely followed the religious instructions; so, he was both *abid* and *zahid*. He was a 'high level' (*buland*) dervish.

We also learn about these Sufis from their relationship with the other Sufis. One such interaction Abu Bakr had was with a disciple of a famous Chishtiya Sufi. All these 'stories' have implication to the assessment of the social status of Qalandars.

Baba Farid's first Khalifa, Sheikh Jamalu'd-Din Khatib of Hansvi, used to visit Abu Bakr and respected him for his spiritual accomplishment. Both of them had cordial relations. Sheikh Jamalu'd-Din was himself a profound and reputed scholar, yet he had great regard for Sheikh Abu Bakr. Whenever Sheikh Jamalu'd-Din visited Delhi to pay his respect to the Chishti saint, Bakhtiyar Kaki, he used to stay with Sheikh Abu Bakr at his Khanqah. *Mehfil-i-sama'* was organized whenever he visited, and sometimes Hazrat Nizamuddin Auliya also came to the Khanqah to attend the *majlis* (assembly).

Sheikh Jamalu'd-Din composed a verse in Persian in praise of Abu Bakr (see *Diwani Jamalu'd-Din Hansvi*, Vol. II: 42-3). He also gave the title Shah Baz-i-Safed ('White Falcon') to Sheikh Abu Bakr for his 'rare mystical achievements' (*Siyar ul-Arifin*, p. 67; Rizvi, 1978: 307). Hussain (1960: 22) thinks that perhaps it was because of his complexion that this title was given to him. He writes (*Ibid.*):

> Khorasan is a cold country. The people of Khorasan are fair-complexioned. Abu Bakr Tusi must have been extremely fair with handsome features and face (*khush indam*).

After they had reached the Khanqah, the *qawwali*s began. Although the *qawwal*s were singing with great involvement and attention (*tawajjuh*), they were unable to raise the emotional and ecstatic level (*qaif*) of the audience. As no one seemed to enjoy (*lutf*) the song, Hazrat Nizamuddin requested the singers to stop singing for a while. Addressing the audience, he said that there were three prerequisites of a *qawwali*-session. The first is *akhwan* (the 'listeners'); the listeners must share the same body of thoughts (*hamkhyal*), paying uninterrupted attention (*mutawajjah*) to the *qawwal*s. The second condition is *makan* (the 'place') – the site of *qawwali* should not be close to the place of residence or the mosque so that the listeners do not have any distraction. And, finally, the *zaman* – (the 'time') – it should not be dinner time, or prayer time, or bed time.

Hazrat Nizamuddin said that all the three conditions stated above existed at the Khanqah of Sheikh Abu Bakr, yet the *mehfil* was unable to produce ecstasy. He averred that there must be some reason behind this of which he was unaware. In such a situation, the Sheikh continued, we must stop the *qawwali*-session and listen to the stories of our revered saints (*Auliya-i-qadim*), and he started narrating stories from the lives of some of them. Sheikh Nizamuddin Auliya's narration generated the 'waves of ecstasy'. At that time, Sheikh Ali Zanbali looked at Sheikh Nizamuddin Panipati, gesturing him to move to the place where the *qawwal*s sat and start singing. The backdrop for *sama'* had been created. Sheikh Nizamuddin Panipati was all prepared to sing, but since he was alone, Sheikh Nizamuddin Auliya asked Khwaja Muhammad Imam (who had come with him) to join him. Both of them began with a *ghazal*, and when they reached a verse (*sher*) which went like this 'in case you meet anyone at night, please keep him away from me until dawn,' Sheikh Nizamuddin Auliya entered into a state of ecstasy (*wajd*) and started dancing. The other Sheikhs were also entranced and they all performed the *wajd raqs* (the 'dance of ecstasy'). Khwaja Jahan Ahmad writes that Haydari dervish Sheikh Ali Zanbali also danced.

In this entire episode, the focus is on Nizamuddin Auliya. Abu Bakr is in the background, except for the fact that all this happened at his Khanqah. Whether or not he performed the *wajd rasq* is not pointed out. But, this incident makes it clear that he was popular with the Chishti Sufis and the latter (whether Nizamuddin Auliya or the disciples of Baba Farid) often visited him. In fact, Jawaliqs, Qalandars, and Haydaris visited Sheikh Nizamuddin's Khanqah. Despite the arrogance and insolence with which they sometimes behaved, the Chishti Sheikhs treated them courteously and fulfilled their demands (Nizami, 1991: 77). Nizamuddin Auliya is believed to have said (*Fawa'id-u'l-Fu'ad*, p. 48):

But more than this, he says, 'falcon' symbolizes the 'spiri Compare this with Lal Shahbaz Qalandar, who was called 'r Hussain (1960: 22) writes:

> Once we meditate on Allah, our materialistic lust is transcended fc as a result of which the human body becomes incredibly light ar 'fly' anywhere.

So, if 'white' stands for 'complexion' and 'purity', 'falcon' is of 'lightness' and 'supernatural flight'; thus, the title 'White Fal an insight into the 'character' of Abu Bakr, as constructed b Jamalu'd-Din.

'Abdu'l Haqq (in *Akhbaru'l-Akhyar*) refers to another inci shows the closeness of Sheikh Jamalu'd-Din with Sheikh Abu Bakr. Husamuddin was a disciple of Sheikh Jamalu'd-Din. Once wher to meet Sheikh Abu Bakr, the latter told him that he was planning *haj*. When he returned to Hansi and met Sheikh Jamalu'd-Din, th first question was regarding the welfare of the 'White Falcon' (1960: 8).

Mehfil-i-Sama'

The literature we cited earlier often has entries on Nizamuddin visit to the Khanqah of Abu Bakr, frequently attending audition but it does not say anything about the nature of interaction these twc had. The context of such meetings used to be the *sama'*.

Hussain (1960: 29) begins the description of *sama'* at Abu Khanqah with the following words: 'Sheikh Abu Bakr, though a be the Shariat, was also a lover of *sama'*. Implicitly, he is hinting at the between the Shariat and the practice of *sama'*; however, he soon tells the *mehfil-i-sama'* at his Khanqah was of a high religious order. It expectations of the Chishti saints who vehemently opposed those au which did not rise above simple secular enjoyments. We noted ear these musical concerts were not for all; they were for trained and spi developed people. Mir Khurd (p. 201) gives an account of one of the *i-sama'* at Abu Bakr's Khanqah. Khwaja Jahan Ahmad Ayaz in *Nizam* (1945: 214-5), a book on Nizamuddin Auliya, also mentions this inc

Once Sheikh Abu Bakr invited Hazrat Nizamuddin for a *mehfil* other Sufis and dervishes had also come to attend the musical concert. Nizamuddin Auliya asked Khwaja Sayyed Muhammad (Imam) a brother, and Khwaja Jahan Ahmad to accompany him. After *magi namaz* (prayer answered after sunset) and *iftar* (breaking of fast), the ca (*kafila*) consisting of about fifty-sixty people left for the Khanqah. S Nizamuddin went in a palanquin (*palki*).

> This sort of behaviour [the behaviour of the Beshara sects] should also be tolerated. Many people come, place their hands at the feet and bring presents. Such people should also be there and should be allowed to come and speak whatever they like.

Earlier, we stated that the policy of the Chishti saints towards the Qalandars was one of accommodation and reconciliation, and visits to the Khanqah of Abu Bakr substantiate this point. At the same time, it should be remembered that the latter saint was not a wandering dervish, he had a Khanqah. Thus, in many aspects of his lifestyle he bore similarity to the Chishtis, for example, in organizing and participating in the *mehfil-i-sama'*.

CONTROVERSY

One very unfortunate incident in which Abu Bakr was involved was the execution of Sidi Muwallih. One of Abu Bakr's disciples mortally wounded another Sufi, the founder of the Muwallih path, Sidi Muwallih, a saint who came to India from the Upper Country, during the reign of Jalalu'd-Din Khalji. The story as narrated in Ziya'u'd-Din Barani's *Tarikh-i Firuz Shahi* (c.f. Lal, 1967: 23-7; Rizvi, 1978: 308-9; Digby, 1984: 67-8, 91, 106) is as follows.

Sidi Muwallih, on his way to Delhi from Persia, met Baba Farid (at Ajodhan) some years before AD 1265 (*Tarikh-i Firuz Shahi*, p. 208). Baba found him exceptionally ambitious and advised him to keep himself away from the company of the political elites (Sultans, Shahzade, Amirs, Maliks), for 'such associations were calamitous for dervishes' (Rizvi, 1978: 308). *Tarikh-i Firuz Shahi* (p. 209) records Farid's advice to Sidi:

> Saiyyidi! You are going to Delhi and wish to keep an open door and earn fame and honour. You know what is good for you. But keep in mind this advice of mine. Do not mix with *amir*s and *malik*s. Consider their visits to your house as calamitous. A saint who opens the doors of association with *malik*s and *amir*s is doomed.

But, Sidi did not heed Baba's advice, and during the reign of Balban, he bought his way into the elite circle and established contacts with prominent people, but to no avail. During the reign of Mu'izzu'd-Din Kaiqubad, he was more successful and gathered around him an entourage of followers. His popularity further rose during the reign of Sultan Jalalu'd-Din Khalji. The Sultan's eldest son, the Khan-i-Khanan, became Sidi's ardent devotee, whom Sidi treated as his 'son'. Besides him, many other outstanding nobles and religious functionaries (*qazi*) used to visit his Khanqah.

But, mystery surrounded the source of Sidi's wealth. He accepted neither land grants nor any other largesse. Although he himself led a simple life, his guests were looked after very well. They were fed lavishly, and bestowed with gifts. He maintained a *langar*, where delicacies were served, which were beyond the means of *amir*s and Khans (*Tarikh-i Firuz Shahi*, pp. 208-10). The story goes that whenever he wanted to pay somebody, he would ask him to reach a specific spot where they would find freshly minted money (*tanka*).

In his personal habits, Sidi had his own eccentric ways. He did not go to the mosque to offer Friday prayers. Though he offered his obligatory prayers regularly, he did not join the congregation. But he was not wanting in strenuous spiritual exercises. He did much penance and did not spend anything on his personal comfort. Clad in a blanket, he lived a simple and unostentatious life. He did not have a personal servant or a slave girl to look after him. *Tarikh-i Firuz Shahi* (p. 209) says that he was 'free from all desires of the flesh.' It is said that nearly ten thousand people had associated themselves with him and had joined the circle of his admirers. He was an enigma to all, and the news spread that he was a 'magician', a 'sorcerer', and an 'alchemist' (having the knowledge of *kimya-o-simya*), for he was believed to create wealth.

When Sidi's popularity grew, some intriguers and mischief-mongers gathered round him and sought to exploit the situation to their advantage. A man notorious for his mischief, known as Qazi Jalaluddin, began to visit Sidi's Khanqah regularly. His presence there converted the Khanqah into a hot bed of sedition and conspiracy. Many scions of displaced families of Balban's court, who nursed several personal grievances against the Sultan, also congregated there, charging the atmosphere with chicanery. A former *kotwal* named Brinjtan and a wrestler of Delhi, Hatya Paik, also had an opportunity to fan the flames against the Khilji Sultan.

Soon a conspiracy was hatched to kill the Sultan and install Sidi on the throne. Brinjtan and Hatya Paik were to kill the Sultan, when the latter came to the mosque for prayer. A daughter of Sultan Nasiruddin was to be married to Sidi in order to elevate his status. Qazi Jalaluddin was to be honoured with the title of Qazi Khan and given the *iqta* of Multan. Others were also promised with posts and offices.

This plot to assassinate Sultan Khalji was exposed by a conspirator. Sidi Muwallih was alleged to have hatched it. He was arrested along with his accomplices. Barring Sidi, the others were transferred from the capital as they denied conspiracy in the plot.

However, a debate ensued regarding an appropriate punishment for the arch-conspirator, Sidi. The Sultan ordered him to pass through the ordeal of fire, as was practised in south India in ancient times, in order to prove his innocence. Trial by fire was ruled out on the ground that the Shariat did not sanction it. The Ulema also declared that the 'function of fire is to burn – it will burn the truthful as well as the liar'.

To pass an appropriate sentence on him, the Sultan had called a number of nobles and religious personnel for consultation. Sidi was brought before the throne in fetters and shackles. Elephants were also brought out of the enclosure, since one of the punishments used to be that the offender was trampled to death under this animal's feet. Some nobles argued that since there was only one witness to the conspiracy, charges against Sidi remained unproved and legally no action could be taken on a solitary testimony. However, the Sultan ordered the execution of *kotwal* Brinjtan and Hatya Paik.

The Sultan's assembly included Abu Bakr Tusi and his disciples. The presence of Sidi "threw Qazi Jalaluddin into a rage and he addressed Sheikh Abu Bakr Tusi thus: 'O Dervishes! Get me justice from Sidi Maulah'" (Lal, 1967: 26). At that point of time, Bahri Haydari, a reckless follower of Abu Bakr, rushed towards Sidi and attacked him with his razor and *juwal-doz*. Sidi, wounded, fell forward. Just then, the other son of Jalaluddin, named Arkali Khan, signalled to a mahout to trample Sidi to death.

The orthodox deplored this execution. Unfortunately, a number of natural calamities (dust storms, failure of the monsoon, drought and famine, and devastating floods the following year) followed Sidi's death, and the Sultan was unequivocally blamed for this. Due to dearth of food, people drowned themselves in river Jumna (Yamuna) (*Tarikh-i Firuz Shahi*, p. 212). To the Chishtis, the moral was clear: the Sufi should distance himself from politics and power struggle. And, to Barani, the lesson was that 'no king could afford to kill a dervish' (Rizvi, 1978: 309).

'Isami's *Futuhu's-Salatin* (1948) argued that the Sufi impostors (*khirqa-poshan-i kham*) falsely accused Sidi. Yahya Sirhindi says that Malik Ulghu concocted the charge of conspiracy against Sidi. The actual conspirator was the Khan-i-Khanan, a contender with Arkali Khan for the throne. Sidi's finances came from the merchants and the Sultan's son, the Khan-i-Khanan. The widespread belief that Sidi was obtaining wealth from magical practices was a myth. In this power struggle, Arkali Khan enlisted the support of many Sufis, Sheikh Abu Bakr being one of them. Rizvi (1978: 309) concludes from this that Sheikh Abu Bakr was also 'ambitious', but we do not know what his ambitions were.

This incident clearly shows that although the Haydari-Qalandari had settled down in Khanqahs, they continued to keep with themselves the objects (the razor, the sewing-needle), the symbolic characteristics of their path. In the case of Abu Bakr, the number of his followers decreased due to his role in the execution of Sidi Muwallih. This also showed that he lacked the qualities of a leader, since one of his disciples, without seeking his permission, just ran berserk to attack Sidi. All this antagonized public opinion against him and Haydari-Qalandars. This incident also throws light on the enmity and ill feeling between the Haydari-Qalandars and the Muwallihs (the followers of Sidi), as also ill feeling against the *silsila-i-ishaqia* of which Yar Parran was a member.

Cultural Practice

Most of the Sufi shrines are popular for the institution of free distribution of food. Take the example of the shrine of Mu'in al-Din Chishti at Ajmer. The *dargah* administration distributes food to the destitute and others twice a day from the *langar khana*. In 1974-5, the annual expenditure on *langar* was Rs. 54,410 (Currie, 1989: 122, 183). In fact, Chishti foundations have always believed in distributing food to the needy (Nizami, 1991). In 1567, Akbar granted to the Ajmer *dargah* the revenue of eighteen villages, and a levy of one per cent on the sale of salt at Sambhar, to pay for the *langar* (Currie, 1989: 174). The practice, then established, is continuing till date. When we enter the *dargah* of Nizamuddin Auliya (or Mu'in-al Din's *dargah*), the *pirzade* persuade us to enter our names and addresses in the register. Their aim is to inform us by post about various celebrations in the *dargah* and seek our contribution towards meeting the expenses of the shrine.

Sheikh Abu Bakr's Khanqah, quite like its counterpart in Chishtiya path, also had a *langar*. Food was distributed to all. Hussain (1960: 25) conjectures that there were no beggars at that time. All those who were poor (*fuqra*) thronged the Khanqah, devoted themselves to the glory of Allah, and were dependent on the free kitchen. Food of extremely good quality was cooked there, but Sheikh Tusi liked simple food (*sada giza*). He was extremely fond of roasted horse-gram (*bhune chane*). A part of the lore of Matka Pir is that he used to take *bhune chane*, rub them between his palms, blow off the husk, and eat them. His followers and devotees used to bring *bhune chane* for him, and this explains why even today, it is an important part of a devotee's offerings at the shrine. We are not aware of any other Sufi whose offering includes roasted horse-gram. Today, the Matka Pir does not have the institution of *langar*, but on all the three days during his *'urs* celebration, a free kitchen is set up.

It is said that Sheikh Abu Bakr was very fond of sherbet. His visitors and followers used to bring it for him in earthen pitchers (*matkey*), water-pots of clay (*lutia*), oval long necked water containers (*kunde*), and the rich people brought it in silver kettles. It is not known what used to be the fate of these pots at that time: were they disposed off, or did people take them back, or did they lie in the corners of his Khanqah, or were the metal ones kept and the rest thrown away? Perhaps, they were not thrown away, kept in one corner of the Khanqah.

The tradition of keeping the pots at the shrine and suspending them from the branches is dated to September 1947 (Hussain, 1960: 29). During those months of looting, plundering, and massacre, thousands of Muslims took shelter near his shrine. The earthen pots lying there were used by them to store water and also for cooking. In order to keep them safe, the people used to cut the branches of trees, make them stand on earth, and then place the clay pots atop them. At that time, Hussain (*Ibid.*) writes, the entire land used to appear like a 'city of water pots'. We also learnt that in those months of the Partition, a man suspended one such pot on a branch of a tree, and many others followed. Since then, it has become a tradition to suspend earthen-pitchers from the branches of trees. This also gives an exotic touch to the shrine; you find earthen pitchers wherever you go. Hussain (*Ibid.*) also writes that the standard item brought as an offering to the shrine was an earthen pitcher, but sometimes kettles made of brass, copper, and silver were also offered. The latter were kept with the administrators of the shrine and displayed during the *'urs* celebrations of Sheikh Abu Bakr.

It is because the Sheikh liked sherbet, its ingredients (milk, sugar, jaggery) are included in the list of offerings one should bring after the fulfilment of a vow (*mannat*). An earthen pot is another important item. During my fieldwork at the shrine, I did not come across any devotee offering a silver pot (or of any other metal). Notwithstanding their economic status, all those whose vows were fulfilled brought earthen pitchers, which they invariably bought from the shops at the foot of the shrine. However, the quality of the sheet they brought for the *mazar* greatly varied. The administrators of the shrine advise the visitors to bring the sherbet ingredients as oblations, rather than the prepared sherbet, but if a devotee brought the latter, it was also accepted. Often, on Thursdays, people brought sherbet and distributed it as blessed food (*tabarruk*) to others.

Miracles (*Karamat*)

The hagiography of a saint is incomplete without the stories of miracles that he is believed to have performed. The ability to perform miracles, what is known as *karamat*, is an essential characteristic of a saint.

The stories of miracles may be divided into two categories: first, those which were performed when the saint was alive, and the other includes those which took place after his demise. In this section, we are concerned with the first type. Later, we shall have a look at the experiences of the devotees from which they conclude that the saint is present among them.

Let us begin with a *karamat* of Tusi Baba, which is known to each of his devotees. Once, during the reign of Ghiasuddin Balban, a 'disrespectful' (*bad aqide*) man, with an intention to test the power of Sheikh Abu Bakr, brought iron balls (*lohe ke chane*), which resembled the horse-gram (Bengal gram). He brought them in a platter (*tashtari*) as an offering. He was cynical of the Sheikh's power, since chewing the 'iron' horse-gram was nigh impossible, the falsity of the 'power' of the saint would be exposed (*qalandari kirkiri ho jayegi*). Hazrat Abu Bakr picked a fistful of these grams, rubbed them between his palms, blew off the husk – as he would have done with the 'real' horse-grams (*kale chaney*) – and ate them. The man, who had intended to belittle him, was thoroughly ashamed of his action. He apologized profusely and became a follower of the Sheikh. Since then, a well-known saying about Sheikh Abu Bakr is:

Abu Bakr Tusi, khaye chane, udaye bhusi.
[Abu Bakr Tusi, [he] eats horse-grams, blows off husk.]

Another version of this is:

Abu Bakr Tusi, mare phunk, ude bhusi.
[Abu Bakr Tusi, when he blows on it, the husk flies off.]

The above-mentioned story is not only repeated by the administrators of the shrine, but has also been recorded by Hussain (1960: 28). There is another one of the same type, but it has not been recorded anywhere. A man sent horse droppings (*ghore ki leed*) in an earthen pitcher to the Sheikh, again with the intention of testing him. When the cloth covering the pot was removed before Hazrat Abu Bakr, everyone saw that it had *gur* (jaggery). The man who had played this prank apologized and became his ardent follower.

In both these stories the poetic justice was that the miscreants learnt their lesson and ended up joining the entourage of Sheikh Abu Bakr. These stories abundantly establish that the Sheikh is *karamati* (producer of miracles), he can give an evidence of his power, and whenever and wherever he likes, even after his death.

There is another story. One day, a thirsty traveller approached Abu Bakr. The saint offered him water from an earthen pitcher. The man then told the Sheikh that he was suffering from an ailment for which no one could find a cure. The saint agreed to pray for him. A few days later he was cured.

Besides these, we did not come across any other that reiterated the Sheikh's spiritual powers. Nor is there any dealing with the austerities that he undertook during his lifetime. But, it has been seen that as the saints' popularity grows, more such stories are added to their respective hagiographies. For the believers, they are real; they must have happened. Today, many people claim to have felt the Sheikh's presence in the mausoleum; and such experiences, when shared with the crowd, reinforce the structure of the belief.

Respect for the Shariat

Earlier, we noted the distinction between the Bashara and the Beshara sects, and an example of the latter is the Qalandari path. The Qalandars (and also, the other related groups) were criticized by the orthodox for not adhering to the Shariat. They were also accused of defiling the sacred objects of the Bashara Sufis (remember the case of the Qalandar who threw a preparation of Indian hemp on the prayer-carpet of Baba Farid). But, once people (including the orthodox) start venerating a sedentary Qalandar saint, he is presented in a different light.

This is exactly what has happened with Sheikh Abu Bakr. Hussain (1960), perhaps an orthodox scholar, tries his best to conclude that although Sheikh Abu Bakr was a Haydari-Qalandari, he was not only respected, but also, closely followed the Shariat. Hussain quotes many scholars to support his point. For instance, 'Abdu'l-Ha'i in *Nazhatu'l Khwatir* (p. 123) writes: 'Abu Bakr was a Qalandari but abided by the Shariat.' Amir Khurd in *Siyaru'l-Aulia* (p. 181) says:

> Sheikh Abu Bakr was a loving dervish. He was attached to the Haydariya and Qalandariya order. He was a wearer of chains (*zanjir posh*) and according to the Haydariya tradition he used to keep the objects associated with it on his person. But, in his appearance and demeanour (*ahal-i-hazir*), he was not dirty (*aluda*), nor poor (*ma'siyat*) like the Qalandars. Sheikh Abu Bakr observed all the prayers and strictly followed the Shariat. He had a thorough knowledge of Islam. The Auliyas used to respect him.

Dervish Jamali writes in *Siyaru'l-'Arifin* (p. 67) that though Abu Bakr was a Qalandar, he used to observe all the five prayers (*salat*) in a congregation (*jamat*).

From these observations, we learn that the Sheikh wore chains and kept with him the objects which were associated with his Qalandariya path and he also wanted his disciples to follow the rules of the order. That his disciples kept razors and sewing-needles can be inferred from the story of the attack on Sidi Muwallih. Perhaps he was celibate. He was not a peregrinating dervish. He was not anti-Khanqah. The mere fact that he had established his Khanqah near the banks of Jamuna shows that he was like the Chishtis in many respects. If we follow Rizvi's conclusion from the Sidi episode that Sheikh Abu Bakr was quite 'ambitious', it is likely that the Sheikh in order to win over the orthodox and the political elite, which was guided by the orthodox, followed the Shariat ardently, thus distancing himself from the 'pure' Qalandari path, but at the same time he retained allegiance to the order in which he was initiated. Therefore, Sheikh Abu Bakr Tusi was a *Bashara* Haydari-*Qalandari* saint. He mediated the structural opposition between the Qalandar and the Shariat.

HISTORY OF THE SHRINE OF SHEIKH ABU BAKR

Historical information on the mausoleum of Abu Bakr is scarce. The contemporary administrator does not know much. Whatever written material (for instance, the genealogy of the family of the *mujawars*) he might have had was destroyed in a fire. However, the *sajjadanashin*, a man in his fifties, spells out whatever little he knows about the happenings at the shrine in the last thirty years. The publications on Delhi and her monuments give reference to the mausoleum of Abu Bakr, but in any case it is not more than a few paragraphs. However, in some of them, a reference to him is grossly missing; for instance, Spear's *Delhi, its Monuments and History* (1943 [1997]) has a chapter on Purana Qila, but it does not refer to Abu Bakr's shrine.

We noted at the outset that till July 2008, there was no information on it in Hindi or Urdu for the visitors. Recently, a small booklet on Sheikh Abu Bakr has been published by the *sajjadanashin* Naseem Sultani. Hussain's booklet of 1960, which is out of publication and can only be found in private collections, is perhaps the only source so far as the history of the shrine before and after 1947 is concerned.

Before Delhi expanded, the area beyond Delhi Gate, till perhaps Lodi Road, had several burial grounds (*qabristan*). Around the shrine of Abu Bakr, there were many *qubur* (graves), some of which are now objects of veneration. In the neighbourhood of this shrine are Purana Qila, the *mazar* of Bhure Shah, the ancient temple of Bhairon-ji, and another temple of Dudhadhari. Opposite the shrine is a beautiful gate built by Shershah Suri. Passing through this, we reach the remains of shops which constituted the Meena Bazar or Moti Bazar of Shershah. Near this is a mosque called Khair-ul Manazil, which was built by Akbar's 'putative sister' (*dharam behn*). Near it was a school (*madarsa*) set up by Akbar's stepmother. Close to it is the *mazar* of Hazrat Bibi Fatima Sam, about whom Rizvi (1978: 402) writes that she considered Baba Farid and his brother, as her own brothers. To quote Rizvi (*Ibid.*):

> Little else is known about her except that she would say that feeding the hungry and giving water to the thirsty was more meritorious than hundreds and thousands of *namazes* and many days spent in fasting.

It is also said that Hazrat Nizamuddin Auliya used to visit her tomb to offer prayer.

On the north of Abu Bakr's *rauza*, was a vast and dense jungle, which was later cleared to provide temporary accommodation to the employees of the postal department. Today, it is the site of Pragati Maidan. A platform at the meeting place of the Khanqah and the road was used to conduct prayers (*namaz*). There used to be an old well (*qadim kuan*) containing brackish water. Near the road was a cement wall which does not exist any longer. We surmise from Hussain's description that the mound where Abu Bakr's mausoleum is located had retained some of its old architectural design at least till 1947.

Outside the Khanqah, a majestic gate had been erected, called *bahishti darwaza* ('gateway to heaven'), which, according to Khan Maulavi Sayyed Ahmad (in *Firahang-i-Asafiya*, 1918; c.f. Hussain, 1960), lay between the *mazar*s of Sheikh Abu Bakr and Sheikh Parran. When the road was being laid, it was pulled down. The *sajjadanashin* of the shrine claims to have seen its remains when the telephone lines were being laid and the road was dug up to facilitate them. A common belief about the *bahishti darwaza* was that if the corpse of a non-Muslim (*ghair Muslim*) was carried through this gate, it did not burn. God-fearing people wished that after death, their bodies should pass through this gate, for this would ensure them against the 'fire of hell' (*atish-i-dozakh*). The *sajjadanashin* claimed to have learnt from his elders that when this gate was being constructed under the supervision of Sheikh Abu Bakr Tusi, Amir Khusrau asked Hazrat Nizamuddin about the need to construct it. The latter said that whosoever passed under that gate would be heaven bound.

Hussain (1960: 50) gives a description of the Abu Bakr shrine in the late 1940s. Earlier, an uneven (*nahamvar*) and circular (*chakradar*) path led to the shrine. The courtyard was also small and the wall around the *mazar* was made of a type of brick called *lakhori*. The construction and repair work was taken up by the Dargah Committee, which was formed during this period. There used to be a one-foot tall boundary wall made of red stone around the shrine, which was gravely damaged during the riots of 1947. This was also re-erected by the Committee. The area of the *mazar* was 4'x 8', and it was made of red stone. Towards the headrest, the plaque (*loh*) of the *mazar* had been installed. On this was inscribed:

Sheikh Abu Bakr Tusi Qalandari qadas
sarah mashrib-i-Qalandariyya dasht.
Sheikh Jamaluddin be-ghayat muwarrat
bud-o-Sultan alam sheikh neztar Khanqah
hazir shude. Majlis wasle 22 Rajab 700
azeen jahan pardo-namud.

[Sheikh Abu Bakr Tusi was affiliated to
the order of the Qalandars. There existed
great affection between Sheikh Jamaluddin
and him. And, Sultans and Sheikhs used to
visit his Khanqah and participated in the
assembly. He left the mortal world on 22
Rajab 700 AH]

On the eastern side of the courtyard existed the *mazar* of Auliya Sulaf which was of lime and clay. In front of the courtyard there was a private room (*hujra*) covered with iron sheets, but it was not an old structure. The shrine was generally unattended.

Taking advantage of the situation, a Hindu renouncer, Aughar Nath Saini, established his 'renouncer's fire' (*dhuni*) there. He declared that the *mazar* of Sheikh Abu Bakr was in fact the grave (*samadhi*) of a Hindu mendicant. The renouncer said that this was revealed to him in his dream. Hussain (1960: 51) remembers that those days he used to cross Mathura Road quite often with his brother, Hakim Sayyed Hussain. They noted that a *sadhu* (renouncer) was in the process of usurping the shrine, so they informed the members of their community of what was going on in the absence of surveillance exercised over Muslim shrines. The community members approached the *sadhu*, tried to convince him, but he was adamant. Eventually, they had to seek the help of the state administration. The *sadhu* was arrested and a case of trespassing and illegal occupation of the shrine was registered against him. Then, with some aid from the state, the *taveez* (inscription) of the *mazar* was cemented and installed, thus eliminating any future occupation of the shrine by Hindu mendicants.

At that time, the *rauza* was in shambles. The highly fluid Committee – which called itself the Sheikh Abu Bakr Tusi Dargah Committee – started the construction work slowly. It appointed a *chowkidar* (watchman) for the *mazar*; this was perhaps the first appointment made by the Dargah Committee before 1947. A big pitcher for storing water was also placed there. One of the duties of the *chowkidar* was to give water to the visitors and keep replenishing the pot. Besides looking after the *rauza*, the *chowkidar* also kept an eye on the vast tract of land (measuring about 40 *bighas* [a quarter of a hectare]) around the mausoleum. But, at that time there was no shelter in the vicinity of the shrine where the *chowkidar* could have escaped from the heat of the sun or inclement weather. Later, the Dargah Committee constructed a temporary structure for his residence.

The next person to settle down here (around 1946) and serve the shrine was Nur Muhammad (son of Ghasita), who hailed from Pali Unnao (in Kanpur) and was affiliated to the Qadiri order. He volunteered to work as a *mujawir*. Because the Dargah Committee urgently needed a man to 'administer' the shrine, no one raised an objection to his appointment, or the order to which he belonged. On the other hand, the members of the Committee extended him all possible help. He was totally dedicated to the shrine and a grand *'urs* celebration was organized under his guardianship. He also decided to get the *rauza* repaired. He arranged for the red stone and other material needed for construction. But before this work could take off, the 1947 riots began; this entire area of Purana Qila became an 'ocean of people'.

The shrine was damaged during the riots of 1947. The tin sheets of the private cell were stolen. Miscreants razed the *mazar* of Auliya Salaf to the ground. The southern portion of the boundary wall was demolished. The pillars of the outer chamber (*baradari*) of the shrine and its fencing (*katghara*) was broken. The *mazar*'s plaque was destroyed and its tablet (*taveez*) was taken away. Not only that, the Sheikh's *mazar* was also disfigured at places.

After the riots, the Dargah Committee once again started the repair work. The first major celebration they conducted was the *'urs*. Maulana Ikhlaq Hussain Dehalvi, the author of the booklet on Sheikh Abu Bakr, advertised the details of the programme of *'urs* celebration in newspapers. His brother, Hakim Sayyed Hussain Dehalvi and another friend of theirs, Muhammad Yunus Langri, worked untiringly to make it a success. Financial and social support also came to them from the state. Both Hindus and Muslims attended the *'urs* celebration. But, on the whole, they were not like the one that took place when Nur Muhammad was the *mujawir* of the shrine.

At that time, a person (whose name is not given) claimed that a faction of the visitors to the shrine of Abu Bakr desired that he serve it as its *mujawar*. Thus, the entire responsibility was entrusted to him, but he was unable to fulfil it. Almost a year passed, during which the shrine was further damaged. None came forward to take up the charge of management. Then, many members of the Dargah Committee, which till then had a fluid structure, thought that it should be formalized and strengthened.

In 1949, the time for celebrating the *'urs* of Sheikh Abu Bakr drew closer, but none volunteered to discharge the duty of organizing it. Hakim Sayyed Hussain published the *'urs* dates in the newspapers. Once again, timely help came from Muhammad Yunus Langri. Cleaning of the shrine was the first task to be done. When the refugees camping at the Purana Qila and neighbouring areas, saw some people cleaning the *rauza*, they volunteered their services. The arrangement for the *'urs* was timely, nevertheless the enthusiasm of the participants was 'sky-high'. Not many shelters were available, so at night, when the weather became inclement with hailstorm and incessant rain, the visitors had no place to go. Hussain (1960: 59) describes the difficulties the people had that night, but the following morning, their enthusiasm was unfazed. They decided collectively to work for the development of the shrine. In informal meetings that followed, certain suggestions came up: for instance, a person should be appointed to take care of the shrine; Dargah Committee should be properly constituted; it should not just be a closed group; it should be the duty of the Committee to look after all the works in the shrine; the *'urs* should be organized under its direction; and it should explore the possibilities of raising funds. On one of the *'urs* days of 1949, the Dargah Committee was formally created. What existed earlier, for which the same term was used, was an informal group of Akhlaq Hussain and his brother, and their friend. The Committee formed in 1949 had the offices of the President and the Secretary; Akhlaq Hussain occupied the former, while the latter office was entrusted to Sheikh Abdul Haq Pracha Dehalvi. The members of the Committee were Hakim Sayyed Hussain, Muhammad Ismael Nuri, and Muhammad Yunus Langri. During the meetings that followed, the Committee was requested to approach the community of Sunni Muslims and the Waqf Board for assistance, in undertaking repair work and new constructions. Because of people's involvement, the *'urs* of 1949 was quite successful. The assistance rendered by the state administration and police was also satisfactory, and around four hundred people attended the three days' *'urs* celebrations. The number of people who attended the earlier *'urs* is not known because no registers were ever kept.

In the late 1940s, Delhi had not expanded beyond the walled city. The place where Sheikh Abu Bakr's shrine is located was uninhabited at that time. Therefore, not many people came forward to serve the shrine as *mujawar*. Muhammad Ismael was appointed as *mujawar* in 1949-50. He served the shrine with devotion and commitment. He was attacked many times by unsocial elements, and on one occasion, he suffered head injury. Although he survived, he did not enjoy good health any more. Yet, he continued to render his services till 1954, when Mansur Khan became the *mujawar*. He was very old, and was fast losing his eyesight; so, he kept his sister's son, Mendhu Shah, as his assistant. Mendhu Shah was a dynamic and hard-working young man. The condition of the shrine greatly improved after that.

However, the income from vows and oblations (*nazr-o-niyaz*) was not much. It was barely sufficient for the *mujawar* and his family. If in a given year, it was good, some of its portion could be set aside for meeting expenses on repair and *'urs* celebrations. Otherwise, for *'urs*, the entire expenditure came from the contributions made by the well wishers (*ahal-i-khair*) of the shrine. Gradually, more people started visiting the *rauza* and the income also increased. From 1958, the Dargah Committee decided to set apart the income of the month when a large number of devotees visited the shrine, for expenditure on the *'urs* celebrations. The maximum number of people came to the shrine from 21 Jamadi to 22 Rajab on their way to Ajmer Sharif to attend the *'urs* of Mu'in al-Din Chishti. This pattern continues till today. Throughout this month, buses loaded with pilgrims are parked at the foot of the shrine. These pilgrims, whether they are from India or neighbouring countries (Pakistan or Bangladesh), also visit certain *dargah*s in Delhi, such as that of Nizamuddin Auliya, and Sheikh Abu Bakr's mausoleum is one of them.

Hussain (1960: 58-9) writes that between 1949 and 1960, the popularity of the shrine increased. But, factionalism also intensified. Some employees also tried to pocket the offerings. One of them issued false receipts and collected money (around Rs. 200). In spite of opposition and problems, the Dargah Committee was able to work successfully. Earlier, as we saw, the path to the shrine was uneven, and at places, dangerous. The Committee constructed a cemented staircase leading to the courtyard. The *mazar* of the Khalifa of Sheikh Abu Bakr, damaged during the Partition riots, and the outer chamber of the mausoleum was also repaired. An iron gate was erected at the mausoleum to ensure its safety.

There was a deep pit between the shrine and the road. Several hundred trucks of debris were unloaded to fill it. As a *maidan*, it became the site of *qawwali*-performance and *langar* at the time of *'urs* celebrations. Hussain (1960: 58) writes that there was another pit which, at the time of writing the booklet, was being filled up. The well of brackish water was also treated with an appropriate technology so that it could become potable. With the active intervention of the Dargah Committee, an Imam was appointed for the mosque which stood at the entrance of the shrine. He was also given accommodation at the shrine complex. The silver pots offered to the Sheikh were also kept safely, and exhibited during the *'urs* celebrations; however, those of brass and copper were sold off, and the money thus generated was spent on other activities of the shrine. Hussain (*Ibid.*) says that 1959 was extremely good from the point of view of income. After expending for the *'urs*, whatever money was left was spent on publishing Hussain's booklet on Sheikh Abu Bakr.

The Dargah Committee consisted of five people (including the President and the Secretary) in 1949 when it was formalized. On 5 December 1959, four more members were added, keeping in view the enlargement of the activities of the shrine. In February 1960, there were nine members of the Dargah Committee.

From the description given above, it could be guessed that the Dargah Committee was bound to become stronger over time. But, the opposite happened. It seems to us that somewhere between 1960 and 1965, it lost its control, with the result that today an extended family looks after the shrine. Today, there is no Dargah Committee to look after the shrine of Abu Bakr.

CHAPTER 5

The Shrine of Hazrat Sharfuddin Bu Ali Shah Qalandar of Panipat (Haryana), One of the Two-and-a-Half Qalandars

Imam Mohammad believes that there have been two-and-a-half Qalandars of the highest spiritual status and divine zenith, namely, Bu Ali Sharfuddin Qalandar of Panipat, Lal Shahbaz Qalandar of Sehwan (Sind), and Rabia Basri. According to Canon Sell (1928 [1985]:51), the Qalandar order was introduced in India by its founder Ali Abu Yusuf Qualandar, known as Bu Ali Shah Qalandar, a thirteenth century saint of Panipat, who was believed to be a native of Spain.

Panipat is a well known historical as well as industrial town of Haryana in India. It is believed to have been founded by Arjuna of the Mahabharata fame. New Delhi is ninety kilometres south of Panipat (one-and-a-half hours by road) and sixty-five kilometres away is the legendary town of Kurukshetra.

Panipat has been known for its culture and civilization. Many illustrious Ulema, *muhaddisin*, *mufassirin* (commentators of Hadith and Quran) and *qurra* (readers of the Quran) have lived here. The teaching of Qirrat in Panipat is known all over the Muslim world. Ustad Hali, the famous nineteenth century Urdu poet, also lived here. It is well established that in 1947, it had 365 mosques, dozen or more *madrasa*s (schools of Islamic learning) imparting training in Qirrat and was a centre of Islamic learning and arts. Not only men but women reciters of the Quran could be found here.

Today, Panipat is a highly industrialized town, known for its blankets and carpets. After 1947, handloom and handicrafts are its main produce. Most of the workers involved in producing tapestry and upholstery material, curtains, bed covers and bedsheets are Muslim. Panipat is also a place of pilgrimage for the Muslim and many Hindus; the *ziyarat* (worship) of the *mazar* of Hazrat Sharfuddin Bu Ali Shah Qalandar is the most important in their itinerary. Kabul Masjid (built by Babur), Sultan Ibrahim Lodhi's tomb and the Kala Aam Bagh where the third battle of Panipat was fought between Ahmed Shah Abdali and the Marathas, and the Devi temple are the other tourist sites.

Khwaja Suhail Ahmed Ansari (the writer of a booklet on Bu Ali Shah Qalandar) has written a poem about the glory of the city of Panipat. It is reprinted in an undated, locally produced booklet, written by Bashir Ansari Alkhamoshi, titled *Auliya-e-karam Panipat*; an excerpt from this is rendered below:

khench lai Sayyid-e-Mahmud ko teri zamin
aankh ki thandak Iraqi ko mili aakar yahin
Hazrat Sharfuddin Qalandar sahib-e-jazb-o-suluk
fakhr se qadmon mein jis ke sar jhukate the maluk
teri agosh-e-muhabbat mein wo lal-e-be baha
parvarish pakar bana tha zeb-e-taj-e auliya
shauk ke alam mein jab hota tha woh nagma sara
dil pe khel jata tha saut-e-sarmadi ka majra
uska andaz-e-tagazzul Qudsiyon ko bha gaya
shair ke parde mein asrar-e-junoon samjha gaya

[The land of Panipat has drawn to it many a Saiyyed and Mahmud,
Iraqi (supposed to be Bu Ali's father) found contentment here,
Bu Ali Qalandar, the master of passion and attraction,
He to whom many bowed their heads in respect,
In your lap of love, the distressed child found peace,
It's in Panipat that Bu Ali was nurtured,
And became the uncrowned king of saints,
In the state of longing when he broke out into a song,
The hearts of even the brave clamoured for help,
His style of rendering *ghazal*s pleased the Qudusi,
In the garb of his verses, he taught them the secrets of passion.]

A Karnal based NGO, HIFA (Haryana Institute of Fine Arts) has chosen a novel way of promoting communal amity and harmony in celebrating what they call a national level festival in memory of Bu Ali Shah Qalandar at the historical town of Panipat. Referring to the life and times of this revered saint, HIFA has adopted in their charter four key aspects in recalling *guru-shishya parampara* (the tradition of the relationship between a teacher and his pupils), documenting architectural impressions as in the *dargah* of Qalandar Sahib, projecting the subtle nuances of Sufi music, and promoting unity and brotherhood after the ways and means adopted by Amir Khusrau in adopting Brij Bhasha, a facet which was very close to the heart of Bu Ali Shah.

DESCRIPTION OF BU ALI SHAH'S SHRINE

A seventeenth century hagiography depicts Bu Ali stating that 'the kettledrum (*naqqara*) of Qalandari has sounded in the whole world and sky' (*Sharaf*, p. 35).

Sharfuddin Bu Ali Shah Qalandar, sometimes also referred to as Abu Ali, the patron saint of Panipat and the first of the Qalandars in India, has his final resting place (*aramgah* or *dargah*) in Panipat. The road next to the bustling Haryana Roadways, Panipat Bus Terminus leads, after many twists and turns to the shrine of the revered saint. Surprisingly, if one asks the route and location of Bu Ali's shrine, one is given an uncomprehending look, but if one asks politely where Baba Qalandar or Qalandar Sahib's *dargah* is to be found, many are willing to lead you there.

The grand mausoleum of Sharfuddin Bu Ali Shah Qalandar has a marble dome and the *kalasa* on the finial is made of gold. The gallery around the *mazar* is beautifully carved in gold. The terrace (the *chajja* or eaves) has exquisite carvings and etchings. The railings around the grave used to be of silver and gold. It is believed that when Nadir Shah came to India, he visited the *mazar* of the Qalandar, and seeing the ornate silver and gold railing, exclaimed, 'This is not the grave of a Qalandar'. Thus, his soldiers removed all the precious metal. What Nadir Shah meant was that the Qalandar's shrine should be simple, austere, and non-ostentatious as their lives.

As it stands today, the railing is made of very ornate and delicately chiselled wood and steel. The inner chamber has an alcove in the centre of each wall. The roof has the Star of David designed in the centre and a silver plated chandelier hangs down. Four fans and lamps can also be seen suspended from the ceiling. The wooden frame around the raised grave is covered in green coloured plastic or rexine sheet. There is a large clock on the right wall. There are also two pillars on either side of the *qabr* (grave) painted bright blue. There are no posters, except the names etched in the walls: Ya Ali, Ya Mohammad and Ya Momin. To the steel railing encircling the grave are tied hundreds of locks, of all shapes and sizes, iron ones, steel ones, brass and aluminium, large fancy ones and very tiny ones, with their keys intact. There is an anteroom leading from a door in the left, which is a storeroom (*tosha khana*), and is kept locked.

Just behind the *mazar* of Bu Ali is that of his dear friend, Prince Mubarak Khan. His grave, covered in a green and blue sheet, is inside a square chamber, surrounded by a wonderfully carved wooden railing. The roses are so beautifully depicted that they seem almost real. An ornately designed headrest and an iron box 2 ft x $3^{1/2}$ ft is the other furnishing in this cell. This is a collection box. The four walls have posters stuck on them proclaiming glory to Baba Bu Ali Shah in Devanagari script:

Hazrat Ilahi Bu Ali
Shah Baba Qalandar Sahib ki Jai

[Glory to Honourable Bu Ali Shah Qalandar]

And, then a couplet praising his kindness, which reads thus:

mere baba hain kitne dayalu
ek bar sar jhuka ke to dekh
pal bhar mein bhar denge jholi
jholi phaila kar to dekh

[My lord is extremely kind,
Bow your head in obeisance,
In a moment he'll grant all that's in your mind,
Spread your lapels at least once.]

Five out of the six posters pasted on the walls had the word *Jai* (from *Shah Baba Qalandar Sahib ki Jai*) scratched out by some miscreants. The wooden door leading to these two inter-connected sepulchral chambers is large and roughly carved. On either side of the wall is painted Ya Allah and Ya Mohammad. And, in the centre, above the wooden frame is calligraphed Ya Haq, Haq, Haq, Haq. Below this is written the Fatiha and Bismillah, and finally a couplet in Persian supposed to have been penned by Bu Ali himself.

The verandah (*dalan*) outside the chambers has a black and white tiled floor. It has many fans (with 'Jai Baba Shah Qalandar' written on its blades in red paint) and bulbs, and as many as six large and four small wall clocks adorning its two major walls. In fact, one of the clocks tells international time. The ceiling has such beautiful inlay work and golden *minakari* that it is really breathtaking. On the extreme right of this covered verandah is a small room, 8 ft x 8 ft, where the keeper (or the caretaker) of this shrine, Bashir Ansari, has his office. A small wooden desk (floor type), a mat on the floor, two or three refilled mineral water bottles, a couple of hand fans, a few books scattered haphazardly, a dusty telephone and a mobile phone, few glasses, steel stainless dishes, a red mattress, and a blue *gaotakiya* (bolster), and a steel almirah make up the furnishings of this humble office. It has the Indian flag and a dirty poster declaring 'My next car is a Swift' placed on the low table.

The *dalan* is said to have been constructed by Jehangir in 1071 AH, as is stated on a plaque placed there. The inlaid stones are both precious and semi-precious. Eight square pillars of Zehermora stone (called *kasauti ka pather*), extremely beautiful with golden embellishment, support the arched ceiling, so that those going inside 'can be spiritually tested', whether they are of 'pure conscience'. In other words, those who have the ability to read the subtle changes that surface in Zehermora when a person moves through the verandah can say whether the visitor has come to the *dargah* with a spiritual and religious motive, or if he has some nefarious thought in mind.

The doorways leading to the *dalan* are cuspated and arched, with lattice work. This whole structure is topped by a huge dome and has four minarets on all four corners of the roof. Outside this *dalan* is a very large courtyard, laid with red sandstone tiles. On the western side is a large raised tank, with a fountain in the centre and artificial flowers floating in it. In the centre of this tank is a crescent and stars made of moulded iron. Since this tank is a raised one, it has on one side many water taps. I counted as many as twenty on two sides. There is a garden on the other side of the tank and few trees. The main door leads to a *deorhi* (passage) which opens into the courtyard.

On the same side as the tank, but behind it, is a library called the Altaf Hussain Hali Library. On the eastern side of the courtyard is the lattice-work enclosure, housing the *aramgah* or tomb, after whom the library is named, a contemporary of Mirza Ghalib. On the left of the *mazar* is a plaque on which a *qasida* is written by a Hindu poet of Panipat, Amarnath Ashaftat. On the other side is another plaque on which a couplet of Hafiz Shirazi is written:

bar zameen ke nishan kafe paye to bud
salha sajda sahib nazare khwabid bud

On the other side of the main structure is a mosque and two large halls, also with an intricately worked and designed ceiling built by Muqarrab

Ali Khan, In-charge of the Royal Storehouse, whose father was Ikramullah Khan, the Wazir of Akbar. Their family graves are in the same premises.

On the far western side are a series of quite dark and dingy rooms for wandering *faqirs*. For visitors, there are some large rooms and newly constructed guest rooms, with modern facilities. A number of bathrooms, eastern and western style, have recently been constructed. An unkempt, unruly garden is also visible. This whole structure (that is the *dargah sharif* of Bu Ali Shah) is inside what once was a fort. Outside the *dargah* is a *naqqara khana* (drum house). It has two accesses: one is from the busy main road, which is in fact a very bustling market with lots of shops and a large modern restaurant. Facing this restaurant is the slightly modest entrance to the *dargah*. Most of these shops are owned by Punjabis (in fact one by a Sikh gentleman, since 1950). They sell pictures of the shrine, booklets about the saint in Hindi and Urdu, *prasad*, flowers, *elaichi dana*, incense sticks, rice puffs, cassettes of songs and *qawwalis* in praise of Shah Baba, oil and wicks, and sundry other items. These shops also sell sheets and posters (with *Haji Malang, ho nigah-e-karam* written on them). The other entrance is from a bylane; only the locals can locate this entrance since its approach lane is not apparently visible.

The *dargahs* of Haryana and Punjab were administered by the Punjab Wakf Board. Now, the Haryana Wakf Board administers all *dargahs* in the state. There are a number of rooms in the *dargah* premises housing the offices of the Estate Officer (one Mr. S.Y. Sarolvi) and the representative of the Haryana Wakf Board. The Estate Officer sits in room number 20. There is also a collector above him, who keeps the account of the collections made at the *dargah*. The *akhrajat* (collections) are carried to Ambala, and then disbursed by him, according to the demand made by the keeper of the shrine. There are a few direct employees of the state or the collectorate or the Wakf Board. Many work voluntarily and do not get any honorarium except free board and lodgings. The keeper of the grave (*mujawir*) gets a paltry sum for his personal expenses. He grudgingly states that he is given a pittance of rupees one thousand per month.

BU ALI SHAH QALANDAR'S KINSHIP

The case of Bu Ali is less well attested. He does not find mention in the *Fawaid al-fuad* or *Siyar al-Awliya*. A late seventeenth century *tadhkira*, the *Siyar al-manaqib* of Sheikh Hamid claims to draw upon earlier written sources as well as upon oral tradition at the shrine (*Tazkira Auliya Pak-o-Hind*).

Bu Ali Shah's descent is traced to Imam-i-Azam Abu Hanifa. His patri-genealogical tree reads thus:

Noman
|
Sabat
|
Imam Noman Abu Hanifa Koni
|
Wang
|
Mohammad
|
Abdul Rahim
|
Abdur Rehman
|
Faras
|
Abu Bakr Ghazi
|
Salar Aziz
|
Maulana Fakhruddin Zubair Iraqi
|
Bu Ali Shah Qalandar

(Reference: *Tazkira Auliya, Auliya-e-Karam Panipat*, by Mirza Mohammad Akhtar Dehlvi [in Urdu], p. 132).

Auliya-e Hind aur Pakistan (1981) offers another geneology of Bu Ali.

Imam Abu Hanifa
|
Danak
|
Mohammad
|
Abdur Rahim
|
Faras
|
Abu Bakr
|
Salar Aziz
|
Salar Hasan
|
Maulana Fakhruddin Zubair Iraqi
|
Bu Ali Shah Qalandar

These two genealogies differ with respect to the number of generations before Bu Ali. The first genealogy counts eleven generations before him, whilst the second records nine generations before him. It is difficult to have a consensus about the preceding generations and the actual patrilineal relatives. In fact, dispute exists with respect to the name of Bu Ali's father. However, most of the writers agree that Bu Ali's father was also a Qalandar. His name was Shaikh Fakhruddin Zubair Iraqi, and his son, who was named Sharfuddin, was born at Panipat. Later, Sharfuddin earned the title of Bu Ali Shah. His mother's name was Bibi Hafiza binte Jamal; she was the daughter of Maulana Nemat-ullah Hamdani. The other name given of his mother is Bibi Fatima (see, *Tazkiratul Auliya*). The name of Bu Ali's mother may indicate a claim of decent from the poet and Chishti Khalifa, Shaykh Jamaluddin Hansvi, but this is not made explicit by the *Sharaf al-manaqib* (by Hamid al-Din). Some sources say that Sheikh Jamal Hansvi was the son of his mother's sister. Chronologically neither of these claims regarding Bu Ali's parentage appear well founded.

Though Bu Ali was born in Panipat, his *mazar*s are at Panipat, Karnal and Buddha Khera (*Tazkira Auliya*; *Akhbar-ul Akhyar*, p. 279). The year of his birth was 606 Hijri. Most agree it was AD 1200 (in the reign of Qutubdin Aibak). His date of death is given as 9 Ramzan 724 (i.e., 30 August 1324) at an alleged age of 122 lunar years. Given the importance of the date of death at *'urs* festival, we may accept this date as possibly genuine. Bu Ali would therefore be a Qalandar of early thirteenth century when this order had considerable power and prestige in north India, who had established himself as a charismatic figure at Panipat (*Sharaf al-manaqib*, pp. 8, 35). From the *Sharaf al-manaqib*, it is clear that Bu Ali was not a member of a wandering Qalandar band. He was born at Panipat, where he established his Khanqah and his wanderings do not appear to have taken him farther afield than the neighbouring capital city of Delhi.

Bu Ali's father has been identified with the illustrious scholar and famous dervish Fakhr al-Din Iraqi, the meritorious poet. This identification is made in a variant of the anecdote regarding his joining a Qalandar band and his reception as a *murid* by Sheikh Baha al-Din Zakariya of Multan. If one may trust the rather fanciful biography, which prefaces his Diwan, he grew up in Hamadan in south-west Persia as a model of adolescent piety, industry, and learning. At the age of seventeen, after completing *char abru* (shaving off the head, beard, eyebrows, and moustaches), when a group of Qalandars passed through Hamadan, his eyes fell upon a beautiful boy among them. After they had set out again from Hamadan, he threw away all the books on Islamic sciences and religious discipline, and caught up with the Qalandars travelling through Khorasan. He later accompanied them when they decided to go to India. They went on to Multan and took refuge in the Khanqah of Sheikh Bahauddin Zakaria (*Auliya-e Hind aur*

Pakistan). The Sheikh perceived the inner strength of Fakhruddin and decided to separate the young man intoxicated by spiritual energy from the peregrinating Qalandars.

The following day when the group decided to move on to Delhi on way to Somnath, a great storm arose in the deserts of Rajasthan, separating them all. Iraqi returned to Delhi and after parting from his friend, decided to settle down in the Khanqah of Zakaria. The force of the Sheikh's personality made Iraqi forget the young boy, and he began to live in a cell that the Sheikh assigned him as a spiritual retreat. The Sheikh was aware of the happenings, and one day, he called Fakhruddin and embraced him. It is said that when their 'hearts met, all traces of Qalandarism disappeared'.

Fakhruddin was included among other *murid*s of the saint. His spiritual accomplishments so impressed the saint that he married off his daughter to him. Soon after, his wife died. He left Multan and went to Iraq, where he married the sister of the popular scholar, Sayyid Nematullah. His son, Nizamuddin Iraqi, was born there. Nizamuddin grew up and wished to carry out trading activities. For this purpose, he came to Hindustan, and settled in Panipat. His parents, unable to stay away from their son, also came and settled there. It is said that the younger brother of Nizamuddin was Sharfuddin.

Fakhruddin Iraqi and Jamaludin Hansvi were contemporaries, the latter being acquainted with some of the *ghazal*s of Iraqi and wrote *jawab*s (replies) in the same metre. These *ghazal*s are dated to the early period of his life spent in the Khanqah of Zakaria in Multan and Delhi.

Against this background, one has reasons to doubt Bu Ali's paternity (whether he was Fakhruddin Iraqi's son). Nevertheless, if the claim that Bu Ali was the son of the poet Iraqi was possibly made by him or during his lifetime, it helps to explain his identification as a Qalandar. Many of the *manaqib* recorded of him, his lack of association with any band, his sedentary life in a particular locality, would make him fit better into the category of a Majdhub (*Sharaf al-manaqib*, p. 7).

Bu Ali's founding of the Khanqah at Panipat established his claim to a local territorial *wilayat* similar to that exercised by more orthodox Sufi sheikhs during their lifetimes. An anecdote of *Sharaf al-manaqib* describes Bu Ali engaged in a levitatory contest in which he vanquished a Jogi and established his control over a subsidiary sacred site in the vicinity of Panipat. To this day, the seat of Bu Ali and the grave of the Jogi are found on that hill and are a pilgrimage place.

SPIRITUAL TRAINING OF BU ALI

Sheikh Khizr Rumi's *silsila*, known as Chishtiya Qalandariya, is present in India. The renowned saint of this *silsila* in India was Qutub-din Bakhtiyar

The shrine of Bu Ali Shah Qalandar at Panipat (Haryana), India.

The inner courtyard where the *qawwals* sit and sing. The architecture is Indo-Persian – the trabeate combined with the arcuate.

The marble plaque outside the carved outer walls of the shrine proclaiming the date of the *'urs* of the saint Bu Ali Shah and other saints of Panipat (Haryana).

A close up of the locks attached to the lattice grill inside the *dargah*. After the vow is fulfilled they are unlocked and removed.

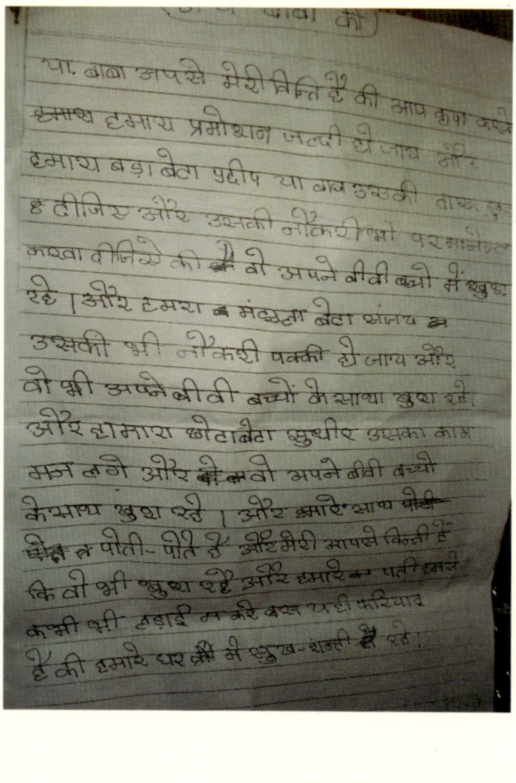

बाबा की

या बाबा आपसे मेरी विनती है की आप कृपा करके
हमारा प्रमोशन जल्दी हो जाय और
हमारा बड़ा बेटा प्रदीप
दीजिए और उसकी नौकरी भी परमानेन्ट
करवा दीजिये की वो अपने बीवी बच्चो में खुश
रहे। और हमरा मंझला बेटा संजय
उसकी भी नौकरी पक्की हो जाय और
वो भी अपने बीवी बच्चों के साथ खुश रहे।
और हमारा छोटा बेटा सुधीर उसका काम
मन लगे और वो अपने बीवी बच्चो
के साथ खुश रहे। और हमारे साथ
पोती-पोते है और मेरी आपसे विनती है
कि वो भी खुश रहे और हमारे पति हमसे
कभी भी लड़ाई न करे बस यही फरियाद
है की हमारे घर में सुख-शान्ति रहे।

An appeal made to the *pir* to help in getting employment, promotion and well-being of the extended family.

The *qawwal*s rendering their musical offering to the saint and asking for his blessings.

The sanctum sanctorum – the *mazar* (grave) – of the revered saint. Women are allowed here.

A shop selling ritual ingredients outside the shrine, such as flowers, *elaichi dana*, *chadar*, *itr*, pictures of the saint and his shrine.

The administrator of the shrine of Bu Ali. In the background are the ritual implements of *jhar phoonk* to drive out the evil spirits.

A class going on at the *madrasa* in the precincts of the shrine of Bu Ali.

Kaki (d. 572). Sheikh Qutub-din and Sheikh Rumi influenced each other. Sheikh Rumi's influence is seen mainly in the episodes of *karamat* (*Akhbar al-Akhyar*). He wore leather, was always in a state of intoxication and ecstasy, and performed lengthy prayers. One of his Khalifas was Bahari Qalandar, who brought Bu Ali Shah into this *silsila* (*Roz-al Azahar*, p. 168). The details of this are recorded in his life history. The other Khalifa of Sheikh Rumi was Hazrat Saiyyid Najmuddin who brought popularity to this *silsila*.

Different opinions exist with reference to the order to which Bu Ali may be appropriately classified. H.A. Rose (1919) places Bu Ali Shah to the Chishti order and mentions his shrine as one of the important Chishti shrines in India. Subhan (1960: 323) and Schimmel (1979: 16) have also assumed that Bu Ali was a member of the Chishti *silsila*. Lawrence (1979: 53) says though Bu Ali is sometimes linked to the Chishti *silsila*, he seems to have had no formal attachment to a *pir* like other Qalandars; according to Lawrence, he belonged to the Uwaysi tradition. It is said that Jamal Shah, the Qalandar who appeared soon after his birth, taught Bu Ali love for Allah.

Rose (1919) also notes that one is not clear as to who was Bu Ali's mentor: some holding that he was the disciple of Khwaja Qutubdin Bakhtiar Kaki and others, Nizamuddin Auliya. Bu Ali wrote many works on Sufism, and in one of them, the *Hikmat Namah*, he gives a short autobiography. Among his numerous disciples were Jalaluddin Khilji and Sultan Alauddin Khilji. In his *Hikmat Namah*, he says that at the age of forty, he left Panipat for Delhi, where he was entrusted with the office of *mufti* and taught Islamic law for twenty years. When his abstractions increased, and he became extraordinarily philosophical, he gave up teaching and his position and spent the rest of his life as a Qalandar. He accepted no presents from disciples. He performed many miracles and died on the thirteenth Ramzan 724 AH (11 January 1324) (*Khazinat ul-Asafiya*, pp. 826-8; *Ansar-i-Aksar*, pp. 100-1, *Miftah ul-Tawarikh*, Persian text by Beale, p. 79). It is also said that after having connected with the Bektashi and Chisti orders, he finally left them both, and organized an order of his own. In his travels, he ultimately came to India, and settled down at Panipat near Delhi. The tomb of Bu Ali is the chief shrine of the order he founded.

Other scholars have also made attempts to identify his spiritual authority with a Suhrawardi or a Chishti lineage. It is stated that he had professed allegiance (*ba'iat*) to Qutubdin Bakhtiyar Kaki or to an obscure Suhrawardi saint (whose tomb is also stated to have been at Delhi), Shaikh Shihabal-din, Khalifa of Imam-al-din Abdali.

Abd-al Haqq (*Akhbar al-akhyar*: 124-5), however, is suspicious of the traditions that link the saint either to Bakhtiyar Kaki or Nizamuddin Auliya. Bu Ali's namesake Sharfuddin bin-Yahya Maneri is said to have met him and been impressed with his spiritual powers during his visit to Delhi (AD 1326-27). In the twelfth chapter of *Ma'dan al-Ma'ani*, Zainal-din Badr-i-Abadi, presumably on the authority of Sharfuddin himself, states that the saint visited Delhi during the lifetime of Nizamuddin, met the resident *pir* of Ghiyaspur, but preferred the Firdausi Najib al-din. Since the date of death of Najib is AD 1291 in *Munisal-qutub*, as compared with 1300 in *Ain-i-Akbari*, and 1322 in *Khazinat al-asafiya*, the likehood is that Sharfuddin did visit Delhi well before the death of Nizamuddin and lived till 1379. *Makhdum ul-mulk* does not link Bu Ali to the Chishti order (according to Saiyyid Shah ibn-'Ali, 1334 AH, M. Tayyib Abdali, 1975, pp. 18-19).

Sharaf-al manaqib also rejects both these founts of authority, that is, Bu Ali being a Chishti or Suhrawardy saint, stating that he received instructions from the pure spirit of Hazrat Ali, son-in-law of the Prophet. He states that Abdal Haqq had written in the *Akhbar al-Akhyar* that there is no mention of his allegiance to either of these *buzurg*s, but Bu Ali was in the habit of attending the assemblies of Qutub al-Din. There is however no notice of Bu Ali in the AH 1209 edition of the *Akhbar al-Akhyar*, and Qutubdin Bakhtiyar Kaki predeceased Bu Ali by 91 lunar years. The connection, therefore, appears to be a much later hagiographical invention. The same is probably true of the accounts of his relations with his contemporary at Delhi, Nizamuddin Auliya, as these find no mention in the fourteenth century Chishti sources. A more interesting connection is made in the account of his parentage.

It is believed that the saint received his spiritual training from Sheikh Shahabuddin, the Khalifa of Sheikh Imamuddin Abdal, who in turn was the Khalifa of Sheikh Badruddin Ghaznavi, the Khalifa of Khwaja Qutubdin. It is said that Imamuddin Abdal received his Khirqa-e-Khilafat from the Khwaja. There is a legend that Bu Ali Qalandar received his initiation directly from Hazrat Sultan al-Mashaikh (i.e., the Sheikh of Sheikhs, used for Hazrat Ali) himself.

The author of *Tazkira Auliya-e Pak-o-Hind* writes that Bu Ali Qalandar in the hope of meeting his mentor stood for years in the river. It is said that the fish ate away the flesh of his calves. When twelve years elapsed, a voice came from the heavens (*ghaib*): 'Sharfuddin, your prayers have been accepted by me, say what you want?' Sharfuddin replied: 'Oh! Parvardigar-e-Alam Al-Ghaib ('The invisible God of the unseen world'), I desire nothing but you, otherwise I will keep on standing at this very place and give up my life in your love.' The unseen voice said again: 'Come out of the water, I have a lot of work for you.' Bu Ali Qalandar replied: 'You take me out of the water with your own hands, I will not step out of this ocean of love myself.'

He then slipped into an unconscious state. Coming out of his trance, he found that an old man had picked him up from the water and placed him on the bank of the river. Sharfuddin opened his eyes and addressed the old man thus: 'What have you done? You have washed away years of my effort and patience. I was just about to attain my desire.' The old man replied: 'Do you not know me, I am Ali, Yad Allah (the hand of Allah).' On hearing this, Sharfuddin bent down on his knees to offer a prayer of thanks to the Almighty and then kissed the feet of Hazart Ali, who offered him some divine secrets, and words of wisdom and soon disappeared. Sharfuddin became *mast-al-mast* (regularly lost in spiritual wonderment). His heart was filled with heavenly light. And, he illuminated the whole intellectual world with his knowledge. He was then onwards addressed as Bu Ali Shah Qalandar ('Boo Ali' meaning the 'fragrance of Ali').

Several chronicles opine that he did not pledge obedience to a holy man, but was admitted directly into the fold by Hazrat Ali. Some link him to Mahboob-e-Ilahi whereas others bind him to Hazrat Qutubdin Bakhtiyar Kaki and Sheikh Shahbuddin Suhrawardy.

This story of receiving initiation directly from Hazrat Ali is repeated in many sources. *Tazkira-e-Ghausia* (1977: 394-7) notes that a *majdhub* had helped him solve a curious problem of the reigning King. As a consequence, he threw away all his books and went out in search of the saint, who had left a note for him in his school. On the third day, he succeeded in locating him. He was none other than the great Sufi saint, Bakhtiar Kaki. Sharfuddin prayed to him to accept him as his disciple. However, the saint refused to do so, for he said he was not authorized. But, he assured Sharfuddin that he would take him to his *pir-o-murshid*. Saying this, Kaki placed Sharfuddin's hand in the hand of Hazrat Ali Murtaza (*Amir-ul Momineen*). Hazrat Ali revealed to him divine secrets. On receiving them, Sharfuddin became 'intoxicated' (*majdhub*). Since than his *laqab* (popular name) became Bu Ali. The saint Hazrat Ghaus Ali Shah Panipati emphasizes that the *pir-o-murshid* of Bu Ali could have been and was none other than Hazrat Ali. There is a verse related to Hazrat Ali and Bu Ali.

Bu Ali la maim wa maula Ali
Bu Ali bashad Ali maula-i-ma

(Oh Bu Ali, we are just dead bodies, in fact not even corpses.
We are no body, our Lord is Ali and He is everything.
He is the Lord of us slaves.)

It is not amazing that this event occurred since other saints have also received *bait* (initiation) and *faiz* (glory) in the aforesaid manner; for instance, Khwaza Abul Hasan Khirqani received *bait* from Bayazid Bistami though the latter was dead for over a hundred years (*Akhbar ul-Akhyar*, pp. 279-282). Bu Ali then wrote the following couplet in Persian in honour of Ali (*Auliya-e-Hind-o-Pakistan*, pp. 71-90):

Hayderum, Qalandarum, mustam,
banda-e-ur murtaza Ali Hastum,
Peshwa-e-Tamaam Rindan num,
key sagae kuo-e-sher-e-yazdan num.

The other closely related legend is that once in a state of intense devotion to God (trance), Sharfuddin appeared in the *majlis* of the Prophet (Mustafa), where Hazrat Ali was also present. Rasool-e-maqbool (the Prophet) called out to Ali and asked him to instruct Sharfuddin in the divine secrets (*israr-e-ghaibi*). Ali revealed all Khafi and Jali secrets, and then took some of his saliva and rubbed on Bu Ali's tongue. He then gave him the name Bu Ali and disappeared.

There is another story. Proverbially, Hazrat Bu Ali may have gone 'beyond fifty thousand dark veils, achieved the goals of twenty thousand illuminated veils.' He tried to go further spiritually, but realized that without a *murshid*, it was impossible to accomplish this feat. He was abject, and the following day, he presented himself before Sheikh Nizamuddin Auliya and requested for his spiritual mentorship. Nizamuddin smiled and said: 'You have sojourned to the seventh heaven without the guidance of a *pir-o-murshid*. Do you really think you need one now? I do not think you need to become a *murid*.'

On hearing this, Bu Ali became despondent and depressed, and narrated the whole incident to his elder brother, Nizamuddin. He pacified him and explained that the Sheikh must have had reasons to refuse to initiate him. 'Please do not let it affect you so much, wait for the decision of Allah,' he said.

Soon after, Bu Ali left the peaceful environs of Panipat and came to Delhi. He established himself near Qutub Minar at the Quwwat-ul Islam Masjid, and took up the activities of teaching and discoursing. He also performed the duties of a *mufti*. Besides this, he did not give up his own spiritual quest and spent time in prayer and study. Whenever Bu Ali planned to leave Delhi, the local residents and intellectuals requested him to stay back and solve their problems. Thus, Bu Ali stayed in Delhi for almost twenty years. However, there is no doubt that Bu Ali was a fourteenth century saint. An indirect evidence is that like Masud Bakk and Ashraf Jahangir Limani, the other fourteenth century saints, he also regularly quoted verses of *Mathnavi* or the *Diwan-i-Shams Tabriz*.

The Qalandariya Chishtiya legends claim that the celebrated Qalandar, Sheikh Sharfuddin Abu Ali Qalandar of Panipat, was either the disciple of Shah Khizr Rumi or that of Najmuddin. This also links him with Bakhtiyar Kaki (*Nafahatul Ambariya*; Rizvi, 1979: 304.). Some say he was fourth in the line of succession from Bakhtiyar Kaki (see Rastogi, 1982). In *Akhbar ul-*

Akhyar (pp. 21, 33), Qalandariya Chishtiya is treated as one of the fourteen sub-branches of Chishti order.

ANECDOTES AND MIRACULOUS FEATS OF BU ALI

All saints are attributed with the power to create miracles. In case of Qalandars, the source of power lies not only in their wanderings, but also, paradoxically, in a minimal to negligible observance of the requirements of the religious law. Since Qalandars were wandering dervishes, in some parts of India, a set of beliefs emerged according to which if vows were made to Qalandars before commencing a long distance, often hazardous, journey, then everything would go well. Sweets were quite often used as a viaticum; the widely travelled Bu Ali Qalandar was also among those to whom one vowed sweets before a journey.

A large number of tales are related with Bu Ali. The significant point is that they are not only recorded in literature (popular as well as historical) available, the devotees consider their narration, in howsoever unrefined and non-literary way, as endowing them with religious merit. A sample of such stories is being presented here.

Once, it is said, Bu Ali Shah was sitting on the wall of a building when a *faqir* riding a lion drew near. The Shah ordered the wall to pay its respect to him, whereupon it moved up and down in token of respect. So, the people founded a fair in honour of the Shah. It is also said that he used to ride about on a wall, eventually settling down at Panipat. The river called Jamuna (Yamuna) then flowed by the town, and Bu Ali continuously in prayer found it convenient to stand in the river and wash his hands without moving. After seven years of performing this penance, his body stiffened; the fish ate his legs; so he asked the river to step back seven paces and let him dry. In her hurry to oblige the saint, she retreated seven miles, and there she is now. It is also said that he gave the people of Panipat a charm which drew away all flies from the city. But then, they grumbled, and said that they rather liked flies; so he brought them back a thousand fold. The people later repented.

How Bu Ali Qalandar reacted to the Shariat may be gauged from the following anecdote recorded in *Akhbar-ul Akhyar* (pp. 279-82). Since he was always absorbed in prayers, he was unmindful of his physical appearance. Once his moustaches assumed large proportions. None of his *murid*s had the courage to comment on their length or to suggest that they be trimmed. Once Maulana Ziyauddin Samnani, the *mufti* of Panipat, a strict follower of the Shariat, chanced to visit him. On seeing his condition, he called for a pair of scissors. Holding Bu Ali's beard with one hand, with the other he trimmed his moustaches. According to the Shariat, the size of the moustaches should not exceed the length of a grain of rice. It is believed that from then onwards Bu Ali Qalandar used to kiss his beard and make this statement: 'The moustaches have been caught in the path of the Shariat (*Shariat ki rah mein shahid ho gayeen*).'

The Story of Amar Singh

Another oft-repeated tale is of a lad named Amar Singh, who was greatly impressed by Bu Ali, and wished to become his *murid*. Since his mother was alive, he could not do anything without her bidding. Hazrat Bu Ali advised him to go back and seek permission from her whether he could embrace Islam, and return with her consent.

The boy went home. The mother thought that he probably had not been able to get a boat to ferry him across the river, that's why he had returned so soon. When she learnt the reason that her son wished to embrace Islam, she wanted to hear the details of the conversation he had had with Bu Ali. While they were in the midst of this conversation, Amar Singh found Bu Ali standing beside him. He called out to his mother and said that this was the saint who had given him an invitation to convert to Islam. The mother looked at the saint and before she could say anything, the saint told her to give her son permission to join his faith.

The woman was greatly attracted towards the saint, but she had a problem. She told Bu Ali that Amar Singh was her only son, and if he turned a Muslim, her kinspersons would break off all ties with her. The saint smiled and said: "What if your whole clan turns Muslim, then you would have no problem with maintaining ties with your kinsmen." The mother then requested Bu Ali to convert Amar Singh right there and then. As soon as she said this, Bu Ali disappearead.

When Amar Singh reached the bank of the river, after receiving his mother's acceptance, he was dumbfounded. As usual, Bu Ali was standing in the river offering his prayers. Amar Singh placed his head at his feet and begged him to make him a Muslim since his mother had permitted him. Bu Ali converted him and named him Amarallah Khan. Some time later, his ancestral property was also returned to him and his relatives also took to Islam. He also got married in his own kin group. He was blessed with three sons: Shihabuddin, Daulat Khan and Shahbaz Khan. These children also settled in Panipat.

It is said that Bu Ali undertook regular teaching and propagation of Islam. Hundreds embraced Islam because of him. The Rajputs, who lived in the vicinity, were the greatest beneficiaries. He left a deep impact on the royal dynasty of Delhi, and advised them to always maintain good conduct.

The Story of the Servant's Son

Whenever Bu Ali was engrossed and absorbed in prayer and meditation, he would often forego his meals. In this state, the only person permitted to come close to him was his personal attendant. He would stand at a distance, and enquire with great fear and trepidation in case of being rebuked, if the master wished to partake of food. If Bu Ali desired food he would state 'bring food, the person will eat', and in case he did not wish it, he would admonish, 'Allah, the merciful, does not eat.'

Once his servant had gone out on some errand, and he instructed his young son to perform his duties. When the lad asked the saint if he wished for food, the saint agreed. When the meal was brought to him, he took only few morsels and left the rest. He told the boy to throw the leftovers into the well.

The boy mulled over it. It was the leftover of the saint; it was 'sacred food', he thought, why waste it by throwing it into the well. He ate that meal. He had but finished the last bite that he fell sick. By the time he reached home, his condition deteriorated. The father came home to find his son in a critical state. On enquiring he found that the boy had partaken of the saint's leftovers instead of throwing it as instructed. The boy's condition became worse by the minute and he died.

The servant did not bury his son. He very carefully preserved the body. The following day when he went to offer food to the saint, he had tied the dead boy to his body. Placing the platter on the dead boy's hands, he called out, "Sir, the meal is ready." The saint replied, "Bring it, I'll eat it." The saint's last words were hardly uttered when the boy regained consciousness and ran with the meal tray to serve the master.

The Story of the Marriage Procession

Bu Ali would often traverse the peaceful jungles near Panipat, called Buddha Khera, for meditation, devotion and prayer. Once while so absorbed, he was disturbed by the cacophonous, raucous sound created by a wedding procession (*barat*). He did not like it and got enraged. In a fit of anger, he inverted a cup lying nearby. As soon as the dish was overturned, the *barat* disappeared in a haze of a dust storm.

This incident upset the arrangements, created an uproar and panic. Three days and nights, the family searched high and low for the *barat*, but had absolutely no clue of its whereabouts. Despairing and despondent, the families of both the bride and the groom went to a dervish and related to him the whole episode of the missing wedding procession.

The dervish informed them that he was unable to help them, but a distance away, he said, was a dervish of great spiritual attainment who was deeply involved in devotion at the time. 'When he is free from his devotions, lay your problem in front of him,' he advised them. He would definitely find a solution, by the grace of God and His mercy.

Thus, they arrived in the service of the revered saint and related to him the incident of the lost *barat*. Bu Ali asked them if they were willing to offer three maunds of *niyaz* (offering) in the name of Allah, for this would solve their problems. They were delighted to do so. As soon as they assented, Hazrat Qalandar instructed them to close their eyes and witness a miracle of nature. And what they saw was the whole *barat* coming along with fun and gaiety. The people were astounded. After the wedding celebrations, they appeared again and offered as promised, one maund of meat, one maund wheat flour leavened bread (*chapattis*), and one maund of yoghurt in the service of the saint. The saint advised them that whenever they were in any problem or crises, they should remember this *faqiri niyaz* and offer this to servitors, employees, poor, dependant and wise men. God willing, all their obstacles would be removed. However, they should remember that money should be rightly earned.

THE CASE OF BU ALI VERSUS THE *MUFTI*

The fallibility of the saint, who too is human, is clear from the following anecdote, but the underlying message is profound. One of Bu Ali's *murid* was issueless. He tried to apprise his *murshid* of this problem, but could not will himself to say it. One day, he said to Bu Ali that he and his wife wished to invite him to their house to share a meal with them. He further added that his wife had a request that when he visited their house, she would like to 'wash' his hands. Hazrat Bu Ali looked at his *murid* with a glint in his eyes, and replied, 'I will come to your house, partake of the repast, and will fulfil your wife's wish too.'

When the saint reached the *murid*'s house, the *murid* had another request: 'My wife and I desire that you kindly pray for the well being of our children.' Meanwhile, the *murid*'s wife busied herself in cooking dinner for her esteemed guest. After she had finished cooking, she took a bath and wore a clean dress. Then, with a ewer in one hand and a pitcher in another, she entered the room to help Bu Ali wash his hands. The woman was strikingly beautiful. As soon as Bu Ali set eyes on her, he went into a state of trance. He neither ate his food, nor remembered to pray. Only one thing he recalled, only one phrase he uttered: *be-aib zat Allah ki* ('Only Allah is faultless') and *Allah bas, baqi hawas* ('Only Allah is best; rest is all lust'). In this state of attraction and intoxication, Bu Ali forgot everything, *namaz* (prayers) and all the rules of the faith. When people asked him why he had foregone prayers, he would say *'la salala bi huzuril qalb'* ('If the heart is not present, there is no *namaz*').

The people were quite concerned about his condition. They informed the *mufti* Ziyauddin Samnani, appealing to him that Bu Ali should be forcibly made to perform *namaz*. Ziyauddin came to Bu Ali's abode and asked him, 'Oh Bu Ali, what have you done to yourself? See what a deplorable state you are in!' Bu Ali replied: *be aib zat Allah ki, baqi hawas* ('Only Allah is faultless, rest is all lust'). The *mufti* said: 'Whatever it be, *namaz* is obligatory upon us. It cannot be bypassed.' Bu Ali replied: 'Mufti Sahib, kindly mind your own business, and let me do mine. I have been excused from *namaz*.' The *mufti* was enraged and said: 'You have no knowledge of these things, even the Prophet was not excused from it, how can you be excused?'

Hazrat Bu Ali responded by begging the *mufti* to leave him in this state of affairs: 'I am *mast-al-mast* (intoxicated).' He refused to perform mere lipservice when his mind and heart were engaged elsewhere. The *mufti* insisted, so Bu Ali accepted his order on one request: 'Tie my waist with ropes and I will forever do what you wish, but if you are unable to bind me, then please leave me in peace in future because I am without bonds (*beqaid*), I am free. Do not thrust me into bondage.' Accepting the condition, the *mufti* tied Bu Ali's waist tightly with a rope, but was astounded to see that the rope opened by itself, and lay far away. Bu Ali was free, miraculously.

The *mufti* felt quite embarrassed. Bu Ali then explained: 'I am a lover, engrossed and involved only in love. Which *namaz* are you forcing me to read? If you are insistent and adamant, I will pray with you.' With these words, Bu Ali prepared himself to read the *namaz*. The *mufti* was delighted, for he had been successful in bringing the violator to book. Now the *mufti* became *imam* and Bu Ali was ready to follow him in prayer.

When the *namaz* began, Bu Ali went into a state of meditation. The *mufti* finished the prayers, but Bu Ali continued to remain in a state of prayer. The *mufti* asked him: 'The *namaz* is over, yet you are still standing in the position of *niyat* (intent to prayer).' On hearing this, Bu Ali recited a couplet. Those present there could not understand its meaning, so the *mufti* asked him to explain why he did not continue his prayers having intended to do so (repeated the prayer formula, *niyat bandhna*).

Bu Ali replied that even the *mufti* was not present there during the *namaz*. Bu Ali explained that the *mufti*'s mare had given birth to a foal and they were in the *mufti*'s house in a room where wheat had been stored in a pit (*gaddha*). Throughout the duration of the *namaz*, the *mufti* was worrying over this: 'God forbid the foal falls into the pit where grain is stored.' Bu Ali said: 'I do not follow this type of *namaz* where mind and heart are absent. I am a stranger to myself; I am a slave who is sunk in the ocean of love for God and remain silent, since slaves must not speak.'

The *mufti* felt ashamed of himself and left the place. In retaliation of this embarssment, he enlisted the support of the *ulema* and residents, and prepared a *mahzarnama* (decree) accusing the saint of violating the precepts of Islam (Shariat) and not performing *namaz*. Bu Ali was asked to improve his demeanour and shed his Qalandari way of living. This was mentioned in the *mahzarnama* that Bu Ali was a renowned scholar and was involved in study, research and teaching in Delhi since forty years, but on returning to his homeland, Panipat, he had become completely oblivious to the regulations of the Shariat, therefore he was guilty and should be punished.

Bu Ali replied: 'You follow your duty, let me do mine.' The *mufti* remarked that obligations were followed even by the Prophet; even they were not excused. Bu Ali said that he was aware of everything, but he was in a state of intoxication, as a consequence of which he was not even aware of his own existence; and the state he was in was a gift from God, and he was doing what God wanted him to do (*mujhe lazzat-e-khudi dekar, who chahate hain ki main apne aap mein na rahoon, wo haraf raaz ke mujh ko sikha gaya hai junoon, khuda mujhe nafs jabreel de to kahoon*). Besides the *mufti*, there were other renowned people who had signed the *mahzarnama*. When this document reached the office of Khwaja Ali Ansari (and his two sons, Khwaja Nasiruddin and Khwaja Masud) for his final decision, he tore up the petition. The *mufti* was enraged and he filed a case against the Khwaja. When the Khwaja was taken to the court and asked the reason why he had torn up the *mahzar*, he read an *ayat* from the Quran, the meaning of which was 'Do not perform *namaz* in a state of intoxication or inebriation' (when you are not in your senses). The court declared that Qalandar Bu Ali was not in his senses, then how could he be bound by the limits of the Shariat. Thus, the *mufti*'s case fell flat. After this, Bu Ali prayed that Khwaja should always remain in Panipat. People say that his prayer was accepted, and till today, his descendants have their abode in Panipat.

This case brings out many aspects regarding the relationship between the Qalandars and those holding religious or religio-political authority. The Qalandars listen to the dictates of their heart. They believe in the reality of ecstasy, love, and mystic experience, and they wish to be in this state, of love and mysticism, forever. They acknowledge human frailty, faults, and weaknesses. Look, how Bu Ali 'falls' for the beautiful wife of his disciple. But this amorousness is not an instance of lust. Bu Ali is not desirous of the woman, but he wants to remain in the state of 'intoxication' and 'bliss' (*mast*) that comes with her sight. This is the state of Qalandarism, which makes him unmindful of the mores of Shariat, which was the cause of his argument and conflict with the religio-political authority. This state is understood as a gift of God. That those in the Qalandari state are exempted from the Shariat indicates the accommodation that scriptural Islam has historically made, thus yielding variants of popular Islam. The intensity of ecstasy and intoxication that came by way of Bu Ali was more than that had been experienced by others. Love, losing oneself in its pleasure and depth, makes the status of the travellers on the path of Qalandariya higher than that of those who immerse themselves in Sufism.

The Story of a Curd-Seller

A beautiful young woman with a clay vessel of curds on her head passed by Bu Ali Shah's residence, calling out to people to buy her sweet yoghurt. Bu Ali asked her if she would give him some and enquired the price. She said laughingly that it was very expensive, and he would not be able to afford it. 'How much?' 'One gold coin (*ashrafi*),' she replied. He offered her one coin. Everyday, from then on, he would present her with an *ashrafi*. She told her husband about it and soon they became very wealthy.

Her husband asked her to beg Bu Ali to bless them with a child. The saint asked her to bring with her the next morning all those women desirous of a male child. The following day, when they arrived, the saint was chewing *pan* (betel leaf). He spit out the chewed leaf and gave some of it to each of the women gathered there and blessed them. Each of them, except one, ate the offered *pan*. She felt disgusted and hid her share under a stone. The following year, each one was blessed with a son, except that particular woman. She asked Bu Ali why was she the unfortunate one? He asked her to go to the same place where she had thrown the spittle. On reaching there, she was amazed to find an infant. She repented and begged forgiveness of him.

It is also said that Bu Ali composed a *rubai* (verse) in praise of the curd-seller:

ai gujri dar husne latafat chun hi
eein deg-e-dahi war sar-e-to taj-e-shahi
ab lal-e-labt shiro-shakar mi barad
har gah ke wa goi, dahi lo ji dahi

(Oh maiden! The earthern pot on your beautiful head is like a crown. When you call out time and again, 'buy my yoghurt', the sound of your voice is like honey dripping from your lips.)

Blessings to the Ansaris

The forefather of the Ansaris of Panipat was Malik Ali Ansari. His sons, Nasiruddin and Masud Ali Ansari were married to Makhdum Jalaluddin Kabirul Auliya's two daughters on the behest of Bu Ali, and he also blessed them that till the Day of Judgement their generations would reside in Panipat. And, many illustrious saints and intellectuals would be known from their clan.

Coincidentally, once Bu Ali arrived at the very mosque they were staying in. The two brothers treated him very respectfully and welcomed him warmly. Bu Ali was touched by their modesty, humility and respectful behaviour, and blessed them. As he had predicted, many amazing and honourable Auliya and intellectuals were born to them, and their generations have stayed in Panipat in peace and contentment.

Bu Ali's Meeting with Nizamuddin Auliya

Sayyara Digest (Auliya-e-Karam Number, pp. 161-81) notes that Bu Ali Qalandar had great affection for Mehboob-e-Ilahi Nizamuddin Auliya. Whenever he visited Delhi, he used to pay his respects to him at his *dargah*. Many a times he thought of requesting the *pir* to accept him as his disciple but something would hold him back. He always thought of receiving *bait* from such a person who was respected in the Heavens also. Everyday, during deep meditation and devotion, he found that in a state of trance he witnessed Nizamuddin Auliya engrossed in prayer in the first Heaven. On the second day, he saw Nizamuddin in the second Heaven. On the third day, in the third Heaven, fourth day saw him in the fourth Heaven, and so on. On the seventh day again, he saw the Sheikh in deep prayer in the seventh Heaven. Bu Ali was amazed to see the spiritual height and status of the saint.

Hakim Liaqat Ali Suhrawardi's *Adhai Qalandar* has recorded the interaction that Bu Ali had with Nizamuddin Auliya.

> Nizamuddin Auliya: What brings you here?
> Bu Ali: Why do you ask me, Sir, you know better than me what brings me here.
> Nizamuddin: I know you have sojourned to the seventh heaven. Now why do you need me? Go back, you have not traversed the whole path to my door. Go and journey some more.
> Bu Ali: You did not let me remain in the heavens; now are you turning me back from your door too?
> Nizamuddin: Yes! Go back, Sharfuddin, the fire is raging, you'll need water; go near the Jumna.

Once Nizamuddin sent Bu Ali a verse in Persian:

> O righteous! Guidance! I'm in difficulty and want the answer to this.
> People say that when there was nothing, God was there,
> but if there was nothing, then where was God?

Hazrat Bu Ali Shah Qalandar wrote a couplet also in Persian in its answer:

> I'm unconscious about the world and the people.
> Everything belongs to God, and God, and God cannot be defined.

If you want to know about the secret,
then look at your soul, how it is existing in your material body.

Such exchanges created affinity between Nizamuddin and Bu Ali. Five years later Nizamuddin again created a stir in Bu Ali's life. He said to Bu Ali: 'Come, lower your head.' Putting his cap on Bu Ali, he made him his *murid*.

Soon after, Sharfuddin went to the grave of Qutubdin Kaki. He had hardly finished his prayers that he found himself in the assembly of dervishes of Delhi. One of them said: 'Kindly give us a discourse on Qaza Kursi (a recitation from the Quran) since you are well versed in it.' Sharfuddin bowed his head and agreed: 'Your wish is my wish.' They were very pleased with him. They took him to Darul Qaza and placed him on its seat (*masnad*). He remained there for twenty years. One day, a *faqir* came and reminded him of his finality and vows: 'How long will you remain like this, you have forgotten yourself, forgotten love. Besides the path of love, there are many worlds of which you are unaware' (*ishq ki taqvin mein asar ravan ke siwa, aur zamane bhi hain jin ka kahin koi nam nahin*). This exercised great impact on him; he threw his books in the river, and left for Panipat in search of the other 'worlds'.

Bu Ali and Prince Mubarak Khan

Hazrat Bu Ali was very fond of his *murid* Mubarak Khan, son of Alauddin Khilji, Sultan of Delhi. His birth was considered to be a blessing of Bu Ali. Mubarak Khan also had an intense, extreme, unlimited respect for Bu Ali. Strange of all, in spite of being a royal prince, he lived in penury and poverty with Bu Ali. An army officer was smitten with the young and handsome Mubarak. He wished that Mubarak should leave Bu Ali and join him. He made many attempts, but all failed.

One day, the army officer was informed that Mubarak had embarked on a hunting expedition. He considered this to be an apt opportunity to satiate his desire. He kidnapped Mubarak, and took him to his residence. Bu Ali waited all evening for Mubarak's return. There seemed to be no sign of him. He meditated and divined that he was in the custody of the officer. He reached his house, and waited for him to return. The sun set and darkness enveloped the area but neither the officer nor Mubarak returned. Bu Ali closed his eyes and started reciting the verses of separation. His singing had a great effect, darkness increased and the night grew long, so long that the city got fed up with its length. The people tried to find out the reason for this unusual occurrence. They sent their investigators to various stations, who reported that Bu Ali was standing outside the door of the military officer's house and said that he would not move until Mubarak returned.

The night would not end unless he returned. The *alims* (the learned) went in search of both of them. Thus, Mubarak returned to Bu Ali. The sun rose again.

The meeting between Alauddin Khilji and Bu Ali has been recorded by Mohammad Iqbal in his *Aahang* in the form of a poem. This poem is part of his famous Persian essay 'Asrar-i-Khudi and Ramoz Bekhudi'. In this, Iqbal narrates the merits of Bu Ali of Hind (*ba to mi goyam hadis Bu Ali, dar swad Hind nam-o-jali*).

One day, Alauddin Khilji, while on a hunting expedition wandered into Panipat and presented himself at the Khanqah of Bu Ali. The saint requested the Sultan to construct a dome and a tomb for him. He warned him to be careful in having it constructed by a Hafiz-e-Quran. Sultan Alauddin, who considered this wish as a blessing, accepted the condition and forthwith proceeded to have the tomb built. He had fine food prepared by his chef and sent the choicest to the saint's table. Hazrat Bu Ali tasted a little of each savoury, bit into one morsel of meat and sent for his favourite Mubarak Khan to throw the leftover into the well. Instead of throwing the piece into the well, Mubarak partook of it, considering it a *tabarruk* (grace) of his *pir-o-murshid*. He did not realise the grave consequences of this act, i.e., eating the food left by his *pir*. As soon as he put the morsel in his mouth, he became restless and uncomfortable and soon breathed his last.

When Bu Ali was informed of his friend's death, he read a prayer over his dead body. He wept bitterly and cried out, "O Friend! Congratulations for your journey into the assembly of your beloved. I thought you were to be my support in old age. My heart is broken, my friend. I will soon follow you." The tomb that Alauddin had prepared for Bu Ali became the last resting place of his son, Mubarak Khan. The *mujawirs* (administrators) of the shrine of Bu Ali narrate this story to all visitors, and guide them to pay their respects first at Mubarak Khan's grave, and only then proceed to the grave of Bu Ali. Bu Ali had told Alauddin to prepare another dome and tomb for him towards the left of Mubarak Khan's *mazar*. He is believed to have said: "My days are numbered, both *friends* will stay together."

Notwithstanding what history says about the death of Prince Mubarak Khan, the belief is that he died after eating the leftover food of his *pir*, which was instructed to be thrown into the well. Earlier, we recorded a similar story of the son of Bu Ali's servant, who also died after eating the leftover food. But, the difference is that the servant's son returned to life, courtesy the saint, whereas Mubarak departed forever.

Two interpretations may be offered here. First, the saint's leftover food is laden with such spiritual power that an ordinary man cannot afford to eat it. The moment this food comes in touch with the palate, the spiritual energy imbued in it will play havoc, taking the life of the person. But this concept, though observed cross-culturally (Babb, 1986; Parry, 1994), is antithetical to the idea of transvalued food (*tabarruk, prasad*). The second interpretation, more plausible, is that both the servant's son and Mubarak died for not following the instruction of the master, howsoever non-rational (and wasteful) it may be. The pivot of the master-discipline relationship is that the disciple must obey the master unquestionably, in the same manner as the corpse in the hands of corpse bearers.

Hazrat Amir Khusrau and Bu Ali Qalandar

The literary skill of Bu Ali is clear from his interaction with Amir Khusrau, the poet laureate and the disciple of Nizamuddin Auliya. Sultan Alauddin Khilji wished to pay his respects to Hazrat Bu Ali Qalandar, but the saint did not accept any offerings of the Sultan. Thus, he requested Amir Khusrau to take the gift and present it to him. Before departing from Delhi, Khusrau wished to visit Nizamuddin to seek permission to proceed on his journey. The Sheikh permitted him with this advice: 'O Khusrau, whatever the Qalandar states, consider it your good fortune and well being, and accept it. Do not refuse or refute anything.'

When Amir Khusrau reached the hospice of Bu Ali and presented the gifts sent by Sultan Alauddin, the Sheikh responded on seeing him: 'Are you called Khusrau?' Bu Ali addressed Amir Khusrau in Punjabi: '*Khusrau, pheri kotra*?' ('Khusrau, What have you come for?').

Khusrau, as was the custom, removed his cap and placed it at Bu Ali's feet, folded his hands, greeted him and prayed: 'Yes, this servant is called Khusrau.'

The saint desired of Khusrau to recite a *ghazal*. Khusrau recited a *ghazal* in such an attractive and pleasing manner that Bu Ali was ecstatic. The *ghazal* was as follows:

aanche goi hech sukhne juz firaq-e-yar nist
chun umid-e-wast aan hamchuna dushwar nist
aashiqan ra dar jahan yaksan nawashud rozgar
jan ke angushtaha-e-dast-e-man hamvar nest
khalq ra bedar bayadbud zeaab-e-chashm-e-man
ei ajab a waqt mi girem ke kas bedar nist
yak kadam bar nafs dano digardar kue dost
har che chini durust been ya ein-o-anat kare nist
che mi goi baro junnar vand-e-but Parast
war tan-e-Khusrau kudami rag ke aan junnar nest

[Whatever I state will be about the separation from the beloved. Besides this, I will say not a word.
Since I am hopeful that I will meet her, this is not impossible nor difficult.

For lovers in this world, it is not the same state that they remain in.
Just as the fingers of the hand are not the same size.
The creation should awaken by my tears.
It is surprising that I weep when no one is awake.
Keep one foot on your baser instincts and the second one on the doorstep of your beloved.
Whatever you see, consider it proper, do not waver.
How many times should I say 'O infidels, go and tie the sacred thread.
Which part of Khusrau's body is not a sacred thread of the Brahmins'.]

In response to this evocative *ghazal*, Bu Ali also recited one.

wahim Khusravan waraan fel astarast
Khusrau kase ke khalat-e-tajrid darwarast
si murg war rue-fahm man waqaf-e-ishq
ko arife ke ba nazar-e-u-arsh-e-akbar ast
aql kulast ilm-e-ladduni wa arifa
ein aqlo ilm hisi darsi mahzar ast
darse shaf habuwad alwah-e-abjadi
loh-e-jamale dost mara u ra barabar ast

[The crown of the king is like the sole of the footwear for such a person.
The monarch is he who has worn the garb of a renouncer,
like the *simurg*.
I address myself to Qaf;
where is the wise man whose sight is towards the great heavens.
In comparison to the knowledge given by Allah the intellect of the wise is nothing.
This knowledge and learning can be understood only through the sensory organs.
Sharfuddin's calculations are not at the mercy of mere tablets.
The beauty of the beloved is enough, proper and right for this.]

Amir Khusrau wept bitterly as he heard the words. He was inconsolable. Bu Ali addressed him in the Punjabi language: 'Khusrau, will you continue to weep, or will you explain why you weep so?' ('*Rounda hunh, kuch bujhanda hun*?'). Khusrau placed his headgear at his feet and exclaimed: 'O saint, I do not understand, therefore I weep.' On hearing Khusrau's answer, Bu Ali was delighted. It was after this that Amir Khusrau presented the offering sent by the Sultan.

Reference to the Interaction between Bu Ali and Ghiasuddin Tughlaq

Ghiasuddin Tughlaq, with his son and nephew, visited the Khanqah of Bu Ali. The three of them ate together in one platter with great zest as if the food was *manna* from heaven. Bu Ali was greatly pleased to see their love and unity, and commented spontaneously: 'See, today, three kings are dining together in the same platter. Ghiasuddin Tughlaq, Juna Khan (Mohammad Tughlaq) and Feroz Tughlaq.' Mohammad Tughlaq presented a *rubai* to Bu Ali.

ghai rast kunad surat makhi wazni
ghai bash kunad ei tilism jani watani
kis nist ke ustad qaza ra par sad
qaz bahar che sazi wa chara mi shakni

[He sometimes takes on the shape of a man or woman,
sometimes the saint of the land.
Sometimes breaks the spirit and body's attraction and charisma;
there is no one who can question the lord of death, as to why
does he create if he has to destroy.]

In reply Bu Ali wrote thus, which humbled the prince, and this further shows his literary skills:

shart ast kedar agar khuddam tar ni
ei noi ke gufti na tu mard mi nazani
gulrache majal ast be par sad zakalal
kaj bahrcha sazi wa chara mi shakni

[You should not grumble or complain against God's plans.
That you have had the nerve to question shows that you are
neither a man or woman.
How dare the clay, earth question the potter:
Why he creates and shapes her and why does he destroy his creation?]

There is another reference to the interaction between Sultan Ghiasuddin and Bu Ali.

The Sultan desired a son desperately. In this desire, he had many daughters. He had vowed that each girl born to him would be killed. In this process, he lost many girls. At that time, Bu Ali was in Delhi.

Then, the Sultan married a beautiful girl. Whenever he wished to consummate the marriage, she would start bleeding (as in menstruation), whereas he was fine with his other wives. The Sultan was greatly perturbed by this strange turn of affairs. He invited all intellectuals of his kingdom to solve this matter for him. This was a problem no one had heard of and so they could not gave a satisfactory reply to the Sultan. Full of wrath, the Sultan ordered that if the intellectuals were not able to explain why his new bride was having this condition, he would hang them. Everyone was petrified and started pleading and begging of Allah to help them resolve this problem.

That very day, at the Khanqah of Bu Ali, an old dervish made an appearance. He asked the pupils there about their teacher. The students replied that the Sultan had called him for an urgent problem. The dervish asked them to bring him a copy to write in. He then wrote a detailed answer to the problem concerning the Sultan's new bride, and told the pupils that when their teacher returned, they should give him the paper and inform him of his visit.

When Bu Ali returned, the students related the whole incident to him. He immediately read what the dervish had written:

> The beautiful girl that the *badshah* has married is his daughter! A long time ago, the *badshah* had turned out one of his wives on some frivolous pretext. She had gone to the jungle. Seeing her in this plight, a washerman (*dhobi*) took pity on her and gave her refuge. In his humble abode, a daughter was born to her. After seven years, she died. The washerman was childless. He cared for the girl as his own child. When she attained puberty, she became more beautiful. Stories of her beauty travelled far and near. The *badshah* also heard of it and thus brought her into his harem. Since the Sultan was a Muslim and a *naib-i-rasul* (Deputy of the Prophet), Allah prevented him from performing the sinful act by making the girl bleed every time the Sulan came near her. In case of suspicion and lack of veracity in my story, the Sultan can call the washerman and confirm my assertion. The *begum* (the girl's mother) on her death bed had related of her misfortune and disclosed her identity to the *dhobhi*.

Bu Ali was so glad to read the message that the next day, he related the whole matter to the Sultan. The Sultan called for the washerman, who confirmed all doubts. Thus, all wise men, who had been consulted about this problem, and who had received threats of death, heaved a sigh of relief.

Bu Ali returned to his abode and was so annoyed with himself for the futility of the knowledge and learning that he had amassed over the years that he threw all his books into the river, and went in search of that dervish. On the third day, he found him. The dervish was the great Sufi saint, Hazrat Bakhtiyar Kaki. Bu Ali requested him to initiate him in his path. The dervish refused and explained that he did not have the inner strength to teach him anything. But he promised to take Bu Ali to his *pir*. The story goes that after this, he placed Bu Ali's hand in that of Hazrat Ali, and that is how, as we saw earlier, he became the 'fragrance of Ali' (Bu Ali).

Shamsuddin Turk and Bu Ali

After Makhdum Sabri's death, Shamsuddin Turk came to Panipat. On reaching the city, he sat in the shade of a wall. Bu Ali was in his private chamber at that time. He came out, went to the market, and bought sweets from the confectioner (*halwai*). The *halwai*'s son asked him as for whom he had bought sweets. Bu Ali replied that the 'spiritual territory' of Panipat now belonged to another, who had arrived to claim it. Bu Ali said that he was looking forward to meeting him. The boy said that he also wished to pay his respects to him. Bu Ali told him that he should go and deliver the sweets to the saint, and also gave him direction as to where he would find him.

Bu Ali, however, met him separately when Shamsuddin made his presence felt in Panipat. He sent a cup of milk through his servant to Bu Ali. The Sheikh smiled and picking up a few rose petals, he placed them on the brimming cup of milk gently and sent it back. On seeing the rose petals, Shamsuddin also smiled. On being questioned by the members of the assembly the reason for the same, he replied that sending a cup of milk to Bu Ali meant that this area had been allotted to him by his Sheikh as his spiritual territory, which was completely filled by his presence. The rose petals on the cup meant that he would have no concern with the other's spiritual area and would stay on in Panipat in such a way as rose petals on a cup filled to the brim.

Relation with Sheikh Jalaluddin Mahmud

Sheikh Jalaluddin Mahmud Panipati was a *murid* of Bu Ali. Once Bu Ali was sitting by the roadside when Sheikh Jalaluddin went past seated on a horse. Sheikh Bu Ali remarked, *zahe asp waz hai sawar*. On hearing this, Jalaluddin lost his senses, dismounted, changed his garments and left for the jungle. For forty years, he wandered in the forests and interacted with many *faqir*s and *alim*s. When he returned, he became a *murid* of Bu Ali. The Sheikh commented, 'Ah! Farzand-e-aziz, your problems have been solved due to the arbitration of another.' Thus, when Shamsuddin came to Panipat, Bu Ali sent Jalaluddin to him to pay his respects.

Incident of the Lion

One day, a disciple of Shamsuddin Turk went to the city on an errand, and saw Bu Ali riding a tiger. On returning, he retold the episode to his teacher. Shamsuddin Turk said to his disciple, 'Go to the residence of Bu Ali Shah and if you see him riding the tiger, tell him, the tiger should live in the jungle.' The disciple obeyed, found Hazrat Bu Ali in the condition and conveyed his teacher's message. He rose from his place and immediately prepared to leave Panipat and proceed to the jungle.

A saint of Panipat, Sheikh Jalaluddin went to the Bhagwati jungle to meet Bu Ali Shah. On the way to the forest, he saw a fierce lion. He addressed the lion, 'Oh lion! This is the habitat of the lovers of Allah, what are you doing here?' On hearing this, the lion turned towards the place in the Bhagwati jungle, where the saint was encamped. The Sheikh followed the lion to the *hujra* (a cell, a private chamber). On the way, he saw four lions moving in the same direction.

Seeing this fearful scene, the Sheikh felt apprehensive. He had hardly moved a few steps forward that Bu Ali appeared and stated, 'You are among my confidantes, come I'll show you a spectacle of the lions.' Sheikh Qalandar asked Jalaluddin to accompany him to this abode. There, Sheikh Jalal saw four lions playing with each other. When the two Sheikhs approached, they fell at their feet and started behaving like tame cats. The Sheikh asked 'Where is the fifth one here, there are only four of them.' Bu Ali replied that the fifth lion was he himself. When he saw that Sheikh Jalal was frightened, he realized that there was no need to test him further. Therefore, he revealed his true self soon after.

Stories of saints (such as Rabia Basri) meditating in the company of fierce animals and changing into them for a while to escape from the public, come from other religious traditions as well (Laidlaw, 1995; Srivastava, 1997). A message here is that the saints have tried to demolish the difference between men and animals, showing that all creations of God can exist in harmony. It also shows the victory of saintly virtues over the world of ferocity and aggression. In other words, with their radiance and compassion, they can domesticate fierce and blood-thirsty animals. There are stories of saints transforming meat-eating animals into vegetarian, thereby spreading the message of peace.

Some Other Anecdotes

- *Tarikh-i-Habibi Urdu* (p. 107), drawing upon an earlier source, notes in the context of Bu Ali that young boys were driven out of his Khanqah when their beards began to grow. An element in the traditions regarding him, which appears early in the narrative, is his attraction to young boys and his relations with them. Like a crazed lover (*ashiq*), he was stoned by them at which he is believed to have remarked that he was in the seventh heaven where angels were honouring him and blowing trumpets. Boys would come to live in the Khanqah but he would turn them out when their beards began to sprout. He did not marry, and the inheritance of the shrine appears to have been transmitted through his brother's children. The author of *Sharaf al-manaqib* claimed descent from his brother, Sheikh Nizamuddin Iraqi.
- Once, a pilgrim offered an excuse for not fulfilling his vow saying that the right kind of meat was not available. Bu Ali was highly enraged and he told him this, 'If you cannot find any cow's meat, then do the *fatiha* with your soul's meat.' This anecdote is reported in M.A.H. Alawi Habibi's *Tazkira-i-Mashaikh-e-Kakori al fiqr-al-gharib be zikral* (1927). Even today, three maunds of *niyaz* are offered at the *dargah* of Bu Ali.

- Hazrat Bu Ali's disciple Shah Shafiuddin is regarded as the first Sufi of this order to enter Bengal.
- In his passion for God, Bu Ali experienced seventy orgasms in a night. (Incidentally, the same number is mentioned in case of Rumi also.) Thus, for several nights he performed ablutions seventy times. From washing with cold water, his body 'split' and 'cracked' – and in 'such a place'. The unseen voice told him that by God and by the Prophet, he was exempted and excused (*muaf*) from the performance of prayer.
- Once Nasiruddin Mahmud came to Bu Ali's Khanqah, folded his hands and stood at the doorstep. Bu Ali asked him how long he had planned to stay. Mahmud replied, 'Three days.' Bu Ali said that he was wrong. He would stay there for four years. The Sultan distributed a lot of his wealth. Once in a state of semi-consciousness, he recited the following couplet: *waqt khairat kar diya aur duniya ka kul mal-o-mahal jo kuchch bhi mere paas tha sab ke sab luta diya* (I have given up time; whatever wealth and palaces I had, I have given up everything).
- Once a saint named Ahmad Yahya asked Bu Ali to pray for a progeny. Bu Ali told him to promise that he would name his son Sharfuddin, so that when he grew up, he also becomes the best *wali*. This child grew up to become Sharfuddin Maneri, the eminent saint of Bihar.
- Sultan Jalaluddin Khilji had great respect for Bu Ali, so he joined his sect. The company of elders of his religion made him kind-hearted and self-respecting.
- Lal Shahbaz Qalandar met Bu Ali Shah Qalandar and received spiritual blessing from him as well. He came to Sind on the instructions of Bu Ali Shah Qalandar and made Sehwan his headquarters.

An Anecdote of Bu Ali's *Karamat* in Contemporary Times

A family from Ahmedabad was visiting the shrine of Bu Ali. They were sitting near the well in the courtyard of the *dargah*, having their food. Their one-and-a-half year old son was playing nearby. He however wandered near the well (seventy feet deep) and fell in it. There was panic all around. The boy was however rescued and rushed to the nursing home nearby. After two days, he recovered and was well. The residents of Panipat attributed his miraculous escape from a watery grave to Bu Ali's *karamat* (*Auliya-e-Karam, Panipat*, 2000).

BU ALI'S DEATH

Irrespective of the religious order, the saint's death is invariably a matter of controversy and dispute. This begins with different factional groups claiming right over the saint's body and deciding to bury him according to their wishes. It is particularly the case where people of different faiths venerate the saint during his lifetime. One is reminded here of the dispute that surfaced after Kabir's death, when both the Hindus and Muslims lay claim to his body.

In the last years of his life, Bu Ali Shah left Panipat for the jungle of Budha Khera. Here, he became free from discussions with the *qazis*, *muftis* and intelligentsia. He stayed here for a long time. There was however a great deal cf trouble about Bu Ali's funeral. He died near Karnal, and there he was buried. But the people of Panipat claimed his body. When they opened his grave, he sat up, looked admonishingly at them till they felt ashamed.

The people of Panipat were prevented from removing his body by some supernatural portent. They merely dug up a few bricks from his grave that they carried in a coffin to Panipat. Their intention was to found a shrine in Panipat, but when they got to Panipat and opened the coffin, they found his body in it. So, now, he lies buried both at Panipat and Karnal. His *'urs* is also celebrated at both places from the ninth to the twelfth day of Ramzan with music festivals and illuminations. This is recorded in the *Ain-i-Akbari*.

One day, a person questioned Shaikh Ghaus Ali of Panipat as to how come Bu Ali's *mazar* is at three places: Panipat, Karnal, and Budha Khera. The saint replied that it was because the devotees and visitors can take advantage of the saint's grace from any place.

But the story is that Hazrat Hafiz Sirajuddin Makki was told that when the *faqir* died, he should be buried near the *mazar* of his *farzand* (son). Some days later, Bu Ali felt quite out of sorts, so he left Panipat for Karnal. In a barren place, away from settlement, he died under a tree – it is said that he died 'standing, just like that' (*khare khare hi intaqal ho gaya*). When people came to know of his demise, they buried him at Karnal itself. In the meantime, Hazrat Sirajuddin was reminded of the saint's will in his dream. The Prophet said to him, 'The Saint has died on way to Karnal. Go forth, bring him here and bury him at Panipat.'

Hazrat Makki went to Karnal and tried to bring the body back, but the people of Karnal refused to part with the body. A lot of heat was exchanged. Finally, Makki carried out a false funeral procession to Panipat, placing a brick of Bu Ali's *mazar* in the coffin. He reflected that if the saint is an *insane-e-kamil*, he would himself enter his coffin. On nearing Panipat, a person happening to pass by, enquired as to whose *janaza* (funeral procession) it was. When informed that it was that of the Qalandar sahib, he wished to perform *ziyarat*. He lifted the sheet to look at the Qalandar and found that his body lay in the coffin. He was then buried at Panipat also (*Tazkira-i-Ghausia*, pp. 394-7).

The date of his death is not certain. *Auliya-e-Hind-o-Pakistan* (pp. 71-90) places it on 9 Ramzan 724 Hijri (AD 1324) at the ripe old age of 122 years, whereas according to *Sair-ul Aqtab*, he died on 17 Ramzan 724 Hijri at Budha Khera, but lay to rest in Panipat instead. It is said that he was alone at the time of his death. It was on the third day, when some *murid*s desirous of seeing him found that he was no more. They informed others at Karnal. They were preparing for internment of the body, when Sirajuddin Makki, to whom this unfortunate event had been revealed in a dream, proceeded to Budha Khera with Khwaja Nasiruddin Ansari, Sheikh Ahmad Zinda Pir, and other luminaries of Panipat. The people of Karnal disallowed them, saying that Karnal was the place of Bu Ali's *wilayat* and it was their great fortune that he be buried there.

Sheikh Makki remonstrated with them, giving them the evidence of his dreams. Bu Ali had appearead in his dream and asked him to release him from the clutches of the people of Karnal, since he wished to be buried in the vicinity of his friend, Prince Mubarak and a *chhatri* and *gumbad* had already been built there in readiness for his final residence. Makki reiterated that his descendants and relatives also wished the same. The people of Karnal said that he belonged to all Muslims, and all Muslims were his heirs. Finally, in exasperation, Makki said, 'Why do you not ask the holy body itself where it wishes to be buried?' The whole night the people of Karnal and Panipat sat on either side of the body, reading the *darud* and *fateha* and *sura ikhlas*.

Then, Sirajuddin Makki, addressing Bu Ali Shah's mortal remains, said, 'Oh, Lover of Allah, give us any signs so that we may follow your wish.' Hardly had he said that when a voice was heard, 'Panipat and Karnal both are my *guzargah*; I traverse on both the paths; I am in both these places. Even now, I'll do the same. I will be present both here and there. But, I wish to remain in Panipat permanently.'

Coincidentally, Bu Ali Shah's favourite *qawwal*, Valadat Mal reached the site of dispute. He started singing *qawwali*s in *kos ragini*. Suddenly, the body started moving and the hand came out of the shroud (*kafan*). Makki asked the *qawwal* to stop singing, and addressed the gathering thus, 'Who soever can lift the coffin, he should take it where he pleases for burial.' The people of Karnal tried their best, but the body could not be lifted. It had become as heavy as a rock. They then withdrew. Then, the Panipatis moved forward, lifted the body with ease, as if a flower, and took it to Panipat. He was buried to the right of Mubarak Khan in the same precincts.

There is however another version. One day, Maulana Sirajuddin in a state of deep reflection and meditation saw that Bu Ali had departed from the mortal world and wished to be buried in Panipat. On reaching Karnal, he found that the saint was dead and the Karnal residents had made preparations for his burial. The body had been bathed and wrapped in a shroud. They were unwilling to send the mortal remains to Panipat for burial. After a great deal of dissussion and argument, they agreed that he be buried at his place of birth.

Alauddin Khilji's sons, Shadi Khan and Zafar Khan, built the mausoleum of Bu Ali Shah. It was expanded later in Emperor Jehangir's reign in 1661 by Rizkallah Khan. The glory of the *mazar* of Bu Ali is great. Four hundred slates of marble and innumerable precious stones have been used here.

WORKS ASSOCIATED WITH BU ALI SHAH

Bu Ali Shah is credited with some dazzling verse, appropriated by a mainstream Sufi group, the Indian Qalandar order centred at Kakori near Lucknow. Bruce Lawrence (1978: 79-82) reviews the skepticism about Bu Ali's Chishti affiliation and also the translation of an excerpt from the famed *Mathnavi* altributed to him.

Bu Ali was a model of self-mortification, but also of overflowing love and enthusiasm. He was widely travelled. He even visited Konya (Turkey), and perhaps even saw Rumi's son Sultan Valad. From his *Mathnavis*, it is clear that he was acquainted with Rumi's work, a book that was to inspire kings, poets, mystics and mullahs alike.

Suffering in love was Bu Ali's ideal and he adhered to the traditional Sufi triad of 'little food, little sleep and little talk', and a fourth tenet, i.e., endurance of people's oppression. And when Rumi classifies the ascetic as one who seeks mercy (*rahma*), while the lover seeks pain (*zahma*), Bu Ali exclaims,

The way of the ascetic is nothing but the way of purity.
The way of the lover is nothing but the palate of a crocodile.

In his letters, he spoke with the tongue of enthusiastic love and charity, comprising spiritual knowledge and realization of the profession of divine oeness, of giving up the world, and love of the Lord, as Abdul Haqq Dehlavi states in his *Akhbar-al Akhyar*. In addition to his contribution to Persian and Urdu, he also made an important contribution to Hindavi, as is evident from his verses (*doha*), one of which is (see Nagori, 1997: 128):

sajan sakare jayenge aur nain marenge roye
bidhna aisi kijiyo ke bhor kadhi na hoye

(My beloved will depart at dawn; And my eyes would weep to death;
Could we devise some means that morn dawns not.)

This *doha* shows that in the early part of the fourteenth century, the Hindavi language had become an effective medium of expression and had acquired the grace and beauty of a cultured language.

The following works are associated with Bu Ali:

1. *Maktubat Benam Ikhtiyaruddin* (Epistles)
2. *Hukumnama-i-Shaikh Bu Ali Qalandar* (The Commands of Bu Ali Qalandar)
3. *Masnavi Kanjul Asrar*
4. *Risala Ishqia*
5. *Hikmat Namah* (The Book of Wisdom)

Maulana Abdul Haqq Muhaddis Dehlavi writes: 'One of its *maktub* titled *Ishq-o-muhabbat* has Ikhtiyaruddin's name which is associated with *tauhid* (unity), *tark duniya* (renunciation), *talab akhrat* (desire for afterlife), love of Allah and full of *haqaiq-o-maarif*.' In *Khazinat-ul Safiya*, it is mentioned: 'The *maktubat* that are named after Ikhtyaruddin are in the form of a book and are a collection of knowledge of unity.' Sultan Iltutmish's Hajib was also called Ikhtiyaruddin. Probably they are in his name.

Lawrence (1979: 53) thinks that Bu Ali Shah's alleged works such as *Hukumnamah* and *Hikmatnamah* are most certainly spurious, while others, specifically the famed *Mathnavi* and *maktubat*, bear all the markings of authenticity. Both the latter works suggest that the scholar who came to disdain books in much the same manner as his spiritual brother from Anatolia, Jalaluddin Rumi, nonetheless learned much from these books before discarding them. In style, the *Mathnavi* and *maktubat* are concise and direct, yet they retain a lyrical softness even when the saint's mood becomes sardonic. Bu Ali compares this world to an ugly, deceitful hag, a shrewd and cunning woman who lures men away from God, righteousness and the true path. Have a look at the following passage from the *Mathnavi*:

hast dunya pirzal-o-purfareb
mi kunad pir-o-jawan ka nashkib

[The world is an aged and deceitful hag;
She excites every man, young and old.]

arifan dadand-ra sad talaq
har ke aashiq shud bar-o-gashtaq

[The men of God have divorced her a hundred times;
For to be her lover is to be faithless to God.]

ein sukhandar gar gosh jandar ei jawan
maulvi guftah z rah imtihan

[Keep this in mind, young man;
The great *maulvi* (Jalaluddin Rumi) spoke from experience
(when he said).]

ham khuda khwa hi-washum dunyai don
ein khyalast-o-malsat-o-junun

[If you want both God and this world;
That is foolishness, absurdity, lunacy.]

behr din dil kunad az dunya Ali
aan Ali shud wali mulk nabi

(About Hazrat Ali, his mentor, *pir-o-murshid*)
[For the sake of his faith, Ali turned his heart from this world;
That is why Ali was made heir to the kingdom of the Prophet.]

an wasi Mustafa sher khuda
an Ali zoj balol parsa

[The right hand of Mohammad, that lion of God;
He became the noble husband of virtuous Fatima.]

zal dunya rachanan zad pasht pa
ta nya yad dar nikah auliya

(He explains how Ali discarded all material things.)
[He kicked the world with such force;
That she never entered into marriage with the saints.]

bhar dunya aan Yazid nakhalaf
din khud karda barai-o-talaf

[But that rascal Yazid married her (the world);
He made this world his religion and for her sake he plundered.]

zal dunya chun daramad dar nikah
karad bar khud khun aan mibah

[Having married this old hag;
He justified shedding the blood of that Saiyyid (Imam Hasan).]

dad bari hamchu kas ra pirzal
bard aura dar do alam paimal

[Whomsoever this old hag befriended;
She destroyed him in both the worlds.]

chun khudi pas khurdai khune Yazid
talakh gardan kam az nan Yazid

[Why then do you eat the remnant from the table of Yazid?
And make your throat bitter with the bread of Yazid?]

gar baraftad parda az ravi mubhaz
nafsati giri z zal haila saz

[When the veil is lifted from the face of illusion,
then will you hate this deceitful hag.]

zasht ravi-o-chu ayad dar nazar
az khuda khwahi aman ei be khaber

[When her ugly face comes into view
Then will you beg mercy from God, O foolish one.]

atishi azdor chun gulshan bud
dar haqiqat sarbasar gulshan bud

[Fire from a distance may look like a rose garden;
But close up it proves to be an oven.]

nakhut ard mar tera mal-o-manal
gasar nadari az thedasti manal

[Wealth and status bring naught but pride;
So if you have nothing, don't feel empty-handed.]

The equation of this world or worldiness with an elderly woman of low taste is hardly novel in the history of Sufism or Persian poetry (Schimmel, 1979: 428-9). But the further suggestion that the meretricious spinster is the spouse of Yazid and that the Sufi's struggle with the world is akin to that of Ali with Yazid, and marks an advance over conventional imagery. Bu Ali enters the world of literary conformity, just as his reclusive but chiding presence must have affronted the comfortable Muslim saints of the Punjab. In the words of Lawrence (1979: 53), he is 'fresh, outrageous, and uncompromising.'

His *maktubat* (*Maktubat Akhbar-ul Akhyar*, pp. 279-282) have been written under the pseudonym Ikhtyar-al-ddin. The topics covered in it are the following;

(a) *tauhid ke ma'aruf-o-haqaiq* (The noted rights of unity)
(b) *tark duniya* (Renouncing the world)
(c) *talab-e-aakhrat* (The desire for the end)
(d) *mohabbat-e-ilahi* (Love of God).

Another *risala* (journal) of Bu Ali, also very popular among the people, was the Hukumnamah Shaikh Sharfuddin, but it was perhaps written by some other person. Let us have a look at some of the excerpts from his *maktubat*. Bu Ali begins each *nasihat* (advice) with 'O! Brother', and then follows it with the message.

(1) O! Brother, When God bestowed his mercy on you, he filled your heart with feelings and saved you from being selfish (*khuddar*). He then filled your heart with love and made you see the varied facets of beauty. When you realize and recognize love, then you will become the *haqiqi aashiq* (spiritual lover) of your beloved. When the lover and beloved meet each other, then you should follow their footsteps, the methods of the beloved and the duties of the lover, so that you are able to recognize the beloved through the lover.

(2) O! Brother, God has created the beloved in your image. He has sent the beloved unto you so that you are led on to the right path.

(3) O! Brother, Allah has created both heaven and hell, and promised that he would fill both. The beloved with her lovers would enter heaven and the Shaitan with his followers will be hurled into hell.

(4) O! Brother, In the heavens, the lovers would be allowed entry on the basis of their beautiful and sublime love and their baser love. Paradise is the place where friends would meet (*manafiq*) friends, and hell, that destination where enemies would be separated (*firaq*). Separation would be for non-believers (*kafir*). For the lovers of Prophet Muhammad, it would be a moment of union (*wisal*).

(5) O! Brother, Open the eyes of your heart and see what the lover has created with his immense love. How the world is a playground! He kept his beauty hidden in the 'tree way'. He created varied fruits and nuts of life and also gave different flavours to each of the fruits and nuts. He did not even let the tree be aware of its own fruits and flowers. He made the sugarcane sweet for you. The sugarcane itself does not have any knowledge of its own sweetness. He placed the musk in the navel of the deer; the deer unaware goes round and round, trying to locate the source of this fragrance. From the sea horse he created amber, from the musk deer he created *jabad*. Both are ignorant of their bounty. He created a plant which produces camphor and the camphor has no intent of it. He created the sandalwood for your consumption and the tree is unaware of its rarity.

(6) O! Brother, Become a lover and transform this world into the beauty of the beloved. Consider your person as the incandescent beauty of the beloved! The lover has created you out of his love so that his glorious efflorescent beauty is reflected in you and displayed. Allah is in your glory. Remain a lover, continue to observe beauty always! Look up on the world in this way and the Day of Judgement is the last day in the territory of the Lord and the Prophet. Learn about both of them, the world and the Prophet; why has each been created, what is the reason for its creation?

(7) O! Brother, Realize your baser instincts. Once you have done so, you will be able to understand the reality of the world without help.

Similarly, recognize and realise your spirit, your soul (*rooh*), because it is on this knowledge of the *rooh* that the knowledge of Qayamat or Akhrat is based.

(8) O! Brother, In this world beauty that is given is *kufr* (infidelity) and *ahl-e-kufr* (infidels) can be recognized only by the lovers, therefore whosoever loves this world, his beloved is *husne kufr* (false beauty), i.e., infidelity.

(9) O! Brother, Are you aware of the uncountable suffering that *kufr* (disbelief) (because of passionate beauty) has made the people of this world undergo, how it has made them lovers?

(10) O! Brother, Realise your identity, your person. Gain true knowledge. Once you become familiar with your true self, the various secrets of love will by themselves be revealed to you. You'll see love loving your beauty and find every tongue pronouncing your name. In short, become a lover and find your beloved within you. See the immense beauty reflected in the mirror of your own heart. The beauty of this world lends more force to the thought that this is the ultimate. Involved, lost and absorbed in such a thought, we visit the houses, tap the doors of every lover of the world. The lovers and beloved walking on this path, both will tread a path leading to humiliation and insult, but they, lost in the glamour, glitter and bright lights of the world would remain unware of this total loss of person, so much so that they would not be able to distinguish between right and wrong; to whom they should declare their undying love and whom they should shun. Their condition becomes so unrestorable that they do not even fear death; these lovers of the world become completely absorbed and lost in the attraction of the world, that they forget that world is controlled by the lover of the world. He will do what he desires. Lovers of this world even forget or ignore the fact that they have to travel the path towards the Last Day of Judgement.

(11) O! Brother, Think and worry and focus on this fact that you need a person who understands, sympathises, and helps you understand the world. Remember, you have become the slave of the baser self (instinct) and your personal desires. Try to get out of this person you have trapped yourself in, for this you need some help to come out of your senses, and try to get rid of the situation you are in.

(12) O! Brother, Take a piece of *gur* (jaggery). Divide it into a hundred balls and name each one differently, for example, horse, elephant, etc. As long as these objects remain in the forms and names that you have given them, till then they will be known by their acquired names separately. Once all the forms are combined, the names will also merge and only the lump of *gur* will remain.

(13) O! Brother, I know not why Allah has created man? What are the men doing what they will do and what ought they to do? I am involved all the time in this dilemma, I am unable to understand; sometimes I reflect that God is cleansing the mirror of our hearts so that the lover can see his glorious image in it and the love lorn lover is made to understand that 'I am the Beloved.' The duties of a lover and his responsibilities are that they obey the various instructions of their loved one and follow the method shown by the Beloved. He should fill his heart with love and the beauty of his Beloved should reflect from his eyes. Besotted with the beauty of his Beloved, the lover should entrance everyone. Whatever is happening in the unseen world, he should be able to see and follow its path.

(14) O! Brother, Whenever the thought of our baser self (*nafs*) comes to mind, immediately man gets involved in the material world and the humdrum routine of this world. Do you know that the thought alone would take you to the depths of degradation? At this moment you are not aware of your plight, but when misfortune and bad luck become apparent then you will find out that this misfortune is caused by the bad thoughts and one's own baser self.

(15) O! Brother, I know not what I am saying or what I am doing. I know not of my past or future. Although my tongue is in the control of Allah, I want that I never speak a word which is not accepted or liked in both the worlds.

(16) O! Brother, Create *khudi* (self-esteem) in yourself. Rise above the mundane. Try to desire and achieve selflessness Allah has desired and Allah has created. Whosoever wishes he will get what he wants. No one has the right to interfere in His decision or determination.

Before offering an analysis of his *maktubat*, I wish to present below a sample of Bu Ali's verses. As said earlier, he wrote the famous couplet in Persian in praise of Hazrat Ali.

Hayderium, Qalandarum, mastam
banda-e-Murtaza Ali hastam
peshura-e-tamaam rindon num
kay sagae kuo-e-sher-e-yazdan num

Some of his verses are:

aan shahad mani ki talib a vind
hum ausat ke az chadre to sakhta sarposh
dar badiye hijr chera band bemanim
dar ain salim nigar ast dar agosh

(He is a lover who has many seekers.
That is he who has covered his head with your sheet.
Why should we go to the jungle to assuage the pain of your separation?
When my beloved is in my arms.)

az me hubb-e-shah sar mastam
banda-e-Murtaza Ali hastam
man baghair az Ali nadanistam
Ali Allah az azal guftam
Haiderium Qalandaram mastam
banda-e Murtaza Ali hastam

(From wine of love of God I am afflicted;
I am the servant of Murtaza Ali;
Without Ali, I do not exist;
From Allah, the great, I from infinity declare;
I am Haider, I am the carefree Qalandar;
I am the servant of Murtaza Ali.)

jam mehr Aliyat dar dastam
bada zan jam khurda mastam
rinde be bak-i-Haidari hastam
kamar andar qalandari bastam
Haiderium Qalandaram mastam
banda-e-Murtaza Ali hastam

(From the cup of kindness of the Great I partake;
of the wine of His, just a small cup intoxicates me;
I am the fearless wine bibbler of Haidar;
I reside inside the Qalandari garb.)

az Ali bad lamshana khwanam
shah aqleem hal ata khwanam
malik takht-e-qul kafa khwanam
waris-e-tajeinma khwanam

(Ali, Of the existence and praise of the Great I know;
King of the weak and dispenser of Justice, I know;
Master of the throne of Almighty, I know;
Inheritor of the Crown of God, I know.)

In total, three hundred sixty-two verses are attributed to Bu Ali, some of which have also been adopted by the singers (*qawwals*) at his shrine (see Appendix III). The word Qalandar figures prominently in the verses. But, interestingly, the *maktubat* are largely free from the imagery of Qalandarism. In verses, the Qalandari approach to religion is extolled, which is not the case with Bu Ali's *maktubat*. The latter are highly philosophical. They do not lend credence to any other lifestyle except the one that God has ordained. As is with the *Mathnavi*, here also the world is considered an illusion, a beautiful mirage, which makes men run astray. They lose the true path, and tread the one that the devil (Shaitan) has laid down. Such men succumb to their baser instincts. Eventually, they are distanced from God and would suffer the fire of the hell on the Day of Judgement. The singular message from Bu Ali is that although the world is beautiful and the satiation of baser instincts looms primary in the minds of men, they should realize earnestly that this would cause their downfall, waylaying them to hell. One can control this with right thoughts that only come from Allah, who has been kind enough to gift them to human beings.

In line with the Sufi ideology in general, Bu Ali's thoughts spread the message of unity of human beings, thereby contributing to the integration of different religious communities. To illustrate this, the example of the lumps of jaggery that Bu Ali gives in his *maktubat* is particularly good. Each piece of jaggery may come to be known by a different name, but when they are all merged into one, what results is the unified jaggery. The same happens with human beings. Each being may be called by a different name, and may belong to a different religion, but the essential humanness is not lost.

These ideas bring him closer to those Sufis who respected and followed the Shariat. At the same time, he donned the label of Qalandar, by which he is known till today. We said earlier that his shrine is popularly known as the 'dargah of Qalandar sahib'. People do not know him as Bu Ali but as 'Qalandar sahib', or 'Qalandar baba', or simply, 'Qalandar-ji'. When he was born, the dervish who came to his door was believed to have told him, 'Qalandar, you have come to the world, now open your eyes.' Maybe, because of this, the appellation Qalandar came to stay with him, although he did not wear the diacritical marks of Qalandar. We shall return to this point later when we shall make a distinction between 'Qalandar in theory' and 'Qalandar in practice.'

CHAPTER 6

Organization and Practices at the Shrines

A chasm of time separates us from the subjects of our study. The worldview of the pre-modern Persian Sufis was different, and it has continued to exist despite vast changes that have occurred. In approaching their study, we are limited by evidence, and also, some of us, by the language (classical Persian) in which the literature is available. Further, our problem multiplies, as there is no secure frame of reference, no uncontestable or incontrovertible facts. To understand how a major shrine functioned in the past, we have to look for evidence, both genealogical and literary. Without documents that provide us the history of how the shrine emerged, who considered it significant enough to have it maintained and restored, we are reduced to a positivist testing of biographical information. The ethnographic approach in this context is concerned with how a shrine functions at a given point of time and what people managing it say about its functioning in the past.

Right from the inception of the *dargah*, there must have been a permanent band of caretakers, *khuddam* or *mujawir*, at the shrine, performing necessary rituals and devotions throughout the year. In the context of Bu Ali's shrine, no systematic and comprehensive attempt was ever made to consolidate the details of pilgrims' activities over the ages or assess the significance of service performed by the successive generations of custodians. Hagiographical literature does not supply sufficient material either about the routine religious rituals at the shrine or any detail with regard to the number, class, character and moral springs of crowds of visitors each year. That Bu Ali was visited by Alauddin Khilji, his son, Mubarak Khan, Ghiasuddin Muhammad Tughluq is borne out by history. The visit of Amir Khusrau is also recorded. That other Sufis and *alim* visited him is also verified. The *shijrah* (spiritual pedigree) is of the utmost importance in all Sufi orders, for the ultimate question is that of the link upward, tier by tier to the Prophet, and after him to one's *pir*s placed in the particular Sufi order. Bu Ali's *shijrah* is very much clear till his birth but of his descendants there is no record. Today Bu Ali's shrine, as stated earlier, is managed by the Waqf Board, which has its office inside the premises.

Let us take up the case of Abu Bakr's shrine. As was mentioned earlier, our historical knowledge of Abu Bakr and his *dargah* is scanty. We know of certain events from his life (recorded by the historiographers of his time) because of their political importance, whether it was his brief conflict with Sheikh Parran or his role in the Sidi episode. We do not know much about the administration of the *mazar* after his death. Controversy also exists about the year of his death. Hussain (1960: 54) notes that the original plaque, which was destroyed by miscreants during the riots of 1947, bore the date of his death as 22 Rajab 700 AH (AD 1280), and according to the plaque now placed in the mausoleum, it is 20 Ramzan 655 AH (AD 1235). The administrators of the shrine know nothing about the discrepancy of dates. Moreover, these controversies do not interest the visitors to the shrine. What is of utmost importance to them is that the saint works miracles. For most visitors to the shrine, desperately searching for supra-empirical solutions to their crises, especially those created by incurable illnesses, it is of no importance that the 'miraculous' saint is Muslim. The celebrations at Matka Pir shrine are sometimes glorious; at other times, they are humble. The belief is that sometimes the saint wants seclusion (*khilwat*) at his place and, thus, everything becomes subdued and modest, and at other times, he prefers to have congregation (*jamat*) and crowd (*hujum*), and one discovers that his *mazar* acquires popularity. This is the belief of people, but the administrators play an important role in raising the popularity of a shrine. As the charisma of a leader is built up, in the same way the cults are 'built up' and become popular.

Against this backdrop, we may compare the two shrines. Earlier, we noted that notwithstanding the historical importance of Bu Ali, his shrine does not have the kind of popularity it deserves. In fact, many do not know his name. Popularly known as the Qalandar Baba, or Qalandar Sahib, it is on the *'urs* celebrations that his shrine is frequented by visitors from other parts of the state of Haryana and Punjab. Otherwise, the visitors are local people, who come to the shrine with the same degree of regularity, as they would do in the case of a temple or mosque. The caretaker of the shrine is always on his toes getting the shrine cleaned or getting the errands done, but his job is not to tell people about the saint and the miracles he performed during his lifetime. Actually, it seems that he has scant knowledge of the saint, for his job is not to attract people to the shrine but to keep it clean and orderly. It really does not matter if the number of visitors to the shrine declines or increases. Although he and other members of the Waqf Board are interested in getting Bu Ali's shrine included in the 'famous tourist spots' of Haryana, they have done virtually nothing to spread the popularity of the saint. The basic reason is that for them, the shrine is not a 'commercial proposition'. It is not a source of earning.

Compare this with Abu Bakr's shrine. The extended family that looks after it is particularly interested in spreading the stories of miracles that the saint has performed during his lifetime and later. Whenever an affluent looking outsider, or someone genuinely interested in the life history of the saint, comes to the shrine, the caretakers make every effort to tell him the lore of the saint, and the miracles that keep on occurring in the lives of people because of his grace. The caretakers call themselves the 'spiritual descendants' of Abu Bakr, so they are also of the Haydari-Qalandari order. Being in the saint's line, they also have the power to create miracles in the lives of people by extending them supernatural help. Abu Bakr's shrine is one of their main sources of earning and, therefore, they have to 'advertise' it as much as possible. They often call the TV channels to cover the *'urs* celebrations for the media. Pamphlets are distributed highlighting the events. Posters are pasted all over and booklets on the saint's life and miracles distributed.

THE EXTENDED FAMILY AT ABU BAKR'S SHRINE

The Sheikh transmits his spiritual authority (*wilayat*) to his chosen disciple (Khalifa). The latter inherits various personal insignia (*amanat*) of office from his Master, such as the *sajjada* (prayer carpet), the *'asa* (staff), the *khirqa* (cloak), and sometimes, sandals and the begging-bowl. These insignia are also called *tabarrukat*. In case of Sheikh Abu Bakr, the *tabarrukat* were inherited by Sheikh Rahimuddin Iraqi. Besides this, we do not know much about the latter's life. Whether he established himself in Delhi or somewhere else is not known. His Khalifa, who usually migrates to another locale and establishes his Khanqah or *jamat khana*, perpetuates the spiritual tradition of the Sheikh. This practice was especially strong among the Chishti; for instance, Qutb al-Din, the Khalifa of Mu'in al-Din Chishti, did not live in Ajmer but established himself in Delhi. His Khalifa, Baba Farid Shakarganj sought his Master's permission to live at Hansi, then he went to Ajodhan, and finally, spent his last years at Kathwal in Multan. By sending Khalifas to different parts of the world, the aim of the Sheikhs was to spread (*tabligh*) Islam and familiarize people with the Sufi way of life.

The charisma of the Sheikh was believed to be transmitted to his Khalifa. Besides him, there were two others which also acquired the saint's magical properties: the Sheikh's charisma remained in the physical site of his burial which became the object of veneration; and his lineal descendants were also believed to carry his charisma. Descendants of the saint looked after his grave, thus carrying forward his cult. The community of people which lived at the shrine was led by the man who was closest and most directly descended from the saint. For this man, the term used was *sajjadanashin*, but he in all cases did not inherit the Sheikh's 'prayer carpet', as the term implies. In terms of its definition, the *sajjadanashin*, 'was believed to represent the saint on earth and to symbolize the saint's continued activity and interest in the lives of the devotees' (Currie, 1989: 148).

Literature on Sufi shrines is replete with acrimony, intense rivalry, and ceaseless litigation between different claimants to the office of *sajjadanashin*. Jeffery (1981), in her study of the *dargah* of Nizamuddin Auliya, documents various ceremonials at the time of *'urs* which were disrupted by members of the rival factional groups. They wanted their differences with other factions to become public, rather than remaining concealed. There could not be a better occasion to make these differences and claims public than the occasion of *'urs* celebrations because it was attended by people of enormous diversity, from different parts of the world.

In comparison to the *dargah*s of Mu'in al-Din Chishti and Nizamuddin Auliya, which have a complex pattern of administration and a detailed set of rituals, the shrine of Abu Bakr is in an embryonic state. From Hussain's (1960) description of the Dargah Committee, one believed that it would flourish further. On the contrary, somewhere between 1960 and 1965, it declined sharply, with the result that today, the Dargah Committee does not exist nor is there any attempt to found a new one. As we shall see later, the present *sajjadanashin* is not favourably disposed to the idea of a Committee. He is a staunch supporter of centralization not only in *dargah*s but also in temples.

The *sajjadanashin* introduces himself in the following manner: 'I am Sufi Pir Muhammad Naseem Sultani, Sajjadanashin, Matka Pir.' One is constrained to ask him: 'How could any one be the *sajjadanashin* of a saint without a *khilafat namah*, or a descendant? The saint was celibate and there is no knowledge about his blood relatives.' As an answer to this question, Muhammad Naseem Sultani points to the *khilafat namah*, hanging from a nail in the wall, and says: 'I have the *khilafat namah* from my father.' One may say at this point: 'But, *khilafat namah* from one's father, who himself was not the Khalifa or spiritual successor of the saint, does not make one a *sajjadanashin*.' After sometime, one realizes that it is not a gainful exercise pursuing the argument on the meaning and exposition of the term *sajjadanashin*. Notwithstanding its meaning, which he knows full well, he calls himself so, and is so addressed by others. He says that all his brothers are the *gaddinashin* ('occupants of the throne') of Matka Pir, and therefore, can occupy the 'seat' (in his absence, but he is the only *sajjadanashin*). Irrespective of what he calls himself, he is an 'administrator' (*mujawar*) of the shrine. After him, his eldest son will normally inherit this office, but in case he thinks that one of his other sons, or any other agnate, is more suited for the position, he will appoint him, and issue *khilafat namah* in his name, even if it displeases his eldest son.

The collocation of different Sufi orders may be noted in case of the *sajjadanashin* of Abu Bakr's shrine. He says that all his agnates are Haydari-Qalandari, because his grandfather was from that order. But his father also had his initiation in Faridi order; so, he was Faridi Haydari Qalandari. And, the *sajjadanashin* also has his initiation in Sultani order, initiated by a saint from Rampur; so, he is Sultani Faridi Haydari Qalandari. He dresses up as Sultani saints do.

This case amply shows that no conflict exists between different orders: one may be spiritually affiliated to different orders at one time. Thus, if one develops spiritual concordance with a Sufi of a different order, and feels attracted towards him, there is no hesitation in receiving initiation in that order, but it does not replace one's earlier spiritual affiliations acquired through lineal connections. So, Muhammad Naseem and his family members say that they are all of the 'order of Matkey Shah.' From them, one hears a different story of the administration of the Matka Pir. They say that their family has been tending the *mazar* of Abu Bakr for the last five or six generations, but an important observation is that none of the names of the elders of this family figure in Hussain's (1960) booklet. Muhammad Naseem also does not remember the names of his elders beyond his grandfather's generation; and beyond it in the ascending generation was a person called Kallan; thus, Muhammad Naseem's family is also called 'Kallan Miyan's *khandan*' (extended family).

Belonging to Bulandshahr (in Uttar Pradesh), Muhammad Naseem's ancestors migrated to Delhi five or six generations ago. They settled here on the mound, which those days used to extend for several miles. Their main occupation was animal husbandry. They used to tend buffaloes, sell animals and milk. In addition, they raised rabbits and pigeons. Those days, a large animal fair used to be held at Dalai Pur and they would participate in it. When the army was stationed at what later became the site of Pragati Maidan, the Kallan family used to sell milk to them. When Sundar Nagar and Kaka Nagar came up, their milk business flourished. Alongside, they looked after the shrine of Abu Bakr.

In fact, Muhammad Naseem did not say anything about the Dargah Committee in the initial interviews, but when I mentioned that there used to be one, his answer was that it was long time ago, before the Partition, and that it did not function for long, and the shrine remained unattended. At that time, Naseem's family used to live in a hutment.

In 1965, there was a massive fire, which reduced their house to ashes. The deadly fire began from the family hearth. Naseem's grandmother used to sweep the courtyard of the shrine and would throw the garbage into the fire. On that fateful day, the spark caught the ceiling made of thatch and bamboo, and engulfed all the huts in a short time. Besides Naseem's hut, hundreds of *jhuggi*s of other migrants were also gutted. Nothing remained. Fortunately, there was no casualty. Muhammad Naseem recalled that in this fire valuables were destroyed which also included the genealogical chart of the family.

The state administration had built some rooms and wanted Naseem's family members to stay at the foot of the shrine, but they had no intention to leave their original abode. They rebuilt their houses, this time of cement, and with the assistance provided by devotees to the shrine, they also constructed thirty-five rooms (locally called 'quarters') to accommodate pilgrims from other states. But, their plan to expand the activities of the *dargah* received a setback when in 1971 the Delhi Development Corporation (D.D.A.) decided to clean up the area in the wake of a World Exhibition planned for 1972 (Asia '72). Not only did the demolition squad of the D.D.A. raze to the ground their houses and guest rooms, and hundreds of *jhuggi*s that had mushroomed all around the mound, but also the boundary wall of the shrine. Muhammad Naseem, who was a student of sixth class at that time, recalled that when the *qubur* (graves) were bulldozed, the bones came to the surface. The then Vice-Chairman of the D.D.A. supervised the operation. Naseem remembered that when the squad was heading towards the *mazar*, his father, Haji Pir Jan Muhammad Faridi Haydari Qalandari, was so angry and agitated that he slapped the highest official of the D.D.A.

Although the shrine was not greatly damaged, the D.D.A. lowered the mound, and removed the unauthorized construction from the entire area. At the foot of the shrine, it built three 'quarters', one for Naseem's father, the other for his father's younger brother, and the third was to be used for *langar* at the time of *'urs*. But, Naseem's father declined to shift to the new accommodation. He wanted to be given the right to build his houses in the vicinity of the shrine, as he had been serving the shrine all these years. Haji Jan Muhammad approached various officials of the D.D.A., and finally, the Vice Chairman authorized the family the right to stay on the mound, close to the shrine. After this persuasion, the Haji thought of repairing the *astana* (resting place) of Abu Bakr, for which he spent Rs. 3000 from his savings. Contributions also came from regular visitors. Earlier, the tomb was made of red stone. It was replaced by white marble. Finally, on 17 September 1987, the repair work was over and the mausoleum had a new look.

The D.D.A. repaired the staircase. At the foot of the shrine, it built some shops and a fountain. As Naseem's family refused to shift to the 'quarters' built for them after the demolition of their huts, they were rented out to the Imam of the mosque and his assistant. The third 'quarter' was given to a *chowkidar* working for the D.D.A. The entire property at the foot of the shrine belongs to the D.D.A., and for shops, tea stalls, garage, and residential accommodation, it charges a nominal rent. The boundary of the shrine was marked in 1992. It includes the shrine and its pathway and their one-storied residential accommodation, high upon the mound. For the 'time being', it belongs to the family of the *sajjadanashin*. However, no floor can be added to it, for this would mean approximating the height of the shrine, which is a sacrilegious act. Therefore, the housing complex can only expand horizontally, but there is a limit to this. Already, Naseem's extended family members are facing the problem of space, and they are trying to construct cubicles wherever they can. The shed where goats and fowls were kept has now been converted into a room, given to one of the married sons.

As it is now, the shrine of Abu Bakr has nothing to do with the structures and appurtenances at its base. However, to a person who does not know the history of the shrine and the role of the D.D.A., the entire complex, consisting of flower-shops and the mosque, appears a single unit, administered by the same management, and in that sense, it may be termed a *dargah*.

Naseem's grandfather, Sufi Pir Amir Baksh Haydari Qalandari, who looked after the shrine, died forty years ago. He and his younger brother, Sufi Pir Wazir Ali Haydari Qalandari, were experts in supernatural treatment. Naseem learnt the lore from them. Sufi Amir Baksh had two sons, Sufi Ibrahim Haydari Qalandari and Naseem's father, Haji Jan Muhammad. Sufi Ibrahim died young, so the charge of managing the shrine was given to Haji Jan Muhammad. Two sons were born to Sufi Ibrahim, Abdul Rahim and Abdul Karim. None of them showed any interest in administering the shrine. Not only that, after marriage, they have moved to their respective in-laws' houses. Both of them are employed elsewhere. They visit their relatives sometimes, but so far they have not staked their claim in the property of the shrine or its income.

Sufi Wazir Ali, whom Naseem called Chote Dada, had only two daughters, whose children, mainly settled in Uttar Pradesh, have nothing to do with the shrine. Haji Jan Muhammad's line continues with three sons, Sufi Muhammad Naseem, Sufi Muhammad Salim, and Sufi Muhammad

Tahseen. These three brothers are affiliated to the Sultani order. Haji Jan Muhammad died on 3 October 1992, and after him, his eldest son, Sufi Muhammad Naseem, became the *sajjadanashin*, although he had received the *khilafat nama* in his name earlier. An interesting point is that the term *sajjadanashin* was not used by Muhammad Naseem for his father and grandfather. Naseem's mother is alive and plays a conspicuous role in managing the affairs of the shrine.

Muhammad Naseem is the father of four sons. His eldest, thirty-two years' Sufi Muhammad Na'im, has received his training in supernatural cure from his father. When his father is not home, or is resting, then he attends the clients. Although so far, he has not received the *khilafat nama* issued in his favour, in all likelihood, he will be the future *sajjadanashin*. Naseem's three younger sons (Muhammad Qayoom, Shakil Ahmad, and Muhammad Arif) are also gradually learning the lore of supernatural healing, but it seems that they will branch out in other occupations in future. Muhammad Naseem's third son has political ambitions. When he was seventeen years old, he had become the Secretary of the New Delhi branch of Samajvadi Party. Before him, Muhammad Naseem held this office.

Sufi Muhammad Salim has two sons, Muhammad Sahib and Muhammad Sarfaraz. They are both young and attend school. The youngest son of Haji Jan Muhammad, Sufi Tahseem, has three daughters.

All men of the generations of Muhammad Naseem's father and grandfather earned their livelihood through tending animals. The traditional occupation of the family came to an end in 1971, although it had started declining much earlier. The income from the shrine was negligible, and was spent on managing it. Once their paternal occupation was disbanded, and administrative problems had surrounded the shrine, the number of the visitors also fell sharply and the family had to spare its own resources for running it. Therefore, it became imperative for Muhammad Naseem, being the eldest son, to search for a job.

After great effort, he got a job with the Delhi Transport Corporation, and is presently posted at the Haqiqat Rai Interstate Bus Terminus on the Ring Road at Sarai Kale Khan. Because of his preoccupations at the shrine during the day, he has opted for night duty. For many years, his monthly salary was a substantial portion of the family income. His younger brothers opted for business. After the D.D.A. had constructed shops at the base of the shrine, both of them took one shop each. Muhammad Salim has a provision store, while Muhammad Tahseen runs a petty food-stall. On Thursdays, they keep themselves free of all engagements, for they have to sit in the *dargah*, by turn. Sufi Muhammad Na'im, the eldest son of the *sajjadanashin*, was till quite recently in 'balloon-advertising'. Now, he is exploring alternate business avenues. His father wants him to spend more time at the shrine, and take the work of supernatural treatment more seriously, because it brings 'respect as well as money', in addition to 'earning good wishes from people'.

Earlier, we noted that the *sajjadanashin* and his brothers at Abu Bakr's shrine are not like the full-time *pirzade* of the *dargah*s of Mu'in al-Din Chishti and Nizamuddin Auliya. They have their own, independent occupations, thus not dependent upon the income from the shrine. As I learnt from interactions with them, they all want to diversify in different occupations. One of Naseem's sons is now in TV cable business.

Let us now have a look at the role of the *sajjadanashins*. They organize the festival of *'urs*. In other shrines, they also organize some more, for instance, Basant Mela at Nizamuddin Auliya. They maintain the shrine, keep peace within it, and initiate developmental tasks. The *sajjadanashin* of Abu Bakr's shrine also said that one of his prime duties is service. The people are made familiar with the teachings of the Quran and the hadith. If people approach them with problems, it is their utmost duty to extend the maximum help they can render. It is not only that the Sufis wish to extend 'supernatural aid' to people, and make some extra money, but also, the latter themselves expect such help from those who are supposed to be the 'descendants' of the saints. By virtue of that, they are believed to be endowed with 'power', 'grace' (*baraka*). Therefore, they have to prepare amulets (and other 'supernatural' preparations, like charmed water) when their clients approach them for success in business, marriage and children, favourable verdict in court cases, illness, preventing calamity, job, and several other problems of life.

THE *KHADIM*

The meaning of the word *khadim* (or, its plural, *khuddam*) is 'one who serves the others', 'one who carries out the acts of *khidmat*'. This term is used for both males and females, unlike *sajjadanashin* and *pirzada*, the offices which can only be occupied by the male. Large and important shrines not only have a number of *khuddam*, but the activities they carry out in the social and religious life of the *dargah* are also highly differentiated. For instance, in case of Ajmer Sharif, in 1976-77, there were 1400 members of the *khadim* community, and some of them claimed to have descended from the saint himself (Currie, 1989: 145-6). With so many people dependent upon the shrine for their livelihood, it is obvious that the rota system would be followed. Emperor Jehangir introduced this system in Ajmer Sharif. He knew that if this was not done, the consequence would be bloody competition (*Ibid*.: 141). Further, ritual activities carried out by the *khadim* community at that shrine are also elaborate (*Ibid*.: 141-3).

In comparison, small shrines have fewer *khuddam*. Bu Ali's shrine has five, whereas Matkey Shah, has four. Here, there is a male whose duty is to sit in the shrine on all days as a 'ritual officiant', and also to keep it clean. Bu Ali's shrine does not have such an 'official' for any other day except Thursdays. In Abu Bakr's shrine, then, there is another person who sweeps the courtyard outside the grave, the lower courtyard outside the rooms of the family of *sajjadanashin*, and the staircase. A person serves water to visitors; and another looks after their footwear. These positions are not hereditary, as is the case with Ajmer Sharif. A *khadim* can move from one *dargah* to another, and also, from one occupation to another. When I started my fieldwork at Abu Bakr's shrine, the *khadim* at the shrine was a man named Anwar. Some months later, he went back to his village in Uttar Pradesh, and his position went to another man. But, some *khuddam* do stay at the shrine for a long time. Bu Ali's shrine has a *khadim* who has been working there for more than a decade. At Abu Bakr's shrine, the woman, who tended footwear, had been there for the last twenty-six years. Another old man at this shrine was Raju whose duty was to offer water to visitors, but most of the time he helped Bhajni in keeping shoes. He came to the shrine six years ago.

In both the shrines, the *khuddam* were single and largely cut off from their families. In other words, they were free from responsibilities. In theory, they could move from one shrine to another, or take up another occupation, but in reality, they remained attached to the shrine for life. Loyalty to the saint and his shrine was especially high among them, for they thought that this was ordained by the saint. As they had voluntarily taken up the work, they did not receive any salary from the administrators of the shrine, but their survival needs were adequately taken care of. They received food, clothes, medicines, and other things of utility from the shrine and its devotees.

None of the *khuddam* asked for money, but it was customary for pilgrims to give a few coins to them. I have rarely seen people giving more than a rupee to them. Often, they would bring with them coins or loose change of lesser denomination than a rupee for distribution among the beggars. The *khuddam* did not have any right over the money offered at the shrine. If a pilgrim gave some token money to the *khadim* stating categorically that it was for his personal use, only then he kept it. If this were not made clear, it would be considered an offering to the shrine. In case of Abu Bakr's shrine, the *khuddam* were considered 'members' of the *sajjadanashin* family. Housing was not worrisome, since they could spread their cot in a corner of the shrine. In fact, Bu Ali's shrine, having a large area and a number of big halls, old and new, all fitted with bulbs and fans, provided shelter to a large number of old, diseased, mentally challenged, infirm, destitute and helpless people.

Earlier, in Abu Bakr's shrine, when the courtyard had not been roofed, the male *khuddam* slept in the open courtyard during summer and spent monsoons and winters in any available covered shelter in the residential complex of the *sajjadanashin*. Since the courtyard has now been roofed, the *khuddam* sleep here, but when Bhajni was alive, she had her own private cell contiguous with the other rooms. The *sajjadanashin* made it clear that those without family were considered for the position of the *khadim*, for lack of space. On way to Ajmer and during the days of the *'urs* of Matkey Shah, the pilgrims sleep in the courtyard outside the *mazar*. If a pilgrim wants to spend the night outside the *mazar*, with an aim of undertaking certain austere measures, he is permitted to do so. The visiting pilgrims to Matka Pir or Nizamuddin Auliya are also permitted to spend the night there. At the base of the shrine, at night one can see beggars huddled. Besides the courtyard, there is no other place for *khuddam* or pilgrims to stay. Moreover, there are no public toilets or bathrooms. The *khuddam* are, however, accommodated with the extended family of the *sajjadanashin*.

We observed earlier that a *khadim* is always available at Abu Bakr's shrine. He is around even on those days when not many people visit the shrine. On Thursdays and Sundays, when a large number of pilgrims visit the shrine, a member of the *sajjadanashin* family sits at the shrine to receive offerings to the saint, and the *khadim* assists him. In fact, the former occupies the space on the left, while the *khadim* is pushed to a tight space in the corner, on the right. Thus, temporarily, the male relatives of the *sajjadanashin* become *khuddam*. At Bu Ali's *dargah*, the *khadim* sits at the grave on Thursdays, and receives offerings for both the shrines. No one takes his role as there is no *sajjadanashin* at this shrine.

The *khadim* takes the offerings the pilgrim has brought with him. In case, he has brought a sheet, the *khadim* helps him in spreading it properly over the *mazar*. The *khadim* advises the pilgrim to offer flowers, and he may assist the latter in the ritual offerings. At Abu Bakr's shrine, if the devotee has brought an earthen pitcher filled with roasted gram and *ilaichi dana*, it is given to the *khadim*, who empties some of its contents in another earthen pitcher, which is kept before him. They are then mixed and a fistful of them is given to the pilgrim as *tabarruk*, which contains a random mixture of roasted gram, *ilaichi dana*, and rose petals. While offering the gifts to the saint on behalf of the pilgrim, he reads the Fatiha. Some visitors request that the Fatiha be read by the *sajjadanashin* himself, thus they wait hours for him to arrive. Bhajni sometimes used to wait for weeks for the *sajjadanashin* to give her time and read Fatiha when she offered an earthen pitcher to Abu Bakr. People think that when an offering to the saint is mediated by one most closely related or associated with him, the chances of receiving the saint's grace increase manifold. That is the reason that they want the help of the *sajjadanashin*. Such a belief is obviously not there at Bu Ali's *dargah*.

The *khadim*'s day begins before dawn when he unlocks the entrance gates of the shrine. He enters the inner sanctum to perform *khidmat* (service). He removes flowers and *chadar*s which were offered to the *mazar* the day before, leaving the *chadar* that originally was there. He does not offer a new *chadar*, but fresh flowers are presented to the grave. Then, he sweeps the floor of the mausoleum with a broom of peacock feathers. He also wipes the floor with a moist cloth and dusts the marble arches. He reads the Fatiha while performing these tasks. All this shows the Islamic character of the shrine. Then, he is ready to provide ritual services to the visitors. In the meantime, the other *khuddam* are at work. The *khadim* may sweep the floor of the mausoleum several times during the day. Often, the pilgrims may clean the courtyards of the shrine, as happens in a large shrine like that of Bu Ali's, but not the inner sanctum, which is the *khadim*'s prerogative. On Thursdays and Sundays and days of the *'urs* celebration, in case of Abu Bakr's shrine, the male members of the family also share the work with the *khuddam*. On other days, just one *khadim* seems to be enough, because not many pilgrims come during the day, and very few in the evening hours. But, for Bu Ali's shrine, which is spread over a large area, many *khuddam* are needed for cleaning it. On Thursdays, if the number of visitors is more, few friends of the *sajjadanashin* may volunteer their services. The *mazar* of Sheikh Iraqi at Abu Bakr's shrine has a 'ritual officiant' (another *khadim*) on Thursdays only. No elaborate rituals are performed by the *khuddam* at the shrines of Abu Bakr and Bu Ali, as their counterparts do at Ajmer Sharif (such as, the ritual of carrying the unlighted candles to the mausoleum, reciting Persian verses, or ringing the bell) (Currie, 1989: 142).

In other words, the income of the *khadim* at Bu Ali and Abu Bakr's shrine is not much. In large *dargah*s, such as those of Mu'in al-Din Chishti and Nizamuddin Auliya, the *khadim* arranges and provides accommodation to the pilgrims, escorts them to the various ritual ceremonies held at the shrine, and takes them around the sacred places of the city (Currie, 1989: 142-3; Pinto, 1995). So, they also may have a lasting relationship with pilgrims, almost similar to *jajmani* ties, and they write to them in advance about the ceremonial dates, and send them money order forms for their contribution to the functions at the shrine. When their clients confirm the date and time of their arrival, the *khadim* goes to the railway or bus station to receive them, provides them a reasonable accommodation, and acts as their escort throughout their stay in Ajmer. In other words, the *khadim* is the link (for religious as well as secular purposes) between the pilgrim and the shrine, or even, the city. The *khadim* is always in search of new clients. It does not happen in Delhi, but in Ajmer, for instance, one can see hordes of *khadim* waiting at the railway station, or the interstate bus terminal, or the hotels and guest houses, or at the main highways leading to the city, for prospective clients. The pilgrim also knows that once he is under the patronage of a *khadim*, all his problems will be taken care of, in exchange for some lucre. Haggling and bargaining is part and parcel of this exchange, but the pilgrim is linked almost permanently to the shrine.

Compared to small shrines where there are few servitors, in large shrines, they are dependent upon the pilgrims for their livelihood. They raise their families from the money their clients give them. One does not find such a system in small shrines. At Matka Pir and Bu Ali's shrine, almost all the visitors are from neighbouring areas. At Abu Bakr's shrine, one meets pilgrims from other parts of India *en route* to Ajmer or Nizamuddin Auliya's *dargah*. Also, during the days of *'urs*, some come from nearby towns and cities. Abu Bakr's shrine figures on the itinerary of pilgrims to Delhi and Ajmer, but so far an exclusive pilgrimage to Matka Pir is not undertaken. The same could be said about Bu Ali's shrine, although it has larger popularity in comparison to Abu Bakr's. Against this background, one may easily infer the poor economic condition of the *khuddam*. Those without any family responsibilities can hope to survive here, but not those who have to look after old and ailing parents or have to bring up children.

When we step into the lower courtyard of Abu Bakr's shrine to meet the *sajjadanashin*, we invariably see him advising clients on various matters. He is always seated on his *gaddi*. Durries are spread on the floor of this roofed courtyard. Resting his back against the wall is a thin, bearded fellow, in *salwar kameez*, the typical dress of Muslim males. Like the *sajjadanashin*, he is also seen advising his clients. Muhammad Naseem calls him his 'son'. This unmarried man, known as Chand, calls himself a *khadim* of Baba Abu Bakr. His *khidmat* is in terms of *ruhani ilaj*. He also lives with the family of the *sajjadanashin*. A Brahmin from Bihar by birth, his original name was Chandra Kant Sharma. He has been in Delhi for the last three decades. Before he became a *khadim*, he used to be a carpenter. From the beginning, he was deeply interested in occult knowledge, especially as held and practised in popular Islam. For acquiring knowledge of talisman and amulets, he not only read books on this subject, but also prayed at various Muslim shrines. His abode those days was the Bagh-i-Bedil. He used to visit the shrine of Abu Bakr regularly and consulted Muhammad Naseem, whom he addressed right from the beginning as Babu or Babu-ji, an honorific term for an elderly male. One night, while praying at the shrine of Sheikh Abu Bakr, he fell asleep, and spent the whole night there. When Naseem came to know about this, he advised Chand to live at the shrine and perform *khidmat*. Naseem said that Chand could afford to spend the entire night at the shrine of Abu Bakr because he 'was chosen to do so by the saint himself.'

This happened fifteen years ago. Chandra Kant embraced Islam, became Chand, started learning the lore of *ruhani ilaj* under the supervision of Muhammad Naseem, and later, assisted him in his work. Today, he also takes up the cases of his clients independently. Being Naseem's 'son', Chand also calls himself Qalandar, but like the others, he does not wear any outward signs of Qalandars. For him, a Qalandar is one 'who is not afraid of anyone except Allah. He does not heed to the advice given by others, except those which come directly from Allah. If we are not afraid of anyone (animals and human), but Allah, then we are all Qalandars.' He made a distinction between those who are Qalandar by 'tradition', those whose first affiliation was with this *tariqa*, and those who became Qalandar by choice. He placed himself in the latter category.

The example of Chand makes it clear that the concept of *khadim* should not be restricted to one who looks after the ceremonial life of the shrine and its maintenance. Those rendering spiritual help to pilgrims are also *khadims*. But this meaning of *khidmat* is contested at the shrine of Bu Ali, where, as stated earlier, the caretakers and servitors do not provide any supernatural aid to the visitors.

SINGING OF *QAWWALI*

All Sufi orders have a common outlook, but vary in spiritual practices, like *aurad* (reciting verses from the Quran), *sama'*, certain festivals, institutions like veneration of shrines, etiquettes of visiting them, and devotion to certain leading personalities of the order. In Indian context, *sama'* blends with classical music and creates a particular kind of singing called *qawwali*, in which songs of Sufi poets composed in Persian, Urdu, and Hindi, and dialects like Brij and Purbi are sung. Poets whose songs are sung are Maulana Jami, Hafiz Shirazi, Rumi, Shams Tabrezi, Hazrat Amir Khusrau, and other Sufi luminaries. These songs are sung in a fluid style alternating solo and group passages, characterized by repetitions and improvisations. A barrel shaped drum (called *dholak*) accompanies singing, which is reinforced by hand clapping. The lead singer plays on a small, portable harmonium. Originally *qawwali* was accompanied by the *daf* (a Mid-Eastern instrument); then came *dholak* and *tabla*, and harmonium, and with the passage of time, *qawwali* singing became more complicated as Indian classical compositions (*ragas*) were incorporated in it.

Today, the tradition of *qawwali* singing is an integral part of every Sufi shrine, even when the specific saint during his lifetime was opposed to it. In Chapter One, we said that *sama'* is an integral component of the Chishtiya order, although some Sufi orders and orthodox Muslims criticized it. The ideology of *sama'* is based on three premises: (a) the words must be powerful; (b) they should be effectively repeated to create impact; and (c) they ought to be lyrically and musically rendered. Undoubtedly, *sama'* can be created through *dhikr*, but the Chishtis added to this the practice of singing the religious composition, a tradition continuing till date. The professional singers (*qawwal*s), as said earlier, sing the verses that the Sufis have composed, or that they themselves have composed, to the accompaniment of primarily two musical instruments, namely harmonium and *dholak*. Often, to the verses of Sufi saints, the individual *qawwal*s add their own lines, sometimes signature tunes. Therefore, each *qawwali* keeps on expanding, and eventually comes to be multi-authored. The individual writer is merged in collectivity. While singing, the verses are repeated several times to create an impact on the listeners. Time and again, the Chishti saints reminded the audience that *sama'* was a serious spiritual exercise, and laid down norms and conditions under which this was to be practised. The 'focus in the *mahfil-i-sama'*, instead of being on the music, remains on the listener and on his ability to draw spiritual benefits from it' (Qureshi, 1986: 137).

The most important function during the *'urs* at the *dargah*s of Chishti saints is the *mahfil-i-sama'*. How elaborate this function would be depends upon the historical importance and the popularity of the shrine; for instance, at Ajmer Sharif, it is perhaps the most elaborate (Currie, 1989: 126-9; Moini, 1989: 71-2). The function is supervised by the *sajjadanashin*, who, although the living representative of the former saint, represents 'the Mughal king rather than a religious dignitary', and he comes to the *mahfil* 'escorted by the torch-bearers and mace-bearers wearing Mughal costumes' (Moini, 1989: 72). *Mahfil-i-sama'* also takes place each Thursday, under the tutelage of the *sajjadanashin*, but he does not symbolize the king on this occasion. Women and young boys are excluded from the *mahfil-i-sama'*, 'because of the temptation their presence constitutes' (Qureshi, 1986: 141). However, in modern times, they are permitted to listen to the music in case it is relayed by a loudspeaker system or is available in the form of cassettes (Currie, 1989: 126).

The Qalandars originally did not have the tradition of *qawwali* performance, but some dervishes having sympathy for them improvised their own *sama'* sessions. One may refer here to the descriptions of the *sama' khana*s of the followers of Jalal-al Din Rumi. The 'whirling' and the 'dancing dervishes' tried to have ecstatic experiences using their own techniques. Because the Qalandars adopted the lifestyle of wanderers, they could not have had the *sama'* sessions of the type of Chishtis. *Mahfil-i-sama'*, in many ways, was associated with settled living, in the Khanqah, *jamat khana*, *zawiya*, or *dera*. Once the Qalandars sedentarized, they adopted the traits of a settled Sufi living. Among them were *mahfil-i-sama'* and *qawwali*.

From the hagiography of the two saints under study, it is clear that both were fond of *sama'*. Whenever the Chishti Sufis visited them, they organized the *mahfil*s. It is not known from where the musicians and singers came and where came the verses they sang. Earlier we learnt that Nizamuddin Auliya attended one such occasion at the Khanqah of Abu Bakr. After Abu Bakr's death, it is not known whether this practice was continued at his *mazar*. We learnt from the administrators of the shrine of Abu Bakr that earlier *qawwali* performances did not take place. Sometimes the eulogies of the Prophet (*na't*) were organized.

Haji Jan Muhammad was least interested in popularizing the shrine of Abu Bakr. He was unenthusiastic about meeting the reporters from newspapers who came to the shrine to cover it in their writings. His single aim was to serve the shrine, for which he thought there was no need to have publicity. He also did not engage or permit any *qawwal*s to sing at the shrine. After Muhammad Naseem became the *sajjadanashin*, he realized the need to popularize the shrine. Since he knew the lore of *ruhani ilaj*, he came in contact with those who helped in building up the cult of Abu Bakr. Documentaries on the shrine were made for the national television channel. Since the early 1990s, the *'urs* is covered in great detail. Naseem was also instrumental in starting the *qawwali* session on Thursdays and the *'urs* because 'it attracted people'.

Today, two teams of *qawwal*s perform at the shrine of both Bu Ali and Abu Bakr. On Thursdays and the days of *'urs*, both these teams perform by turn. On other days, a couple of their members perform either just before noon or in the evening. Each team consists of three or four members – one or two on *dholak*; the main singer is seated in the middle. He plays the harmonium. There may be another harmonium player; and one or more persons who sing in chorus and clap in tune with the music. In fact, two persons – the main singer on harmonium and the *dholak* player – constitute a viable *qawwal* group. The group beyond the dyad is quite flexible. More and more singers may join who do not play on musical instruments. Young boys, some only six to seven years in age, are also apprentice members of the *qawwali* group. Harmonium and *dholak* are the main instruments of a *qawwali* performance, but sometimes other instruments, like *sarangi* (a stringed instrument played with bow) may also be added (Baljon, 1989: 194). Although women are shown in films singing *qawwali*s and participating in *qawwali* competitions, they are abstained from singing at Sufi shrines. In the past, they were not permitted to attend the *'sama* sessions. Now, they can sit in a corner of the shrine and listen to the *qawwali*s, but they are not expected to go into trance, or shower praise on the singers, or nod in approval. They are expected to be quiet listeners.

The *qawwal*s, like the *khuddam*, do not get a salary from the shrine. Their work is also interpreted as *khidmat* and is voluntary. They are barely able to make their ends meet from what they get from the pilgrims. The usual practice is that before starting a singing session, the *qawwal*s spread a large kerchief before them. They keep a little *prasad* and some rose petals over it. After having visited the shrine, the pilgrims place a little money and *prasad* on the kerchief for the *qawwal*s, who raise their pitch and beat the drums faster on seeing someone approaching them with money. The usual practice is that some visitors to the shrine put little money on the harmonium of the singer, or tuck it under the *dholak*, or leave at the feet of the *qawwal*. Some visitors divide their offering into two: the harmonium and *dholak* players are offered money separately. The offering is extremely small; rarely it is of more than ten rupees. One of the *qawwal*s quickly dispatches notes of smaller denomination and coins to his pocket, leaving higher currency notes (like of ten rupees), but not more than two, on the kerchief. The idea is that if a large number of currency notes are visible, the pilgrims may resist from giving them more, assuming that the *qawwal*s have already received quite a lot. But, this does not happen at the shrine. Currency notes and coins lie in heaps at Abu Bakr's shrine, and they are gathered after mid-night. On a weekday, the earning of a *qawwal* party is not more than twenty to thirty rupees. On Thursdays and Sundays (or holidays), it is around one hundred and fifty rupees. Many visitors to the shrine in fact do not take note of the *qawwal*s. They pray and leave.

Barring one, none of the *qawwal*s of the shrines is employed elsewhere. In other words, singing is their full-time profession. One of the senior *qawwal*s at Abu Bakr's shrine is luckier than others, for his *qawwali*s have been recorded and cassettes released. But this cassette is not dedicated to Abu Bakr. This singer also sings at private gatherings. The employed *qawwal* keeps himself free after office hours. In Bu Ali's case, a private music company has released a set of cassettes of *qawwali*s in honour of the saint. The lyric writer and singers happen to be Hindu. The *qawwali*s have borrowed the tunes of the famous cine *qawwali*s (see Appendix III). During the *'urs*, the *qawwal*s perform on the first day in the evening from five to nine. On the second day, they perform from eleven in the morning to two in the afternoon, and then from five in the evening till nine. On the last day, it is only during the pre-noon hours that they sing. The *qawwal*s halt their singing at the time of prayer. If some other parties of singers also volunteer to sing during the *'urs*, the *qawwali* schedule is chalked out well in advance accommodating all of them.

The *qawwali* session at Abu Bakr's shrine during the *'urs* celebrations is supervised by the *sajjadanashin* who comes to the gathering wearing a tall green headgear. At Bu Ali's shrine, some dignitary, often the district collector, is invited to preside over the function. The symbolism one finds in the dress of the *sajjadanashin* of Ajmer Sharif and his entry to the *sama' khana*, is not seen in Abu Bakr's shrine. The *qawwali* sessions on Thursdays are generally not attended by the *sajjadanashin*. Moreover, there is hardly any audience when the *qawwali* performance is held on other days. As said earlier, those visiting the shrine seem to be in hurry. They leave almost immediately after having performed the rituals and proceed to the *sajjadanashin* quarters for redressal of their mundane problems. During the *'urs*, however, one encounters serious audience, but, as Currie (1989: 127) found in Ajmer Sharif, many appear to be bored with music, some find it lifting, and some react to it ecstatically (like, falling prostrate on the floor and pointing a finger upwards, towards the 'world of Allah', or dancing). It may be noted here that the Sufis have warned against feigning ecstasy (*Ibid*.: 128).

Separate *qawwali*s for Abu Bakr, which narrate aspects of his life and miracles, have not yet been improvised, but his name figures in many verses: for instance,

Baba ke dar pe sir jhukane aye hain;
Matke wale Baba pe chadar chadane aye hain.

Bin mange mile sab ko Baba ke dar se;
Kami hai kya mere Baba ke khazane me;
Mazar-i-Baba mein matka chadane aye hain.

([We] have come to bow our head [i.e., to pay our respects] at the threshold of the Baba;
[We] have come to offer a sheet [after the fulfilment of vow] to Matka Pir.
[We] get everything from the Baba without asking for it;
There's no dearth in Baba's treasury;
[We] have come to offer a clay pot at the Baba's grave.)

Or, a *qawwali* ends with words such as:

Jo lena hai woh Matkewale Baba se lenge
(Whatever we want, we shall take it from Matka Pir.)

Like in case of Abu Bakr, a number of *qawwali*s sung at Bu Ali's shrine include a line where favour is sought from the saint. There are no *qawwali*s that narrate the life history of the saints or their feats. Besides them, the *qawwali* sung with great enthusiasm at the Qalandar shrines is *dama dam mast Qalandar*, which, as we said previously, is in honour of Lal Shahbaz Qalandar of Sehwan (Sind, Pakistan), but is sung because of its reference to the Qalandar tradition, and also, because of its popularity. Another *qawwali* sung here is based on the famous verses of Amir Khusrau, which he created in a state of love for his mentor, Nizamuddin Auliya: *chap tilak sab chini mose naina milaye ke*. The recent addition to the repertoire of the *qawwali*s is *mera piya ghar aya*, sung by Nusrat Fateh Ali Khan. But, to all these *qawwalis*, the individual singers add couplets that they have composed, and thus, the song becomes a little different from its original rendition. Sometimes, the *qawwals* embellish their songs with Persian verses. Songs are also structured after popular Hindi film songs (see Appendix II): one I heard was based on a song of an old Hindi film, Qismat, *kajra muhabbat wala, ankhiyon mein aisa dala, kajre ne le lae meri jan, hai mein teri qurban.*

In conclusion, we may say that in the absence of a distinct *qawwali* tradition evolved in honour of Abu Bakr or Bu Ali, the *qawwals* pick up popular film songs and compose lines to sing on those tunes. In contrast, at Ajmer Sharif and Nizamuddin Auliya, there exists a separate set of *qawwalis* especially created and sung. At the time of the *'urs* of Mu'in al-Din, the *qawwalis* are sung not only at the shrine, but also in the houses of the *pirzade* and *khuddam*, the lodges where the pilgrims stay, and at different places in the city. The entire city of Ajmer becomes a ritual theatre and the sound of *qawwali* resonates all over. Each *qawwali* is devoted to Mu'in al-Din. In this rich tradition, it is inconceivable that the *qawwals* at the *dargah* of Ajmer will sing a song written in honour of a Qalandar saint, or one based on the tune of a popular Hindi film song.

ECONOMY OF THE SHRINE

The Waqf Board manages the shrine of Bu Ali; so it provides all the expenses required for its upkeep, and it has full right over whatever the pilgrims leave in the donation-box (*dan patra*). In addition, as was noted earlier, the visitors also give some money to the *khuddam*. The caretaker whom the Waqf Board has appointed also secretly extends supernatural aid to his clients for which he receives payment, both in kind and cash. The economy of Abu Bakr's shrine is interesting because the family of the *sajjadanashin* manages it.

The family of the administrator does not keep any financial records or accounts of expenses incurred. It was virtually impossible for me to trace the records of the earlier accounts that the Hazrat Abu Bakr Tusi Dargah Committee had kept when it was active in the 1950s. As stated earlier, the D.D.A. (Delhi Development Authority) had given the right to the family of Muhammad Naseem to live on the mound and manage the shrine. The boundary of the complex was drawn in 1992. The shrine of Abu Bakr does not have any endowment (*auqaf*). Also, there is no record of a Muslim prince or noble or state giving it a grant to defray the cost of the *'urs*. The institution of regular *langar* ended after the death of Abu Bakr. It has not been revived. It implies that perhaps those managing the shrine earlier did not approach the affluent devotees for contribution. None of the shops at the base of the shrine is under the administration of the shrine; therefore, the latter receives neither rent nor commission on sale, as in other shrines.

The large *dargahs* (and Bu Ali's is one such example) need a lot of money to meet the expenses on the distribution of food, the lighting of the mausoleum, prayer carpets, flowers for the tomb, prayer leaders (*imam*) for the shrine's mosques, servants of the shrine, for those who recite the Quran, running other institutions in case they are attached to the shrine (such as, dispensaries and hospitals, educational institutions, libraries, etc.), and also for carrying out various other social welfare tasks (such as a health camp, construction of road, etc.). The Waqf Board takes care of all these tasks at Bu Ali's shrine. Abu Bakr's shrine has no employees on its roll; the servitors are all voluntary. Except the *qawwals*, the other *khuddam* get a place to stay and food from the *sajjadanashin*. They meet their pocket expenses from whatever they get from the pilgrims. It is important to note that none of them demands money for the services they provide. As no institution is attached to the shrine, the question of its maintenance does not arise.

Thus, the income of the shrine consists of the offerings made by devotees. Keeping in mind the example of Ajmer Sharif, I made enquiries on the content of offerings. Was there gold and silver jewellery, precious gems and stones, watches, foreign currency? On one occasion, during the *'urs*, there was a gift of a watch. Otherwise, devotees offer only money. As pilgrims from foreign countries are an exception, so extremely rare is the foreign currency. Equally uncommon is the offering of a silver pot, or one made of some other metal. And, it is also not known if ever a royal personage or political entity visited Abu Bakr's shrine, or made a handsome offering. About Ajmer Sharif, the gifts given to it by Emperor Akbar, or the visits of Zia ul-Haq and Parvez Musharraf are a part of the lore. The visit of an important public figure is an addition to the popularity of a shrine.

The monetary offerings to Abu Bakr's shrine are spent not only in managing it, but also for the extended family of the *sajjadanashin*. The major expense of the shrine is on electricity, not only because of the number of lamps, fans, air-conditioners, and air and water coolers (in the mausoleum, the *sahn*, and the housing complex), but it is substantially lit throughout the night. Moreover, electricity has become quite expensive these days. The *sajjadanashin* does not keep an account of the daily *chadhava* (offerings); he says that whatever they get from the shrine is sufficient for managing it.

I inquired about the procedure of emptying the donation box (*golak*). In other religious institutions with which I am familiar, there are norms clearly laid down. At Bu Ali's shrine, it is emptied in the presence of Waqf officials. It was stated earlier that one such official is permanently stationed at the shrine. At Abu Bakr's shrine, any member of the family, who later deposits money with the *sajjadanashin*, opens the *golak* every second or third day, irrespective of whether it is full or not. Moreover, I observed that devotees do not generally put money in the donation box; they prefer to place it on the *mazar*, for they think that it would please the managers of the shrine and as a result, they would be able to receive their favour. This would explain why the amount collected in the donation box is abysmally low. The *khadim* serving the shrine collects in the evening or midnight (depending upon the day of the week), the money offered at the shrine. He hands over the entire collection to the *sajjadanashin*. No *khadim* ever tries to pocket some of this money, as he knows that in case he is caught, he would lose his livelihood. The *khadim*'s existence is so open and public that if he has extra money it would be known to everyone.

After setting aside the amount needed for the expenses of the shrine (electricity, flowers, sheet, food for the *khuddam*, etc.), the rest is divided among the brothers. Although I did not come to know the total average income from the shrine, my estimate is that it may be below twenty thousand rupees a month, the bulk of which comes on Thursdays. The three days of *'urs* yield fifty to sixty thousand rupees. The number of people attending the *'urs* celebrations is estimated from the number of leaf-plates (*pattals*) used for feeding them. On average, around five thousand people eat on the first day of the *'urs*, but it should be kept in mind that some do not stay for the meals or eat at *langar*. In three days, roughly eight to ten thousand devotees visit the shrine. Close to one lakh rupees is generally spent on *'urs*, and almost the entire amount is contributed by devotees, some of whom are Hindu businesspersons of old Delhi; prominent among them is one Dinesh Mehra, who in fact is the first one to offer *chadar* on the first day of the *'urs* celebrations.

Those who have been visiting Sheikh Abu Bakr's shrine for years know that in the last five years, phenomenal changes have been brought about in the material aspects. I have been in touch with the shrine and its developments for the last more than ten years (from August 1996). In this period, the large courtyard (outside the mausoleum) and the inner courtyard (outside the houses of the *sajjadanashin*) have been roofed; the houses of the family members of the *sajjadanashin* have been repaired and painted and a couple of new rooms have been added; lamps and fans have been fitted in the upper courtyard; and air and water coolers have been installed. For none of these additions was money spent from the income of the shrine. These developmental works might have been initiated by the *sajjadanashin*, but finances for them came from the devotees, who were all Hindus. One, who bore the cost of covering the lower courtyard, believes in the concept of 'concealed donation' (*gupt dan*), and so his identity is not disclosed to anyone. One of the businesspersons from Old Delhi was a 'disciple' (*murid*) of Haji Jan Muhammad. He has contributed greatly to the developmental works at the shrine. It is believed that he has flourished in business because of Sheikh Abu Bakr's blessings. In Bu Ali's shrine also, individual devotees can make their contribution but after seeking permission from the Waqf Board. A common practice is that people vow that if their problems are solved, then they would donate a particular amount of money to the shrine or get some developmental work done. In this way, the shrine keeps on expanding.

Whenever I spoke to the *sajjadanashin* about the administration of the shrine, a question that came to my mind concerned the possibility of reconstituting the Dargah Committee. But, he was opposed to this idea, and so were his brothers. He thought that religious institutions collapsed because of these committees, as in each one of them, its members tried to maximize their gains. Furthermore, conflicts between members take place because of their personal interests. For him, the concept of a 'selfless' committee is utopian. Therefore, each *dargah* should be managed by the *sajjadanashin*, and the income, after deducting all the expenses, should be equally divided among the descendants of the saint. He was hopeful that the system operating at his *dargah* could be adopted even when the *pirzade* numbered in hundreds. However, he forgot about contesting claims to a position in the saint's genealogy. He can opt for the system of centralized control now because his family is not large and his brothers and sons are not yet a threat, but as it will enlarge, it is likely to pose problems of succession, inheritance, and division of the income of the shrine.

In addition to the income from the shrine, the brothers of the *sajjadanashin* have their own sources of livelihood. The *sajjadanashin* is also gifted cash (and material things, such as clothes, sweets, grain, etc.) from his clients who have benefitted from his *ruhani ilaj*. He never asks compensation for the service he renders. I have seen some clients offering him hundred rupees, and others who simply touch his feet after receiving the spiritual advice. As in the shrine, the clients leave the monetary gift at his feet or tuck them under the *gaddi*, so that it is not obvious to the others. Sometimes, the currency notes are tightly folded before offering. This is another way of ensuring the secrecy of the amount. The individual tries to strengthen his ties with his patron by such devices. The point is that the clients reinforce the idea that the patron provides help without exchange of money. For him, all are equal. But then, the kindness of patron must be acknowledged. The ways to do it are both material and non-material. Touching his feet, which is un-Islamic, is one way; paying him in kind or cash is another. Since he may refuse material gifts, one has to give them without his knowledge. That is the reason why money is tucked under the mattress on which he sits or gifts in kind may be left in one corner.

At Abu Bakr's shrine, Chand, one of the *khuddam*, the 'fictive' son of *sajjadanashin*, also receives gifts in the same manner, for he also independently serves the clients, but he gives his entire collection to his mentor. The latter redistributes it to Chand to pay for his immediate needs. Being unmarried and having no parental (or familial) liability, Chand does not need much. Since he has embraced Islam, his family members have severed ties with him, but sometimes his parents come to see him. He needs some money at those times.

Although clients come to the *sajjadanashin* and Chand almost every day, there is quite a crowd on Thursdays and Sundays. On average, sixty to seventy people come for consultation each Thursday and Sunday. A large number of these clients are from poorer sections, thus the monetary gift they leave for the specialists is also meagre. Rarely does it exceed twenty rupees. Some do not leave any money; they simply touch the feet of specialists and leave. People from middle and professional classes (bureaucrats, accountants, doctors, etc.), are rarely seen. However, I have come across school teachers and clerks as clients of the *sajjadanashin*.

These clients tend to pay more, fifty or even a hundred rupees. Furthermore, far more women come for consultation than men. If men are seen around, one can be sure that they are merely accompanying their wives, mothers or sisters. Women tend to spend more time with the specialists, telling them many things about their households that may have a little bearing on the problem for which they want redress. Often, they become hyperemotional and cry. As clients, men are more focused in the description of their problems. For women, a visit to the specialist performs the cathartic function, for it provides them with an opportunity to talk about their personal lives, thereby giving vent to their emotions. Further, women unhesitatingly talk about their problems in presence of other clients, mostly women. In this way, they create a bond of affinity with others, who may be having similar problems. Many women felt 'light' and relieved after talking to the *sajjadanashin*, who listened to them carefully and patiently. The specialists never seemed to be in a hurry. They gave a lot of time to each of their clients. Male clients, on the other hand, were apprehensive and hesitant relating their problems in the presence of others. Since it was difficult for them to have absolute privacy, they spoke in hushed tones. On a couple of occasions, when clients were not many, a male visitor would request the *sajjadanashin* to give him a private hearing. In that case, the *sajjadanashin* would take his client to a secluded corner of the courtyard. In a nutshell, women shared their problems with other women; men did not. Women did not protest against a collective hearing, i.e., stating their problems in presence of other women. Men were individualistic – they always wanted a private audience. Women discussed their problems with other women, and sought their counsel; men did not. Women continued to stay at the shrine after they had received 'treatment' from the specialists; men left immediately. Gender differences were also related with payment. Men generally took less time of the specialists, and always paid. Women took more time, and tended to pay less money than men. Sometimes, they did not even pay. The idea they conveyed was that since they were in the midst of a plethora of problems, it was impossible for them to make a substantial payment to the specialists. On the contrary, they wished compassion and blessings from them.

The point I intend to submit is that income from consultations is meagre. My estimate is that it rarely exceeds seven or eight thousand rupees a month. This is the personal income of the *sajjadanashin*. His brothers have no share in it.

THE SAINT IS ALIVE; HE IS THE INTERCESSOR

It is reiterated that the people after Bu Ali's death, especially the *khuddam* of Panipat, helped to retain the centrality of the shrine, as a perpetual source of spiritual sustenance and inspiration. The motives, which inspire pilgrims to visit the shrine, vary from person to person, according to his perception and circumstances of life. It is true that a majority of believers come to pay respects to the shrine to invoke the blessings of Bu Ali for fulfilment of their mundane desires simply because such needy and poor people have no succour or help, notwithstanding the opposition from the orthodox. Then, there is another group of believers, howsoever small, who come to stay for a longer period solely to meditate and pray at the shrine to cover the stages of spiritual development in their mystic path. Whatever the category of pilgrims, the fundamental fact is that the shrine is regarded as a religious place and reverence for it is deeply rooted in their hearts.

The visitors to the Sufi shrine may be divided into four categories: first, the regular visitors, they visit the shrine regularly, some are daily visitors; some come on Thursdays or Sundays. Second, the travellers: they visit the shrine since it happens to be on the itinerary of a tour. They may vow to come again, but their first visit happens to be a part of the programme. The third category comprises those who visit the shrine in moments of crises. They have heard from others the 'miracle-stories' about that saint, and visit him for good luck and a solution of their problems. The last category is of people who have a 'sudden, strong urge, as if someone is advising them to visit a shrine.' Although the ritualistic behaviour differs in each one of them, the grave and the area (the 'sacred complex') around it become a site of reverence.

One of the questions often asked is why graves become the object of veneration and why people approach the graves as if they are 'animated'?

The Deoband School of Islamic Thought has strongly opposed the worship of graves. Shah Waliullah's criticism of this is well known (Baljon, 1989; Gaborieau, 1989). But, an examination of the composition of people who visit the graves with an explicit aim to venerate them, or as pious Muslims would say, 'to read' there (*padne ke liye*, meaning 'reading certain verses from the Quran'), reveals that the orthodox Muslims are as much present there as are the liberal ones. Mahmood (1989: 40) recalls the names of many Deobandi *ulama*, who used to visit the *dargah* of Sayyed Salar Mas'ud Ghazi.

I remember one of my first visits to the shrine of Abu Bakr, with a family friend of ours, a devout Muslim, who is critical of the 'keeping of graves', which has become, according to him, a 'commercial proposition'. Although orthodox in many ways, he, like many other Muslims I met during the course of my work on the Sufis, visits the *dargahs* of prominent saints, as and when he 'feels' like visiting them, and his ritual includes no offerings' (of flowers, scented-sticks, sweets, etc.). He does not bow before the saint or kiss the grave. His practice is confined to 'recitations' from the Quran.

I had sought his help in establishing rapport with the 'caretakers' of both the shrines under study. On that day, after he had 'read' at the *mazar* of Abu Bakr, he told me that he had the feeling that 'the saint was present'. I asked him to describe this remarkable experience, but he said 'it was ineffable': in his words: 'You have a strong feeling in your heart (*qalb*) that the saint is present there.' He says that he has not fixed a particular day to visit the *dargah*, but whenever he has a strong 'feeling', he knows that he has to visit the saint, who could be from any order, and his shrine could be located in any part of the city. Whenever he has this 'feeling', he takes out time from his busy schedule to visit the nearest Sufi shrine, and recite certain verses of the Quran there. I learnt the same from many other visitors to the shrines of Abu Bakr and Bu Ali. Many claimed to have 'seen' the saint. They all believe that the saint is alive and alert (*zinda jawed*).

Stories of the miracle of omnipresence of saints are common in other religious traditions (see Babb, 1986; Laidlaw, 1995; Srivastava, 1997). Chand (the servitor at Abu Bakr's shrine) described one of his experiences. One day, he was handling the case of a woman who was possessed by an evil spirit. She was in Dehradun and it was virtually impossible for her kin to bring her to Delhi. Chand had to go there to perform the rites of exorcism (*utara*). When he started 'reciting' the verses from the Quran, it became clear to him that the 'dangerous' (*khatarnak*) and 'sullied' (*gandi*) entity was extremely powerful. Then, he had a strong feeling that Shaikh Abu Bakr was present there: 'he was sitting on a cot,' and continued to be around till the rituals of exorcism were in progress. The woman was cured after the ritual. Chand ascribed the success of the ritual to the presence of the saint.

Mohammad Naseem told me one of his experiences, which would also illustrate the concept of Qalandar. Once, while he was rendering supernatural aid to his clients, three women (from Reghar Pura, Karol Bagh) came to the shrine. They had brought with them a clay pot that was empty. Naseem told them that the earthen pitcher was never offered empty, and advised them to fill it with a fistful of roasted horse-grams or sweet balls of cardamom (*ilaichi dana*). The women knew of this, but had brought an empty pitcher on the advice of a saint who had appeared in the dream of one of them. The moment the women finished saying this, he saw an old Muslim gentleman (in shirt and trousers) standing behind them. Presumably, he had come for prayers, he thought.

The man had a magnetic personality. Even when Muhammad Naseem was reading the Fatiha, while offering the women's oblations at the shrine, he was transfixed. The man sat on the parapet. Naseem was extremely keen to speak to him. Just a few moments before he had finished the ritual (of distributing the 'blessed food'), he saw that the man was stepping down the staircase. Immediately, he ran after him, went even up to the main entrance gate to the shrine and the road beyond it, but that man was to be seen nowhere. The man 'became invisible', Naseem said. He shared this incident with his father, who remarked that the man was a saint. That night, in a dream, Naseem received a confirmation of his father's conclusion about the identity of that man.

He saw three old men sitting on a wooden cot. The one in the middle sat crossed-legged. Naseem paid homage to them. They stood up and asked him to follow them. The entire pathway was brightly lit. Suspended to the branches of small trees were lamps. Naseem wanted to touch them but the elders advised against it, warning him that if he did, the whole place would be engulfed by fire. They asked him not to follow them any further and return. Suddenly, Naseem's woke up. The old man seated in the middle had a receding hairline, but long wavy hair; he sported thin moustache and beard, wore *kurta* (shirt) and *tehmad*. On his chest were iron chains (quite like what the prisoners are made to wear), and in one of the chains around his neck was suspended a big locket. Unmistakably, he was a Qalandar.

The following day, he did not feel like going to work, although he had committed to help his three friends teach a lesson to their officer who had troubled them no end. Since Naseem absented himself from office, the others went ahead with their plan of waylaying the officer and thrashing him. The injured officer lodged a complaint with the authorities, and the three disgruntled fellows had a hard time saving their jobs. Naseem reached his office the following day and was told about the misdeed of his colleagues. The interpretation of all who listened to Naseem's proclamation of supernatural experience was that it was the divine intervention by Sheikh Abu Bakr (the saint standing behind the women in one episode and one sitting in the middle, in the other) which saved him from disgrace.

I asked people why they visited shrines. Many of them told me of the incredible experiences they have had of 'feeling' the presence of the saint. Many claimed to have benefited from the guidance the saint provided them in their dreams. The belief of the people is that the saint is alive; he is *zinda* and *jawed*. Findings of other researchers who have studied Sufi shrines corroborate my observation. For instance, Pinto (1989: 118) writes:

> Continued interviews with those who visit the *dargah* regularly... revealed their unshakeable faith that Hazrat Nizamuddin is alive. They often said, 'He is not dead. He has only put a veil between himself and us, ordinary mortals. That is why we cannot see him.' But sometimes he is believed to appear to some people. These appearances are taken as a mark of special favour and love.

The belief is as follows. After leaving the body, the soul (*ruh*) of ordinary mortals rests at one of the two places (*muqam*), Illin and Sijjin, which lie beyond the 'seventh heaven'; on the Day of Judgment (*roz-i-mahshar*, *qayamat*), their destination would be known. But, the souls (*arwah*) of saints do not ascend to the places meant for ordinary mortals; they go to the Ka'ba, from where they travel, on their own volition, to places they like most, and one of them is their grave. The bodies of ordinary beings rot ('they are eaten away by worms') but those of saints remain as they are: 'they are beyond the process of decay.' One of my respondents, quoting from the Quran, said: 'The Holy Book pronounces that they are not dead who have sacrificed themselves in the path of Allah. They are alive, but you do not know this fact' ('*mat kaho unko murda, jo Allah ki rah mein shahid ho gaye; halanki woh zinda hain, tumhe is bat ka sha'ur nahin*'). On Thursdays, when shadows lengthen, the souls of all dead descend to their graves, wherever they are located. They expect their relatives to visit them and light candles. That is why, Thursday is regarded as extremely important for visiting graves of saints. As they are likely to be there, they may fulfil the wishes of their visitors and devotees.

We noted earlier that the equivalent in Arabic language to the English word 'saint' is *wali* (plu. *awliya*). The terms *wilayah* or *walayah* may be translated as 'sainthood'. There is no passage in the Quran explicitly recognizing the institution of sainthood. It repeatedly emphasizes that Allah alone is the *wali* of the believers. The latter are strictly warned against seeking help from any but Allah. The Quran disallows intercession (*shafa'ah*) by any but Allah; there is neither *wali* nor *shafi* (intercessor) except God. But, scholars submit that the idea of 'saint' as *shafi* is indeed present in the Quran. The verse 62 of the Tenth *surah* is: 'As for the friends (*awliya*) of God, no fear shall come upon them, nor shall they grieve.' Its interpretation is that there is a 'select' band of people. They possess esoteric knowledge, and have also been guarded against committing major sins. Such people are most dear to God because of their complete devotion. These pious souls can act as *shafi*, but with God's permission. The Sufis have also drawn attention to a number of hadiths that delineate the qualities and privileges of *awliya*.

From this interpretations has developed the idea that if a person 'prays fervently to the Sufi, he will in turn present his petition to God' (Jackson 1988: 251). The presumption is that like the 'visible world' (*al-duniya*), the 'invisible world' (*al-ghaib*) is also hierarchical. The Sufi is Allah's *'ashiq* (lover), and so he stands in a different relation to Him, than those who are merely *'abd* (slaves) (Subhan, 1970: 321-2). Currie (1989: 139) puts this idea in the following words: 'To petition Allah, it is necessary first to approach an intermediary, just as to petition the local Deputy Commissioner his inferiors had first to approach the door-keepers.' One may remember here the story of Musa Shahi Suhag, a Suhrawardi saint. When it did not rain, people wanted Musa to pray to Allah. He prayed thus: 'O my husband, if you are not going to send rain at once, I am going to deprive myself of these bridal ornaments.' When he was about to break his bangles, suddenly dark clouds appeared on the sky, and it rained! (Subhan, 1970: 248).

The model of ranking in this world is extended for the other world as well. But, here is a caveat. The petitioner can always approach Allah directly, and fulfilment will come from Him and Him only, and none other. But, by submitting his petition through the intercession of a saint, the petitioner is only trying to ensure that it will be heard, for the saint is 'nearer' to Allah. Gaborieau (1983) quotes a scholar (from Lahore) who said: 'God has made the saints the governors of the universe.' Similarly, Pinto (1989: 122) concludes from the opinion of the pilgrims and the *pirzade*: 'Hazrat Nizamuddin is ... the mediator between the pilgrims and God.' A large number of people attend the *namaz* at the mosque inside the *dargah* of Nizamuddin Auliya on Thursday evenings, and on Friday and Sunday afternoons, believing that the saint prays with them and makes up for 'defects and deficiencies in their prayers' (*Ibid.*).

The saint loves all, even those who do not visit his shrine. But, sometimes he may test his devotees. When petitions are not heard, the devotees feel that the saint is testing them. They keep visiting the shrine regularly, waiting for the divine intervention. The saint may also mildly punish in order to make one a devotee. A woman (Mrs. Kalra) working in a Delhi library told me how her husband developed faith in Abu Bakr. He used to go down Mathura Road almost everyday on way to work. One of his friends told him about the shrine of Abu Bakr and the stories of his miracles, but he was skeptical. On his friend's insistence, he went to the shrine, and to show his disbelief, he kicked an earthen pitcher that had already been offered to the saint. He tossed and turned, and lay awake all night. The second night he writhed in pain, as if someone was yanking his hair. He told his mother what he was passing through. She immediately guessed the cause and advised her son to apologize to Abu Bakr. Since then, he, and later his family members, have been visiting the shrine every Thursday for the past thirty years. Each time, they distribute home cooked food (generally, *roti* and vegetables) to beggars. They believe that the saint has been very kind to them.

The list of people who attribute their success or cure to the saint's grace is long. A shopkeeper (Radhey Lal) from Old Delhi told me that a decade ago, his business suddenly collapsed. The sale reduced drastically and debts multiplied. He was able to pull on for some months, eking out his livelihood by selling his wife's jewellery. Initially, his relatives extended some help, but since they also had modest means, they could not continue to help. When his condition worsened, he decided to mortgage his small house. At one point of time, he also thought of committing suicide.

One day, when he was in Chandni Chowk looking for a job in a shop, he heard a man telling another how he recovered from penury after his visit to Abu Bakr's shrine. Immediately, Radhey Lal returned from the market, and asked his wife to accompany him to the shrine. Since they were short of money, they decided to walk. It happened to be a Thursday. Both of them prayed, asked for forgiveness, and vowed to visit the shrine to seek its grace from then on. He remembers that as they were leaving the shrine after having spent more than two hours there, they were feeling better and optimistic. It seemed to them that their problems were going to end, and so it happened. Within a week, he saw some signs of improvement; his economic condition improved and soon, he returned to his good, old days. Radhey Lal attributes all this to the saint. Since then, he visits the shrine every Sunday and also requests his kith and kin to seek the saint's blessings. But he completely avoids any counsel with the *sajjadanashin*, saying that it is not a part of the saint's worship. In fact, he is critical of the idea of supernatural cure, but then is grateful to the *sajjadanashin* and his family for looking after the shrine.

Let us take some more cases. A mentally deranged person brought by his sister to the shrine every week, is now cured. A girl who could not find a suitable match for many years, started praying at the shrine, and within a few weeks of her regular attendance (*hazri*), she got a good husband and caring parents-in-law. After her marriage, she went there with her parents and in-laws to thank the saint. Another married woman was greatly harassed by her husband. A neighbour of hers (who was a regular visitor to the shrine) advised her to pray to Abu Bakr; she followed the advice and now her husband has been transformed into a gentle and loving person. Before appearing for an interview for the post of a teacher at a public school, a woman prayed for her appointment, standing at the foot of the shrine. She got the job, and since then, she has been visiting the shrine regularly.

Some visitors (like Radhey Lal) to the shrine place their requests and wishes before the saint, and after distributing the food or *prasad* among other visitors and beggars, leave without meeting the *sajjadanashin*. They believe that only Allah hears petitions and grants them. The saint, at best, can intercede on behalf of the pleader. They do not believe in approaching the *sajjadanashin* (or, any other 'spiritually qualified' person) for help. Some of my respondents did not have faith in supernatural therapies that *pirs* give. They believe in approaching God directly, perhaps through the intercession of the saint. The others were not skeptical of the power and efficacy of the supernatural treatment, but of the people who claimed to be providing it.

However, there were cases of those whose primary motive was to come to the shrine to seek supernatural solution to their problems. A university teacher I met had come to thank the *sajjadanashin* for helping him in retrieving his daughter's dog, an expensive Pekinese. It so happened that the neighbour had his eyes on this lovely dog, and once while it was unattended, the man took it away. Since it was the teacher's married daughter's dog, it perturbed him no end. He visited the *sajjadanashin* who gave him a piece of paper with a verse of the Quran written on it, and asked him to fold it and keep as heavy a weight on it as possible. The gentleman kept a chest of drawers on it. On the third day, the man who had stolen the dog brought it back, apologizing and very fearful. He explained that for three days and nights, neither did the dog eat or drink, nor did it sleep, nor did he himself eat or sleep. He lay awake restless and full of trepidation. At that time, he thought that the best solution to all this would be to return the dog and tender a profuse apology. The teacher did visit Abu Bakr's grave, but it was *sajjadanashin*'s fame that had brought him there. But this does not happen at Bu Ali's shrine, since the caretaker does not advertise his ability to render supernatural help, although the objects and ingredients used for this cure are kept in his office.

Some of my respondents were against getting the amulets and talismans prepared by the so called *pirs*, for they were ill-qualified and were using their little knowledge in commercial pursuits. About the *sajjadanashin* of Abu Bakr's shrine, some of my respondents said that he did not know the art of writing *tawiz*. He wrote all of them, irrespective of the problem of the client, with the same pen (ball-point), and did not care to follow the rules about time, place, and material for writing. The type of amulet depends upon the nature of the problem. Above all, the amulet-writer should be a pious Muslim, who practices austerities, and has transcended the commercial motives. My respondents said that highly qualified amulet-writers, possessing the required characteristics, certainly existed, but those who worked at the *dargahs* and *mazars* had half-baked knowledge. Their aim was to make as much money as possible. Not only should they be avoided, but also the gullible public saved from their ruses. Devotees of Abu Bakr belonging to these two categories desist from cultivating a relationship with the *sajjadanashin*, and they follow the same pattern in other *dargahs* that they visit. By comparison, there are visitors who have unshakable faith in the treatment that the *sajjadanashin* provides. They primarily come to seek his counsel, and not to visit the shrine. However, they think that going away without paying their respects to the saint may make them lose out on the saint's blessing. Some feel that this may annoy the saint with disastrous consequences. Nevertheless, there are a few who leave soon after consulting the *sajjadanashin* or his disciple.

From a comparative study of the visitors to the shrine, we can arrive at two models of intercession between human beings and God. The first is that the saints are the intercessors; the second is that the *pirs*, the 'officials' at the shrine (the *sajjadanashin*, the *pirzade*) are the intercessors between their clients and the dead saint, who in turn links them to Allah. In other words, the *pirs* mediate the relation between the individual and the saint; and the latter mediates the relation between the *pir* and Allah. Some approach Allah through their *pir*; some through the saint; and some approach Him directly, without any intercession. The saint's nearness to God is derived from his dedication and performance of austerities, whereas the *pir*'s influence over the saint is derived, in addition to devotion, from his purported links of kinship. The visitors are free to choose from these models, but which of these they choose depends upon their intellectual level, social background, peer and relatives' group, and the nature of their problems.

BEHAVIOUR OF PEOPLE AT THE SHRINE

A visit to the tomb is called *ziyarat*, a word that comes close to denoting the place itself. Muslim visitors read the Fatiha and, sometimes, the last three *suras* before making a personal request. One of the most common reasons for the devotees to visit the shrine is to seek a child. In many of the shrines, unmarried women pray so as to get suitable grooms. Quite often, as we saw earlier, strings, rags, and green bangles are tied to the latticed windows (*jali*) in the shrine while seeking the boons. Miniature cradles too are hung on trees to remind the saint of one's wish while seeking children. In the shrine of Bu Ali, two betel leaves (*pan*) are offered – one is left there and the other is to be eaten by the childless couple. New crops are offered and hung in the *dargahs* after the harvest is over. In some of the shrines, the new milk of the cattle too is offered.

There are standardized ways of behaving at the shrine, irrespective of the community to which the visitor belongs. As in mosques, the visitors should cover their knees and heads. A cap or handkerchief is used for covering the head. Hindus generally do not wear caps; they make use of their handkerchief. Women cover their heads with wraps. These rules are relaxed for children. The visitors may go to pray at the shrine without taking with them any offerings. They may make a monetary offering after the prayer. They may take with them offerings even when they have not made any petitions or their wish has not been fulfilled. But, once wishes have been fulfilled, it is expected of them that they would redeem their pledge. The quality of offerings may vary. For instance, the sheet for the grave may be from coarsest and cheapest material to richly worked embroidered silks and velvets costing several thousand rupees. This depends upon the economic condition of the devotee. Similarly, at Abu Bakr's shrine, the earthen pitcher may be a clay one, a metal one, or may be jewel-studded.

Performance of a brief ceremony around the grave of Bu Ali and Mubarak Khan is a distinguishing feature of their visit. This includes supplications and prayers to the tomb, sprinkling perfume on it, burning incense sticks, and lighting lamps (particularly on Thursdays). It is customary to strew a handful of rose petals or chains of flowers or nosegays over the tomb. Some visitors may also be given dried flowers as blessing to be swallowed. With all this, they wish to please the saint, and be near him. Some visitors will not only touch the railing around the grave, but also kiss it or kiss the threshold. To sweep a saint's tomb is a meritorious act, often performed in fulfilling a vow.

Once this is done, the rest of the time is spent in offering prayers, reciting the Quran (if Muslim), meditating, etc. Given the sacredness of the place and its serene atmosphere, the devotees feel blessed when engrossed in worship and prayer within the precincts of the shrine. The casual observers, who are mainly attracted to ceremonies, customs and conventions in practice at the shrine without understanding their deeper significance, have generally overlooked the religious aspect of the pilgrimage.

It appears that certain rules and regulations at the shrine were based on Sufi traditions and local customs to maintain discipline and orderliness among visitors, particularly during the performance of *'urs*. This unwritten code of behaviour prescribed for a devotee or a casual visitor concerned the manner and style of performing rites, making prayers and reciting the Fatiha. For instance, the system of *kalid bardari* (key keeping) of the shrine is directly borrowed from the practice at Ka'ba (Mecca) and also, on the routine of many a famous temples of India. The setting of the *qawwali mehfil*s during the *'urs* days and on every Thursday, and the frequent use of the terms and words in the daily working and routine of the shrine (such as *toshak khana* [store room], *nima* [inner cloth sheet], *chanwar* and *farrasha*s [sweeps made of peacock feathers], and *bangla* [tying of floral net around the grave]) indicate the *adab* (honorable convention) that was borrowed from the court of a ruler. The system of cooking food in a big cauldron (*deg*) was probably borrowed from the practice at Ajmer Sharif.

The modes of worship differ. Hindus do not kiss the steps to the shrine; they touch them with their foreheads or with their hands that they bring to caress the forehead. When inside the mausoleum, they stand in a corner with palms joined, or arms crossed, or arms hanging in front with their hands crossed. Rarely do they kneel down, cupping their palms in an action of prayer. They do not know the Fatiha, but if they wish it, then the servitor reads it on their behalf. Muslims, on the other hand, kiss the steps, the gate, the pierced-screens, and the pendentives of the arches. They read verses from the Quran. Prostration before the grave and its circumambulation is common to both Hindus and Muslims. For Hindus, it is *parikrama* (moving around the deity), which is an important temple ritual. Both Hindus and Muslims lift the consecrated sheet covering the shrine and touch their eyes with it, or pull it over their heads. Many visitors sit in the vicinity of the shrine in passive and receptive silence. In this way, they try to absorb the grace of the saint, who is 'present there'. Others meditate there. Many simply reiterate their petitions and vows. At Bu Ali's shrine, one may also see people reading the Quran, as is common in other shrines (Currie, 1989: 120). In other words, there are similarities in the modes of veneration; at the same time, people blend it with their own symbols. For instance, for Hindus, the Sufi shrine is 'like a temple'. I have come across both Jains and Sikhs visiting the shrine. Christian visitors have been rather insignificant.

We noted earlier that people come with petitions and requests to the shrine. Some of them are written on chits, concealed in small pieces of cloth, sewn, and then tied to the grills. Threads or strips of cloth (called *herak*) are also tied. At Bu Ali's shrine, people also put locks. The practice of tying threads or putting locks to the grills of the shrine performs two purposes. It is a gentle reminder to the saint of their petitions. Also, the people remind themselves of the commitment they have to keep in case their requests are granted. After the fulfilment of the wish, the person is expected to visit the shrine with the offerings (of food, sweets, or the special items) and unknot the thread he had tied. He is permitted to untie any of the threads tied there. At Bu Ali's *dargah*, he will open any lock with the keys hanging therein.

Women are permitted entry in both the Qalandar shrines. However, in the inner chamber, none other than the servitors can go. But I learnt that earlier, at Abu Bakr's shrine, like in any other *dargah*, women were not allowed to go inside the *mazar*. The change came after the D.D.A. demolished its outer wall. The then administrator of the shrine decided not to impose the taboo. It only reflected the spirit of the changing times. Some of my respondents thought that Qalandar saints were different from others, as they did not keep a gender distinction. One of the explanations was that because the number of Hindus attending the shrines was far more, and in their temples, no prohibitions were imposed on female entry, this would restrict the number of visitors. However, there is a flaw in this explanation because the number of Hindus attending Nizamuddin Auliya's shrine is also very high, yet there are restrictions on women there. Some Muslim respondents of mine said that if the administration of the shrines becomes more Islamized, the taboo on women's entry is bound to come. But women are not in favour of any custom that disallows their entry. In spite of orthodox Muslims favouring ban on women, it does not seem likely to come in force in the near future.

Situated on a mound, Abu Bakr's shrine is a pleasant place to spend a summer evening or winter day. Similarly, Bu Ali's shrine has a vast courtyard. Visitors come with their families and spend few hours there. Other authors (see Jackson, 1989: 110) have also noted that visits to *dargah*s on Thursdays and *'urs* are also considered as 'outings'. In many contexts, these are also market days (see Siddiqui, 1989: 22). A petty bazaar comes up at the shrine. At Abu Bakr's shrine, on the days of *'urs* some kind of a fair (*mela*) is held. On Thursdays, the two shops selling ritual ingredients extend their counters. A few balloon and ice-cream sellers stand outside the entrance.

Some authors (Rose, 1919, for example) say that from the perspective of Muslim visitors making a pilgrimage to a Sufi shrine is an act of worship comparable to seeing the Holy Ka'ba. The pilgrims adore the shrine in the same way as one worships Allah in the Ka'ba. They spread covers on the graves, kiss them, and circumambulate them, reciting vocal or silent *dhikr*. They make vows to the saint; they sacrifice animals in his name, though we did not come across this at either of the shrines under study. They consider the water used to wash the grave as a benediction comparable to the water of Zamzam well. Coming in processions to the shrine, with standards (*alam*), musicians, dancing girls, drinking alcohol and consumption of drugs, they, after their canonical prayers, take away relics, parts of the offerings or a bit of veils, or handful of earth. The core of these rituals at the *'urs* (such as prayer inside the saint's grave) is similar to Islamic pilgrimage in the Middle East.

We saw many of these things happening at the shrine, but the devotees were neither drunk nor drugged. The processions sometimes included musicians, but never did we come across dancing girls. People bought mementos; took with them *tabarruk*, but not parts of the veils. Taking a bit of the earth was also not a common practice.

Currie (1989) says that pilgrims to the grave shrines are also engendered by the possibility of pollution emanating from the holy grave, and, therefore, fragrant essences are used at the shrines. Such fragrant odours are used to endow pilgrims with blessings. Desai (1989) writes that a fragrant sandalwood paste is thus smeared on the tomb and then washed with water. This water is collected in a basin and distributed as *tabarruk*. The sheet offered to the saint is green, since this colour symbolizes the House of the Prophet, signifying sanctity. People give offerings in order to show respect and deference for the dead to gain merit, forgiveness and blessings, to endow the grave area with an aura of sanctity, to appease the soul of the dead, and to gain an insight into their fate. Flowers combine both pleasant smell and attractive colour to create a powerful and sacred symbol (Siddiqui, 1989). Flowers as offerings, left on the grave, then taken back and given to pilgrims are charged with the mystic power (*baraka*) of the saint. In West Bengal, writes Roy (1983), women are given amulets (*maduli*) containing dried flowers from a saint's grave.

CELEBRATIONS AT THE SHRINE

The shrine closes for the night with a small ceremony, which is connected with closing of the doors. The whole shrine is cleaned, and all the flowers, dust, and ash of incense sticks, are collected in a special dustbin, later distributed among the visitors as *tabarruk*. Every Thursday evening, a special gathering is arranged in the courtyard, in front of the shrine, and a sheet of cloth (*farsh*) is spread for the people to sit on. The Fatiha is recited and then the *qawwal*s sing religious and devotional songs in praise of the saint.

The major function at a Sufi shrine is the *'urs* of the saint. Celebrated for three days, at Abu Bakr's shrine, it begins on 21 Rajab. It symbolizes the 'marriage' (or, union) of the saint with God, which is possible only after death (Jeffery, 1981: 167). It is a moment of celebration; that is why, it is referred to as *'urs mubarak*. Compared to the *'urs* celebrations at the *dargah*s of Mu'in al-Din and Nizamuddin Auliya, or even at the shrine of Bu Ali, those at Abu Bakr's shrine are simple and informal.

Three days prior to the annual *'urs* at Bu Ali's shrine, people in new clothes gather in the courtyard, Qalandars and *faqir*s arrive from Delhi, and other parts of Haryana and Punjab, with sticks (*charri*s) and big and small flags. The *khuddam*, devotees, and others form a procession at the gate, accompanied by a troupe of musicians and pay homage. The schedule changes during the three days of *'urs*, i.e., 9 to 12 Ramzan. The grave is bathed (*ghusal*) twice a day with rose water, perfume (*itr*) is sprinkled, and the doors opened then for the general public. All the three days, a *sama'* ceremony is held. The people offer cash to the *qawwal*s. In other parts of the shrine, devotees may be seen praying, or listening to the musicians, or meditating quietly. The unending stream of visitors comes with garlands or bunch of flowers, or a sheet. In the evening, the shrine is illuminated. Large tents are put up, and the local tent shops provide (some of them, without any charges) durries and sheets, chairs, fans, loud speakers, mikes and lights for this occasion.

Food is prepared in large quantity, and distributed to one and all. The cost of food and cooking is met by the donors and rich merchants or devout, though the Waqf Board covers these expenses as well as the expenditure incurred in the maintenance of the *dargah*. During *'urs* days, the whole area looks like a fair (*mela*) with vendors, hawkers, wayside shops selling wares and memorabilia associated with Bu Ali. Local dignitaries, social and political leaders, are invited and felicitated by the *mujawir* and members of the Waqf Board. Special entertainment programmes are held to keep the audience busy and enthralled through the night. On the third day, *na't khwani* is held for the closing of festivities. The pilgrims and devotees are given enough *tabarruk* (flowers, sandal powder, *ilaichi dana*, thread) of the *'urs* so that they can distribute these back home.

At Abu Bakr's shrine, on the first day, early in the morning, the grave is bathed (*ghusal*) with rose water and sandal paste is applied to it. No special class of people is appointed for this purpose. The male *khuddam* perform this ritual. Since I knew that because of my gender, I would not be permitted to participate in this ritual, I requested if they could allow my husband to see how the grave is washed. The answer that I received from the caretakers was that '*ghusal* takes place in an enclosure' (*ghusal parde mein hota hai*) and no outsider, except the *khuddam*, is expected to be present there. A bath is a private ritual, and more so, because of the belief that the 'saint is alive'. And, what is public is the water used for bathing. It is collected by the caretakers, and then distributed among the devotees as *tabarruk*. There is no tank at the bottom of Abu Bakr's shrine where the consecrated water could be collected, as exists, for example, in the *dargah* of Salar Mas'ud Ghazi (Mahmood, 1989: 37-8). After bathing the grave, it is covered with new sheets and fresh flowers, specially roses.

In the evening of the first day of *'urs*, groups of people, from different parts of city, carrying baskets of flowers and sheets (*chadar*) on their heads, come to the shrine. At Abu Bakr's shrine, big processions of people carrying sheets come from the National Sports Club, Katra Neel (in Chandni Chowk), and Bhairon Mandir. The caretakers and *sajjadanashin* of the other *dargah*s also arrive. After offerings, the devotees perform veneration. Then, food is served, which continues till late night when every visitor has eaten. The most important official function of *'urs* is singing of *qawwali*s, which is held every evening. It is also held during day on the second and third days of the *'urs* celebrations. The 'singing of *qawwalis*' is also known as *mehfil-e-sama'*, as it induces among the listeners a state of ecstasy and trance. The singing commences after an elder (or, *sajjadanashin* in the case of Abu Bakr's shrine) has read the Fatiha.

After the *mehfil* ends, people prepare to sleep in the courtyard of Bu Ali's shrine. But, since Abu Bakr's shrine does not have an adequate space, visitors hailing from Delhi go home to return the following morning. On the second and third day, the proceedings are normally delayed because the visitors get up late, after having remained awake for a longer part of the night. Food is served to visitors in late afternoon. The *qawwali* session takes place in the evening, which continues till early morning. The ceremony of Kul Sharif, in which *na't khwani* (eulogy of the Prophet) takes place, is performed on the third day, followed by the Fatiha. Then, like the two preceding days, food is served. After this, the pilgrims start to leave. However, some may continue to stay for a few more days at the shrine. A couple of days after the *'urs*, the grave is bathed again. Then, the shrine returns to the normal ritual status.

Since Abu Bakr died on 20 Ramzan, the month of fasting, the devotees break their fast after prayer. All Muslim celebrations also take place at the shrine. Though, officially, there is no *langar*, invariably, a devotee of Abu Bakr, organizes the distribution of food at the shrine. Both Diwali and Holi are also 'celebrated' here. The shrine is lit up on Diwali. During the day, Hindus come in large number to pray. On the day of Dulhendi (when people play with colours), several Hindus play *holi* with the saint, which again reinforces the idea about his being alive. They smear the shrine with colour. A Hindu family from old Delhi distributes clothes to beggars on the occasion of Holi. Visits of Hindus to the Sufi shrines on the days of their festivals has been a well known practice in the past also. At Bu Ali's shrine, the celebration of Hindu festivals is less conspicuous.

Although Abu Bakr was a Muslim, his shrine, however, has become a meeting point of two religious communities, the Hindus and Muslims. As noted earlier, Jains and Sikhs also come there, but they mostly consult the *sajjadanashin*. It is well known that the eunuchs go in large number to Bu Ali's shrine. As said previously, most of the people who come for consultation with the *sajjadanashin* and Chand are from lower economic strata, but visitors to the shrine are highly diverse. I have met both highly educated and non-literate people at the shrine. Almost seventy to seventy-five per cent visitors to Abu Bakr's shrine are Hindu and eighty per cent of the contribution to the developmental and charitable works comes from them. Other writers (for example, Sleeman, 1858; Crooke, 1897, 1968; Rockey, 1913; Schwerin, 1981) have also drawn attention to the presence of a large number of Hindus at Sufi shrines. Mujeeb (1993: 405) wrote:

> I remember that shortly after the orgy of violence in Bihar I visited the grave of a Sufi on the banks of the Ganges. The Muslims living in the *dargah* had fled and the place looked desolate. But soon a group of Hindu women appeared. They performed circumambulations and prostrations, as if nothing had happened that affected their sentiments of veneration for the tomb of a Muslim saint.

Moini (1989: 63) noted that in the Ajmer Sharif, non-Muslims had held important positions of *mutawwalli* (custodian) and *amin* (revenue officers).

Let me now take up the question of why Hindus come to Sufi shrines in a large number. The usual answer that among the Muslims, there are two divisions, one of those who favour veneration of dead saints, and the other, which is opposed to such practices. The former has two categories: the first includes those favouring Sufis who are the 'people of the Shariat' (the Bashar saints), and the second is of those having respect for Beshar saints (such as Bu Ali, Abu Bakr). If one follows this division, assuming equality in each category, it is clear that only twenty-five per cent Muslim would favour Qalandar shrines.

But, let us look at this from the perspective of one of the major distinctions between Islam and Hinduism, which is with respect to the conceptualization of God. Islam adheres to the tenet that there is no God except one and Muhammad is his messenger. By comparison, although having the concept of monotheism, Hinduism is pluralistic, polytheistic, and syncretic. It is far easier for a Hindu than a Muslim to accept a divine entity for veneration, regardless of the religion (or sect) to which he may belong. It is well known that Hindus hold the deities of Jains, Buddhists, Sikhs, and even Christians in great respect. Against this background, for a Hindu to 'worship' graves is in line with his pluralism.

Let us look at the characteristic features of a Sufi shrine in India. First, its appeal transcends the boundaries of community and caste by attracting people drawn from different sectors of society. It consequently acts as a powerful syncretic force in a world that has variety in religion, belief and custom (Roy Burman, 2002). The shrine serves to bridge the gap between elites and masses of all religions by attracting both to a common centre in different ways. Second, the shrine acts as a means of integrating local cultural systems into a larger one. Third, the shrine owns and controls considerable economic resources like property, land, cash, and income. Lastly, it becomes a symbol of power, both spiritual and secular. It is spiritual in the sense of its association with God and fulfillment of earthly desires through acceptance of prayer. It is secular in the sense that economic wealth and social status could be transmitted to the individual or individuals concerned with its administration.

The *dargah*s also develop a composite culture through the elaborate cultural programmes, which also provide entertainment and recreation to people, during the *'urs*. Donations are collected from members of all communities, and they are expected to participate. The rituals performed on the days of *'urs* are shared by Muslims and Hindus, and embody faith in the power of the saint to mediate between the local people and the supernatural, and it is sustained by local syncretic traditions.

Furthermore, the cultural significance of *dargah*s provides a holistic dimension to human existence. In many of the *dargah*s, especially that of Rabia Basri and Bu Ali, we come across the myth of the saints having tamed tigers or ridden on fishes and horses. Often, these shrines are located in forests and sacred groves (we know, Bu Ali lived in the jungles of Buddha Khera in the later years of his life). They throw a subtle message of cohabitation with nature, thus reinforcing the moral principles of social existence, biodiversity and conservation.

Sufi shrines also offer solace and psycho-medical cures and remedies to people. One can also offer silken or satin covers, or pieces of cloth that are put over the grave, and then taken away to be presented to some high-ranking visitors. Smaller pieces of cloth that have been in touch with the grave are often given to girls for their trousseaux to secure the saint's blessings. The visitors may also receive some sweetmeat (*mithai*) as *tabarruk*. At Bu Ali's shrine, once the vow is fulfilled, the devotee is supposed to offer *niyaz* of cooked rice, mutton and yogurt. Many Khanqahs have been popular in the past for certain dishes. It is believed that saints feel pacified when certain particular gifts are given to them – for instance, to Salar Masud, a flag is offered. Some saints prefer white roosters or goats. Emperor Jehangir dedicated one of the huge cauldrons to the sanctuary where he had been born. To offer something at Mu'in al-Din's tomb, or have it repaired, embellished or enlarged, could form the contents of a vow in times of dangers or ailment. The dust of Burhanuddin Mahmud's tomb is given to children for intellectual progress. Sher Shah of Multan is a protector of persecuted lovers. Special rites add to the general blessings obtained by the visit. Pilgrims squeeze under the Bhishti Darwaza (Abu Bakr's shrine) to enter the sanctuary that secures the future entrance to the Paradise. At the *'urs* of Qadir Wali Saheb in Tanjore, pots with milk and rice pudding (*kheer*) are smashed on the sea shore and people rush to get a drop of the liquid, for it aids the fulfilment of their wishes. These examples show that the *dargah*s can also be analyzed psychologically, from the point of view of their function to keep the mental stability of people intact in times of crises.

Concluding Observations

The Islamic resurgence can be traced to the Middle East War of 1967 and Iranian Revolution (also known as Islamic Revolution) of 1978-79. In its wake, it has brought a wide range of Islamist and neo-fundamentalist movements into the public sphere. It has also occasioned a revival of Sufism and other related devotional movements. Most scholars agree that Islamist ideology and movements are a distinctly modern phenomenon. Sufism, on the other hand, has been presented and has often presented itself as anti-modernist and anti-reformist. It had long been taken for granted that Sufism was largely disappearing and retained a foothold among backward, often rural, segments of the population. Arberry (1950: 122) and Baldick (1989) thought that Sufi orders in many places were attracting the 'ignorant masses, but no man of education would care to speak in their favour.' Geertz (1960, 1968), Gellner (1969, 1981, 1992) and Ahmed (1988, 1992, 1993) examined the inevitable shift from the 'classical styles' of Islam (or 'maraboutism') centred on rural miracle-working saints and mystics to 'scripturalism' (or 'scriptural Islam') of urban scholars. For Geertz and Gellner, Sufism was moribund, destined to decline once and forever, with passing away of the traditional society. Gilsenan (1967, 1973, 1985) argued that the functions performed by Sufi orders in the past were now being ably executed by other institutions, such as trade unions, political associations, schools, etc.

In opposition to this, a different argument concerning the relationship of Sufism and modernity has been made. Ansari (2001) and Voll (1972, 1980,

1995) have taken note of the worldwide wave of Sufi-led *jehad* movements against colonial powers of the late nineteenth and early twentieth centuries. Their militancy in these cases contrasts with the peace loving, tolerant, and inclusivistic attitudes commonly attributed to Sufis.

Further, during the last three decades or so, the academic study of Sufism and Sufi orders has experienced a remarkable expansion. Several publishing houses (Hurst & Co., Curzon) have initiated book series dedicated to Sufism. A number of specialist journals have emerged (such as *Journal of the Ibn Arab Society, Ayn-al Hayat, Journal of the History of Sufism, Islam and Muslim Societies*). Some neo-traditional scholars (such as Seyyed Hossein Nasr, Syed Nagiub Al-Attas) have contributed to a renewed appreciation of Sufism among Western educated Muslims. Several encyclopaedia and compendia have been published on Sufism (like the *Encyclopaedia of Sufism*, or the volume edited by De Jong and Radtke, 1999). In other words, Sufism has gained tremendously in modern and modernizing settings. It has become a conspicuous aspect of urban middle class religiosity. Many believers express their interest in and sympathy with the mystical tradition in Islam, which they think is more open, inclusive and tolerant of others. In contrast to the fundamental versions of Islam, Sufism is believed to create unity in a multiethnic world. It is indeed a remarkable fact that Sufism has adapted well to the global world, producing a whole genre of works, compositions, arts and crafts, poetry and music.

My work on the antinomian Sufi cult is situated in this context. What has inspired me to study it is the vibrancy of Sufi shrines. In other words, the practices, institutions, and intellectual traditions associated with Sufism have adapted well to modernity. I have also explored in this work the adequacy of various analytical frameworks to account for the observed manifestations of contemporary Sufism. Why does Sufism appeal to urbanites and others at the forefront of vast changes appearing as a consequence of globalization? One of my objectives in this work has been to explore the meaning that Sufism has in a multicultural and plural society.

Let me here distinguish an anthropological study of religion from a theological one. For a theologian, religion is real and true, a divine revelation, or a message that an incarnation of God delivered. The words of God, his messenger or incarnation, are infallible and unfaultable. They transcend time and space, and are eternally applicable to all human beings till their species exists in the world, which once again depends upon the divine wish that none knows. For a theologian, the subject matter of study is the complex of words and messages of God, and their earnest interpretations by 'blessed' scholars, which are now assembled in texts what earlier were transmitted orally. A theological study is not only based on texts, but also borne out of the fact of 'believing in divinity'. A theologian reposes his faith in the world of divine beings he studies. In other words, a theologian is concerned with the truth or falsity of religion.

By comparison, an anthropologist studies the religious beliefs and practices of people from a distance, dispassionately and without taking sides. He begins with the premise that religious beliefs and rituals are 'real' and 'truthful' for people who sincerely subscribe to and live by them. But for their anthropological investigation, they are treated as 'as if real', and need to be studied with as much of objectivity as possible. The anthropologist is neither a believer nor a non-believer. He begins with the idea that what he is studying is real for people, who have firm faith in their religion, in its efficacy, in the powers of gods and goddesses, but for him, they are neither real nor false. The anthropological task is to find out the meaning that religious reality has for people, the mass of believers.

Furthermore, an anthropologist is aware of the fact that in a literate society, a vast corpus of literature exists on peoples' religious beliefs and practices. The commands of God for men, the pieces of advice that spiritual intellectuals have given from time to time, and their myriad interpretations, some sincere, some blasphemous, have been well documented, and are available for research and understanding. The sole aim of an anthropologist, however, is to study how people actually live in accordance with the scriptural knowledge. Are deviations permitted from it, and if they are, to what extent?

This question is investigated in each anthropological study of religion, but more so, in the anthropology of Islam, for Islam offers the paradigm of a unified religion – one God (Allah), one Prophet (Muhammad), one Book (the Quran), and one set of 'Five Pillars' of faith (*khatmul ambiya*) (belief in the oneness of God and finality of the Prophet; praying [*namaz*] five times a day; paying welfare tax [*zakat*]; fasting during Ramadan, the ninth month of the Islamic lunar year; and performing the annual pilgrimage [*hajj*] to the Ka'bah once in one's adult lifetime). For being a Muslim, one is required to have full faith in them. Here, we come across the claim and belief of some Muslims that there is no other reality except what has been revealed in the Holy Book, and in the sayings (hadith) and deeds (*sunnah*) of the Prophet. Juxtaposed with this is a vast majority of Muslim communities all across the world, which, while not swerving from scriptural Islam, brings in a host of other beliefs, customs, and practices to amicably coexist with it. One such tradition, the Islamic moorings of which are rarely doubted, is Sufism. Many Muslim respondents of mine were hesitant in including Sufism within the framework of Islam. Some thought that Islamic principles have been diluted due to the Sufi onslaught. Thus, today Sufism is known more than Islam (see, Chaudhary, 1998).

Regardless of what die-hard adherents to scriptural Islam think, the fact is that today Sufism has swayed the world. Not a day passes when a reference to Sufism does not come in media in one context or the other – it may be the celebration of Jalaluddin Rumi's *Mathnavi*, or the recital of a Sufi master, or the *'urs* of a saint, or the former prime minister of India offering a sheet to Mu'in al-Din Chisthi's *dargah*. Contemporaneously, Sufism has become, what I would call, a 'canopy term', comprising a wide variety of thoughts and practices, different 'specializations' (from singing to dancing, from painting to healing), some explicitly religious, some manifestly secular. A man, who gives up drinking alcohol and smoking, and non-vegetarian food, is said to lead a 'Sufi life', regardless of the fact that many Sufi masters ate meat, drank wine, and smoked. Folk dances of Egypt are conveniently classified as 'Sufi dances', although many of them have nothing to do with the dance of 'whirling dervishes'. A *ghazal* singer from Pakistan is advertised as a 'Sufi singer', and perforce she sings a Sufi couplet to justify her label. Moreover, Sufism is not just confined to Muslims – a number of Sufi saints, discoursers, poets, painters, dancers, singers have been from other religious communities, particularly from the Hindu in India.

Cruising through the literature on Sufism, I found that the foci of attention of scholars and investigators have been the well-known shrines (such as of Mu'in al-Din Chishti, Nizamuddin Auliya), especially the ones that enjoyed royal patronage in medieval times. Here, it may also be pointed out that many popular shrines having specific healing traditions have not been the objects of a full-fledged ethnographic investigation. At best, one comes across short articles on them. And, in so far as Pakistan and Bangladesh are concerned, which have some well-known shrines (such as of Golra Sharif, Baba Farid, Bahauddin Zakaria, Data Ganjbaksh Ali Hujwari, Lal Shahbaz Qalandar), we do not have an anthropological study of any one of them.

Thus, one of my first observations is that notwithstanding the contemporary popularity of Sufism, and the media being saturated with it, anthropological studies of Sufi shrines can be counted on fingertips. In fact, anthropology of Indian Muslims is rather a thin discipline. And, most of the studies that have been carried out on Muslims have been by Muslim investigators. When even well known shrines have not been studied, what to speak of their lesser known counterparts, which are spread all over the length and breadth of the country and are culturally effervescent places of veneration, counselling, and healing. Of course, some writers (like Roy, 1983; Roy Burman, 1996, 2002) have tried to prepare their catalogue in a specific region, rendering a short account of each one of them.

My other observation is that Sufism is presented in media and popular works as a homogeneous movement. Indubitably, the meeting point of all

Sufi traditions is their argument in favour of the unity of all human beings. They have time and again stated that God has created all beings, privileging them with equal rights. Thus, the distinctions between them, some of which are highly discriminatory and rancorous, are human-made. That is the reason why Sufism has promoted not only integration in a plural society, but has also kept alive the enormous diversity of cultures. So, when a Hindu goes to a Sufi *dargah*, he folds his palms, suggestive of the ritual action of salutation (*namaskar*), before the saint, seeking his blessings in the same way as they would do in a temple. Standing proximate to a Hindu in the same shrine may be a Muslim, who spreads his palms in the ritual action of prayer (*dua*). Both close their eyes to seek the saint's favour by rendering prayers according to their respective religious traditions. While a Hindu may recite a holy litany (*mantra*) in a Sufi shrine, a Muslim would read a *kalma*, or *ayat*, or *durud* from the Quran. Both are seeking the saint's blessings, but in different ways. Sufism has encouraged diversity to perpetuate. People are permitted to follow their own ways of entreating the saints. They transport ritual actions from their respective religions to Sufi shrines.

But, it does not imply that there is no standard procedure to be followed in the shrine. For instance, there is a uniform method of offering Fatiha and taking the vow (*mannat*). Similarly, set procedures exist for meditation. Certain beliefs and practices are commonly shared, like visitation of souls to their burial sites, lighting lamps on Thursdays, etc. These uniformities exist because the Sufi saints are Muslim believing in the oneness of God. One of the Sufis' aims has been to serve people with the teachings of Islam. The Sufis are believed to have treated all their visitors equally, since they are Allah's *bande* (people). They knew that unless they furthered the idea of the unity of all religions, without compromising with the basic tenets of Islam, they would not succeed in making impact in a multi-religious society. Subhan (1970) and Rizvi (1978) have noted that many Sufis referred to Hindu religious texts and ideas in their discourses. The contemporary *pir*s are well versed in the philosophical traditions of different religions.

However, this should not lead us to conclude that Sufism is undifferentiated and monolithic. In fact, it consists of a myriad of schools and philosophical traditions, beliefs and practices, and spiritual lineages, as I have tried to show in the first three chapters of this work. Sufi literature has been produced in different languages, such as Turkish, Arabic, Persian, Urdu, and Hindivi. Thoughts from different religious streams have been appropriated in Sufism, returned to established religions for scrutiny and absorption. In other words, pluralism is a characteristic of Sufism.

Of many distinctions within Sufism, a distinction of far-reaching importance is between those Sufis who follow the Islamic law and way of life, and those who do not. The former live according to the Shariat, the sacred body of Islamic tenets and principles, and thus are called Bashara, that is, 'living according to the law'. Those who prefer to live in ways antithetical to the Shariat are known as Beshara, 'without the law'. The Beshara is also a heterogeneous category. Comprising it are loosely organized groups of saints (or mendicants), each known by the names of their eponymous founders, practicing their 'unusual', 'eccentric', 'different', and idiosyncratic actions, having no fixed abode or spiritual descendant. Because of their loose organization around an individual, rather than a belief, we prefer to call them 'cults'. These people usually travel their path without the comforts of a spiritual community and basically alone with God. The Beshara groups, which have been recorded in India, are the Dawla Shahi, Haydari, Ismail Shahi, Jalali, Lal Shahbaziya, Madari, Malamati, Makhdumi, Miran Shahi, Musa Suhagiya, Qalandar, Rasul Shahi, and Siyahposh. Now, one rarely comes across the adherents of all these cults. However, once in a while, on the occasion of *'urs* of a saint, one may come across a mendicant, differently dressed, with an unpleasant appearance, who identifies himself with one of the lesser represented orders. Otherwise, the most popular of them is the order of Qalandars.

In fact, if there is any popular term after Sufism, it is Qalandar. Generally used as an idiom for a freely led lifestyle, despising social conventionalities, in which a person experiences a state of ecstasy (*masti*), Qalandar is one of the central imageries of Sufi music and songs. An evening of Sufi singing is incomplete unless the singer sings the celebrated Qalandar number *dama dam mast Qalandar, Ali da pehla number, Ali dam dam ke andar, dama dam mast Qalandar*, sung by all singers who claim to be Sufi in their style. Please note in this song the use of the concepts of *mast* and Ali, the Prophet's son-in-law, who is believed to have initiated Qalandar saints. In many traditions, it is believed that the first Qalandar was Hazrat Ali himself. Further, focus on the imagery of *mast* states that the Qalandar saint is always self-absorbed, in a state of bliss, unaware of himself, 'intoxicated', not in his senses – he is *mast*, thus experiencing the streak of divinity in him. I have observed during the course of my fieldwork that the audience waits patiently to listen to this song, and wishes that it never ended, with the singer adding more stanzas to it and repeating those that have been sung earlier. This song is believed to infuse trance and elation (*sama'*) among the listeners. At one time, this song was sung exclusively at Qalandar shrines, but now, because of its popularity and ability to make people go into rapture, it is included among the *qawwalis* sung at Chishti *dargahs*. In fact, *sa'ma* sessions used to be an important feature of the gatherings of Qalandar saints.

The Shariat does not legitimize the concepts of *masti* and *sama'*. Not only that, scriptural Islam forbids music, dance, and poetry, except what is required for a proper rendition of the Quran. The Beshara saints also indulge in activities – such as drinking alcohol, consuming barbiturates, smoking intoxicants – tabooed in the Shariat. In an idiosyncratic style, the Qalandar also shave off the hair on their heads, beard, and moustaches, and also their eyebrows (*chahar abru*). Some of them also wear iron chains (*ahan posh*), black clothes (*siyah posh*), and peregrinate from one place to another seeking alms. Non-observance of the mores of cleanliness has also been observed among some. Since they indulge in activities prohibited in the Shariat, the term 'antinomian cult' may be used for them. They have also been termed 'rebellious Sufis' and 'unruly friends of God.'

But this antinomianism does not imply a rejection of the cardinal tenets of Islam, and like their Bashara brethren, they believe in the oneness of God and finality of the Prophet in Islam. During my fieldwork, I found many *khadims* and *pirs* from the shrines emphasizing the definitive markers of Islamic identity – the importance of observing 'prescriptive' Islamic ritual activities like *namaz* and *ramazan* on the premises of the shrines, and the importance of studying the Quran. Most shrines also have a mosque on their premises. Muslims (and also, people from other religions) visiting the *mazar* of the saint cover their heads. If it is time for *namaz*, they read that in the premises. The separation of men and women, especially in formalized ritual settings, and among women, the definition of themselves as being in *purdah*, also seems to hint at the importance of the visitors' identities as 'good Muslim first and foremost.' The *mujawir* is usually an orthodox Muslim, following the code of ethics, morality and dress as conveyed in the hadith, like *pyjama* above the ankles, no moustache but a beard, a skullcap, and a cloth on the shoulder. Yet many of these people, who visit *dargahs*, are lax about following certain practices prescribed in the hadith and *sunnah*. They adhere to practices which Islam expressly condemns or forbids: the practice of divination, different forms of magical intervention, curse or boon (*jadu tona, jhar phunk, tawiz*), numerology (*abjad*), veneration of deities from other religions, etc. They have all been regarded as examples of 'superstitions', and the Wahabis and Tablighis consider it their religious duty to eradicate them from people's way of living, thereby making them 'puritan Muslims': 'Islam is in danger, let's go back to Islam, let's convert – *dar-ul harb* into *dar-ul Islam*.'

Orders classified as Beshara are 'notorious', in the language of scriptural Islam, for blatantly deviating from the Shariat, but even the Bashara have been the butt of criticism. In fact, the orthodox and conservative elements in Islam have often criticized, chastised, and persecuted Sufis in general.

All those movements within Islam that have tried to revitalize the 'Islam of the Book' or the tradition of the Prophet have invariably denounced Sufism because of its moderation, tolerance, and 'open-door policy', that is accommodating people from a variety of faiths in its fold without concertedly advising them to divorce their own. Orthodox Islam has censured the practices of revering and worshipping saints and their graves, or reposing complete trust in their *pir-o-murshid.*

As a consequence, the Sufi identity has been fractured into 'privileged hereditary caretakers of famous shrines', 'mystics', 'miracle workers', 'healers and faith generators', and 'good Muslims.' Notwithstanding the opposition of orthodox Islam to Sufism, there has not been a single respondent of mine who believed Sufism to be not Islamic, and even those associated with antinomian orders did not think of deviating from the central Islamic practices. It is against this background that I argue in this work that antinomianism might be more a state of mind than an actually practised lore.

Of the different antinomian orders, the most famed and represented are the Qalandars. It is through the case study of their shrines that I have tried to comprehend the nature of antinomianism in Islam. The widely held belief is that there have been two-and-a-half Qalandar saints in the world, namely, Lal Shahbaz, Bu Ali, and Rabia Basri, of whom the *dargah* of Bu Ali is located in Panipat (Haryana) in India. Some Qalandar saints also have their affiliations with other Beshara orders. For instance, Abu Bakr Tusi of Ḍelhi is a famous collocation of Hayḍari-Qalandar order. Thus, I have devoted this work to a detailed and comparative study of the two popular Qalandar shrines in India – one of Abu Bakr and the other of Bu Ali.

Let me enlist the similarities and differences between these shrines. Let us take the similarities first.

Both are regarded as Qalandari shrines, notwithstanding the tag of Haydari attached to Abu Bakr; however, none of these has any outward signs of Qalandarism, such as *mujawir*s wearing iron chains or with shaven heads. Both the saints had settled down in their Khanqahs in Delhi and Panipat, rather than remaining in a state of peregrination, and started their Khanqahs, where they often entertained the Sufis of other orders, Bashara as well as Beshara. They also visited other Sufis, especially the famous Chishti saint, Nizamuddin Auliya, and earned his compliments. In other words, in spite of their antinomianism, the Bashara saints were respectful towards them. Throughout their lives, both were immersed in their respective cogitative and contemplative practices, extending help to their needy visitors, but did not establish a line of spiritual descent. Surely they had friends and admirers. However, they were not men of their spiritual lineage. Today, both the shrines have *mujawir* (caretakers), not the spiritual successors of the saints. And, like the other Sufi saints, both had links with the seats of political power, often exercising influence on rulers as and when the need arose, but they tried to avoid them as much as they could.

The first difference between the two shrines, however, is in terms of their location. Abu Bakr's *dargah* is located on the main road, near Pragati Maidan, in the cosmopolitan city of Delhi. Situated on a mound (*tila*), it has a big parking space near it, where visitors to Pragati Maidan park their vehicles. A number of kiosks are also located here where food items (such as *biryani*), comparatively inexpensive, are sold, attracting people from all walks of life. Out of curiosity, quite a few of them visit the shrine, and make offerings. Because of its location, it generates more revenue than the shrine of Bu Ali, which is located three kilometres inside from the main Panipat-Delhi road, near the State Bus Terminus, and one has to hire a rickshaw to reach it. In other words, since it is located inside old Panipat, it is not easily accessible, and thus fails to attract stray visitors. Barring the occasions of *'urs* and Bada Khara festival, on the other days, the callers to this shrine are usually from the neighbourhood. Anyone would be struck by the more urban nature of Abu Bakr's shrine. This also indicates that more Hindus than Muslims visit Abu Bakr's shrine. Further, it is also situated on way to Nizamuddin Auliya's *dargah*. Coaches taking pilgrims to Ajmer Sharif stop at the shrines of Abu Bakr and Nizamuddin Auliya. In addition, pilgrims coming to attend Nizamuddin's *'urs* also visit Abu Bakr's *dargah*.

With respect to their structures, Bu Ali's shrine is an example of medieval architecture. It has a large area where stands an elaborate complex of guest rooms, garden, well, Hali's library, mosque, fountain and pond, besides the *dargah* of Bu Ali and also, graves of his friends and admirers. The huge tank and a garden laid out of deep reverence for Bu Ali are respectively called Baba Ka Hauz and Baba Bari. A large *langar khana* is also built in the premises, where the devotees and needy are fed on Thursdays, Sundays, and during the *'urs*.

In comparison, Abu Bakr's shrine has a more restricted area. Bu Ali's *dargah* is completely administered by the Waqf Board, which appoints a caretaker on a paltry salary. In comparison, an extended family manages the Abu Bakr shrine. This family has added splendourous rituals, and pomp and show, during *'urs*, aiming to attract more visitors. Because of Waqf administration, the organization of Bu Ali shrine is quite streamlined, which is not the case with Abu Bakr, where the family looking after it often takes decisions in its interest. The nature of their administration has important implications for the character of these shrines. Each *dargah* develops its own tradition and a diacritical mark: Abu Bakr's shrine is known for its offerings of earthen pitchers, displayed all over its space. At Bu Ali's *dargah*, as a mark of promise to return once their wishes are fulfilled, the devotees put locks on the iron grill around the grave.

We know that *shijrah* (spiritual genealogy) is of the utmost importance in Sufi orders, for the ultimate question is that of the link upward, tier by tier, to the Prophet, and after him to one's *pir*'s place in the particular Sufi order. Bu Ali's *shijrah* is very much clear till his birth, but of his descendants, consanguines and affines, there is no record. With respect to historical information, we find that less material is available on Abu Bakr. He finds no mention in *Akhbar ul-Akhyar*, which is not the case with Bu Ali. As we have seen, a lot of information is available on Bu Ali's family, his early training, Islamic learning, austerities and penances performed, devotees, and his literary works. The verses, which are recited daily at the time of *roshni* (candle lighting) ceremony at the shrine at dusk, were most probably composed by him. About Abu Bakr, we do not know as to who initiated (*bai'at*) him, and how much Islamic learning he had received. Interestingly, there are stories of rulers and other dignitaries testing him to determine whether he was endowed with supernatural powers. This, however, is not the case with Bu Ali as doubts regarding his spiritual attainments are almost non-existent. This is closely linked with the observation that Bu Ali has produced a vast amount of splendid literature, some of which bears close resemblance to that of Rumi's. Well known to the students of Persian and Urdu literature are the erudite exchanges that had taken place between Bu Ali and Nizamuddin Auliya, and the latter's *murid*, Amir Khusrau. Bu Ali's *Mathnavi* is also a richly quoted and referred work. Abu Bakr does not lay claim to any such literary accolades.

A common sight at Abu Bakr's shrine is that its caretaker (who calls himself the *sajjadanashin* of the saint) and sometimes his brothers and assistants render supernatural aid to visitors, for which they do not charge any fee, but accept whatever the client offers. On a Thursday, which happens to be the day when saints are particularly revered, the *sajjadanashin* sits on his seat in formal attire (a long green robe), with a long cap, which he usually does not wear on other days, to receive clients thronging to him for supernatural assistance. A visit to Abu Bakr shrine in the afternoon of any day would bring one face to face with a crowd of visitors waiting for their turn to receive supernatural cure (*ruhani ilaj*). For these people, what is important is a personal interview with the *sajjadanashin*, who would listen to their problems and suggest appropriate remedies. And, what is secondary is a visit to Abu Bakr's *mazar*. In many cases, the *sajjadanashin* advises his clients to pay respects to the *mazar* before leaving. In some cases, the treatment suggested for the problem is a daily floral offering at Abu Bakr's shrine. In other words, the tradition of supernatural healing and solutions that the *sajjadanashin* (and his family members) provide takes precedence over the worship of the saint.

On the other hand, Bu Ali's shrine does not have a publicly advertised tradition of supernatural cure. At first instance, the caretaker and his assistants vehemently deny that they render any supernatural help to anyone. They say that people come to the shrine to pray before the saint and seek his blessings. They place their petitions before him, and it is he who intercedes with God on their behalf to grant favours. However, once rapport is established with the caretaker, one comes to know that he gives all possible supernatural aid to his clients, but secretly. He charms water for them, makes talismans and amulets, prepares chits of paper (*purza*) with sacred words from the Quran inscribed on them, which people are asked to wear as talismans, or partake the water in which it is dissolved or stirred. Each time, he advises his clients not to disclose this practice, justifying it by taking recourse to the plea that he cannot but help those in a state of hopelessness. The Waqf Board has clearly prohibited the practice of rendering any kind of supernatural help at the shrine, for it is un-Islamic. We may hypothesize here that Islamization of a Sufi shrine begins when the Waqf Board takes it over. This would also explain why Abu Bakr's shrine is less Islamized than that of Bu Ali's.

Women make up a substantial portion of the total number of pilgrims who patronize the shrines for various reasons and frequently. Women come alone, from far and near, in case the matter desires secrecy, or with families, to participate in large public festivals, like the *'urs* and *milad-un nabi*. They visit local shrines for matters, both mundane and spiritual. They come for healing, advice, and to obtain amulets from the *pir-o-murshid* or *sajjadanashin*. They come to read the Quran and to pray alone or in groups. They seek the saint's intercession through prayer and ritual supplication. They come to make vows (*mannat*), to fulfil them, or to give thanks for prayers answered. Women appear as pilgrims, clients and *murid*s.

The shrine is a space in which women have little influence in terms of shaping ritual life. In certain shrines, they are not permitted to enter the sanctum sanctorum, whereas in others, they are. In Qalandar shrines, they are permitted to go right up to the grave; although not restricted, women generally do not touch the grave, an act that Muslim men generally do. Mindful of the gender mores regulating physical distance, women pray from a distance. They come to seek help in conceiving children, particularly sons, advice regarding marital relationship, and medical treatment, especially gynecological problems. Whereas men seem to visit shrines for social reasons, out of respect for the saint, and for reasons which have to do with their own well being and prosperity (such as legal matters, promotion, job), women, however, come with their families in mind, particularly children. A large proportion come for reasons related to their roles as wives and mothers. During *'urs* festivals, which are celebrated on the shrine's premises, women prepare the food. They also redistribute the food brought into the shrine as gifts. Women also sell goods at the shrines. They apply henna to female pilgrims, particularly new brides.

Underlying *ziyarat*, the worship of saints and graves, is the animistic belief that Muslim and Hindu pilgrims fully share – the saint is 'alive' in his grave, the place where he would 'rest' (*aaramgah*) till the Day of Judgement. Physical obliteration of the saint draws him closer to Allah, and he continues to help them through his nearness to God. Godly interventions create miracles. The saint is an intercessor. However, God pays heed to him since he spends his earthly existence, and later his moments in the grave, in revering Him. The belief that the saint will always be 'alive', first physically and later spiritually, makes the caretakers of his grave treat him in the same way as human beings are treated – in other words, the saint rests, wakes up in the morn, is given a bath, and is dressed. Against this background, the grave is animated; the saint is there; and a petition placed before him will be considered favourably.

That is the reason for visits to the shrines of saints. Relics and amulets are also considered effective. It is against this background of the idea that 'saints never die' that one can appreciate the reason for the dispute among the residents of Karnal and Panipat over the dead body of Bu Ali. It was announced that different groups of claimants could come, try to lift his body, and whoever could do that could carry him away. All tried but failed, except those from Panipat, who succeeded in lifting the bier, and thus 'appropriated him'. Even something touched to the saint's grave or his covering, sheet, or shroud produced miraculous effect. Together with the 'divine touch', the soil (*mitti*) from the grave, some of the rose petals scattered over the grave, were considered *tabarruk*.

I came across many Muslims who confined their ritual activity at the *mazar* to reading verses from the Quran. Neither did they prostrate before the grave nor did they kiss or touch it to seek grace (*baraka*). Their view was that the Sufis themselves do not approve of the festivities and celebrations that their followers organize with much fanfare. Some saints, especially of the Qadiri order, prefer seclusion (*khilwat*). They want that their visitors should pray silently and leave. One of my respondents said that a visitor should not stay for long at the Sufi shrine because the saint requires privacy for his own contemplations. In the context of Abu Bakr's shrine, a visitor informed us that when celebrations and singing sessions take place, the saint leaves his abode and goes over to Bagh-e-Bedil, as all this is not in accordance with his wishes.

In this context, I was told a story ascribed to Sufi Shah Abdul Aziz, a Qadiri saint of the sixteenth century, whose *mazar* is situated behind Jai Prakash Narayan Hospital, near Delhi Gate. His two disciples were keen on attending the *'urs* of Nizamuddin Auliya. Although the saint tried to prevent them from going there, his efforts failed and he acceded to their request. However, he wanted to teach them a lesson. So, he gave them a clay saucer with something written on it and told them that on their way to Nizamuddin's shrine, they would come across an old man near Purana Qila. They were advised to give this saucer to the aged and bring his message back.

Abdul Aziz's disciples returned with the message. He read it aloud for their benefit as well as for the others. Aziz had asked the old man why did he not stop people from attending the *'urs* celebrations. The reply was: 'When you can't stop your two disciples, how can I stop a crowd?' The old man was none other than Nizamuddin Auliya.

This story amply conveys what Muslim visitors think the saint's point of view would be on *dargah* celebrations and the ways of *ziyarat*. The rise of Tabligh movement among the Muslim communities has deprecated the holding of *'urs* and the custom of visiting the graves of saints. The Meos of Haryana and Rajasthan provide a fine example, as Marwah's (1979) and Mayaram's (1997) studies suggest. The orthodox Muslims think that *dargah*s resemble Hindu temples, and that is why, they are un-Islamic. But, for a vast majority, consisting of Hindus as well as Muslims, the celebrations at the Sufi shrine help in revitalizing a link with the saint. As we have seen, *'urs*, meaning 'marriage', symbolizes the *wisal* (union) of the saint with Allah, which would only be possible at the time of death. Thus, death is not to be mourned. It is a moment of celebration, indicating that union with God, the goal of the Sufi, follows his physical annihilation. As a sizable number of pilgrims to Sufi shrines are Hindu, they do not object to these celebrations. On the contrary, they want them to be more colourful, mirthful, and elaborate. Earlier, we saw that Hindu pilgrims celebrate the festival of lights (Diwali) and colours (Holi) at Abu Bakr's shrine. Although such celebrations are not held at Bu Ali's shrine, Hindus definitely visit the saint on ritual occasions and thank him for boons granted.

With reference to the question of why people venerate *mazar*s, my data lend support to the thesis of material or practical motives, which implies that people seek help from saints when they are unable to achieve the desired goals with resources available to them. Someone apprises them of the miracles that have occurred in their lives as a result of their investing faith in a saint. The individual, who is already looking for a divine intervention, entertains the idea of visiting the shrine of that Sufi saint to seek a solution of his problem. In many cases, old pilgrims bring new ones, who become regular visitors in anticipation of their desires being fulfilled. Their faith in the shrine is reinforced when their condition ameliorates or their crises are brought under control. They in turn spread the episodes of their experiences at the shrine, particularly of vow-fulfilment, to others. The channel of communication is set up. In course of time, more and more people come to Sufi shrines to submit petitions and to thank saints for their timely help.

A significant number of visitors to the Qalandar shrine are regular. Most visit it every Thursday or Sunday – Thursday, the saint is believed to be present in his grave on that day, because of which the effect of the saint's grace multiplies; whilst Sunday is a holiday. I have also come across people who have promised the saint that they would visit him on a particular day of the week (or fortnight). Such routines are strictly followed, since a promise to the saint must be observed strictly. Some visit the shrine on days and time when it has fewer visitors, so that they can peacefully carry out their veneration, while others come on days earmarked for celebration. The visitors renew their petitions, whereas many think that by praying to the saint regularly, they will be bestowed with long-term welfare. They claim to be living under the canopy of the saint's grace, since they believe that once blessed with it, the saint himself will bring their problems and crises under control.

The saint's grace (*baraka*) is contagious. It may be absorbed by being in its close contact, through a process Currie (1989: 133) has called 'spiritual osmosis'. The belief is that grace permeates everything in the shrine. The *tabarruk* (including the rose petals) he eats, the steps he kisses, the *chadar* (sheet) he touches, the rose water (with which the grave was washed) he drinks, and the air he breathes, all award him with the saint's grace. By keeping the rose petals, he thinks the saint is with him. Those whose petitions have been heard distribute food at the shrine, an activity known as performing the *niyaz*. Accepting it gratefully also implies absorbing grace. My respondents warned that we should not refuse the blessed food, for it brings bad luck. In case we wish not to eat it, we could leave it at a secure place for birds and animals.

The reasons for visiting the shrine vary in relation with education, intellectual stance, class, and general orientation to religious matters. Most visitors happen to be less educated, from lower classes, and they steadfastly believe in the efficacy of supernatural treatments. Sometimes visits to the shrine are a whole day affair – it is a kind of 'outing'. This should not be interpreted as meaning that people from other social backgrounds do not visit the shrine. As I have tried to show that many orthodox Muslims come to the shrine, for they find its environ highly congenial to prayer and thought. Irrespective of the background, when people are in difficulty, one of the recourses they take is to visit a Sufi shrine. Like religious places in general, the Sufi shrine is also hope generating.

Further, the Sufi shrine offers a site where pilgrims experience equality. They clean the courtyard, pray together, eat the same food, sit on the floor to listen to the *qawwalis*, and follow the same round of activities. In this way, they temporarily escape from a hierarchical world. But, the caretakers do not treat all visitors in the same manner. The affluent are accorded a privileged treatment in anticipation of handsome monetary favour. In other words, the Sufi shrines are not free from the values and structural features of the society in which they are located.

During the fieldwork, I came across men highly critical of the *pirs*. They felt that these 'religious men' had become 'commercial'. 'Keeping graves' had become a strategy to encroach upon public land. The *pirs* had no time for contemplation, since they were awfully busy in extending supernatural cure to their clients in exchange of money. Some Sufis were notorious for extorting money from their clients, and for unlawful indulgence in homosexuality. The term *murid* was being used for anyone who came to the *pir* for consultation. The *pirs* were also criticized for their active involvement in politics, and drawing closer to men in power.

The officials and caretakers of both shrines agreed with this criticism of *pirs*, but their defense was that it was on people's insistence that they resorted to supernatural healing. Once their problems are resolved, they recommend the shrine to others. The unending circle forces them to attend to clients notwithstanding the pressure on their time, resources, schedule, energy, and social engagements. Although Sufis should abstain from indulgence in politics, my respondents felt that it was imperative to have political connections, since for every developmental activity at the shrine – be it electricity and water connections, repair, maintenance, sewer lines, construction – administrative intervention is required, which would work favourably provided one knows the 'right politicians'. This certainly is not a new trend. In the past also, the Sufis had to draw closer to the seat of power to get certain grants, and they also received honours, appointments, grants, and land (Eaton, 1973; Gilmartin, 1979; Ernst, 1992; Elias, ed., 2000).

A Sufi cult was never insulated. It had to exist in relationship with the exterior social and religious orders. Theoretically, it might propose an alternative way of living, but when it came down to translating it in action, various problems started surfacing. As a result, the militant and rebellious aspects of living were given up in favour of moderation, particularly when the Qalandar saints settled down and started a Khanqah living. Consequently, they established their relations, cordial and symbiotic, with the Chishti saints. The study of the two shrines shows that the theoretical distinction made between the Bashara and Beshara is actually blurred in reality. Unless one is told that Abu Bakr and Bu Ali were Qalandar saints, their Sufi affiliations are not apparent from empirical studies of their shrines. Social life as conducted in these shrines is similar to Chishti (or other Bashara) shrines.

This in fact is the story of antinomian cults. Against this background, I have shown in this work that Qalandarism is more a state of mind, an imagery of ecstasy, an individuated experience, than an actually led lifestyle continuing for generations.

APPENDIX I

Qalandar in Poetry and Prose

Mysticism has a great relationship with poetry and literature (Chaubey, 1985; Chopra, 1999; Ashraf, 2003). Hafiz, Abdal Rahman Jami, Maulana Jalaluddin Rumi and Amir Khusrau are stalwarts in Persian poetry. Mirza Mazhar Jan-Janan and Mir Dard wrote in Urdu, whereas Shah Mohd. Kazim Qalandar of Kota Nadvi, near Kakori (U.P.), wrote in Hindi.

surat teri pyari pe main balihari
lal ankhen teri lal bast hai
kari kari bin anjan pyari.

....

rakh le laaj do u jag me Kazim ki
de jo mange ye daras bhikhari

His son, Shah Turab Ali Qalandar, wrote in his *Shair ul-Hind* (Maulana Abdul Islam Nadir, *Aithaf al-Akhyar*, p. 419)

nishan us ka kisi se kab bayan ho
wahi pawe nishan jo be nishan ho

....

Khuda jaane woh harjai kahan ho
Turab ustad se malum kar lo
tariqe marifat, gur qudurdan ho (*Aithaf al-Akhyar*, p. 419)

A Khalifa of Shah Turab Ali, Qalandar Shah Imdad Qalandar's *ghazal* is as follows:

tasavvur jis ka har sham-o-sehar hai
bata de koi mujh ko woh kidhar hai

....

hua hai dil hi dil mein kam apna
bhala Imdad yeh kaisa hunar hai

Maulvi Ismail Meeruti, a pioneer in the arts and letters in Urdu, has no equal, whereas Mohsin Kakorvi in the rendition of the *Naat* has no competitors. Allama Mohd. Iqbal's philosophical treatises, his Urdu and Persian poetry, have greatly influenced the minds of people in India and Pakistan.

Maulvi Ismail Meeruti was attached to the Qalandar *silsila*; the famous Qalandar saint Ghaus Ali Shah Panipati was his mentor and *murshid* (*Gul-e-ra-ana*, p. 481). In the words of Maulana Shibali Nomani, after the work of Mohd. Hali, the person worth listening to was Ismail Meeruti (d. 1918).

hai ashk-o-aah ras hamare mizaz ko
yani pale hue is aab-o-hawa ke hain
in bad dilon ne ishq ko badnam kar diya
jo mar takab shikayat-e-jor-o-jafa ke hain

....

khud faroshi husn ko jab se hui mad nazar
narkh-e-dil bhi ghat gaya, janen bhi arzan ho gayeen

Mohsin Kakorwi bin Hasan Baksh bin Husain Baksh Shahid (Ittawa, 1879) ibn Shah Mir Mohd. Qalandar Kakorwi was a poet. Shah Mir Mohd. Qalandar was Hazrat Shah Mohd. Kazim Qalandar Kakorwi's brother (Roz-al Azhar, 176). *Tafrihalaz* and *Tazkira Akhwan-o-ghairah* (1888) are his writings. Maulvi Husain Baksh of the Qalandariya *silsila*'s two important literary contributions are *Ikhtilaf al Basri-o-al Kufeen* and *Fanah-al-Hind*. Mohsin Kakorvi (b. 1884) had an innate sense of poetry (*Caravan-e-Medina*, p. 178). Shaikh Abu Said Abdul Khayr (d. 1048) and Baba Tahir Uryan (d. 1019) are pioneers of Sufi poetry in Iran. Abu Said composed quatrains, Baba wrote *dubaytis* (couplets), which are still sung in Iran on *sihtar* (three string).

Grieving for thee, my heart is ever sad,
A brick my pillow and my couch the earth,
my only sin is loving thee like mad,
surely not all lovers suffer extremeth.

Notable among the mystics and Sufi poets of Sind is Sheikh Uthman (Lal Shahbaz) Qalandar (d. 1274), whose famous lines were cited in Chapter 3.

If one is not aware that the identifying mark of a Qalandar is a shaven head, he will not be able to enjoy the following couplet of Hafiz Shirazi.

dar-in karobare dildar-i-ast
hazaar nukta barik tar zamu injast
na hoke sarbatar ashad qalandari danad

(There's many a subtley, finer than hair,
in this fashion of many a noddle,
head that slave Calendarship, pray who knowest,
just by shaving off one's head and eyebrows,
one does not become a qalandar.)

Mohammad Iqbal (1930; see Kiernan, 1949; Suman, 2004) frequently mentions Qalandar's name in his verses.

mehr-o-ma-o-anjum ka muhasib hai Qalandar
ayam ka murakkab nahin rakib hai Qalandar

....

na takht-o-taj mein na lashkar-o-sipah mein hai
jo baat mard Qalandar ki bargah mein hai

Iqbal's work and message reflects the literary and philosophical aspects of the modern world, yet his poetry clearly reflects his Qalandari leanings; free, unstructured and unbound. In *Bal-i-Jibriel*, he writes.

kiye hain faash ramoz qalandari main ne
ke fikr madrasa-o-khanqah ho azad.

....

pani pani kar gayee mujh ko qalandar ki yeh baat
tu jhuka jab ghair ke age na man tera na tan

....

qalandar juz do harf-e-la-illaha, kuch bhi nahin rakhta
faqia-e-shahreqarun se lughat hai hijazi ka

On the Qalandari path and its customs, he makes it absolutely clear that:

hazaar khauf hon lekin,
zuban ho dil ki rafiq
yehi raha hai azal se,
Qalandaron ka tariq

....

yeh hai khulasa-i-ilm qalandari,
ke hyat khud na gjasta hai, lekin kaman se door nahin

He is thankful to the Qalandari mindset that has made him a poet, otherwise:

khawish aa gayee hai jehan ko qalandari meri
wa gar na shair mera kya hai, shairi kya hai

....

teri nigah se dil seenon mein kampte the
khoya gaya hai tera jazb-e-qalandarana

....

About their free thinking, their *azad* life, without encumbrances, and inhibitions, and of their state of ecstasy, Iqbal is very envious:

yuh haath nahin aata wo gauhar yak dana
yak rangi wa azadi, hai himmat-e mardana

....

He fervently believes that to be a Qalandar is far more difficult than ruling a state, whether he be Sanjar or Tughril or Jehangir. To be like Rumi or Fairabi is a task only a strong-willed person, steeped in the love of Allah, can accomplish:

ya Sanjar wa Tughril ka ain-e-Jehangir
ya mard-e-qalandar ke andaz-e-malukana
ya hairat Farabi ya tab wa tabe Rumi
ya fikr-e-hakimana ya jazb-e-kalimana
ya aql ki rubai ya ishq-e-yad-e-Ilahi
ya heela-e-afarangi ya hamla-i-Turkana
ya shor-i-musalmani, yak der ki durbani
ya naara-i-mastana, kaba ho ke butkhana
miri mein, faqiri mein, shahi mein, ghulami mein
kuchch kam nahin banta, be jurrat-i-rindana

In the *Bang-e-Dara*, Iqbal openly praises the way of the Qalandar:

dam-e zindagi, ram-e zindagi, gham-e zindagi, sam-e zindagi
gham-e ram na kar, sam-e gham na kho,
ke yahi hai shan-e qalandari.

In Persian, in *Armughan-e-Hajaz*, he reiterates his views on this antinomian cult or, what he called the *unruly friends* of God.

Qalandar mel taqrire nadarad
bujuz ein nukta aksire nadarad
azan kashfe kharabe hasil-e-neist
ke ab az khune shabire nadarad

....

Qalandar jarrah bag aasman naha
yeh bal-o-sabak gard giranha
fizai neelgon (nakhchire) gahash
namin gardad bagarad-e aashianaha

He continues in this vein in Urdu too:

Qalandarana adayen, Sikandarana jalal
yeh ummatein hain jahan mein barhana sham shirein.
khudi se marde khud, agah ka jamal-o-jalal
ki yeh kitab hain, baqi tamam tafsiren.

Iqbal now compares 'Sikandari' with 'Qalandari' and concludes: to each his own.

Sikandari ho Qalandari ho
yeh sab tariqe hai sahirana
harif apna samajh rahe hain
mujhe khudayan-e-khanqahi

....

tha yeh Allah ka farman, man ke shikwa-e-parvez
do qalandar, koke hain us mein malukana sifat

The first part of his diwan begins with this couplet.
In *Zabure Ajam*, at one place, Iqbal reveals that:

zabrune dar guzishtam, zorune khana-e-guftam
sukhan-e-na gufta-e-ra che Qalandarana guftam

He reiterates this thought in *Jarbe Kalim*:

firdaus mein Rumi se yeh kahta tha sanai
mashriq mein abhi tak hai wohi kasa wahi aash
Hallaj ki lekin yeh riwayat hai ke aakhir
ik mard qalandar ne kiya raze khudi faash

At another place, Iqbal defines his *afkar* (ideas, notions, thoughts, meditations) as signs of Qalandarism:

tha zabt bahut mushkil sail maani ka
kah dale qalandar ne asrar kitab aakhir

Iqbal's poetry has made the Qalandari notions very popular among the masses, especially their *jalal*. To Iqbal, both the persons following the Qalandari customs or bound by the chain of tradition, are unfree. Followers of the Qalandari custom or followers of Sikandari path are bound by customs, not by spirit. They are both magic or illusion, not the reality or truth (*haqiqat*). That is why in his *diwan*, the initial couplet is:

zabr wanc dar gushistan zardune khana-e-guflurn
sukhana nagufla ra che Qalandarana guftam

In the same *diwan*, these is a complete *ghazal* on the same subject:

Qalandaran ke be taskhir aab-o-gul ko shanad
zishah baz satanad-o-khirqa me poshand

....

bajalwat anad-o-kamand-o-be mehar-o-mah pechanad
bakhilwat anad-o-zaman-o-makan-o-dar agoshanad
baroze-e-bazm sarapa chun par nihan-o-harir
baroze razam khud agah watan faramoshand

At another place, he is in a contemplative mood.

Raaz-e-hayat pooch le khijr-i-khijsta gham se
zindahar ek chuz hai koshish nataman sa

amal se zindagi banti hai, jannat bhi, jahannam bhi
ya khaki apnai fitrat mein, na noori hai na ri hai

taqdeer ke qazi ka ye fatwa hai azal se
hai jurm-e-zaeefi ki saza marg-e-mufajat
kismat ke hain paiband nabadat-o-jamadat
momin faqat ehkam-i-ellahi ka hai paband

fareb-e-nazar hai sakoon-o-babat
tarapta hai har zarra-e-kayanat

yeh alam ye hangama-i-rang-e-saut
yeh alam ke hai zer farman maut
yeh alam ye butkhana-i-chashma-agosh
jahan zindagi hai faqat-khurd-o-nosh
khudi ke ye heh manzil-e-aualeen
musafir ye tera nasheman nahin
bahar ja ye koh giran tod kar
tilsum-o-zaman-o-makan tod kar
jah aur bhi hain abhi be-namud
ke khali nahan hai zamir-e-wajud

If one wishes to familiarize oneself with the Qalandariya *tariqa*, one must read Iqbal's poetry. He looks at both the Islamic faith and Qalandarism in the same manner, their status (*bulandi*), forewarning (*agahi*), selflessness (*bekhudi ka paikar*), openness (*jalwat*), and seclusion (*khilwat*). The Sufi is one who controls the moon and stars (*meher-o-mah par kamand dalne wala*), chains time and space (*zaman-o-makan ko asir rakhne wala*), changes the present, rips off the mask of guile and treachery, and is completely absorbed in or intoxicated by the wine of the love of God. Among friends, he is as soft as silk, in the time of conflict, he is forewarned, fearless, and unselfish. He controls even water and flowers to himself. He receives *khiraj* (charity) from the rulers; but is happy to wear the patched *khirqa* (robe) and is content with his state of affairs. Iqbal says that to be able to find even one pearl in the depths of the dark ocean, one has to become a Qalandar. He is *mast* (happy-go-lucky) in his state of poverty, or plenty or servitude. The Qalandar's look can cause fear in the hearts of people. His slogan is that of freedom, carefreeness and ecstasy.

In a letter written to Allama Saiyid Suleiman Nadvi, Iqbal addresses him as Qalandar: You are a qalandar but of a type mentioned below.

nizam tazah ba charkh do rang mi bakshand
sitara hai khanra janaza bar doshanad
zamana az dikhe farda kashud bande naqab
mashran huna sar maste bada-e-doshand
balab rasid mira aan sukhan ke natwan guft
bakhair tum ke faqiahan-e-shahr khamoshand

Nisar Ahmed Farooqui in his introduction to *Silsila-e-Qalandarriya* says that:

bazaar-e-Qalandari ka rukh karun
aur jo kuch saz-o-barg hai use dao pe laga loon

Hakim Liaqat Ali Suhrawardi is confident that when the world is destroyed, nothing will remain except the Qalandar.

aqbat sanware sanai qalandar
dunya hai fani baqa-i-qalandar

In *Tazkira Ghazi Qalandar* (*Qadiri*), the *murid*, Allama Tariq Mujahid Jhelumi quotes verses in praise of Pir shah Qazi:

pir mera o damdi wala, pira Shah Qalandar
har mushkil wich madad karda dohan jahan andar

In *Nirange Ishq*, Allama Ghanimat Kunjahi writes:

makan us mulk andar, ik sundar
kahande hain pirashah qalandar

In *Qissa Sakhi Khwas Khan*, he reiterates the various aspects of the personality of his *pir*,

rangila us janab da jiu mahtab jahan da pir mera
sakhi mard te dard hatan wala dulo pir shahi jisda mein chehra
nadi ditaha da ghat hai naam jhelum nale shahr zila
os par hai ji othon sab koh tarf pahari wiche
sakhi pir shah da darbar hai ji

In *Mirza Sahiban*, he describes him as:

ohde did te id shahid ghazi har dahonda ho hilal aaya
damdi walda pir shah tahan ghazi kahen da roz te mah te saal aaya.

In *Tohfa-e-miran*,

rahbar us da shahshahan da pira shah qalandar
sada tasarf us da jari do jahanan andar.

In *Shaikh Subhan*,

pir mera jis dunya tajji, chali tekh paramdi
naib hazrat pira shahi khas ghulam mohdi
chhe koh parbat jhelum ghaton khadi mulk wich daera
pak maqam ik pira shahi oh hai maula mera.

In *Heer Ranjha*,

mahaz apne fazl te karam kolon pahlan baksh de mahwer jai de nun
meherban muhammada kar mein le ghazi pir shah mard khalaide nun.

In *Kursinama Pirane Hujwiri Qadiri*,

Hazrat Pirashah ji damdiwala
wich punjab zamin ujala
main haan kutta us dar wala
khidmatgar bhari da.

In *Hidayat-al Musalmeen*,

izzat, sehat, saya, rehmat, dayam baksh Ilahi
dohen jehane rakhein ander khidmat Pira Shahi

pira andar pir ujala Hazrat Pira Shah ji damdi wala
bagh Ali da Khush lala door kare dar ghaflat wala.

Even poets with a Sunni background such as Sanai Ghaznavi and Amir Khusrau do not hint at any specific principle, but refer to themselves as Qalandars (Duggal, 1996). The reference is important as the word Qalandar is used for a group not for an individual.

All those who are not in line with the prevailing mystic orders are relegated to the group of Qalandars. Thus, the Qalandar is not a mystic or a saint. He is also described as a person who does not follow the Islamic laws strictly (*beshar*) or a person other than the jurisprudent (*qazi, faqih*), preacher (*zahid, waiz, ulema*), or interpreter of the Islamic laws, who are chided by the mystics. Even Rumi and Shirazi refer to themselves in their poems as Qalandars, though they meant only to oppose the set and old sectional bonds, and to express themselves in a free and symbolic style. With the passage of time, Qalandarism has become a form of mystic ideology which differs from conventional mysticism.

Hazrat Sayyid Mohammad Gesu Daraz also belonged to the Qalandar *tariqa*. He wrote:

zamin-o-asman har do sharifanad
Qalandar ra darin har do makan neest
hazar dar didha nakas fatahda
ba gar na yar man az kas nahan neest.

A *khalifa* of Nasiruddin Chiragh Dehlavi (d. 1356), Hazrat Saiyyed Mohammad bin Jafar Makki's views can be clearly derived from this couplet:

andar rah ishq sarsari natawan raft
na dida rahe Qalandari natawan raft
khwahi ke pasaz kufr bayabi iman
tazan nalahi be kafiri natawan raft.

Hazrat Khwaja Masud Baq, son of Hazrat Shihabuddin Suhrawardi, and Khalifa of Shaikh Ruknuddin's popular couplet in Persian is presented below:

mahrad shev az din-o-dunya Qalandar
ke rah-e-haqiqat azin har do bartar.

Hafiz Shirazi writes:

hazar nukta darein karobar dildari mast
na ke sarbatar shud qalandari donad

man zatan uryan shudam un az khayal
mi kharanam dar nihayat al wisal.

Sheikh Sadi's opinion of the Qalandars is:

Khaksaran jahan ra be haqarat ma gar
tu che dani ke dar ein gard saware bashad.

Sheikh Fakhruddin Iraqi, the illustrious father of Sharfuddin Bu Ali Shah Qalandar, holds that:

zama rahe qalandar saz-o-war ba man numai
ke daraz-o-daur-o-yadam rahe zuhd-o-parsai.

Sheikh Fariduddin Attar in *Tazkira-ul Auliya* describes the Qalandar thus:

sar be bazaar-e-qalandar barnaham
pas bek saat babazam har che hast

The hymn sung at the shrine of Lal Shahbaz Qalandar is as follows:

dama dam mast qalandar,
Ali dam dam de andar
Ali da pehla number
sakhi Shahbaz Qalandar
sindri da, Sehwan da, sakhi Shahbaz Qalandar
unchara rauza pira tera, heth wage darya wala
jhoole lalan, Sindri da, Sehwan da, sakhi Shahbaz Qalandar

dar te pira teri, naubat baje
nal waje ghariyal, wala, jhoole lalan
char chirag tere balan hamesha
panjwa main balan aayee, wala jhoole lalan

mavan no pira bachre denda
behnan nun denda-e veer mila, jhoole lalan

[On the hilltop is your grave,
And below flows the river at your *dargah;*
The *naubat* (kettledrum) sounds; the drums resound,
Four lamps burn bright at your shrine,
The fifth, my *pir,* will be mine;
You bestow children to childless women,
Sisters you unite with their brethren.]

Bu Ali Shah was regarded as a poet from the Chishtia environment, a model of self-mortification, but also of overflowing love and enthusiasm. He was widely travelled. He is said to have visited Konya and perhaps met Rumi's son, Sultan Walad. From his mystical *Mathnavi* (titled *Gol-o-Bolbol*), it is clear that he was the first Indian Sufi to have referred to Rumi's *Mathnavi*, a book that was to inspire kings and poets and mystics and mullahs alike. Suffering in love was Bu Ali's ideal. He was wedded to the Sufi tradition of little food, little sleep and little talk, and the endurance of oppression. When Rumi classifies the ascetic as one who seeks mercy (*rahma*), while the lover seeks pain (*zahma*), Bu Ali Qalandar exclaims in the same vein:

The way of the ascetic is nothing but the way of purity,
The way of the lover is nothing but the palate of the crocodile.

In his letters, he speaks with the tongue of enthusiastic love and charity, comprising spiritual knowledge and realization of the Divine love, of giving up the world and seeking the other world and love of the Lord.

APPENDIX II

Qawwalis Sung at the Shrine of Bu Ali

Bu Ali Shah's name and fame have not only brought thousands of devotees to his *dargah*, but also inspired many to write and sing verses in his honour. The most popular *qawwali* sung at his shrine is *dama dam mast Qalandar, Ali da pehla number*. It is also the most popular *qawwali* sung at the shrine of Abu Bakr. Most of the stanzas of this *qawwali* remain the same irrespective of the Qalandar shrine where it is sung, but there is a strong likelihood that each singer adds some more stanzas to it. In other words, this *qawwali* has a collective authorship. Further, the length of this *qawwali* may be extended or shortened depending upon the number of people who have assembled to listen to it. As stated earlier, the maximum number of visitors to any Sufi shrine is on Thursdays; that is why the *qawwali* sessions are the lengthiest on this day of the week, and one hears almost all the stanzas (and that too several times) of *dama dam mast Qalandar* on this day.

In addition, several *qawwali*s have been composed based on tunes from old and new Bollywood films. A couple of cassettes having these *qawwali*s (and sung by Kuldip Saini, Vandana Khurana, Taslim and Arif) have also been released. Below are given some of these *qawwali*s with their respective translations.

One of the *qawwali*s is based on the tune from a Bollywood film (*nigahen milane ko ji chahta hai*).

dil ki murad hai, tujh se na kahun to kis se me kahun
ram gaya hai tu Baba nas nas mein, kahun tujh se kahun

tere dar pe aane ko ji chahta hai
sajde pe jaane ko ji chahta hai
woh turbat jise aake lakhon ne mana
us turbat pe aane ko ji chahta hai
hai rutba Qalandar ka duniya me ooncha
woh rutba lubhane ko ji chahta hai
hai alam ka turrah jo pir qalandar
jahan ko dikhane ko ji chahta hai
jahan ke wali tera hai sahara mujh ko
yeh kasam khali lena hai kinara mujh ko
sab zamane se dukhi hoke mein aaee Baba
mujh ko apna ya thukra haq yeh sara hai tujhko
apni ziyarat ka sila do mujhko
meri ibadat ka sila do mujhko
jahan mein batane ko ji chahta hai
alam ka raja tu pir Qalandar
jahan ko dikhane ko ji chahta hai

[I have a boon to ask, but am fearful;
You are in my very being, Baba, I am tearful;
I wish to visit your threshold,
I wish to pay obeisance to you,
That grave which thousands have believed in,
That's what I wish to behold,
The status of the Qalandar is high,
I wish to proclaim it far and nigh,
The crown on the world's head, O Pir Qalandar!
I wish to declare this absolute wonder,
You are the haven of refuge,
I need you as my support in this deluge,
Aggrieved with the misery of the world, let me hide,
Accept me or ignore me, you decide,
Give me the result of my prayer,
Declare my result, I dare,
You are the king of the world,
It's your coming, I herald.]

Then, there is another one based on the tune of a song (*teri mehfil mein qismat aazma kar ham bhi dekhenge*) from the Hindi film, Mughal-e-Azam. The composer of this *qawwali* is Kuldip, so his name occurs in the last verse.

teri dargah pe soya muqaddar jag jata hai
ferishta rahnumai mein qalandar naam aata hai

tera hi naam aata hai
tere darbar mein dukh ka fasana le ke aaye
bade majboor hai baba umeeden le ke aaye
jab ankhon ne jigar ne bhi joda tujh se naata hai
bharosa khas apnon ne qalandar toda hai
kaleje mein mere ik boond tak na chhoda hai
kahon ab Bu Ali Shah kya kaha ab kuchch nahin choda hai
nahin ghairon se kuch shikwa mujhe apnon ne hi maara
rakibon ka nahin gila, rafiqon ka hai sahara
Qalandar pir bin tere nazar ab kuchch nahin aata
mukhalif mujh se duniya ho, mujhe ab khauf kya
mila Kuldip ko saya tera Baba, ab rosh kya Baba
tarane pir ki masti mein han ab gungunata hai

[At your shrine fortunes shine on one;
When angels of kindness' names are taken;
yours is number one.
People come to you with tales of woe,
when eyes and heart maintain kinship with thou,
Helpless, they come to you with hopes galore,
My own have broken my trust,
Not a drop of blood in my body left,
Words do not come easily, my heart will burst,
I have no complaint against strangers,
My own have forsaken me,
My foes have harmed me not,
Save by treachery, guile, my kin have taken me,
You, there is no one besides me,
Let the world turn against me, I care not
'Kuldip' has received your aid, anyone dare not
I sing songs in praise of my *pir* and fear not.]

Another one that Kuldip has composed is based on the Hindi song from Baiju Bawara, a film of the 1950s (*O duniya ke rakhwale sun dard bhare mere naale*).

O Baba Pir Qalandar, mein arz karoon sajda kar
tu rahmat ki varsha kar
daman beshak halka mera
tera bharosa bhari
Bu Ali Shah pir teri shan pe jaon wari
meri wipda haro sari
Panipat wale aaya hun teri shuhrat sunkar

raham dili ka jab hua charcha tera hi naam aya
fakhr hua khud par baba, teri shaan mein aaya
aake daman phailaya
Hazrat Sharfuddin rahamkar, meri khali jholi bharkar
teri chaukhat pe jhukte hain kya adna kiya ala
tujh ko sab sajda karte, kya pandit, mullah, lala
Pir Qalendar main hoon aya dukhon se ghabrakar
chahun mein deedar tera, bas khwashish na jannat ki
Kuldip ak dukhujore laj bas rahe mannat ki
dwar pade ki lajja rakhna bhik raham ki dekar

[Oh Baba Pir Qalandar,
with bowed head I beseech thee,
bless me with your grace,
my cloak is light, my faith is strong,
praise is to your glory, remove all wrong,
hearing your fame, I have come to this place,
when tales of kindness are being told,
your name is taken hundred fold,
I am thankful, I came to you,
and spread my cloth, and been bold,
be kind to me; enrich me with your bounteous grace,
with bowed heads, stand rich and poor,
seek your blessings, pundit, mighty, and moor,
I have come to you, do hear my case,
I desire you only, heaven doesn't appeal,
fulfil my wishes, I beg, do not repeal,
those who come to your door in disgrace,
please listen to their case.]

Some other ones go like this:

alam yeh qalandar wali aaya mein to duniya se nata tod
chaukhat pe teri bechari, tere dar ki ek bhikari
aaee baba duniya se nata tod tod tod
ajab hai teri maya o pir qalandar
tera bhed koi na paya, o pir qalandar
ankhon mein ashkon ke moti khali jholi lekar
aayee baba duniya se nata tod tod tod
nazar pade to teri, to qismat chamke
mahar pade jo teri to qismat chamke
bujhe hue armanon ko phir le kar aaya
mein to duniya se nata tod tod tod

jis par tera saya, woh kya ghabrae
sharan jo teri aya, who kya ghabrae
Pir Qalandar baba mein duniya se shuhrat sunkar
aayee duniya se nata tod tod tod
meine baba ab tujh ko mana
is adne ki Baba tu baat banana
tere liye kuch nahin hai mushkil
baba main dukh sahkar
aaya main to duniya se nata tod tod tod

[O Qalandar, I have come to your grave severing all ties with the universe;
At your threshold, I stand like a slave, breaking all bonds with all, where I traverse;
Your deeds are strange;
You secrets out of range;
With tearful eyes, and empty hands;
Having distanced from kinship and matters averse;
If you bless us, our fortunes rise;
If our grievances redress, our fortunes rise;
With dashed hopes, again, I have come to your threshold, for better or worse;
Those who walk not in your shadow, cheer not;
Those who you give refuge, fear not;
Hearing your fame, I come with naught;
Tearing all worldly ties, wealth all I disburse;
I have accepted you as my mentor;
Keep my faith, abandon me not, be my pastor mentor;
There is nothing difficult for you, no censor;
Abandoning the illusory world, which is a curse.]

Bu Ali Shah Qalandar karam mujhpe kijea,
apni ibadat bakshi yeh ehsaan kiya hai
Pir Qalandar tu hai samundar nanhi si boond deke
milaya tune Baba apne andar
yeh ek nigah tune jo is gharib pe ki hai
karun sau jan nyochavar, karza phir bhi baqi hai
tera dar subhan Allah, tera jalwa nirala hai
tera gumbaz subhan Allah, tera rutba nirala hai
kaliyan dil ki khili baba, tasalli dil ko mili baba
tu hai uncha zamane mein, bigdi baat banane mein
tu adna se aala bana de, tu charnon mein mujhe jagah de
meri soi kismat jaga de, zara apna jalwa dikha de

jo jurrat badhai baba khud tune meri
asha jagai baba khud tune meri
mera sahara tu hai pir Qalandar
aap tera naam hai parvar digar Pir Baba
rahmaton ka tera nahin shumar Pir Baba
tu hi to banda nawaz hai, tu hi to karsaz hai
tere dar pe jo aata hai, na khali haath jata hai
kahoon taqdeer ke baba, julm aur yeh sitam kab tak
kahoon tujh se bhala kaise, kaha kuch bhi nahin ab tak
meri sun nazar zuban se, kahoon kaise mein meherban se
chhupa kuch na tujh se hai mera
mujh ko sandesh aaya hai tera
lakhon ki baba bigdi tune banai
pake bulava socha bari meri aaee
mujh ko bharosa tera pir Qalandar

[Bu Ali Shah Qalandar, you have been bounteous;
You let me in your fold and been generous;
Pir Qalandar, you are like the ocean vast;
A tiny drop like me, you have absorbed in your heart;
Your kind glance on this poor woebegone;
Giving up my life will not repay the loan;
Your threshold, glorious to behold;
Your tomb! Blessed is the womb;
The bud of my heart has blossomed;
Solace, my heart has found;
You are the highest of all;
The redresser of grievances, big and small;
You can make the lowly, elite;
Give me place at your feet;
My bad fortunes change;
Show your blessed grace;
You have yourself given me strength;
You have aroused my hopes at length;
My refuge is you *pir* Qalandar;
Your name is next to God;
Your kindness knows no bound, O Lord!
You are the generous one;
You are through whom the work gets done;
Whoever comes to your door;
Returns not empty handed;
O the master of my fate, till when this silence;

How to tell you, my mind gives my tongue no licence;
Hear my plight through my eyes,
How to speak to my mentor;
Nothing has been kept secret from you;
Some message I have received from you;
You have changed the fortunes of millions;
Now when I am called, I hope my turn comes;
I have full faith in you and doubt seldom.]

O Pir Qalandar nav ko meri par lagana
hai nam tera, kaam hai bigdi ko banana
patwar bhi mera toot gaya, nav hai purani
sahil bhi bada door hai, sagar mein gehra pani
dasne ko paanch nag hain, inse tu mujhko bachana
apne jo mere they, ek, ek kar sabhi roothe
matlab ka jahan sara hai naate sabhi chhute
ghabra ke kahin gir na padoon, mujh ko uthana
apnon ne mujhe chhoda hai baba tu chhod na dena
sadiyon ke mere soye muqaddar ko jagana
kadmon mein tere baba, hai jannat ka nazara
mujh ko parwah hai kya, mila hai tera sahara
bichchda hua tu meet mila mujh ko purana

[O Pir Qalandar, row my boat ashore;
Your name, your fame, your deed is such,
The boat is old and with broken oar,
The shore is far, water in the ocean much,
Five snakes are ready to sting, and much more,
With my very own I have lost touch,
This world is materialistic, all kinship folklore,
May I not fall, lift me I am sore,
My own have deserted me, baba do just this much,
Please wake up my fate, how long will it snore,
At your feet the seven heavens,
I am content at being in your clutch,
My old friend has met me again, I want not more,
O Pir Qalandar, row my boat ashore.]

tujh ko salaam, Baba Pir Qalandar
masti mein gaon tere tarane
dil mera bole har pal bole
Bu Ali Shah mere Bu Ali Shah

sab ka sathi sab ka rahbar
Bu Ali Shah banda parwar
tujh pe qurban duniya hardam
sab dukhon ka tu hai marham

masti me gaon tera tarana
teri ishare pe megha barse
mein aayee hoon jaise ghar se
chand sitare teri nemat
sab bandon par teri rahmat
masti me gaon tere tarane

[My salutations to you, Baba Pir Qalandar,
I sing your songs in merriment,
And my heart chants Bu Ali Shah every moment it pants,
Bu Ali Shah everyone's mentor
Bu Ali Shah, Lord's servitor
We, the world, you are the firmament,
You are the remedy for all ailments,
I sing your songs in enchantment,
Bu Ali Shah, my Bu Ali Shah,
The rain comes down at your sign,
I come out of my house, by your design,
The moon and stars are your blessing,
Everyone, high and low, you are addressing,
I sing your songs and get encouragement,
Bu Ali Shah, my Bu Ali Shah.]

To these *qawwalis*, the singers add some more stanzas, and in this way, they lengthen over time. The *qawwali* tradition is highly creative.

Glossary

Agardani – Plate
Ahat-i-Noor – Enclosure of Light
Alam – Standard
Al-Ghaib – The 'hidden' or 'unseen,' referring to those aspects of Reality which are beyond man's perception; Transcendent realm
Al-hamdu lilla – "All praise is due to God alone"
Allahu akbar – "God is the Greatest"
Batasha – Sugar wafers
Bhishti – Water carrier
Chanwar – Animal hair fan (duster)
Chatris – Canopies
Chilla – Meditation cell
Chobdar – Mace-bearers
Daf – Drum
Dal badal – Special tent
Dar-ul-harb – Land of war
Dar-ul-Islam – Land of Islam
Dastar – Turban
Dhikr – Remembrance of God
Dua – Prayer
Fana – A technical term of Sufism, meaning 'annihilation, dissolution'; 'dying of self'

Fard	–	Obligatory
Farrashas	–	Cleaner of floors
Fatiha	–	First verse of the Quran
Fatwa	–	A religious opinion or decision pronounced by a recognized authority
Fiqh	–	Islamic jurisprudence
Fitnah	–	Confusion, revolt, seduction, discord
Ghusl	–	Bath
Hafiz	–	One who can recite the Quran by heart
Haft chauki	–	Seven groups
Hal	–	Means a 'State'. In mysticism a *hal* is a mental condition, given immediately and momentarily by 'Divine Grace'
Hazrat	–	lit., 'presence'; term of address roughly equivalent to 'Your Honour'
Hazri	–	Attendance
Hijab	–	Veil
Hujrah	–	Cell
Ibn	–	Son; before a proper name, 'son of'
Ijma	–	Consensus
Insan al Kamil	–	'The perfect man'; in Sufism, it denotes the highest type of humanity
Ishraq	–	In Sufism, the doctrine of Truth by illumination, rather than by debate or logical argumentation
Itr	–	Perfume
Jhab	–	Huge baskets
Jibbah	–	Garment
Kalid bardari	–	Key keeping
Karamah, Karamat	–	Miracle
Karka	–	Closing of doors
Khadim	–	Servant/keeper of the shrine
Khalifa (Califa)	–	Anglicized version: Caliph: Successor, lieutenant, deputy, vice regent
Loban	–	Incense
Mannat	–	Boon
Mashalchi	–	Torch-bearer
Mutawalli	–	Custodian
Mujawar	–	Keeper of the shrine
Maqamat	–	In Sufism, a particular spiritual station
Nafs	–	Soul, also lower self (baser self)
Nakkara Khana	–	Place for drums
Naubat Khana	–	Place for drums

Nazrana – Cash offering
Nima – Inner cloth sheet on the grave
Nishan – Flag, standard
Qalb – Heart
Qiyas – Analogical reasoning
Qiblah – The direction toward Mecca (Ka'ba), to which Muslims face when performing *salat* (prayer)
Roshni – Lighting ceremony
Rak'at – Unit of *salat* (prayer)
Ruh – Spirit, 'Breath of life'
Safa – Purity
Saff – First rank
Samakhana – Room for audition
Sanad – Degree
Sawm – Fasting
Sej – Floral garland
Shahada – Declaration of faith in Islam: *Ashadu an la ilaha illa Allah wa ashadu anna Muhammadu Rasool Allah*: "I bear witness that there is no deity except God and I bear witness that Muhammad is the Messenger of God."
Shajara – Lineage of a sufi saint/Genealogy
Shamadan – Candle sticks
Shari'ah – Islamic law based on the Quran and *sunnah* (tradition of Prophet Muhammad)
Shawwal – Afternoon
Shikafti – People of the cave
Sirr – Conscience
Suffah – People of the bench
Tabarruk – Consecrated food
Tafwidh – Submission
Tasha – Aflat drum
Tawhid – Monotheism, the Unity of God – the basic creed of Islam
Tawidh – Amulet
Tosha Khana – Store room
To'widh – Stone structure
Ulema – Scholars, or learned men, especially applied to religious scholars, but often used also for those learned in other branches of knowledge
Umma – Universal Muslim brotherhood
Urs – Marriage/Death anniversary of a Sufi saint

Wajd – Trance
Wazifa – Prayer
Wilayah – Spiritual territory
Ziyarat – Pilgrimage
Zubur – The divinely revealed scripture given to Prophet David

Bibliography

Abdul Hai. 1965. *Nazhat ul Khawatir*. Lahore.

——. 1979. *Maasir ul Umara*. (Trans. M. Beveridge). Patna.

Abdul Haqq. 1914. *Akhbar al Akhyar*. Delhi.

Abul Fazl Allami. 1907-39. *Akbar Nama*. (Trans. M. Beveridge). Calcutta: Biblio Indica.

Ahmad, Aziz. 1964. *Studies in Islamic Culture in Indian Environment*. Oxford: Clarendon Press.

——. 1969. *An Intellectual History of Islam in India*. Edinburgh: University of Edinburgh Press.

Ahmad, Imtiaz (ed.). 1981. *Ritual and Religion Among Muslims in India*. Delhi: Manohar.

Ahmed, Akbar S. 1983. *Religion and Politics in Muslim Society; Order and Conflict in Pakistan*. Cambridge: Cambridge University Press.

——. 1988. *Discovering Islam*. London: Routledge.

——. 1992 *Postmodernism and Islam*. London and New York: Routledge.

——. 1993. *Living Islam*. London: Penguin.

Al-Hujwiri, Ali Usman. 1976. *Kashf-ul Mahjub*. (Trans. R.A. Nicholson) London: Luzac & Co.

Ali, Meer Hasan. 1932. *Observations on the Mussalmans of India*. (Two vols.) London: Parbury Allen & Co.

Alkhamoshi, Bashir Ansari. 1976. *Auliya-e-Karam Panipat*. Panipat: Mohammad Islam Book Sellers.

Allama Tariq Mujahid Jhelumi. 1998. *Tazkira-e-Ghazi Qalandar*. Jhelum, Pakistan: Madrasa Faizan-e-Arif Khari Mujahid ul Islam Dinia.

Alquadri, S.M.S. 1991. 'Saints and its Synonymous Quranic Words'. Paper presented in the International Seminar on Sufism. Delhi: ICCR (November 11-13).

Amir Hasan Sijzi. 1865. *Fawaid ul Fu'ad*. Delhi.
Amir Khurd. 1914. *Siyar u'l Auliya*. (Urdu translation) Delhi: Muhibb-i-Hind.
Ansari, Abdul Haq (ed.). 2001. *Islam*. Publication Bureau: Punjabi University.
Ansari, Sarah F.D. 1982. *Sufi Saints and State Power: The Pirs of Sind (1843-1947)*. Cambridge: Cambridge University Press.
Antoun, R. 1989. *Muslim Preacher in the Modern World: A Jordanian Case Study in Comparative Perspective*. Princeton, NJ: Princeton University Press.
Arberry, A.J. 1950. *Sufism, An Account of the Mystics of Islam*. London: George Allen and Unwin.
Armstrong, Karen. 2002. *Islam: A Short History*. New York: Modern Library.
Asad, Talal. 1986. *The Idea of Anthropology of Islam*. Washington D.C.: Georgetown University Press.
——. 1993. *Genealogies of Religion. Discipline and Reasons of Power in Christianity and Islam*. Baltimore: John Hopkins Press.
Ashraf, Ehsan. 2003. *A Critical Exposition of Iqbal's Philosophy*. New Delhi: Adam Publishers and Distributors.
Attar, Fariduddin. 1993. *Tazkiratul Auliya*. (Trans. Bankey Bihari.) New Delhi: Kitab Bhawan.
Ayaz, Khwaja Jahan Ahmad. 1945. *Nizami Bansuri*. Delhi.
Babb, Lawrence A. 1986. *Redemptive Encounters, Three Model Styles in the Hindu Tradition*. Chicago: University of Chicago Press.
Baldick, Julian. 1989. *Mystical Islam: An Introduction to Sufism*. London: I.B. Tauris.
Baljon, J.M.S. 1989. 'Shah Waliullah and the Dargah'. In Troll (ed.): 189-97.
Batuta, Ibn. 1953. *The Rahla of Ibn Batuta*. Trans. by Mahdi Hussain. Gaekwad's Oriental Series, CXXII.
Ba-Yunus, Ilyas. 2002. 'Ideological Dimensions of Islam: A Critical Paradigm'. In Donnan (ed.): 99-109.
Ba-Yunus, I. and F. Ahmed. 1985. *Islamic Sociology. An Introduction*. Cambridge, MA: Hodder and Stoughton.
Bhajjan, Sam V. 1991. 'Distinguishing Characteristics of Chishti Saints'. Paper presented at the International Seminar on Sufism, ICCR, Delhi (11-13 November).
Bharti, Agehananda. 1976. *The Light at the Center: Context and Pretext of Modern Mysticism*. Santa Barbara, CA: Ross-Ericksen.
Briggs, G.W. 1938. *Gorakhnath and the Kanphata Yogis*. Calcutta: YMCA Publishing House.
Brown, J.P. 1968. *The Darweshes, or Oriental Spiritualism*. London: Frank Cass (Reprint).
Burke, O.M. 1979. *Among the Dervishes*. New York: F.P. Dutton and Co.
Burton, Richard. n.d. *The Arabian Nights (Selections)*. The Programmed Classics.
Chand, Tara. 1922 (1976). *Influence of Islam on Indian Culture*. Allahabad: The Indian Press.
——. 1961 *Society and State in the Mughal Period*. Delhi.
Chaubey, O.B.S. 1985. *Traces of Indian Philosophy in Persian Poetry*. Delhi: Idarah-i-Adabiyat.
Chaudhary, Sahid. 1998. *Sufism is not Islam*. Delhi: Regency Publications.

Chishti, Abdur Rehman. n.d. *Mirat-i-Madari* (Manuscript in Khuda Baksh Oriental Public Library, Patna).
Chopra, R.M. 1999. *Great Sufi Poets of the Punjab*. Calcutta: Iran Society.
Clarke, Wilberforce. 1891. *Sheikh Shahabuddin Suhrawardi's Awaarif al Maarif*. Cairo.
Corbin, Henry. 1993. *A History of Islamic Philosophy*. London, New York: Kegan Paul.
Crapanzano, V. 1973. *The Hamadsha: A Study in Moroccan Ethnopsychiatry*. Berkeley: The University of California Press.
Crooke, W. 1897. *The North-Western Province of India*. London: Methuen.
——. 1968. *The Popular Religion and Folklore of Northern India*. Delhi: Munshiram Manoharlal.
Currie, P.M. 1989. *The Cult and Shrine of Mu'in al-Din Chishti of Ajmer*. Delhi: Oxford University Press.
Darling, M.L. 1930. *Rusticus Loquitur, The Old Light and the New in the Punjabi Village*. London: Oxford University Press.
Das, Veena. 1977. *Structure and Cognition*. Delhi: Oxford University Press.
De Jong, Frederick and Bernd Radtke (eds.). 1999. *Mysticism Contested: Thirteen Centuries of Controversies and Polemics*. Leiden: Brill.
Desai, Z.A. 1989. 'The Major Dargahs of Ahmedabad'. In Troll (ed.): 76-97.
Dhaul, Laxmi. 2004. *The Sufi Shrine of Ajmer*. New Delhi: Rupa & Co.
Digby, Simon. 1984. 'Qalandars and Related Groups'. In Yohanan Friedman (ed.), *Islam in India*. Jerusalem: Magnas Press.
——. 1991. 'Anecdotes of a Provincial Sufi of the Delhi Sultanate'. Paper presented at the International Seminar on Sufism. Delhi: ICCR (11-13 November).
Dihlawi, Abdul Haqq Muhaddis. n.d. *Akhbar-al Akhyar fi Asrar ul Abrar*. Deoband: Kutub Khana Rahimmiyya.
Donnan, Hastings (ed.). 2002. *Interpreting Islam*. New Delhi: Vistaar Publications.
Donnan, Hastings and Martin Stokes. 2002. 'Interpreting Interpretations of Islam'. In Donnan (ed.): 1-19.
Duggal, K.S. 1996. *The Mystic Muse*. Delhi. Abhinav.
Dumont, Louis. 1970. 'World Renunciation in Indian Religions'. In Louis Dumont, *Religion, Politics and History in India*. The Hague, Paris: Mouton Publishers (pp. 33-60).
Eaton, Richard. 1973. 'The Court and the *dargah* in the Seventeenth Century Deccan in India'. *Economic and Social History Review* 10 (1): 50-2.
——. 1978 (1996). *Sufis of Bijapur (1300-1700). Social Roles of Sufis in Medieval India*. Delhi: Munshiram Manoharlal.
Eickleman, D. 1976. *Moroccan Islam: Tradition and Society in a Pilgrimage Center*. Austin: University of Texas.
——. 1978. 'The Art of Memory: Islamic Knowledge and its Social Reproduction'. *Comparative Studies in Society and History* 20: 485-516.
——. 1981. *The Middle East: An Anthropological Approach*. Englewood Cliff, NY: Prentice Hall.
Elias, Jamal J. (ed.). 2000. 'Sufi Saints and Shrines in Muslim Society'. *Muslim World* (Special Issue), 90 (3&4).
Encyclopedia of Islam. Eleven Volumes. 1986-2002. Edited by H.A.R. Gibb *et al*. Leiden: Brill.

Ernst, Carl. 1992. *Eternal Garden. Mysticism, History and Politics at a South Asian Sufi Centre*. Albany: State University of New York.
Fakhry, Majid. 1970. *A History of Islamic Philosophy*. New York: Columbia University Press.
Faruqi, Abdullah. 1981. *Auliya-e-Hind-o-Pakistan*. Delhi: Din Book Depot.
Faruqi, N.A. 1991. 'Ameer Khusro in the Presence of His Mentor Hazrat Nizamuddin Auliya'. Paper Presented at the International Seminar on Sufism, ICCR, held in Delhi (11-13 November).
Fernea, R. 1970. *Shaiykh and Effendi*. Cambridge, MA: Harvard University Press.
Fischer, M. and M. Abedi. 1990. *Debating Muslims. Cultural Dialogues in Post-modernity and Tradition*. Madison: University of Wisconsin Press.
Gaborieau, Marc. 1983. 'The Cult of Saints among Muslims in Nepal and North India'. In Stephen Wilson (ed.), *Saints and their Cults*. Cambridge: Cambridge University Press.
——. 1989. 'A Nineteenth Century Indian 'Wahhabi' Tract Against the Cult of Muslim Saints: Al Balagh al Mubin'. In Troll (ed.): 198-239.
Gardet, Louis. 1978. 'Karama'. In *Encyclopaedia of Islam*. New edition. Leiden: E.J. Brill. (Vol. IV): 615-6.
Gardet, Louis and G.C. Anawati. 1988. *Mystique Musulmane*. Paris: J. Vrin.
Geertz, Clifford. 1960. *The Religion of Java*. Glencoe: The Free Press.
——. 1968. *Islam Observed*. New Haven, C.T.: Yale University Press.
——. 1979. 'Suq: The Bazar Economy in Sefrou'. In C. Geertz, H. Geertz, and L. Rosen (eds.), *Meaning and Order in Moroccan Society*. Cambridge: Cambridge University Press.
Gellner, Ernest. 1969. *Saints of the Atlas*. London: Weidenfeld and Nicholson.
——. 1981. *Muslim Society*. Cambridge: Cambridge University Press.
——. 1992. *Postmodernism, Reason and Religion*. London and New York: Routledge.
Ghazzali, Abu'l-Futuh Ahmad. 1938. *Bawariq-al-lima*. (Ed. and trans. J. Robson.) London: Tracts on Listening to Music.
Ghosh T. K. and Surinder Nath (eds.). 1996. *Peoples of India*. (Vol. XX). Delhi: Manohar.
Ghurye, G.S. 1953. *Indian Sadhus*. Bombay: Popular Prakashan.
Gibb, H.A.R. 1957. *An Interpretation of Islamic History*. Lahore.
——. 1970. *The Arab Conquest in Central Asia*. New York.
Gilmartin, G.S. 1979. 'Religious Leadership and the Pakistan Movement in the Punjab'. *Modern Asian Studies* 13 (3): 485-517.
Gilsenan, Michael. 1967. 'Some Factors in the Decline of Sufi orders in Modern Egypt'. *The Muslim World, 57*.
——. 1973. *Saint and Sufi in Modern Egypt: An Essay in the Sociology of Religion*. Oxford: Oxford University Press.
——. 1985. 'Trajectories of Contemporary Sufism'. In Ernest Gellner (ed.), *Islamic Dilemmas: Reformers, Nationalists and Industrialization*. Amsterdam: Mouton (pp. 187-98).
Goldziher, I. 1967-71. *Muslim Studies*. Trans. S.M. Stern and C.R. Barber. London: Allen and Unwin.
Gross, R.L. 1992. *The Sadhus of India*. Jaipur: Rawat.
Habib, Mohammad. 1950. 'Chishti Mystic Records of the Sultanate Period'. *Medieval India Quarterly* 3: 1-42.

——. 1974. 'Shaykh Nasir at-Din Chirag of Delhi'. In *Collected Works. Politics and Society During the Early Medieval Period*. (Vol. 1, ed. K.A. Nizami). New Delhi: People's Publishing House.

Haeri, S. 1989. *Law of Desire: Temporary Marriage in Shi'ite Iran*. Syracuse, NY: Syracuse University Press.

Hamid Qalandar. 1959. *Khairul-Majalis*. Aligarh.

Hasan, Mushirul and Asim Roy (eds.). 2005. *Living Together Separately*. New Delhi: Oxford University Press.

Hasluck, F.W. 1929. *Christianity and Islam under the Sultans*. Oxford: Clarendon Press.

Hodgson, M. 1974. *The Venture of Islam*. New York: Routledge.

Hughes, Thomas Patrick. 1885. *Dictionary of Islam*. Delhi: Cosmo Publication (Reprint).

Huntington, S. 1996. *The Clash of Civilizations and the Remaking of World Order*. New York: Touchstone Books.

Husain, Yusuf. 1956. 'Sufism in India'. *Islamic Culture* XXXI: 239-262.

——. 1957. *Glimpses of Medieval Indian Culture*. Bombay: Asia Publishing House.

Hussain, Akhlaq. 1960. *Hayat-i-Tayyeba. Hazrat Sheikh Abu Bakr Tusi*. Delhi: Dargah Committee.

Inam Mohammad. 1970. *Hazrat Lal Shahbaz Qalandar of Sehwan Sharif*. Karachi: Royal Book Company.

Iqbal, Mohammad. 1930. *Six Lectures on the Reconstruction of Religious Thought in Islam*. Lahore: Sheikh Mobarak Ali.

'Islami. 1948. *Futuhu's Salatin*. Madras: Usha.

Jackson, Paul (S. J.). 1985. '*Khairal Majalis*, An Examination'. In C.W.Troll (ed.) *Islam in India*. Delhi: Vikas.

——. 1988. *The Mystical Dimension in the Muslims of India, Beliefs and Practices*. Bangalore: Theological Publications in India.

——. 1989. 'Perception of the Dargah of Patna'. In Troll (ed.): 98-111.

Jamali, Kanbah Dihlawi. 1893. *Siyar u'l Arifin*. London: British Library and Delhi: Rizvi Press.

Jami, n.d. *Nafahat ul uns*. Delhi.

Jeffery, Patricia. 1981. 'Creating a Scene: The Disruptions of Ceremonial in a Sufi Shrine'. In Ahmad (ed.): 162-94.

Kedouri, E. 1992. *Politics in the Middle East*. New York: Oxford University Press.

Khalidi, Omar. 1989. 'Qawwali and Mahfil-i-Sima'. In Troll (ed.): 257-61.

Kiernan V.G. 1949. *Poems from Iqbal*.Trans. from Urdu. Bombay.

Kramer, M. 1980. *Political Islam*. Beverely Hills, C.A.: Sage.

Laidlaw, James. 1995. *Riches and Renunciation. Religion, Economy, and Society among the Jains*. Oxford: Clarendon Press.

Lal, K.S. 1967. *History of the Khaljis (1290-1320)*. Bombay: Asia Publishing House.

Lapidus, Ira M. 1988. *A History of Islamic Societies*. Cambridge: Cambridge University Press.

Lapoint, E.C. 1978. 'The Epic of Guga'. In Sylvia Vatuk (ed.), *American Studies in the Anthropology of India*. Delhi: Manohar (pp. 281-308).

Lawrence, Bruce B. 1978. *Notes from a Distant Flute, The Extant Literature of Pre-Mughal Indian Sufism*. Tehran: Imperial Iranian Academy of Philosophy.

——. 1982. 'Islam in India'. In Richard Martin (ed.), *Islam in Local Contexts*. Leiden: E.J. Brill.

Levy, R. 1962. *The Social Structure of Islam*. Cambridge: Cambridge University Press.

Lewis, Franklin D. 2000. *Rumi, Past and Present, East and West*. Oxford: Oneworld Publications.

Liebeskind, Claudia. 1998. *Piety on its Knees, Three Sufi Traditions in South Asia in Modern Times*. Delhi: Oxford University Press.

Madan, T.N. (ed.). 2001. *Muslim Communities of South Asia. Culture, Society, and Politics*. New Delhi: Manohar.

——. 2006. 'Explorations in the Anthropology of Islam'. Department of Anthropology, University of Lucknow, Lucknow. First D.N. Majumdar Endowment Fund Lecture.

Mahmood, Tahir. 1989. 'The Dargah of Sayyid Salar Masud Ghazi in Bahraich: Legend, Tradition and Reality'. In Troll (ed.): 234-43.

Mandal, S. Rahim. 1994. *Dynamics of Muslim Society*. New Delhi: Inter India Publications.

Mann, E.A. 1989. 'Religion, Money and Status: Competition for Resources at the Shrine of Shah Jamal, Aligarh'. In Troll (ed.): 145-171.

Marwah, I.S. 1979. 'Tabligh Movement Among the Meos of Mewat'. In M.S.A. Rao (ed.), *Social Movements in India*. (Vol. 2). Delhi: Manohar.

Marx, Emmanuel. 1967. *Bedouin of the Negev*. New York: Praeger.

Massignon, Louis. 1922 (1997). *Essays on the Origin of the Technical Language of Islamic Mysticism*. Notre Dame: University of Notre Dame Press.

Maulana Obaidullah Koti Nadwi. 2005. *Silsila-e-Qalandariya*. New Delhi: Farid Book Depot Pvt. Ltd.

Mayaram, S. 1997. *Resisting Regimes: Myth, Memory and the Shaping of a Muslim Identity*. New Delhi: Oxford University Press.

Mayer, A.C. 1966-67. 'Pir and Murshid: An Aspect of Religious Leadership in West Pakistan'. *Journal of Middle Eastern Studies* 3: 160-169.

McDonald, D.B. 1903. *Development of Muslim Theology, Jurisprudence and Constitutional Theory*. New York: Free Press.

Messick, B. 1993. *The Calligraphic State: Textual Domination and History in a Muslim Society*. Berkeley: University of California Press.

Moini, Syed Liaquat Hussain. 1989. 'Rituals and Customary Practices at the Dargah of Ajmer'. In Troll (ed.): 60-75.

——. 2004. *The Chishti Shrine of Ajmer. Pirs, Pilgrims, Practices*. Jaipur: Publication Scheme.

Mujeeb, M. 1967. *The Indian Muslims*. London: George, Allen & Unwin.

Nagori, S.L. 1997. *Madhyakalin Bhartiya Sanskriti*. Jaipur: Pointer Publishers.

Nanda, Bikram N and Mohammad Talib. 1989. 'Soul of the Soulless: An Analysis of Pir-Muridi Relationships in Sufi Discourse'. In Troll (ed.): 125-44.

Nasr, Jamil Abun. 1965. *The Tijaniya, A Sufi Order in the Modern World*. London: Oxford University Press.

Nasr, Seyyed Hossein. 1964. *Three Muslim Sages: Avicenna, Suhrawardi, Ibn' Arabi*. Cambridge, Mass.: Harvard University Press.

——. 1972. *Sufi Essays*. London: George Allen and Unwin Ltd.

Nicholson, R.A. 1914 (1975). *The Mystics of Islam*. London and Boston: Roultedge & Kegan Paul.

——. 1921 (1975). *Studies in Islamic Mysticism*. Cambridge: Cambridge University Press.

Nizami, K.A. 1964. *Hayat-i-Abdul Haqq Muhaddis Dehlavi*. Delhi.

——. 1991. *The Life and Times of Sheikh Nizamuddin Auliya*. Delhi. Idarah-i-Adabyat.

Obeysekere, Gananath. 1981. *Medusa's Hair, An Essay on Personal Symbols and Religious Experience*. Chicago and London: The University of Chicago Press.

O'Brien, Cruise and B. Donal. 1971. *The Murides of Senegal, The Political and Economic Origin of an Islamic Brotherhood*. Oxford: Oxford University Press.

Parrinder, G. 1976. *Mysticism in World Religions*. New York: Oxford University Press.

Parry, J.P. 1994. *Death in Benaras*. Cambridge: Cambridge University Press.

Pemberton, Kelly. 1997. *Women, Ritual Life and the Sufi Shrine, North India*. Unpublished Manuscript.

Pfleiderer, Beatrix. 1981. 'Mira Datar Dargah: The Psychiatry of Muslim Shrine'. In Ahmad (ed.): 195-233.

Pinto, Desiderio. 1989. 'The Mystery of the Nizamuddin Dargah: The Accounts of Piligrims'. In Troll (ed.): 112-24.

——. 1995. *Piri-Muridi Relationship: A Study of the Nizamuddin Dargah*. Delhi: Manohar.

Qalandar, Hamid. 1960. *Khairal Majalis*. (Ed. K.A. Nizami.) Aligarh.

Qureshi, Regula Berckhardt. 1986. 'The Mehfil-i-Sima, Sufi Practice in the Indian Context'. *Islam and the Modern Age* 17 (3): 133-65.

Qushairi. 1964. *Ar Rasail al Qushairiyya*. Karachi.

Rabbani, Capt. Wahid Bakhsh. 2005. *Islamic Sufism*. Lahore: Al-Faisal.

Rahman, Fazlur. 1979. *Islam*. Chicago: University of Chicago Press.

Rastogi, T.C. 1982. *Islamic Mysticism: Sufism*. Delhi. Sterling.

Rippin, Andrew. 1990. *Muslims: Their Religious Beliefs and Practices*. New York: Routledge.

Rizvi, S.A.A. 1978 & 1983. *A History of Sufism in India*. (Vols. I and II). Delhi: Munshiram Manoharlal.

Robinson, Francis. 2000. *Islam and Muslim Society in South Asia*. New Delhi: Oxford University Press.

Rockey, N.L. 1913. 'Progress of Islam in Qudh'. *Muslim World* 3: 250-6.

Rodinson, Maxime. 1973. *Mohammad*. Harmondsworth: Penguin Books.

Rose, H.A. 1919. *Glossary of the Tribes and Castes of Punjab and N.W.F.P.* Delhi: Cosmo [Reprint].

Rosen, L. 1984. *Bargaining for Reality. The Construction of Social Relations in a Muslim Community*. Chicago: University of Chicago Press.

——. 1989. *The Anthropology of Justice: Law as Culture in Islamic Society*. Cambridge: Cambridge University Press.

Roy, Asim. 1983. *The Islamic Syncretistic Tradilion in Bengal*. Princeton, N.J.: Princeton University Press.

Roy Burman, J.J. 1996. 'Hindu-Muslim Syncretic Tradition in India'. *Economic and Political Weekly* XXXI (20).

——. 2002. *Hindu-Muslim Syncretic Shrines and Communities*. New Delhi: Mittal Publications.

Ruthven, Malise. 1997. *Islam, A Very Short Introduction*. Oxford University Press.
Sadler, A.W. 1963. 'A Visit to a Chishti Qawwali'. *Muslim World* 53: 287-92.
Said, E.W. 1978. *Orientalism*. New York: Pantheon.
——. 1993. *Culture and Imperialism*. New York: Alfred.
Saiyed, A.R. 1989. 'Saints and Dargahs in the Indian Subcontinent: A Review'. In Troll (ed.): 240-56.
Sehrawardi, Hakim Liaqat Ali. 2005. *Adhai Qalandar*. New Delhi: Farid Book Depot Pvt. Ltd.
Schimmel, Annemarie. 1979. *Mystical Dimensions of Islam*. Berkeley: University of California Press.
Schwerin, Kerrin Graefin V. 1981. 'Saint Worship in Indian Islam: The Legend of the Martyr Salar Masud Ghazi'. In Ahmad (ed.): 143-61.
Sell, The Rev. Canon. 1928 (1985). *Studies in Islam*. Delhi: B.R. Publishing Corporation.
Shah, Idries. 1968. *The Way of the Sufis*. Penguin Books.
Sharda, S.P. 1974. *Sufi Thought. Its Development in Punjab and its Impact on Punjabi Literature (Baba Farid to 1850 AD)*. Delhi: Munshiram Manoharlal.
Sharib, Zahoor-ul-Hasan. 1964. *Dilli ke Baees Khwaja*. Lahore: Hamid & Co.
Sharif, Jafar. 1832 (1921). *Islam in India, or the Qanun-i-Islam*. London: Curzon Press.
Siddiqui, Iqtidar Husain. 1989. 'The Early Chishti Dargahs'. In Troll (ed.): 1-23.
Siddiqui, Mahmud Husain. 1979. *The Memoirs of Sufis Written in India*. Department of Persian, Urdu and Arabia: University of Baroda.
Sleeman, W.H. 1858. *A Journey through the Kingdom of Oudh*. (2 Vols.). London: R. Bentley.
Smith, Margaret. 1973. *Studies in Early Mysticism in the Near and the Middle East*. Amsterdam: Philo Press.
——. 2001. *Muslim Women Mystics: The Life and Work of Rabia and Other Women Mystics in Islam (Great Islamic Thinkers)*. London: Oneworld Publishers.
Smith, W.C. 1957. *Islam in Modern History*. Princeton: N.J. Princeton University Press.
Spear, T.G.P. 1943 (1997). *Delhi, Its Monuments and History*. (Revised by Narayani Gupta and Laura Sykes.) Delhi: Oxford University Press.
Srivastava, V.K. 1997. *Religious Renunciation of a Pastoral People*. New Delhi: Oxford University Press.
Srivastava, Kumkum and Vinay Kumar Srivastava. 1997. 'On Anthropology of Death'. *Economic and Political Weekly* XXXII (16): 827-32.
Stoddart, William. 1986. *Sufism – The Mystical Doctrines and Methods of Islam*. New York: Paragon House Publishers.
Subhan, J.A. 1970. *Sufism, its Saints and Shrines*. New York: Samuel Weises, lnc.
Suman, Sanaullah. 2004. *Iqbal ki Kavitaen*. New Delhi: Markazi Maktaba Islami Publishers.
Talbot, Cynthia. 1995. 'Inscribing the Other, Inscribing the Self. Hindu Muslim Identities in Precolonial India'. *Comparative Studies in Society and History* 37 (4).
Tassy, Garcin de. 1997. *Muslim Festivals in India and Other Essays*. Delhi: Oxford University Press. (Trans. & ed. M. Wasim).
Titus, Murray. 1959. *Islam in India and Pakistan*. Calcutta: YMCA Press.
Toynbee, Arnold. 1961. *A Study of History – Volume XII: Reconstruction*. Oxford University Press.

Trimingham, J. Spencer. 1971. *Sufi Orders in Islam*. Oxford: Clarendon Press.
Troll, Christian W. (ed.). 1989. *Muslim Shrines in India, Their Character, History and Signifiance*. Delhi: Oxford University Press.
Turner, B.S. 1975. *Weber and Islam*. London: Routledge & Kegan Paul.
Uberoi, J.P.S. 1996. *Religion, Civil Society and the State. A Study of Sikhism*. Delhi: Oxford University Press.
Valiuddin, Mir. 1971. 'The Perfect Man'. *Islam and the Modern Age* 2 (1).
——. 1972. 'Virtue is Knowledge'. *Islam and the Modern Age* 3 (3).
——. 1974. 'The Problem of the One and the Many'. *Islam and the Modern Age* 5 (4).
——. 1987. *Quranic Sufism*. Delhi: Motilal Banarsidass.
Van Donzel, E. (ed.). 1973. *Encyclopaedia of Islam*. Leiden: E.J. Brill.
Voll, John O. 1972. 'Mahdis, Walis and New Men in the Sudan'. In Nikki Keddie (ed.), *Scholars, Saints and Sufis*. Berkeley: University of California Press (pp. 367-84).
——. 1980. 'Hadith Scholars and *tariqahs*: An Ulama Group in the 18th Century Haramayn and their Impact in the Islamic World'. *Journal of Asian and African Studies* 15: 264-73.
——. 1995. 'Sufi Orders'. In John L. Esposito (ed.), *The Oxford Encyclopedia of the Modern Islamic World*, Vol. 4. New York: Oxford University Press (pp. 109-17).
Weber, Max. 1963. *The Sociology of Religion*. London: Methuen Press and Co. Ltd.
Westermarck, E. 1926. *Ritual and Belief in Morocco*. (Two Vols.). London: Macmillan & Co.
Yazici, T. 1973. 'Kalandar'. In E. Van Donzel (ed.), *The Encyclopedia of Islam*. (Vol. 4). Leiden: E.J. Brill.
Zaehner, R.C. 1960. *Hindu and Muslim Mysticism*. London.
Ziyauddin Barani. 1860-2. *Tarikhi Firuz Shahi*. Calcutta.

Index